ROADMAP BY MOONLIGHT

A GUIDE TO WICCA FOR LIFE

ABOUT THE AUTHOR

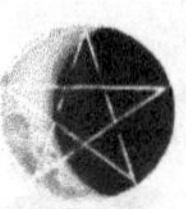

Deborah Lipp's most recent books include *Bending the Binary: Polarity Magic in a Nonbinary World* and *The Elements of Ritual (Revised & Expanded)*. Her earlier works include: *Tarot Interactions, The Way of Four, The Magic of the Elements, Magical Power for Beginners, The Beginner's Guide to the Occult,* and *The Ultimate James Bond Fan Book*. One of these things is not like the others.

Deborah has been teaching Wicca, magic, and the occult for over 40 years. She became a Witch and High Priestess in the 1980s, as an initiate of the Gardnerian tradition of Wicca. She's been published in many Pagan publications, including *newWitch, The Llewellyn Magical Almanac, Pangaia, and Green Egg,* and has lectured on Pagan and occult topics on three continents.

Roadmap by Moonlight

A Guide to Wicca for Life

Deborah Lipp

Chicago, IL

Paperback ISBN: 978-1-968185-12-1
Hardcover ISBN: 978-1-968185-32-9
eBook ISBN: 978-1-968185-17-6

Library of Congress Control Number on file.

Published by:
Crossed Crow Books, LLC
518 Davis St, Suite 205
Evanston, IL 60201
www.crossedcrowbooks.com

Printed in the United States of America.
IBI

DEDICATION

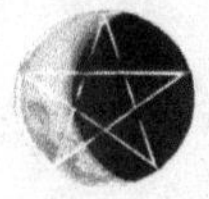

To my Mom

ACKNOWLEDGEMENTS

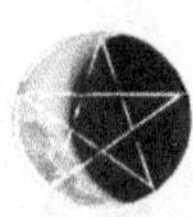

Creating *Roadmap by Moonlight* was more painful than most of my books. My support system has been crucial to me. It encompasses my family, friends, covenmates, and other associates. Black cats were also involved.

If I don't acknowledge Professor Spouse first, the gods only know what will become of me. She loves me, she believes in what I do, and she supports me in any number of ways. A couple of weeks before finishing this book, I had foot surgery, after which the foot was supposed to be non-weight-bearing. She cooked every meal, washed every dish, helped me when my knee scooter got wonky, and washed my hair. If there were Pagan saints, surely she'd be a candidate.

My daughter, she of many names, was also there for me in so many ways, including giving Professor Spouse some much-needed respite. I am very proud of her.

I must thank Barbara Giacalone, Alex Smoker, Ian McKeachie, Maggi Rohde, Erica, Denise, Thumper Forge, Christine Dowling, and Abraham Street. I'd add that if you've shared ritual space with me, I may not be naming you here, but I see you, I see your contribution to my life and to my work in Wicca, and I thank you for it.

I honor the memories of Susan Carberry, Scott Cunningham, Isaac Bonewits, Patricia Monaghan, and Donald Michael Kraig.

I have been blessed to work on different books with two different, wonderful publishers. Blake Malliway has given me support and encouragement when I felt like this book would just be a pile of useless pixels. He understood my direction better than I did. He and his brother Wycke have given me another family that I didn't know I needed.

TABLE OF CONTENTS

TABLE OF ILLUSTRATIONS

INTRODUCTION

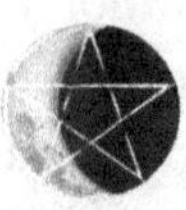

"Sweetness and light." "Basically monotheism." "Elitist." "Homophobic."

There are all sorts of things you may have heard about Wicca, some of which are confusing, some of which are downright nasty. But what is Wicca *really,* and how can someone choose to practice it in a meaningful, fulfilling way?

In these pages, we'll talk about what Wicca is, and what it isn't. We'll explode some myths, tell some truths, and dig into practice in a down-to-earth way. I like mixing theory and practice—you'll get a little history, a little philosophy, and a *lot* of practical guidance.

A Roadmap

Wicca is a path walked alone by each individual practitioner. You may practice in a coven, surrounded by beloved friends, but the path itself is uniquely yours.

When walking a path, a map can help.

If you hike in the woods, your hike is one-of-a-kind, from the exact placement of your feet to the moments you choose to pause, to the things that catch your attention, to the meditations that happen as you commune with nature. Nonetheless, there is all sorts of guidance that will make your hiking experience better. Knowledgeable hikers can guide you to the sturdiest and most comfortable boots, advise you on what to carry with you and what's best left home, point out harder and easier trails, and give valuable safety tips. Maps can show you where rest stations are, what to look for, what to look out for, and your best entry and exit points. Learning as you go is thrilling but also frustrating. A good guide can be your companion and helper, while also allowing you to own your own experience.

I offer myself as that guide, and this book as a map.

It's fair for you to ask what qualifies me as a guide (in fact, it's fair for you to ask that of any prospective teacher). So, let me introduce myself.

I've been Wiccan for a long, long time. I was initiated into the Gardnerian tradition in 1982, and I'm also an initiate of the Minoan Sisterhood, as well as a founding officer of ADF (a Druid organization). Over the decades, I've met thousands of Wiccans and Pagans and participated in innumerable rituals. I've attended at least a hundred Pagan and Wiccan events, on three continents, ranging from one-day public Pagan Pride gatherings to week-long festivals, to convention-style hotel weekends and everything in between. I've interacted with people, from Tennessee to Brazil, from California to Australia, deepening my insight into what Wicca means to them, what works about it, what doesn't, and what a Wiccan life looks like. I've written a dozen books and countless articles, but perhaps more importantly, I've *read* hundreds (or thousands) of books and articles, gleaning wisdom wherever I can find it.

My decades of experience mean I've been Wiccan through every phase of life, as a young woman, as a mother, through marriage, divorce, widowhood, and menopause, through joy and sorrow, through dark nights of the soul and unspeakable happiness. I know what can be sustaining and long-lasting about this path, and what might fall by the wayside.

There is no such thing as an objective author. Each of us brings a unique perspective shaped by our life experiences. Mine is colored by being female, queer, cisgender, a mother, a wife, a computer professional, a Taurus, white, Jewish, and from New Jersey. I can't replace my perspective with yours. I can't be male, or trans, or African American, or any number of other things. It's fair that I acknowledge both the power and the limitations of who I am. I hope this makes me a more trustworthy guide.

Who is This Book For?

- Perhaps you're a beginning Wiccan and you just need help getting started: This book is for you.
- Perhaps you're on a tight budget and you want a lot of information in one place, so you don't need to buy fifty books: This book is for you.[1]
- Perhaps you've begun practicing Wicca, but you're having trouble finding reliable, relatable, sensible guidance. Maybe your sources contradict each other, and you don't know how to sort it out: This book is for you.
- Perhaps you've been practicing for a while but you feel your practice could have more grounding or more depth: This book is for you.
- Perhaps you're already practicing Paganism and/or witchcraft, and you're wondering if Wicca could be part of your practice: This book is for you.

What You'll Find Here

We'll start by exploring what Wicca is, and what it isn't, including the variety of different things that people mean when they say "Wicca," and how it all began. We'll talk about other forms of Paganism and Witchcraft, both to figure out what they all are, and to place Wicca in that context, but we'll stay focused on Wicca. (I'm a big believer that you get better results when you focus, whereas if you try to be all things to all people, you're doomed to fail.)

We'll talk about how you might practice Wicca and with whom. From daily, to monthly, to annual rites, as well as life cycle events, we'll talk about how, when, and why—with examples, of course!

We'll go inside—talking about philosophy and ideas. We'll go outside—communing with the moon, sun, and nature generally. We'll even go shopping, figuring out what the "things" are that make up Wiccan practice.

---

1 I'd never say it's the only book—I love books too much for that! When you're ready to dig further, look to the Recommended Reading at the end of this volume.

Naturally, we'll talk about the gods and supernatural beings, and also about witchcraft—spells and spellcraft. There are some useful charts and correspondences as well, things you'll use in your witchcraft, such as colors, numbers, herbs, and gems.

There's a heavy emphasis on ritual and how it's performed, because I truly believe that performing ritual well is one of the key components to a fulfilling Wiccan life.

Throughout, you'll find stuff you can use now—meditations, rituals, exercises, and the like, so that even though there's lots of reading, it's balanced by lots of hands-on. All of the "how to" is meant for you to adapt to your own life, situation, and preferences. It's a roadmap, remember—I'm not walking it *for* you.

Why This Book

There was a period of time, from the 1980s through the 1990s, when almost every occult book published seemed to be an introductory text on Wicca. I've said more than once that it appeared they were all the same, except for the title and the author. That was frustrating! I wrote *The Elements of Ritual* to change that.

I'm proud of what I wrote then, but times change. A *lot* has changed in forty years. Changes in the world have had a huge impact on Paganism, Wicca, and witchcraft. Language about all of these things has changed. Communities have changed. We have whole new ways of learning and communicating. We have whole new understandings of who people are and who they can be. Our history is better; our research is better. And while some things are better and some worse, many are just different.

One difference is that introductory texts on Wicca, what we once disparagingly called "Wicca 101," are few and far between. Those texts are still needed—perhaps even more now.

My daughter likes to say that I have a knack for writing into a void—for finding something people aren't writing about and choosing to write that. When Wicca 101 was ubiquitous, I found something else to write about. When I had a sudden (and maybe inexplicable) urge to write a book accessible to beginners, I looked around and noticed that there weren't a lot of people doing that. Go figure.

One thing that you'll hear people say is that Wicca is "light." It lacks depth. Some people see it as a sort of "starter Paganism." You start with Wicca and then move on to something considered more substantive. I think there is a certain validity to that argument, if you take Wicca as that thing you find online and don't dive any deeper. This path has been lifelong and life-sustaining for me, as well as for many people I know. After forty years, I hardly even think of myself as an elder, as I know so many people who have practiced for fifty or sixty years. But to stick with it for that length of time, the path has to be rich, detailed, and meaty. The Wicca that I practice is those things, and the Wicca that I teach, in these pages and elsewhere, is those things. In other words, what you're doing today is all well and good, but I want to equip you to continue doing it five years from now without getting bored or restless.

This is a book that will teach Wicca that packs a wallop—Wicca that lasts.

Chapter One:

WHAT IS WICCA?

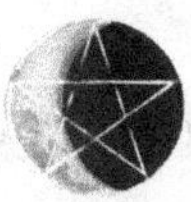

You will hear a lot of answers to this question, some incredibly complex, some so vague as to be useless. I'll give an easy, straightforward, and specific response, then color in the details afterwards.

Simply, Wicca is modern Pagan witchcraft.

Wicca is Modern: Wicca, as we know it, emerged in 1954 with the publication of *Witchcraft Today* by Gerald Gardner. Now, some people will say that Wicca is ancient, and others will say that Gardner made the whole thing up. Neither of those is true. We'll get into more detail about this history a little down the road. For now, it's enough to understand that Wicca is a modern religion, and in that sense, very suitable to modern people.

Wicca is Pagan: Wicca is a Pagan religion and falls into the group of modern religions known as Paganism (sometimes "Neopaganism," although some people find the "neo" insulting). It is Pagan because it is religious, because it is polytheistic (worshiping multiple gods and goddesses, who we'll discuss in more depth later), and because it is rooted in the natural world.

Some Wiccans don't see themselves as connected to the modern Pagan movement, but honestly, that doesn't bear up under scrutiny. Certainly, Wicca is *not the same as* every other Pagan religious path, any more than they are the same as each other, but it fits generally into that category.

While Wicca is religious, practitioners define that word for themselves. There are atheist Wiccans, who view the theology as a metaphor, and that's fine. Because Wicca is *experiential* and based in *practice*, belief doesn't have to come into it: It's what you do, not what you think.

Western culture, because it is deeply influenced by Christianity, tends to think of belief as a central and necessary component of religion, but that doesn't translate well into other religions, many of which perceive things like "belief," and "god(s)" quite differently than what you may be used to. Simply put, not every religion demands belief—just check out Unitarian Universalism sometime!

Wicca is Witchcraft: The word "Wicca" meant "witch" in Old English. To be specific, "wicca" meant a male witch, and "wicce" meant a female witch (the double-c was pronounced "ch").

Wiccan ritual might or might not, on any given occasion, include casting magical spells, but even when no spells are involved, Wiccan practice is inherently magical. We use rituals to alter reality. We'll talk about many such rituals, including those that "turn the wheel" and those that create sacred space. We'll also talk about things more typically associated with witchcraft, like spells, herbs, and charms.

There are people who practice Wicca who say they are not witches, but even in such a young religion, that opinion is incredibly new, and it doesn't hold up to the definition of the word or how it originated. There is no doubt that the first Wiccans understood themselves to be practicing witchcraft and even identified with the victims of the Renaissance-era witch hunts.

Wicca is a unique combination of occultism, folk magic, and worship. It is both a "Craft" and a religion. (Gerald Gardner, borrowing the term from Freemasonry, introduced "the Craft" as a synonym for Wiccan witchcraft.)

Defining Features of Wicca

Many people are Pagan who are not Wiccan. Many people practice witchcraft who are not Wiccan. What is distinctive about Wicca?

Polytheism/duotheism: Wiccans usually worship a single goddess and a single god, although there are some variations on that.

Lunar: Most modern Pagan religions are nature-based, but Wicca is specifically lunar. Primary ritual occasions (*esbats*) are lunar celebrations—usually full moons—although sometimes covens or individuals will have new moon celebrations as well. Many Wiccans won't start an esbat until the sun is fully set because the moon is the most important feature of the sky on those occasions.

Wheel of the Year: Most Wiccans celebrate eight solar/agricultural holidays known as *sabbats,* distributed more or less evenly throughout the year, and these holidays collectively are known as the Wheel of the Year.

Casting the circle: Wiccan ceremonies take place in a sacred space, which is created through the ritual of casting the circle.

Calling the quarters: Wiccan ceremonies include "calling the quarters"—summoning entities, powers, or elements at the four cardinal points of East, South, West, and North, to keep watch over the ritual space and its participants. Usually, the quarters correspond to the four elements of Air, Fire, Water, and Earth. Some Wiccans also invoke the center, which they correspond to Spirit as a fifth element. Some Wiccans, influenced by Native American ways, also invoke up and down.

So, in a nutshell, Wicca is a modern Pagan religious witchcraft that is polytheistic and nature-based. It has lunar and solar festivals known as esbats and sabbats, the sabbats collectively forming the Wheel of the Year. Ceremonies include casting the circle and calling the quarters.

We're going to dig more deeply into just about every word of the above, but before starting all that, I thought it was meaningful to have this as a kind of shorthand definition.

If you're practicing a Paganism that isn't polytheistic, circles are never cast, you don't have eight holidays, and you don't mark moons, I'm going to say you're not Wiccan. Nothing wrong with whatever you *are*, but you're not Wiccan. Words mean things. Waters can get very muddy indeed, especially on a path like Wicca, where there are so many, many variations. I've seen people doing exactly 0% of what I understand Wicca to be while insisting that it's Wicca. I've also seen people practice about 99.9% of what I understand Wicca to be while insisting that it definitely *isn't* Wicca. Maybe I just don't understand people.

Chapter Two:

WHY WICCA?

When I first started outlining what I would write about Wicca, I completely left out *why*. I guess I thought if you were picking up a book, you already knew why. Indeed, the only answer that matters is *your* answer; only you know why you're drawn to a particular path. You may *not* know why you're feeling that draw, but if you feel it, that's what matters.

Regardless, it may help for me to sketch out what *I* see as the unique and beautiful attractions of Wicca, why it might be anyone's home, and why it's been my own home for over forty years.

Wicca combines a number of different streams of thought, feeling, and experience in a unique way. First, there is Paganism. There are many, many ways of walking a Pagan path. There are Paganisms that connect to cultures and practices of the ancient world, like heathenry, Druidry, and Hellenism, and there are more self-consciously modern paths, like the Church of All Worlds. There are also many people practicing Paganism without aligning to any particular group, culture, or style.

They all share a connection to the natural world and to the seasons, and an experience of the sacred in nature. They all perceive divinity as complex, natural, and plural—meaning there are many gods, perhaps infinite gods. Most are pantheistic, finding the universe itself to be sacred and finding spirit everywhere. Pagans might talk to trees, might commune with the ocean; the experience of connection and communication is all around us if we pay attention. Pagan paths are joyful and life-affirming, finding more good than bad in the world. We'll come back to this subject when we talk about Wicca's relationship to nature.

Wicca also inherits a lot of its structure and ritual from Western occultism. While a Wiccan ritual is simpler (usually *much* simpler) than Ceremonial Magic, the two have a definite relationship. You can see it in the circle casting, in the summoning of the Watchtowers that many perform, and in the use of specific magical practices that originate in an earlier century and are often a part of Wiccan traditions.

The combination of naturalistic folkways with more intellectual and structured magical practice is part of what is so delightful about Wicca—it lets you exercise both parts of yourself. When the head doesn't satisfy, go with the heart and the body. Conversely, when "simple" is just *too* simple, the complexity of an elaborate ceremony can be grounding and engaging.

The wisdom of the ages is deeply embedded in Western occultism and its Mystery Traditions. In fact, Wicca looks a lot like a modern Western education, combining Greek and Latin intellectualism with more localized stories, folklore, and culture.

And then there's magic. The knowledge and ability to change the world around us for the better, to place our will in the path of possibility, shifting the odds in our favor, often through simple acts of spellcraft, is a rich and fulfilling part of the life of a witch. The empowerment of knowing *I can change this* and *I can help*, especially in contrast to a world that spends so much time telling us we're powerless, is life-changing.

Just as people can be Pagan and occultists without being Wiccan, there are lots of witches and magicians who aren't Wiccan. Combining these three streams, though, is uniquely Wiccan and is a heady mix.

I know people who have left Wicca to dive more deeply into a purely Pagan path, or into a purely ceremonial magic path, or into witchcraft and folk magic exclusively. I also know people who came into Wicca from each of these three, finding the path they were on unsatisfying. What works for each of us is personal. It's not wrong or right to love the path you're on; it's simply true for you. Wicca has been true for me for my entire adult life and has inspired me to share it with you.

Chapter Three:
TYPES OF WICCA

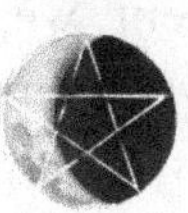

To really understand what Wicca is, we have to get into the different types of Wicca. I'm going to define three basic categories:

- British Traditional Wicca
- Tradition-based Wicca
- Eclectic or freeform Wicca

To understand these, let's step back and see where Wicca comes from and how it developed.

Where Wicca Comes From

At some point, you're likely to hear someone say that Wicca is the ancient religion of the wise and goes back to the Stone Age. This was a very common story back when I first got involved in the 1980s, and it hasn't entirely disappeared. It has no truth to it whatsoever.

You're also likely to hear that Wicca was made up out of whole cloth by a British civil servant named Gerald Gardner, a charlatan and liar who wanted people to believe a silly story about a supposedly ancient religion. This is also untrue.

Gardner said that, in 1939, he was initiated into a group of witches known as the New Forest Coven. He believed they were survivors of the ancient "Witch Cult" described by Margaret Murray. Murray's theory—long discredited—was that the accused witches who were persecuted and killed by the Inquisition were an actual religious cult of surviving pre-Christian pagans. In his novel *High Magick's Aid*, Gardner envisioned the witch cult as the priesthood of a vast underground religion of pagans operating covertly under the Church's nose. (Notice that the name of this religion was "witchcraft," and "Wicca" was a synonym for it. The distinction between the two is almost entirely a product of the twenty-first century; older Wiccans will still often use the words interchangeably.)

Author Philip Heselton has done extensive research, not only finding that the New Forest Coven really existed, but identifying its members and confirming much of Gardner's story. However, like Gardner, the members of the New Forest Coven were occultists and folk magicians interested in reviving the witch cult, not actual surviving members. "The Wica"[2] that Gardner found only predated his involvement by thirty or forty years.

---

2 This was how Gardner spelled it.

In *The Triumph of the Moon*, historian Ronald Hutton places the emergence of Wicca in a cultural context. There was a current in England, for many decades prior, of nostalgia for a pagan past, for finding god and goddess in nature, and associating them with lost folkways. This current was powerful: the New Forest Coven wasn't the only group in England at that time that sought to revive Margaret Murray's witch cult. There was at least one other group—the Pentagram Club—with at least one person being a member of both.

When we mythologize Wicca as ancient, we are partaking of the same current. While it's necessary to understand the true history, it's also important to allow ourselves to feel the beauty and poetry that the false history was trying to express.

Unlike the other members of his coven, Gardner was concerned that witchcraft was dying out and wanted to prevent that from happening. Much to their chagrin and discomfort, Gardner promoted witchcraft, talking to the media and writing as much as he could. He wanted the Craft to grow—and it did.

The witchcraft that Gardner disseminated was not identical to what he inherited from the New Forest Coven. While the original group was content to be insular, shared only among this small group of friends, Gardner had grander plans. He wanted a witch cult that was portable, teachable, and would last. To that end, he initiated multiple priestesses, spreading the seed of Wicca as far as he could. He established a "Book of Shadows" and "Laws" that many covens could have in common.

British Traditional Wicca

British Traditional Wicca (BTW) is the phrase used to refer to those traditions (denominations) that bear a direct lineage from the earliest known covens in England, primarily (but not exclusively) through Gerald Gardner. BTW mainly consists of the Gardnerian and Alexandrian traditions, with a few others that are far less populous.

Two notes on this: First, "British Traditional Wicca" is not a phrase used by British Wiccans. They still refer to themselves as "the Wicca," and a more eclectic practice as "Pagan." Also, British Traditional Wicca is not the same as "British Traditional *Witchcraft*," which is a specific tradition founded by Robert Cochrane.

If you've had any involvement with small communities—Pagan or otherwise—it won't surprise you to learn that there was infighting and interpersonal drama among the occultists of Gardner's day. People denounced one another as fraudulent, as spies, and even sued one another. It was all very juicy, or ugly, or both, depending on how you look at it.

The term "Gardnerian" was coined as an insult by Charles Cardell, a product of one such denouncement. Today, though, Gardnerian witches happily embrace the term.

"Alexandrian" comes from Alex Sanders, who was initiated as a Gardnerian. He (falsely) claimed to have been initiated by his grandmother as a child and founded the Alexandrian tradition, which bears strong similarities to the Gardnerian.

Characteristics of British Traditional Wicca

British Traditional Wicca has several defining features that were once considered to be defining of *all* Wicca. Today, we understand that many of these features do not (or do not necessarily) apply to more eclectic styles of Wicca. This can really snarl communication, as a BTW will say "priestess" or "witch" or some other word, meaning something specific to traditional Wicca, but an eclectic Wiccan will understand something entirely different.

The defining features of BTW, then, are:

***Initiatory*:** To be a Wiccan of such a tradition is to have been initiated by a member of that tradition.

Initiation here means a specific ceremony with a traditional format, which serves as one's ritual admission into the tradition. This ceremony can only be performed by people who are themselves initiates. Hence the saying, "it takes a witch to make a witch." Today, people would call BTW a "closed system" because it is fully accessible only to initiated members, although anyone can petition for initiation.

As a general rule, one becomes an initiate by training for a minimum of a year and a day. Training might be informal or formal, in a group or one-on-one. Most covens require most or all training to be in-person, although some covens do allow distance training. There might be homework, required reading, and hands-on practice. There will certainly be enough time to establish trust and intimacy, and make sure the initiate is a good fit for the existing group, if there is one.

***Lineage*:** In BTW, members know their lineage, and having lineage is a requirement to be considered "valid." Lineage here means a "pedigree" or "family tree" connecting you back to the original source of the tradition. For example, I was initiated by someone, who was initiated by someone, who was initiated by someone, and this line traces all the way back to Gerald Gardner and one of his priestesses.

***Degreed*:** BTW generally recognizes three degrees, and usually you would have to be of a higher degree to be qualified to perform an initiation or run a coven.

***Oathbound*:** Initiation includes an oath of secrecy sworn by the initiate. As I am a Gardnerian, this obviously limits what I am allowed to say in a book like this, but I've written a bunch of books and I'm pretty good at conveying a lot of information without dishonoring my oath.

***Skyclad*:** BTW is almost invariably practiced "skyclad," meaning nude—clad only in the sky.

***Gender roles*:** Polarity energies are considered an important part of BTW and are usually ascribed to gender. That is, male and female energies in balance are considered essential to ritual. Only women can be priestesses, only men can be priests, and there are other rules related to gender. Most BTW practitioners today have an expanded view of gender and polarity,[3] and most covens today welcome trans and non-binary people.[4]

---

3 My book *Bending the Binary* goes into this at great length.

4 And yes, there are some bigots, even in Wicca.

Terminology: Traditional Wiccans sometimes use language in a way at odds with other pagans. For example, they might use the word "witch" to refer to an initiate of a BTW tradition, and "pagan" to refer to a non-initiate. This obviously differs from the way most pagans and witches use those words. A BTW "coven" means a group of initiates (a deeply bonded group of people), whereas many people use the word to mean any group of Wiccans or witches. "High Priestess" and "High Priest" (sometimes "High Priestx") mean someone of a higher degree, usually a coven leader.

Secret God and Goddess Names: In BTW, it is often the case that "the Goddess" and "the God" are not meant as universal, duotheistic entities, but as the titles of deities who cannot be named aloud among the uninitiated. What I mean is, there are probably specific, personal deities worshiped, but their names can't be shared, so a BTW will say "the Goddess" instead of the goddess's name.

Tradition-Based Wicca

Gardnerian Craft arrived in the United States in 1964. This predates the counterculture or hippie movement, and early initiates were often suburban, mainstream, and even conservative. But, in part because the culture was rapidly changing, it was impossible for supply to keep up with demand. With only a handful of covens, there was no way that even a small percentage of the people who were interested in Wicca were going to find it.

So, people started winging it.

People founded traditions based on what they'd read, on what they'd learned from people they met, and sometimes from training received by initiated Wiccans. You'll find traditions where the founder, for example, was a first-degree Gardnerian and then took that material and expanded it. Sometimes that indicates the founder was impatient and egotistical, but maybe the parent coven was the problem. Many are the first degrees left in the lurch when a coven breaks up through no fault of their own!

The derisive term "grandmother story" is used for traditions that claim an ancient family heritage where none exists—Alex Sanders was far from the only person to make up such a story. It's easy to criticize someone like that nowadays, but in the 1960s and 1970s, people were unlikely to accept Wicca as legitimate if it didn't have some kind of heritage, even a made-up one. In other words, be honest and your tradition goes nowhere; fib a little and *voila*! Coven!

From the 1960s through the 1980s, especially, many traditions were founded. Over time, people became more accepting of the idea that a tradition could be valid and powerful without any kind of ancient history behind it. The website *The Witches' Voice* (now defunct), had a Traditions page that listed dozens—and those were just the ones where people bothered to write up a description! Most of these traditions are regional, although people carry their traditions with them when they relocate. The McFarland Dianic tradition, for example, is mainly in Texas, while New York W.I.C.A. is, as the name suggests, primarily based in New York City.

Characteristics of Tradition-based Wicca

Tradition-based Wicca is Wicca that accepts the basic model of BTW. It is initiatory and degreed. There may or may not be an oath of secrecy. There's a set format for conducting rituals, and there's usually a leadership structure. Like BTW, most such traditions are closed systems that require some kind of training or study to gain access to initiation and initiates-only ceremonies and materials.

There are exceptions. Seax Wicca, for example, was founded by Raymond Buckland in 1973 with the specific intention of having no secrecy of any kind and allowing self-initiation—a completely open tradition. His book, *The Tree,*[5] was meant to give people everything they needed to initiate themselves into the tradition.

The earliest "new" traditions adhered closely to the BTW model. However, there are tons of variations, especially now. Some traditions have five or more degrees (BTW sticks with three). Some have more formal study programs, and some treat initiation more like graduation—meaning, if you complete the course successfully, you're guaranteed to be initiated. Many have different structures around leadership, such as elections and terms of office. There might be different magical tools and different ritual norms and customs.

Different traditions have different approaches to gender. Many traditions do not have any rules or customs at all regarding gender. Some have gender-based roles, like High Priestess and High Priest, while others do not. Some traditions are same-sex, such as Z Budapest's Dianic tradition[6] or the Minoan Brotherhood founded by Eddie Buczynski.

Eclectic Wicca

By definition, "Eclectic" Wicca is a Wiccan practice unaffiliated with any tradition. It is an invention of the practitioners, perhaps based on experience with traditional Wicca, perhaps not. Eclectic Wicca might be the product of extensive research, or someone might begin an invented practice with very little background or knowledge. It might be inspired by scholarship, fiction, or intuition, or a combination of all of these. Because it is so varied, it is difficult to define or describe. Indeed, most Eclectic Wiccans practice primarily or entirely alone, so it can be hard even to gauge what's being done.

There have been Wiccans known as Eclectic since at least the 1970s. People invented their own path based on what they'd read and/or public ceremonies they'd attended. Perhaps they'd been with a coven or other circle, but the group thing didn't work out for one reason or another, or, at least, that particular group didn't.

Hybrid things called "eclectic traditions" also exist: Self-consciously invented, purposefully freeform, but having developed, or developing, a body of lore and rituals. Maybe it's a ritual that was performed once and never will be performed again, but someone decided to throw it into that group's version of a Book of Shadows.

Just as there have always been eclectics, there have likewise always been solitary Wiccans in large numbers; I'd venture to say that they've been the majority since the 1970s. However, it used to be understood that those people were solitary by necessity—they had no access to a coven or other group. In the pre-Internet days, especially, finding a group was arduous (it still can be). I am sure that many people then, as now, preferred to practice alone, but it wasn't thought of as a real option except as a stopgap measure. If you were solitary, the assumption was that you were seeking.

5 *The Tree, The Complete Book of Saxon Witchcraft*, was republished in 2005 as *Buckland's Book of Saxon Witchcraft.*
6 There's more than one tradition named "Dianic."

With both eclectic groups and solitary Wicca, there was an attitude through most of the twentieth century that these were inferior practices: both traditionalists and eclectics themselves frequently thought of traditional Wicca as "the real thing."

The breakthrough came in 1989, with the publication of Scott Cunningham's *Wicca: A Guide for the Solitary Practitioner*. For over three decades, this little volume has been one of the best-selling books on Wicca and witchcraft. It fundamentally changed the idea of how Wicca could be practiced. Generations of Wiccans have been influenced by this book, even if they haven't personally read it.

Cunningham's book strongly emphasized that everyone who was truly devoted to the path could be Wiccan, with or without a teacher. Intuition, listening to nature, and opening yourself to the gods were the most important teachers. Although he wanted people to read and research, he stressed experience and communing with the spirits of nature, as higher priorities. This was radical and new at the time.

Controversially, Cunningham talked about self-initiation. To him, "initiation" meant being welcomed on the path of worship by the gods themselves; you could formalize it in ritual, but it would really just happen naturally by opening yourself to them. This is a completely different meaning of the word than is used by traditionalists, who understand initiation to be ritual entry into a tradition, usually after a long period of study. Naturally, two people in conversation, one BTW, one an eclectic influenced by Cunningham, would not understand one another, and feathers could get ruffled all around. I think nowadays, most people understand that different paths use this word differently.

Characteristics of Eclectic Wicca

Because each individual develops their own practice, there are no hard and fast rules as to what is and isn't Eclectic Wicca, except the broad definition on page 15. However, we can generalize about things that are likely to be a part of most eclectic practices:

Minimal formality and repetition: Eclectic rituals are often much simpler than traditional ones and are sometimes created anew for each rite.

Self-initiation: Eclectic Wicca almost never has a formal initiation ceremony, even among those practitioners who have formalized some of their rituals.

Diverse deities: Eclectics might be duotheistic or polytheistic, but will in either case tend to use a wide variety of deity names in ritual. They might use different god and goddess names at each ritual, or have specific names used for specific holidays or occasions. They might also use deity names at the quarters, invoking four additional deities per ritual instead of guardians, watchtowers, or elementals.

Cultural borrowing: The spirit of eclecticism lends itself to picking up bits and pieces from a wide range of sources, both ancient and modern. This might include using Celtic, Slavic, Mediterranean, African, or Native American components (tools, language, practices) in ritual. Wicca is sometimes accused of cultural appropriation, and in some cases, this is an accurate criticism of Eclectic Wicca, although every individual case is obviously different.

Modern: Eclectic Wicca embraces modernity in attitude, structure, and ritual. This can mean many different things. For example, there might be deities or spirits from pop culture on the altar. In a completely different vein, while some practitioners might be more self-consciously timeless by wearing robes, hand-writing rituals, and using candles, eclectics might wear street clothes, read rituals off an iPad, and use electric light.

Naturally, this modernity would extend to social attitudes as well, and eclectics are generally far less interested in things like gender roles or hierarchy.

Post-Wicca: Witchcraft, Paganism, and More

Occultism has always been around, being more or less popular at various times. Gerald Gardner's first non-fiction book, *Witchcraft Today,* published in 1954, helped kick off one of the "more" periods. Even so, occultism remained relatively tiny until it reached the United States and collided with the 1960s counterculture movement. In the 1970s, feminism and the self-actualization movement helped seal the deal, and growth was exponential.

Wicca was the spearhead of this massive growth, and for decades, was the face of the Pagan occult movement. In the 1970s, 1980s, and 1990s, Wicca was something like 85-90% of the modern Pagan world.

That's far from the case today. Witchcraft, in particular, has separated itself from Wicca with a kind of determined fury. There's an "I am *not* Wiccan" voice in the community these days. I've always known people who were more attracted to the simplicity of being a "kitchen witch," who are magical and Pagan but not particularly interested in ritual. What surprises me nowadays is the prevalence of non-Wiccan witches who *are* ceremonially oriented, and who *are* worshiping Pagan deities as part of their practice. To me, the combination of witchcraft, ceremony, and Pagan worship is highly defining of Wicca.

Today, we see a huge population of witches of all stripes: Pagan, monotheistic, and atheistic; ritual-focused and naturalistic; or freeform.

There's also a growing Pagan population that has nothing to do with witchcraft and often doesn't practice any kind of magic.

Many Pagans and witches see themselves as "post-Wiccan"—they understand Wicca's place in the roots of their movement but feel they've moved on.

Wicca, though, is still here.

One of the criticisms of Wicca that is often heard is that Wicca is an invented religion. We've discussed the history, and yes, it is definitely not ancient. But does that matter? The Church of All Worlds is a Pagan organization inspired by a 1961 science fiction novel[7]—is it less valid than, say, a Druid path consciously following in the footsteps of Bronze Age Celts?

The fact is that all contemporary Pagan religions, even the most assiduously reconstructed, are also *contemporary*. They are inspired by ancient practice, sometimes closely following the ancients, sometimes more decidedly modern, but they exist in the present day. You cannot truly be practicing any *ancient* Paganism while living in modernity, driving to rituals, buying your food at the supermarket, and eating things that are out of season, not worried that meat might be scarce or the harvest might be insufficient. You're lighting your bonfire with lighter fluid and checking the weather report on an app.

---

7 *Stranger in a Strange Land* by Robert Heinlein.

Most significantly, you're *choosing* to be Pagan, which is beyond the conception of our predecessors. They weren't even consciously Pagan; they just were themselves, and their practices were not a "religion" separate from any other part of life. Today, we adopt and study a religion in a distinctly modern way. No matter how ancient a specific ritual is, its context in modernity alters it in a fundamental way.

Chapter Four:

THE IDEAS OF WICCA

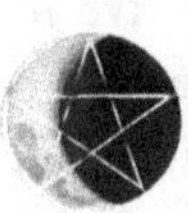

Wicca never tells you what to believe. It is an individual path, and there are no thought police or tests of faith. Nonetheless, there are philosophies, theologies, principles, ideas, and ethics that are common in Wicca. There are also—perhaps unsurprisingly—misconceptions about what some of these ideas are.

As I say, "Wiccans believe..." keep in mind that there are always exceptions, and that you are not required to believe anything. If you find yourself profoundly at odds with everything I describe as a Wiccan worldview, it might be that Wicca is not for you. However, I have known Wiccans who part ways with every one of the ideas I'll discuss yet remain Wiccan.

So, let's dive into these ideas, starting with the veneration of nature.

Nature

Wicca is a religion deeply rooted in nature and the natural world. I know when I say that, some people feel excluded: I grew up in the suburbs and currently live in a city, so perhaps someone like me could ask if "nature religion" is really my cup of tea. I assure you it is.

Nature is certainly found in the great outdoors: in the woods, on the beach, in the mountains. Wild and lonely places where modernity is barely knowable are beautiful and sacred. Getting in touch with the gods and yourself in such places can be life-changing. I will never forget being fourteen years old, walking on a dirt road in the Berkshires, and suddenly realizing there was a presence all around me, that it was alive, and that it was female. I met the Goddess then, and it changed me forever. But such experiences are not all that is meant by "nature."

Nature is the flow of the seasons. In the crowded New Jersey city where I live, I can easily see how different the world is depending on the time of year. As I write today, it is icy cold outside and there's snow on the ground. So much is different than in the middle of July! It's apparent in the sounds of nature—birds and animals are also present in the city, after all—and in the behavior of people. Our energy is different in the summer. When it's cold, we're more insular, as if we were hibernating bears, focusing on inner work or at-home projects. In the warm seasons, we are more external. Even simple things like scraping the snow off the roof of the car, raking leaves, or harvesting tomatoes can connect us to the sacredness of ever-present nature.

The Goddess of Wicca is simultaneously Mother Earth and Lady of the Moon. She is seen as the embodiment of nature all around us, while the Horned God is seen as the cycle of time. The Goddess ebbs and flows throughout each month, while the God brings broad seasonal changes. Speaking of nature in the city: Ask any cop or emergency room worker what happens during a full moon! Natural cycles influence us all.

Nature also means the flow of life, and that flow is seen as *birth-death-rebirth.* Most Wiccans accept reincarnation as a reality. It is typically understood that when we die, we go to the "Summerland," a place of rest and renewal where we await rebirth.

Even while believing in reincarnation, we remain rooted in the Earth and in the present life. Inherent in the idea of an Earth religion is the idea that the next life is not our focus; we're not waiting for death to straighten everything out. After all, our bodies are a part of nature, and therefore this life, and the bodies we live it in, are sacred. While many religions focus on the separation of body and spirit, Wicca is a deeply embodied path. We are not seeking a release from the cycle of rebirth, but a fulfillment of it, through reunion with those we loved before, so that we may love them again. In other words, we're focused on *this* life, and living it well and fully, and loving deeply. The "reward" is not in a heaven, but here. That lends an urgency to what we do in this life, to the integrity of our relationships, to loving passionately and fully, to caring for the climate—all of it.

Embodiment also means that we enjoy our bodies. Wicca believes in the sacredness of pleasure, including pleasurable sex.

Wicca tends to talk a *lot* about sex, sometimes in very heteronormative ways, which we'll talk more about when we get to the idea of polarity. Here, let's just note that the body, and the body's capacity for pleasure, is deeply sacred in the Craft. In part, this is a reaction to many centuries of anti-sex theologies. "Sex is good, therefore don't have it," is one of the stranger theologies that history has come up with, but we sometimes forget how weird it is because it's so prevalent. I've seen variations on this in so many texts, and it is often unexamined: Sex is sacred; therefore, it should be confined to marriage/it must be accompanied by love/it should only happen under the following specific circumstances. The body is sacred; therefore, it should be dressed modestly/we shouldn't run around naked/we shouldn't mark it. None of those "therefores" follow logically and necessarily from sacredness! Saying, for example, that the body is sacred and, therefore, should be covered modestly is practically a non-sequitur. Sacredness does not require a body to be covered or uncovered, celibate or licentious. You could take the idea of sacredness and extract any of these as a "therefore."

Sex and the body are sacred, Wicca says, therefore, enjoy them freely as you see fit. Of course, other people's bodies and sexuality are also sacred, so consent is crucial, and abuse is never okay. But be as sexual or as celibate as you choose, be as naked or as covered as you choose, as tattooed or not as you choose: It's *your* body, and it is beloved of the gods. Wiccans are monogamous, polyamorous, and single. We are straight, queer, and asexual. We are nudists and covered up. We examine and understand our bodies and our sexuality in the context of our religion, and we don't just carry forward ideas from our childhood religions that may no longer fit, but what we conclude is entirely up to each of us.

Nature Exercises

Here are some simple exercises for getting in touch with nature and finding sacredness there. These exercises are accessible whether you're rural, suburban, or urban, and I've noted how each might be adapted to those different environments.

Before any of these simple exercises, it helps to still your mind and breathe deeply. Being open to the world around you is core to what you are doing and beginning in stillness and calm aids that.

Feel free to modify any of these exercises to accommodate your own abilities. For example, if you can't easily walk, use whatever means of movement works for you.

Note that all of these exercises are done in your local environment. I return to the Berkshires at least once a year and take a moment to reconnect to that first experience of the Goddess. I also love visiting the beach; listening to the sound of the waves is like hearing the Goddess breathe in and out, and it can be a deeply meditative experience. But nature isn't someplace you should have to "go" to; it's here and now, all around you. Finding the nature local to you is part of the point.

Exercises

- On a moonlit night, find a spot where you can observe the moon unobstructed. Simply gaze at the moon and allow yourself to experience her beauty and presence.
- Having found your moonlit spot, return there each evening for a full month, observing the waxing and waning cycle of the moon, and communing with her beauty and presence. The weather might not be cooperative; a cloudy or rainy night is still a night you can *be* with the moon, even if she's not visible.
- Return to your moonlit spot monthly after that, noting how she changes position in the sky throughout the year.
- Find a tree that you like. In the city, this may be in a park, or it may be part of urban greenery on any block. In the suburbs, it may be in your neighborhood or more remote—a park or wooded area you like. In the country, it could be anywhere. Build a habit of simply touching that tree, perhaps with your eyes closed, and feeling its presence. Perhaps it communicates with you. Perhaps you might return with water as a gift to the tree. Return regularly and observe the change of seasons with your tree.
- Plant a garden. In my urban apartment, I use a hydroponic planter with a grow light. Many cities have community gardens, and these are wonderful resources, but I don't have access to one. I have herbs I grow myself for cooking, creating tinctures, and using in ritual. In the suburbs and the country, you have more options. Gardening puts you in touch with the reality of nature—the cycles of life and death, the immediacy of harvest (which doesn't wait until you're in the mood), and the pungent reality of soil, water, and rot.[8]
- Find a local spot (in the city, this is probably a park), and explore the greenery and animals found there. Walk there regularly, throughout the seasons, so that observing the changes month-by-month is part of your exploration. Sit—on a bench, on the grass, or at the foot of a tree—and close your eyes, listening and breathing in the nature around you.
- Walk in nature. If you live in the city, walk around your own neighborhood and observe what nature is to be found there, breathing it in. If you live in the country or a green suburb, walk slower than you normally do, and stop to look around. Breathe in the presence around you.

None of these exercises is particularly magical, but they place you in the context of the world around you and help you in the process of connecting to nature and, therefore, to the gods.

8 To be fair, there's no soil with hydroponics, but plenty of water and rot.

For more nature exercises, see my book *The Way of Four*, which has a chapter on elemental exercises in nature.

Philosophy and Theology

We began with the concept of nature and nature worship, but Wicca also has specific ideas about deity.

Almost all Wiccans are *polytheists*, perceiving many deities. Some of us think that all deities are ultimately One—"soft polytheism"—and some think that every individual deity is just that, a unique individual—"hard polytheism." There are lots of gradations and shading between these two.

Wicca is distinctive in modern Paganism for having the concept of *duotheism*. This is the idea that all gods are not ultimately *one*, but *two*. To get there, let's back up and talk about *dualism*.

Dualism and Duotheism

In its simplest form, dualism is a philosophy that understands everything as having a dual nature. So:

Day	Night
Light	Dark
Sky	Earth
Above	Below

...and so on.

In religion, this has often been seen as irreducible (the universe is two and *not* one) and oppositional (the two sides are in conflict). Religious dualism is often moral: Good versus evil. None of this is particularly resonant with Wicca.

There's also Plato's dualism—the duality of mind and body. Here we see something more like:

Gods	Humans
Mind	Body
True	False
Eternal	Ephemeral

Plato saw the mind as eternal and true, while the body, being temporary, was false. This philosophy focuses on the true and eternal. While it doesn't see the body as evil, it does see the body as meaningless compared to the eternal mind and aims toward transcendence.

Here, again, we're going to find little in common with Wicca, which venerates nature and the body as well as gods and spirit.

But there's also the idea of a *dialectic* dualism, a dualism of interaction. Here, every pair that interacts can create a third, which balances or communicates between the two. This third then splits off to create the next pair, in an eternal exchange of energy.

I see that as a kind of dance. Day and night dance together: a give and take that results in twilight, and then dawn, as well as midnight and noon. North Pole and South Pole dance together, mediated by the equator, holding the space of an entire planet between them. This is where Wicca and duotheism come in.

In duotheism, there are exactly two deities, The Goddess and The God, and all deities are aspects of these two. There are different nuances here: some believe that the two are ultimately one, and some do not. Some see these two as vast creative forces, the source of the interplay of energies in the universe. Others see them as more anthropomorphic, an Eternal Mother and Eternal Father.

There's a well-known goddess chant that goes: *Isis, Astarte, Diana, Hecate, Demeter, Kali, Inanna!*[9] The implication is that all of these individual goddesses are faces of The Goddess, a piece, aspect, or manifestation of the Great Mother. Many people believe exactly that. A hard polytheist, on the other hand, finds that concept kind of insulting to the individual beings who are Isis, Astarte, etc.

I'm personally between these two extremes. I see myself as a unique individual, but also part of the vast energy of humanity, and a manifestation of aspects of myself that include gender, culture, and geography. I see deity the same way—which is to say, I see no conflict between a universal "twoness" and individuality.

Another criticism of duotheism is the way that gender plays a part. Dion Fortune[10] said, "All the gods are one god, and all the goddesses are one goddess, and there is one initiator." This seems to divide the universe based entirely on gender and leaves no room for non-binary or non-gendered deity or reality.

But gender can also be seen as part of the dance. Certainly, in the origin of any philosophy that divided the universe into two, gender was going to end up as one of the divisions. Deities can be described *as if* they have bodies, but as universal forces, they really don't. They have natures that are perhaps gendered, perhaps gender-bending, perhaps outside of the construct of gender at all (depending on the specific deity). When we talk about immanence, we'll see how all of this relates to your experience of yourself. For now, we can say that some Wiccans are duotheists who see gender as a significant part of their gods, some Wiccans are duotheists who see gender as an arbitrary label, and some Wiccans are not duotheists.

Note that almost every Wiccan will have a goddess and a god on their altar, even if they're not duotheists. That is, having Gaia and Herne as the focus of your ritual might mean that you're a duotheist: Gaia might represent, to you, the Great Mother, and Herne the Mighty Horned One. On the other hand, you might be a hard polytheist, and Gaia is exactly herself, Herne exactly himself. It is still typical to focus ritual on a pair.

Polarity

The energy exchange of binaries isn't a part of most dualistic philosophy, as we've seen. Moral and Platonic dualisms aren't concerned with interplay. Polarity, however, is defined by that interplay.

9 By Deena Metzger

10 Fortune, page 172

In my book *Bending the Binary*, I define polarity as, "The presence of contrasting energies, forces, or conditions that attract one another, thereby generating power."

So, electrons are attracted to protons and move toward them, generating energy. That's how batteries work. A woman is attracted to a man and flirts with him, generating energy—that's one of the ways heterosexuality works.

Ideas about polarity are ancient, beginning with alchemy. They come to full flower in Kabbalah. In the Kabbalistic tree of life, we see how polar pairs on the left and right interact to form a third in the center, breaking apart into the next left/right pair. This glyph describes the creation of the universe, as polar energies combine and recombine.

Most of the people involved in Wicca's founding were members of multiple other magical, occult, and folklore groups, and many such groups used Kabbalah heavily. So, these ideas found their way into Wicca, where they exist to this day.

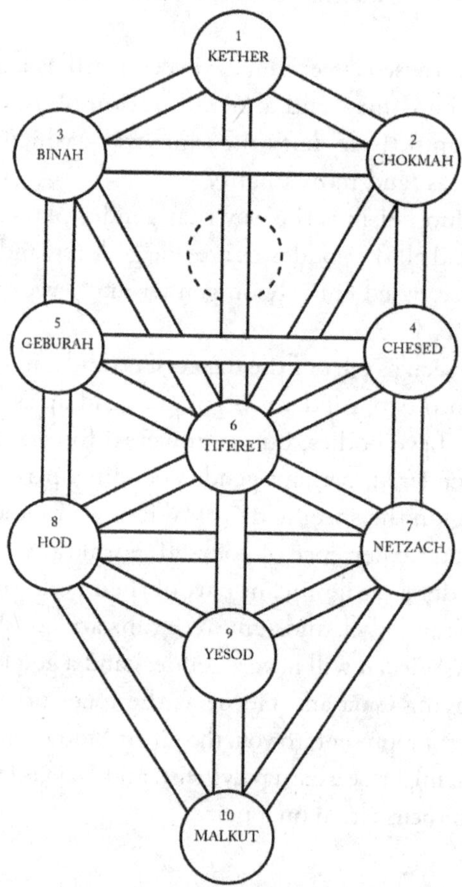

Tree of Life

The polarity of goddess and god is central to most Wiccan thinking and most Wiccan ritual. Many forms of Wicca structure ritual entirely around the movement and flow of polarity energies. Often, but not always, this is gendered. Wicca, historically, has been very heteronormative. The universe was seen as a vast heterosexual interaction, creating metaphysical pregnancy and birth. The fertility of the goddess and god has often been placed at the forefront of Wiccan theology, with physical pregnancy and birth being the whole point. Of course, not all species on Earth reproduce heterosexually (or even in pairs), and most people think of love, joy, and pleasure as energy exchanges at least as powerful as fertility.

The Big Bang is a kind of polarity: Matter and energy breaking apart to create the universe. Many Wiccans see this as the birth of Goddess (matter) and God (energy), and their eternal interplay. Matter and energy relate more directly to Kabbalah (where they are called "form" and "force") than fertility does, and Kabbalah is where our current ideas about polarity come from. This is a very cool observation, both because the entire universe is involved, and because there's nothing very heterosexual about the Big Bang. It's a potent way of seeing polarity energy that is inclusive of all of us queers.

Mythology

Part of how we understand the gods is through their stories. Myth is very important in Wicca, both worldwide myths and those which are unique to the Craft. We don't see these as "just" stories; we see these as deep truths that can only be expressed through storytelling, or universal questions that can only be asked in a story. Myth is an expression of the beauty, dreams, and poetry of religion. We don't take myths literally, and I'd say that religions that take their myths literally are making a grave mistake (Fundamentalism, anyone?). Literalism is a mistake on two levels: First, it takes something as literal that should not be, and second, it debases the true and transcendent meaning of a story to reduce it to its literal meaning. This is easily seen in the Biblical stories that so many of us grew up with. If you take the Exodus literally, you're in the ridiculous position of defending the impossibility that Moses parted the Red Sea, and at the same time, you lose the beauty of a story that talks about transcending slavery into freedom, like passing through a vast sea unharmed. In Wicca, we are conscious that our stories don't need to have happened historically to carry truth.

The creation story of Wicca is something like: In the beginning, everything was one and undifferentiated. But the God so deeply loved the Goddess that he separated himself from her so that he might adore her. This is the creation of two-ness, of the universe itself, and it is the Big Bang.

Is this story limiting us to heterosexuality? I don't think so. First of all, I think the romance of it is breathtaking, even if it doesn't resemble my own romance. Second, the story is both about love and procreation/creation. I'm okay with having heterosexuality as a representation of fertility. Not all species procreate heterosexually, but many do, including ours, so why not? There are those rare Wiccan fundamentalists who are homophobic, because we're "supposed to" be like the Goddess and God, but I feel comfortable ignoring and laughing at people like that. The adoration and devotion of the Goddess and God I worship is beautiful to me, and I've never thought it's somehow the only possible version of adoration or love.

One of the important things about myth is that it personalizes our understanding of the universe. For me, it's not enough to understand deity as some grand cosmic force beyond description. I *need* description. I need imagery, personality, and intimacy. A specific story, about a specific love between a specific goddess and god provides that, but doesn't limit us to mimicking it.

There are two additional Wiccan myths to discuss. The first is "the Descent" or "the Descent of the Goddess into the Underworld." This story bears strong similarity to the Descent of Inanna from the Sumerian myth, one of the oldest stories ever written. In the Wiccan story, the Goddess "would know all things," so she descends to the Underworld to confront the Horned One, the Lord of Death. She demands to know why he causes everything she loves to die. He says "'tis Age and Fate," and declares his love for her. She refuses him, he scourges her, she falls in love with him, and they teach each other "all the mysteries."

This story is profound and complex. It asks, what is love, what is death, and how do they intersect? Many Wiccans spend a lot of time meditating on and studying this short but intricate story.

Finally, let's talk about "the Charge." The book *Aradia* was highly influential on early Wicca, and remains influential, to a lesser extent, today. Folklorist Charles Godfrey Leland published *Aradia* in 1899, saying it was folklore, magic, and witchcraft shared with him by an Italian witch named Maddalena. Scholarly opinions about the work have gone back and forth, and remain divided, with some declaring it an authentic source, and others sure it must be fake. Because we're talking about myth, that doesn't matter too much for our purposes.

Aradia tells the story of Diana, goddess of the moon, and her brother-lover Lucifer, god of the sun. Their daughter, Aradia, is the queen of witches. She appears before the witches and gives them instructions, a "charge," to worship her, to be free, to be "naked in your rites," to dance, feast, make music and love, and to curse and destroy their oppressors.

Modern Wicca tends to remove that last part, but the bulk of Aradia's charge, as interpreted by Doreen Valiente and handed down in Wicca, remains integral to the Craft. In fact, it forms kind of a piece with the Descent: The Goddess descends to the Underworld, then returns to the world enlightened by the mysteries shared with the Horned God, she brings these mysteries to her children, the witches, giving them a charge, and teaching them how to cast a circle, which is between the world of the dead and the world of the living.

There's extraordinary power in this tale, that the circle we cast was brought to us by the Goddess herself, and that we are instructed to seek after her, worship her, and "feast, dance, make music and love," all in her name. There are often times when I am keenly aware of this instruction as I perform my rites and feel connected to her. It's also true that I work extra hard to make my rites energetic and beautiful because they are hers.

Immanence

One of the quintessential ideas of Wicca is that of immanent deity. This means that the gods are within us: Some would say exclusively within us, some would say both within and outside of us, and some would get really metaphysical and say there's no difference between the two. Regardless of the nuance, just about everyone would agree that in Wicca, the gods are within.

Some people are rigidly gendered about this: The Goddess is within women, and the God is within men. I think this idea is rare these days, even among those people who have heteronormative ideas about Wicca. A lot of Wiccans are significantly influenced by the ideas of Carl Jung,[11] and Jung saw both *anima* and *animus* within each person—we are all inhabited by both our own gender and the opposite gender (this is way before anyone was talking about non-binary or third genders).

That said, most of us can most easily find forms of deity inside us whom we relate to: Maybe that's based on gender, maybe on any number of other qualities.

So, I might find the Great Mother within me because I am female, or because I'm a mother, or because I'm as fat as the Venus of Willendorf. Any of those might help me connect to the goddess within. You might find a deity within you to whom you relate because of gender, sexuality, profession, culture of origin, or any other reason. Finding that connection is meant to be helpful but not limiting. It empowers you to open yourself to a beautiful experience and shouldn't cut you off from different, equally beautiful experiences.

Wicca tells us that wisdom, sacredness, and everything we need is within us. This is a good counterbalance to the rules that others lay down on us. If you feel a deep connection to a path, and someone is telling you that you "shouldn't" walk that path, remember the gods within have great wisdom, and that wisdom is capable of overriding a bunch of "shoulds" and "shouldn'ts."

There are some ethical guidelines in the Craft, but not a lot. People who know they have the gods within themselves don't need a list of rules to live moral lives—they just need to listen to that inner voice. You already know the difference between right and wrong and don't need me to lecture you on it, even though sometimes choosing right is damn hard.

Immanence also teaches us to trust people's wisdom and truth about themselves. We can be trusted to know who we are when we listen to the gods within us.

Immanence Exercise

This is a meditation exercise to help you discover the deity(ies) within yourself. You might choose to do this after exploring the centering and grounding exercises under *Mind/Consciousness Work* on page 314, as it will leverage those skills.

This exercise can be repeated as often as you like and can, if you choose, become part of your regular meditation practice.

Begin by calming and relaxing yourself. Make sure the lighting is dim. Your body should be comfortable and unbound. You should be sitting or lying down in a way that makes you feel at ease but doesn't put you to sleep. Turn off your ringer, lock the door, and otherwise ensure you won't be disturbed. Music, if any, should be soft. Incense can add to the atmosphere if you like.

Wiggle your toes and then let them rest, relaxing your toes and your feet.

Wiggle your fingers and shake out your hands, then let them rest, relaxing your fingers and hands.

Clench the muscles in your legs and then let them rest, relaxing your legs.

Tighten and then relax your arms. Feel your arms in a soft, open position at your sides.

Clench your butt and relax it. Relax your groin and hips.

---

11 C.G. Jung was one of the great founding psychologists—a student of Freud's. He was the first psychologist to incorporate mysticism into psychology and worked with Tarot and myth. Much of the recommended reading for beginning Pagans back in the 1980s and 1990s was by Jung or by Jungian psychologists.

Tighten your stomach and relax it. Feel the entire center of your body relax.

Spend a moment relaxing your back, bit by bit. Relax the lower back, the mid-back, and the upper back.

Roll your shoulders and relax them. Feel the shoulders, shoulder blades, and collar relax.

Tighten and release your neck, feeling it relax.

Open and move your jaw, letting it relax comfortably, with your mouth just slightly open.

Squeeze your eyes shut and then open them and allow them to fall comfortably closed, relaxing your entire face and head.

Become aware of your breath. Breathe deeply in and out of your center.

Notice where your center is.

Notice your sense of self, alive and breathing from your center.

There are thoughts, concerns, and feelings scattered about you. Bring each inward and package it up. Wrap it in a package and place it in a spot where you can open it later, at a time of your choosing.

Thoughts of the future are wrapped up in a package and set aside.

Concerns about loved ones are wrapped in a package and set aside.

Persistent memories are wrapped in a package and set aside.

One by one, find each stray thought, wrap it up, and set it aside.

Now ask yourself, *Who am I?*

Take the answer and package it up, setting it aside with the other packages.

Ask again, *Who am I?*

Package up the answer and set it aside.

Continue asking the question and packaging the answer until the moment you feel the voices that insist on answering begin to quiet. Notice they are quieter. You'll know when the moment is right.

And now, simply listen.

What do you hear?

Spend time in that listening place.

Gently allow yourself to return to normal consciousness, slowly reorienting yourself to your body.

You may approach the pile of packages with fresh eyes, choosing to open them or just leave them.

You may wish to journal about this experience.

Laws, Rules, and Ethical Guidelines

Wicca as a whole has no rules, although some traditions have rules that apply to that tradition only. For example, an oath of secrecy, a part of many traditions, applies only to the members of that tradition. Often, people have asked me a question about being a Gardnerian and then apologized if they've violated the oath of secrecy. I always explain that they have nothing to apologize for! *I* am bound by an oath that *I* took—they have no such obligation. They have every right to ask a question, and I will let them know whether or not I can answer.

Some traditions even have a document in their Book of Shadows called "The Law" (also known as "The Old Laws," "The Ordains," or "The Ardanes"), but even those who possess this document typically treat it as something historical, not necessarily something to follow.

Harm None?

The "rule" that most people associate with Wicca is known as the Wiccan Rede: "An it harm none, do what you will."[12]

But is it a rule? "Rede" is an archaic word for "advice," and advice is not the same as law. I *advise* you to drive carefully. It is *against the law* to exceed the speed limit. These are two different things. While it is true that many Wiccans have adopted it as a personal rule, and that there are probably many traditions that have adopted it as their own law, it is not a universal law in Wicca and never was.

But what does it mean anyway?

"An" is another archaic word—it means "if." So, a plain English version of the Rede is "if it doesn't harm anyone, do whatever you want." It's strange to me, then, that people reduce the Rede to two words: Harm none.

There's an idea out there that Wiccans are obligated to never harm anyone. If that's your personal creed, that's great, but it's not what the Rede says *at all*.

The Rede tells us that whatever we do is fine as long as we're not harming anyone. It was originally meant to refer specifically to sex and to act as a counter to Church rules. In other words, while the Church has *all sorts* of prohibitions against doing things—especially sexual things—that harm no one, the Craft has no such rules.

But what does it say about doing things that cause harm? Not one word.

In logic, there are if/then statements: If *x*, then *y*. For example, if it's raining, carry an umbrella. Or, if it's pizza, don't put pineapple on it.

But what if it's sunny? Does the statement above say I *must not* carry an umbrella? What if it's not pizza? Should I understand the statement to be reversed, meaning I *must* put pineapple on all the not-pizza things?

Obviously not. If/then statements don't imply their inverse. Saying if *x* then *y* doesn't mean if *not-x*, then *not-y*.

So, saying *if* harmless, *then* go ahead, doesn't imply, *if* harm, *then* don't do it.

Some people say there's a "full version" of the Rede. This is not accurate. The long poem being referred to, *The Rede of the Wiccae*, was published by Lady Gwen Thompson in 1975; she said it was by her grandmother, Adriana Porter. While this poem's origins are disputed, it's a different animal than the eight-word Rede, not the "full" or "correct" version of the same thing.

The Four Bs

I'm not a big fan of harming people, animals, or property as a general rule. I don't kick my cats or my spouse. But that's my internal moral compass, not the law of Wicca. People use the Rede to say that "Wiccans don't curse," and this is simply untrue. There are times when a curse may

12 "Eight words the Wiccan Rede fulfill, An it harm none do what ye will." This was first published in 1964, quoting Doreen Valiente.

be necessary. I consider it truly a last resort, and no doubt raising all the nasty energy needed to curse someone can have repercussions on the person casting the spell. Like hanging garlic to keep away vampires, it may work, but the house still stinks. To effectively curse, you have to raise and harness an energy that can linger, and not in a fun way.

To me, a curse is necessary only when it is the lesser of two evils—that is, to prevent greater harm. I think cursing because of anger, pride, or envy, lacking any truly *needed* outcome, is deeply unethical.

When it *is* necessary, witches, like law enforcement, should use the minimum necessary force, and for that, I rely on the four Bs. I first heard this as three Bs: "Bless before you bind, bind before you bane." Let's get into that.

Before we do, though, you should first check the locks. If you are considering a curse for protective reasons, don't proceed without first investigating protection itself. Are you, or whoever you're protecting, fully shielded? In day-to-day life, ordinary magical shielding should protect you from most potential harm and help keep you out of hairy situations that may call for curses.

But on with the Bs. It is remarkable how often a negative situation can be diffused by blessing instead of cursing. Blessing a negative person can turn their negativity around. Blessing a space, a community, or a potential victim can also act as a shield. Naturally, the energy raised during a blessing is also nicer to have around.

Banishing is the B that I added to the original formula. Sometimes there's a negative or unpleasant person or situation in your space, and the easiest solution is to use magic to send them far away. I don't think this is a good idea if the person will simply be harmful to others in the new place, but if it's entirely personal between the two of you, then just get them out of your hair and forget about it.

Next is binding, a venerable magical practice where someone or something is bound, prevented from doing any harm, but not harmed themselves. If I bind you so that you may not hurt people, you are completely unhurt; I've just magically "tied your hands." You're free to live your life, as long as you don't resume whatever nastiness made me bind you in the first place.

Finally, "bane," which is a cute way of phrasing the performance of baneful magic—cursing.

The idea here is that yes, as a witch, cursing is in your bag of tricks, but that doesn't release you from the moral responsibility of being very careful how you use it. In fact, it makes you *more* responsible.

Consent?

In the early 1970s, there emerged, from the Pagan and Wiccan community of Northern California, a rule that magic must never be done on someone without their explicit consent. Which is to say, I can't even heal you unless you give me permission. It seems like this was first written down by Aidan Kelly, who attributed it to the late Glenn Turner.[13] In those days, a lot of discussion happened in the pages of Pagan publications like *Green Egg*. As this was all in print, and most of these 'zines were quarterly, discussions were dragged out over quite some length of time.

13 Both people were influential parts of the Pagan community of that era, especially in California. Both were co-founders of the Wiccan tradition known as NROOGD-New Reformed Orthodox Order of the Golden Dawn. Kelly is also known as a researcher into Wiccan history, and an author. Turner also founded PantheaCon, which was for many years the largest Pagan gathering in North America, as well as Ancient Ways, a smaller gathering.

Requiring consent isn't terrible guidance. There are many times when people do things for someone else's "own good" that are unwelcome. Think, for example, about "praying away the gay." I definitely do not consent to anyone praying on my behalf for the purpose of straightening me out.

As guidance, it may be very good, but as a hard-and-fast rule, it can be unreasonably confining. There are many times when someone can't consent. I've done healing work for someone in a coma, and they obviously couldn't consent. I've done magic to find someone who was missing—again, if I could reach them to ask the question, the magic wouldn't have been needed. I've done magic to protect soldiers in war zones, who are also not easy to reach. None of these things would be allowed by sticking rigidly to the rule of consent, and all of them did good.

In general, I want consent for the magic I do. In healing, it is safe to assume that people want to be healed—this is a normal part of medical ethics. Getting consent doesn't hurt, though. For one thing, it can add a little placebo effect to your work, which boosts your efforts. I think it also helps a person who might be feeling helpless to know that their say-so matters.

It's also true that people might have negative feelings about witchcraft and may not want magic done for them, regardless of how much good it might do.

In the absence of an emergency or an impossible situation as I've described above, getting consent is a good way to participate in creating a world in which all of our consent matters. Our culture tends to devalue consent in small ways, from telling children they have to hug relatives when they don't want to or to playing practical jokes; we tend to treat consent as optional in many situations. These tiny bits of disregard for consent contribute to "rape culture," a culture in which marginalized people are continually under threat of having their autonomy stripped away. Every tiny bit of consent, I think, is a blow against rape culture.

Threefold Return?

Another thing you will often hear discussed is the idea that Wiccans believe in "the Law of Threefold Return." This means that anything you put out into the universe, good or bad, will return to you three times (in quantity or intensity, I guess). Some add that this return happens *in this life*.

A lot of people roll their eyes at this one, and rightly so. I feel like people who believe this are also susceptible to multi-level marketing schemes—you simply can't triple things forever. It's also true that any of us can look around and see bad people reaping untold riches, while good people suffer. There's no evidence that threefold return is how the universe actually works—certainly not in a single lifetime.

The thing is, the origins of this idea are known, and they are not what you've been told!

In his novel *High Magic's Aid,* Gerald Gardner laid out many of his ideas about witchcraft and Wicca in fictional form. During a witchcraft ceremony, a character is instructed to return a punishment triply, and then is told, "Thou hast obeyed the Law. But mark well, when thou receivest good, so equally art bound to return good threefold." Here, threefold return is not a description of the nature of the universe, but an instruction as to how to behave. It's not "good and bad will return threefold," it's "good and bad *should be* returned threefold *by you*." That's a very different thing.

So, when did it change? Well, we know that too. It was primarily Raymond Buckland, a well-known author and one of the first Wiccans to reach the United States. And he was pretty explicit about *why* he changed it: For PR.

It's important to understand that up until the late 1990s, almost everyone assumed that witchcraft[14] was malevolent and probably Satan worship. We were evil and we were dangerous. So, it made a lot of sense, not just to tell the world we were harmless, but to tell them we *had* to be harmless, because we believed if we did bad, it would return to us.

So, a rule of behavior became a nebulous law of the universe, entirely for protective coloration. Most of us are less worried about that kind of protection now, and don't need to lie about karma.

But Wait a Minute...

I've just exploded three of the most commonly understood "laws" or ethical guidelines of Wicca. Am I saying there are no ethics in the Craft?

Of course not. First, let's return to immanence. *You already know* what's good and what's right. It's a truth within you. The purpose of following *any* path is not to force yourself to be good when you're not, but to nurture your inherent goodness. After all, we can point to people on any and every path of any and every religion, who are truly evil—people who have thrown away even the pretense of morality. No religion has ever succeeded in turning such people around.

No, it's people who turn themselves around, often reaching for religion to help them do so. The purpose of ethical guidance in Wicca is not to change you from bad to good, nor to stand in the road as a barrier against misconduct. It's to help keep you on a path you can usually already see.

Let's take the example of love spells. Everybody wants one. Everyone who has been doing spells for more than a minute has been asked to cast a love spell. You've probably often heard, though, that love spells are wrong and that Wiccans don't do them. They violate the consent of the person on whom they're cast, they are harmful and therefore violate the Rede, and their harm will return threefold upon the practitioner. *Blah blah blah.*

Are love spells unethical? The late Isaac Bonewits often said the best way to determine magical ethics is to compare the magic to a mundane example. Knocking someone unconscious and raping them is wrong. Therefore, using magic to force yourself on someone is also wrong. But getting a makeover, wearing enticing perfume, and hanging around the favorite haunt of the person you're attracted to is perfectly fine; therefore, casting a glamor on yourself to get your desired one's attention is also fine.

Notice, in this example, that you're using your own inner guidance to determine right from wrong.

Believe me, I've often been sorely tempted to use the magical equivalent of knocking someone over the head. When you're overwhelmed with desire for someone, it's easy to lie to yourself about the ethics of what you want. But somewhere inside you, the voice that knows what's right can be heard.

14 Remember, witchcraft and Wicca were considered synonymous at the time.

What is Sacred?

When we're talking about right and wrong, and discovering our own moral compass, it helps to ask this question: What is sacred to me? To Wicca? What matters to the gods?

I'll start with the Earth. We venerate nature, and we generally consider the Earth herself to be a goddess, or *the* Goddess. Therefore, I'd say that protecting the environment is a moral obligation. Maybe to you this means simply being mindful about consumption, or maybe it extends all the way into environmental activism: The important part is that, if you consider the Earth sacred, you should ask yourself what that means to you on a moral and practical level.

Wiccans also talk about the sacredness of life and of the human body. This can mean wildly different things to different people. I know Wiccans who are anti-abortion because they believe that fetuses are sacred, and Wiccans who fiercely defend the right to bodily autonomy, because the body is sacred, including the right to choose abortion, because immanence tells us that personal choice is sacred. I also know Wiccans who are both—anti-abortion as a personal choice and also in favor of everyone's right to make their own choice. The point, then, is not "the" moral stance, but to look at your experience of the sacred and discern your own moral stance.

So, we look at our own beliefs and practices: What do I think of as sacred? What do I treat as sacred in my ritual life? From there, we ask ourselves these questions: Am I really treating this as sacred in my day-to-day life? If not, how can I do so? This simple act of self-examination can allow us to live more sacred lives, lives more consistent with our own values.

In this chapter, we've looked at the ideas that inform Wicca—beliefs, philosophies, and morals. We've looked at nature, at deity, and laws and ethical guidelines. Most of all, we've looked within.

There are ideas that most Wiccans have in common, while still having enormous personal freedom. There are also vast misconceptions about what Wiccans believe. At this point, though, you should have a good understanding of what's true and false about Wiccan belief, and also, perhaps, some excitement about exploring further.

Chapter Five:

WICCAN "THINGS"—MAGICAL TOOLS

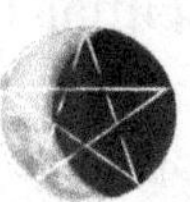

There's an urge, when one starts something new in life, to go shopping. Just me?

Of course, Wicca can be practiced with nothing but your mind and body, if necessary, but tools augment and enhance your practice in innumerable ways.

That doesn't mean you need to run out and buy a zillion things to practice. Wicca has always been meant to be accessible and affordable. Gardner, in particular, understood it to be more folk-oriented, in contrast to ceremonial magic, which was expensive and performed by the wealthy elite with time to kill and money to burn. There are no solid gold tools required, no need to perform magic only on Wednesdays at 1 p.m. when you're at work. A few basic tools are plenty to start with, and you can add to that as time and budget allow.

In this chapter, we'll explore a wide variety of magical tools—who uses them, how they're used, what purpose they serve, and how essential they are or are not.

Tools Are Special

In general, you do want your tools set aside—the things you use for Wicca should be used *only* for Wicca. Your magical knife and the knife you prepare dinner with are two different tools. There are a number of reasons for this.

First, it feels special, and you probably *like* that feeling! Second, that feeling of specialness cues your mind that something special is happening. In other words, because a tool is set aside, the simple act of picking it up awakens your consciousness to the idea that magic is now happening. It is almost like hypnotic suggestion. Many of the things we'll do in Wicca serve this purpose, altering consciousness to place us in an optimal mental, emotional, and spiritual state.

Finally, think about how objects acquire energy. We know that a psychic can pick up an object and get impressions from it—who it belonged to and how it was used. That's because energy lingers on objects. When you use an object for many different things, it has a little bit of all sorts of different energies. When you use it for only one thing, that singular energy becomes concentrated. And it is accessible. Just using a tool that has been used many times before gives you access to the energies contained within that tool and gives a boost to whatever ritual or magic you're doing.

Some Things Aren't Tools

When people refer to "magical tools," what's meant is objects of power—things with symbolic meaning and specific energies, like a wand or sword. Tools are almost always consecrated to a specific purpose (see *Consecrating Tools* on page 49).

But there are other things, both essentials and extras, that are not considered tools. These are things integral to your practice in many ways. Most are simply practical.

For example, candles aren't "magical tools" *per se*, but witches and Pagans use them all the time. And, if you're using candles all the time, I will say that a fire extinguisher is essential to have around, just in case. We'll list these practical items separately.

Essential Tools

These are the tools that almost any tradition of Wicca will agree are needed and will help you kickstart your practice.

The Athame

Just about every Wiccan has a magical knife called an *athame.*[15] Every tradition that I know of asks its initiates to have one.

Traditionally, the athame is a black-handled, double-edged knife, very much like a boot knife (in fact, many, perhaps most, people use a boot knife as their athame). Some traditions are quite strict about this, and some are not. So, you might see someone with a deer-foot handle rather than a black handle, or a wavy kris blade instead of a straight double-edge. If you are interested in joining a particular tradition, you might want to find out what rules they have about your blade before getting, making, or modifying your knife. Once you start working with an athame in ritual, you are likely to develop a strong attachment to it and changing it later might not feel good.

Boot Knife *Kris Blade*

Some traditions require engraving of the handle, so again, if you are interested in joining a tradition, you shouldn't engrave anything in advance.

I have two athames, one for each of the traditions I am an initiate of. That isn't necessary, though, and to be fair, I was initiated into the Minoan Sisterhood over thirty years after I was

15 It may surprise you to learn that no one really agrees on the correct pronunciation of this word. You may hear any of the following: "uh-THAM-ee" "AH-tha-may" "uh-THAME"

initiated as a Gardnerian, so my first athame is the one I think of as "my athame." It is quite simple and plain, and sometimes when I look at people's very fancy knives, I experience a bit of envy, but nothing feels as right in my hand as my own athame.

That's the feeling you're going for: An athame, at its essence, is an extension of yourself and your intentions.

Purpose: The purpose of an athame is to direct your energy. Any time, when doing magic or ritual, that you might use your hands to direct energy, you can hold the athame while doing so. In almost every tradition, the athame is never used to physically cut anything; it is strictly an energy tool. It can cast the circle, call the quarters, summon spirits and entities of all kinds, cut non-physical things (energetic connections, for example), and send power across great distances.

Element: Most people correspond the athame to the element of Air, although some correspond it to Fire.

Polarity: The athame has polarity with the cup.

The Wand

The wand is one of the tools most associated with witchcraft in the public mind, along with the broom and the cauldron.

The size and the shape of a wand vary enormously. Some traditions have strict rules about it, and some do not. Most wands are made of wood, although I've seen metal and crystal wands, as well as wands that combine these materials. Often, I've heard it said that the wand should be about the length of your forearm, measured from the inside of the elbow to the tip of the index finger. I've also seen many wands that don't follow this guideline.

Some folklore has it that a wand should be made from wood that has fallen naturally from a tree, not cut down.

There's a lot of folklore about trees and their magical properties, and many people use this in deciding on the wood for their wand. Some people have multiple wands of different woods for different purposes. Some traditions specify that a wand should be made from the wood of a specific tree.

Although you can certainly buy a wand, it is one of the easiest tools to make since you'll start with a piece of wood that is already wand-shaped. From there, you can carve, shape, smooth, and polish the wand. You might stain or paint it, engrave it, wrap it, glue or otherwise embed crystals or other objects—the sky's the limit on personalizing this tool.

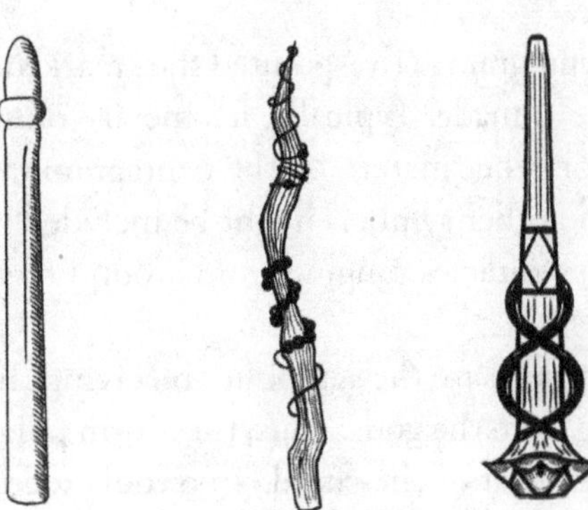

Different Wands

Purpose: Very rarely, you'll find traditions that don't use knives at all, and in this case, the wand is the only tool for directing energy, summoning spirits, and so on. In most cases, though, the wand is a gentler alternative to the athame—you might point a knife at an elemental spirit, for example, but not at a god. It *invites*, while the athame *commands*.

Most traditions say that the athame is an appropriate substitute for a sword, if you don't have one, but I've seen it said that the wand can substitute for the sword. I'm honestly not sure that makes a lot of sense.

Element: Most people correspond the wand to the element of Fire, although some correspond it to Air.

Polarity: The wand has polarity with the pentacle.

The Cup

The cup is a large drinking goblet. I was taught never to call it a chalice—a word associated with Catholicism—but I've since learned that many traditions do use the word. "Cup," though, is easily understood and doesn't need a fancy alternate word.

A cup should be generous in size. It symbolizes the abundance of the goddess and her blessings, so a little sip will simply not do. If you practice alone, you should be able to drink your fill, and if you practice in a group, it should hold enough for sharing.

Because the cup is associated with the Goddess, it is often of a material and color associated with her. Ceramic goblets are common, as they are made from earth, and can be glazed in any color. Silver and pewter are often used as well. Typical colors are green or brown, connected to the Earth Mother, or blue, purple, or silver, connecting to the moon, the night sky, and the sea.

I love having a wooden goblet for traveling—ceramic is breakable. You could theoretically have a wooden cup made from a tree associated with the goddess, but my favorite tree in this case is "flea market." Most people don't make their own cups.

Purpose: The purpose of a cup is as a drinking vessel. It holds consecrated wine or other beverages and represents the blessings of the gods and communion with them.

Element: The cup corresponds to Water.

Polarity: The cup has polarity with the athame.

The Pentacle

The pentacle is a disk with a pentagram (a five-pointed star) marked on it. There's a lot of variation out there in how the pentacle is made. Typically, it's metal—often brass or copper—but some sources call for wood, stone, or other materials. The pentagram might be engraved, painted, or marked in some other way, and other symbols might be included as well.

In terms of size, I've seen pentacles ranging from around four inches in diameter to more than twice that size.

Together, the cup and pentacle are the symbolic "receiving" in a ritual; they hold food and drink, allowing you to receive from the gods. Thus, they form polarity with the athame and the wand, which are the "sending" part of the ritual. Two tools send energy out, two bring it in.

Purpose: Almost every source indicates that the pentacle is a plate, a symbol of food or receiving. Author Jason Mankey[16] says "Pentacles are traditionally gateways from which spirits, demons, and deities emerge" and that it has "unique properties as a window into other worlds and spaces."

Element: The pentacle corresponds to Earth.

Polarity: The pentacle has polarity with the wand.

The four tools above can be considered an essential magical starter set. These are the four suits of the Tarot. (Tarot uses swords, not athames, but a blade is a blade.) They are the four essential tools of many different magical traditions, such as the Golden Dawn. Together, they create a mystical balance, bring multiple polarities to your work, and represent the four elements.

I remember well my first Wiccan training ritual after a particular breakup. I have a set of private tools that I don't bring out for new people. Students were about to arrive when I realized my ex had taken the pentacle we'd used for training rituals. I only had my private one. I grabbed a small ceramic plate, drew a pentagram on it with a Sharpie, and *voila!* Pentacle. I tell this story first, to emphasize that improvisation is great, second, to point out that Wicca shouldn't be expensive, and finally, to say I absolutely would not do a ritual without the four essential tools, even if Sharpies are required.

Book of Shadows

As a fifth essential tool, I'll add the Book of Shadows. This means different things to different people. In some traditions, a Book of Shadows (BOS) is something handed down, conveying the written parts of the tradition. You might receive a BOS upon initiation (in print or digitally), or you might be required to hand-copy such a book. Different traditions (and even different individual covens) have different rules about what can be in the book and how it gets there (inherited, copied by hand, added by the initiate, etc.). Some traditions require you to copy or possess every single thing received from your initiators, including anything they added to the BOS—such a BOS grows, and grows, and grows.

Other people consider the BOS simply a magical journal or scrapbook. Still others place it in between the two—a book containing both inherited tradition and your own, personal rituals, thoughts, and discoveries.

When I add to my BOS, I sign and date my additions to distinguish them from the material I inherited. Over the years, I've added spells, rituals, invocations, notes on trances, passages from books I found meaningful, and more.

While most people do not consecrate the BOS, they tend to consider it sacred, and many consider it essential that the BOS be inside the circle whenever ritual is performed.

Because I'm part of a tradition with a lot of lore about the handed-down BOS and how it is treated, I keep my magical journal separate from my BOS. I write down every ritual, who attended, and what happened. I take notes on magic performed, and I follow up with results.

Purpose: Keeping rituals, spells, and other notes, both personal and handed down.

Element: Most people don't give the BOS an elemental attribution. One could associate it

16 Mankey, page 118.

with Air, as language is associated with Air, or perhaps with Spirit, as it passes down the essence of a tradition.

Polarity: The BOS is not a tool of polarity.

Additional Tools

This next set of tools is not essential, but they're useful and you might want them, as finances and space allow. Over many years of practicing witchcraft, I have gradually built up my tool chest. It's easy to start by wanting everything and envying the fanciest, prettiest stuff. I love acquiring things, but I'm also frugal with my spending. Even after more than four decades, I am not overflowing with magical things, but I do have a lot.

On more than one occasion, I've replaced a plain tool with something more expensive and more beautiful, only to revert to the original. Tools hold energy. Some of that energy, to be sure, comes from aesthetics—when you look at something beautiful that fills you with love for its appearance, that is powerful! But sometimes it's like the difference between attraction and commitment: You might fall for the looks of someone gorgeous but commit to the loving soul of someone whose appearance might be a bit flawed. After a while, the person you commit to becomes beautiful in your eyes.

It's okay to acquire a magical tool and realize it's not quite right for you and replace it. Or to retire a tool in favor of something that represents a different stage of your life. It's also okay not to have every tool.

The Censer

A censer is a container for lit incense: To be precise, it contains the lit charcoal on which the incense is burned. It might be on a chain, in which case it is swung to distribute the smoke, or it might be a fireproof dish of some kind. There are lots of varieties.

Three Different Censers

The censer isn't strictly necessary because you could burn incense sticks or cones in almost anything. However, it's the closest thing to essential in this section. Almost all Wiccans eventually prefer loose incense so that they can create their own blends, and also to control the amount burned. By this I mean, if you light a stick of incense, that's it—it's either lit or unlit. With loose incense, you can add more when you want the atmosphere to be very smoky, or when you're actively using the smoke, and then let it die down. Controlling the atmosphere is handy.

While almost all of the tools presented here are typically consecrated (see *Consecrating Tools* on page 49), some people consider the act of placing incense into the lit censer to be a consecration in and of itself, and so do not consecrate this object.

Purpose: Holding the burning incense.

Element: The censer is the place where Air and Fire are joined together.

Polarity: The censer is not a tool of polarity.

The Sword

A sword can be expensive to acquire, although flea markets and secondhand shops can sometimes yield surprising results. It can also take up a lot of space. I had a sword that I brought home to Professor Spouse's horror. "It's too big!" she said. I didn't believe her until I put it on the altar. Every time I walked past it, I nearly knocked it off the altar, or sliced my leg open, or both. It was simply too long for the space we have available. (I won the sword in a raffle, so I wasn't out a ton of money, but I really did love that sword and wish it were practical to use it. Eventually, I donated it to another raffle, and it graces a larger home today.)

The sword has all the functions of the athame and is also a symbol of rulership. It is said, "whoever holds the sword rules the circle." I think of it like this: As the athame is to the witch, so the sword is to the coven. In other words, the athame is the individual weapon and represents and expresses the will of the practitioner. The sword is the group weapon and represents and expresses the will of the group.

If you have a sword, you generally cast the circle with the sword. If you don't, the athame is a workable substitute. For that reason, the sword is not essential. It is, however, beautiful and impressive. Because less folklore and tradition are associated with the sword, you are freer in your choice of style and decoration.

Purpose: The sword functions like the athame and also represents rulership.

Element: Usually Air, sometimes Fire. Whichever you associate the athame with, you will use the same association for the sword.

Polarity: The sword has polarity with the cauldron.

The Broom (Besom)

In the modern imagination, nothing is more closely associated with a witch than the broom. When I was 24, my stepmother told my 10-year-old sister that I was a witch, and my sister picked up the phone and asked me (in her very cute lisp) if I could fly. I said no. She asked if my broomstick could fly. Alas, still no.

While broomsticks don't fly, they have a significant place in Wicca, witchcraft, and Paganism in three areas.

First, riding. Pagan agricultural and fertility rituals going back centuries include a dance using riding poles, symbolically or literally phallic in nature. The straws of broom might cover a lewd carving, perhaps to hide it from church eyes. The broom in this case would be ridden with the straws facing up.

Second, sweeping and cleansing. Brooms (sometimes called *besoms*) are used in cleansing rituals of all kinds, sweeping out the old, or the negative, or a specific thing that is unwanted. I used a broom often during the COVID lockdown—especially in the early days of reopening—to sweep disease away from my ritual space and from my fellow Wiccans. Sweeping can be used as a routine part of opening a ritual, but the majority of Wiccans don't incorporate this. It can also be used for a specific spell, or as part of a particular rite—the group I trained with didn't use the broom much but did use it annually at Imbolg as part of a spring-cleaning ritual.

Finally, brooms can be used during a handfasting (a Wiccan or Pagan wedding). Some people mistakenly think that "jumping the broom" is an African tradition, and white Americans using it are guilty of cultural appropriation. In fact, the tradition of African Americans jumping the broom to marry began, not in Africa, but in America among enslaved African Americans—it is originally a European Pagan tradition: African Americans and modern Pagans draw on the same cultural source in this case.

My first ritual broom was a fireplace broom. These are short, and I don't recommend them—bending over to reach the ground during a sweeping ritual is hard on the back! Beautiful handmade brooms are available at a reasonable price, and if you're at all crafty, they're easy to make. I've been to several Pagan events where broom-making was taught.

Brooms aren't essential because most people don't use them at every ritual, but they're nice to have, they feel very witchy, and they are a useful magical tool.

Purpose: Riding, cleansing, and handfasting

Element: Earth

Polarity: Brooms have polarity with the space being swept. In a handfasting, brooms have polarity with the newlyweds. As riding poles, brooms have polarity with the rider.

A Cutting Tool

I'm grouping three different tools together, as they have extremely similar functions: The white-handled knife, the boline (or boleen, or bolline), and the sickle. All three are small tools meant for practical, rather than symbolic or energetic, purposes. These tools exist because most Wiccan traditions forbid the use of the athame for actual cutting, but sometimes you need to cut things!

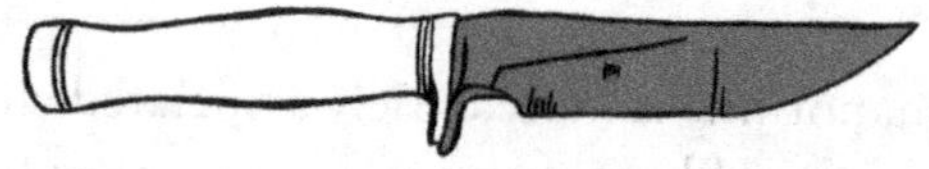

The White-Handled (or White-Hilted) Knife usually has a straight, single-edged blade. As this tool is used for carving and cutting, a single edge can make for an easier grip.

Of the three cutting tools, it's the one most associated with Wicca: Gerald Gardner wrote about it as a necessity in *High Magic's Aid*. This tool is used specifically for creating other magical tools, so some people consider it essential.

Some people only allow this tool to be used in a ritual space, so it could not be used, for example, to cut a branch from a tree to make a wand, or to harvest herbs in the wild. For people who use such a restriction, they may also have a sickle to fill the gap.

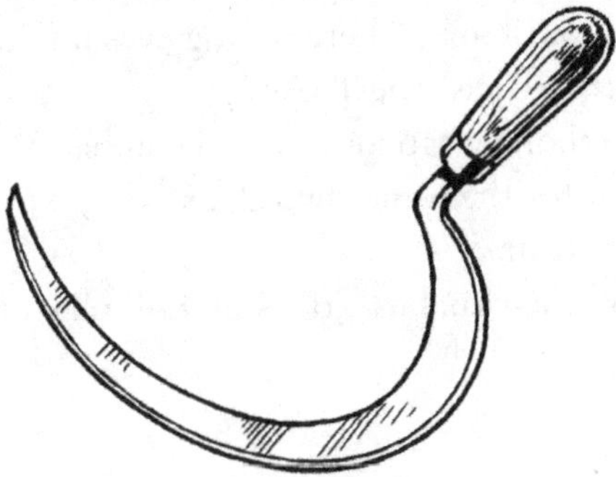

The Sickle is probably more associated with Druids than with Wicca. It is a small tool with a crescent-shaped blade usually used for harvesting herbs. Many Wiccans use a sickle or boleen on their altars, though, instead of the white-hilted knife.

The Boline is sometimes considered synonymous with the white-hilted knife, and sometimes with the sickle. It traditionally is a straighter edge with a curved tip (rather than fully curved like the sickle). However, you'll find knives called "bolines" of many different appearances.

Purpose: Cutting anything magical, from cutting a wand, to engraving, to harvesting herbs, to preparing magical brews.

Element: Earth

Polarity: Most people do not attribute polarity to cutting tools. However, it seems to me that cutting tools have polarity with the items being cut, energizing them as they are cut.

The Staff

If the sword is a "big athame," the staff is a "big wand." Some Pagans have a personal staff, using it as a walking stick—it looks impressive and is handy to walk with at Pagan gatherings and festivals. It's good for drawing attention when leading processions or large public rituals.

With few exceptions, Wiccan rituals don't call for a staff specifically—although it can serve the same function as a wand, as a riding pole, or as a sword. It's especially handy to have a staff if you're doing a ritual outdoors, where prying eyes might be alarmed to see a knife or sword. It's definitely easier to get past the TSA.

I've also used staffs as symbolic weapons in ritual combat.

Purpose: As a replacement for the wand, sword, or riding pole

Element: Fire or sometimes Air

Polarity: Depending upon the ritual use, the staff will take on the polarity of the tool it is being used as.

The Aspergillum

Every Wiccan ritual includes asperging—sprinkling—the ritual space. Sometimes, there is a need for additional asperging. The aspergillum is a tool used to sprinkle water. It is familiar to people who grew up Catholic, as it is used in the Catholic church for sprinkling holy water. It can look like a handle with a tea ball on the end, or it can be just a handle to which fresh herbs are attached. The herbs are then dipped in the water.

In over forty years of practice I have never used an aspergillum—it's perfectly fine to dip your fingers in the water and then flick the drops—however, it's a charming tool if you want one.

Purpose: Asperging

Element: Water

Polarity: The aspergillum is not a tool of polarity.

The Cauldron

Just as a sword is basically a "big athame," a cauldron is essentially a "big cup." Like the cup, it is a symbol of the Goddess and of abundance and plenty.

You will almost certainly never use your cauldron for making witch's brews or potions. It's just not practical. If you look at imagery of witches using cauldrons,[17] you'll quickly realize that they're used over large fires outdoors, or over large indoor hearths of a type that pretty much no one has nowadays. You can't use a cauldron to brew anything on your gas stovetop.

However, the cauldron is still a useful tool. In ritual, it is usually used to hold either water or fire, although sometimes, it can be used as a huge serving bowl for a feast—while you're not typically cooking in it, food can be transferred into it for serving in ritual space.

Mostly, I use my cauldron for fire. It is tremendously handy to be able to create a "bonfire" indoors for rituals when outdoor space is not available. Leaping over the bonfire is part of many festivals (see *Sabbats: The Wheel of the Year* beginning on page 108), but you won't always have a place to do that. A small fire can be built in the cauldron, but this can set off smoke alarms. Alternatively, you can put dirt or sand in a cauldron and then put lit candles in the sand, creating a nice indoor fire for celebrations.

Purpose: Holding abundance—of fire, water, or food

---

17 Such as *The Magic Circle* by John Waterhouse, or just about any image of the witches from *Macbeth*.

Element: Although it depends on what it contains, the cauldron typically corresponds to Water.

Polarity: The cauldron has polarity with the sword.

Crystal

Some people have a crystal on their altar as one of their magical tools. Full disclosure: I don't use one in this way and never have, so my knowledge of this tool is strictly theoretical. I do *like* crystals and am sensitive to their energies. I use them for various magical purposes, but not as a tool on my altar.

Purpose: A crystal gathers and condenses energy. It can be a focal point for meditation, it can be used during magic, it can be used instead of a wand when invoking deities, and instead of an athame or sword when casting the circle.

Element: Typically, the crystal is associated with Spirit and is more likely to be found on an altar when a five-element system[18] is in use.

Polarity: The crystal is not a tool of polarity.

Bell

A bell is an ancient tool of invocation. It makes a pleasing sound thought to attract spirits. When we invoke (see *Invocation: Calling the Gods* on page 345), we use many things—we might use an athame, wand, or something else from the altar, and we use words, gestures, and our voices. Thus, adding the sound of a bell can be seen as superfluous. However, it can be a beautiful addition to a ritual. Bells are also fairly easy to acquire, so for a beginner, it's a lovely way to flesh out your altar.

Purpose: The bell is used to summon and attract spirits and deities. It can also be used to signal beginnings and endings.

Element: Air—the vibration of a bell's sound is carried by air.

Polarity: The bell is not a tool of polarity.

Specialty Tools

Some tools are rarely used. They are usually called for only if you are the initiate of a specific tradition. Some traditions have rules that only initiates can own certain tools. Of course, if you are not a part of those traditions, you are not bound by their rules and can own whatever you like! However, if you intend to join a tradition, it's probably best for you to wait for their instructions as to what tradition-specific tools you need.

Because these tools are often used only in secret, and since I'm not an initiate of every tradition, I'll just list a few here and leave it at that.

- Cord/cingulum
- Scourge

18 Meaning, Air, Fire, Water, Earth, and Spirit, as opposed to a four-element system of Air, Fire, Water, and Earth.

- Stang
- Ankh
- Labrys

The above are samples—I'm sure there are many others, unique to traditions that haven't shared their secrets with me.

Other Essential Items

As I said, not everything is considered a "tool," but that doesn't mean you don't need it. When you're stocking your kitchen with cooking tools, nobody mentions a sink—it's not something you cook with, but you sure do need one in your kitchen!

The Four Elements

Having the four elements of Air, Fire, Water, and Earth present in ritual space is integral to Wiccan ritual. (Some people add Spirit as a fifth element.) Everyone is going to at least have the four elements on their altar in some form or another. I used to really like adding little elemental altars in each quarter (East, South, West, and North), but my space is too small for that these days, and it's not at all necessary.

Air: This is usually symbolized by the incense, or specifically, by the unlit incense. Some people use a feather or a fan to symbolize Air.

Whether you're using loose incense, stick incense, cones, or sage bundles, you'll want a nice container of some kind.

Fire: Some people use a candle to symbolize Fire. While this seems obvious, it's not the only good Fire symbol. There are several other candles in ritual, so I like to separate out my Fire symbol. I use the burning charcoal on the censer to represent Fire and then add the unlit incense/Air to create a blend of the two.

If you have a censer, you probably need a fireproof tile of some kind. If you're using a candle, you probably need a candle holder. And you'll need a lighter or matches in any case.

Water: Almost universally, a dish of water is used. Some people might use a seashell; perhaps a large shell can serve as the water dish.

Earth: Most people use a dish of salt. Especially when working indoors, anything else can be messy. However, pebbles, flower petals, or soil can be used.

Spirit: People who choose to represent Spirit as a fifth element generally use a quartz crystal, a lamp, an ankh, or nothing at all, as the idea of Spirit may be considered invisible. (This isn't something I do personally.)

Quarter Candles

One of the constants of Wiccan ritual is that the quarters are summoned, meaning that at the cardinal points of East, South, West, and North, the entity in charge of that direction is summoned and asked to guard and protect the ritual. In general, the four directions correspond to the four elements.

This necessitates a candle at each cardinal point. Some people start the ritual with the quarter candles lit, while others light them as part of the ritual.

I have placed quarter candles on the floor, but this poses obvious risks. I had beautiful quarter stands that got damaged in a move, now I use the nearest table or other high surface. When outdoors, tiki torches are great.

Because you're using these candles over and over, and since they should stay lit during the entire duration of the ritual, I prefer pillar candles in glass holders. This means that sooner or later, you'll need something very long to reach inside and light them.

Libation Bowl

This is only essential if you're doing indoor ritual. In Wicca, liquid offerings (wine or another drink) are poured to the gods. Where are you pouring them? Outdoors, they're poured directly onto the Earth. Indoors, you use a libation bowl and take the offerings outside later. In a group ritual, this bowl is passed from person to person, so it should be large and deep to prevent spills.

The Practical List of Essentials

- *Candles:* You need a lot of candles: Quarter candles, candles to represent Fire (if that's how you're doing that), altar candles (a pair of candles on every altar for extra light), candles to symbolize other things, and candles for magic. Candles require candle holders.
- *Dishes:* Incense, water, and salt all go in dishes. A libation bowl is also a kind of dish. Extra offerings might require extra dishes. You probably want an ashtray under the altar for used matches and the like.
- *Fire stuff:* You must have a fire extinguisher if you're lighting a lot of fires. I insist. You need lighters and/or matches, charcoals for loose incense, and probably tongs for holding the hot charcoal, as well as a fireproof tile for the censer.
- *Corkscrew:* Most Wiccans use wine in ritual. Plan accordingly.

Additional Items

Here are some additional items (not technically tools) that aren't strictly necessary but which you may want.

Symbols of the Deities

Bless this wonderful Pagan world! When I was starting out, getting a statue of a goddess or god was nearly impossible, and both books and teachers gave you alternatives. Now, they're available everywhere. While you don't absolutely have to have representations of the gods on your altar, they are close to essential—they help you focus and give you a place to direct your energy.

While representations are available, they can be expensive. Here are some options:

Goddess

- Statuettes of specific goddesses, either museum reproductions or those created for Pagan worship
- Generic "woman" statuettes
- Framed pictures
- A representation (picture or statuette) of the moon
- A seashell
- A mirror

God

- Statuettes of specific gods, either museum reproductions or those created for Pagan worship
- Generic "man" statuettes
- Framed pictures
- A representation (picture or statuette) of the sun
- Antlers
- A phallic symbol

I do encourage you to be respectful of artists. If someone created a sculpture or picture, you should not be buying a copy that rips them off.

Some people don't consecrate their deity statues, as they consider the presence of the deity to be inherently consecrating. Others use the consecration as a way of bringing that presence.

Robe

Some people do ritual in street clothes, some skyclad, but most people prefer to wear robes. Changing into something special for ritual (or disrobing) helps you shift into the right mood.

While you could shop online for "Pagan robes," you'll probably find a more abundant selection by using "caftan" as a search term.

Jewelry

Like robes, having special ritual jewelry can help you feel ready for ritual. If you have a necklace, bracelet, ring, etc., only worn during ritual, just putting it on helps you enter the proper mental space.

Musical Instruments

Music, especially rhythm, is one of the easiest and most accessible ways to alter consciousness. Medical evidence is growing that music and rhythm affect things as disparate as breath, focus, mood, and heart rate.

Instruments aren't necessary. Singing, chanting, and toning are powerful. I've done wonderful rituals using "body rhythm," where we clapped, snapped our fingers, tapped our feet, drummed against our legs and chests, and thrilled to the sounds made entirely with our own bodies.

But if you choose to acquire instruments, you can start small and inexpensively. While *djembes* (an African drum) are beautiful and popular in the Pagan community, you can more easily and cheaply acquire or create rattles, finger cymbals, rhythm sticks, and so on.

Consecrating Tools

Consecration is a skill you'll use often in Wicca. You consecrate tools, but you also consecrate things for one-off use. For example, if you're doing a healing spell, you might consecrate the photograph of the person being healed.

To consecrate, you need to know:

- What you're doing.
- How you're doing it.
- That you've succeeded.

What you're doing means you should clearly state your intention. *How* means you should know what power it is that consecrates—the gods, the elements, your will—however you phrase it, it must be present. And then, always finish by declaring *success*.

To consecrate a tool, follow these basic steps:

1. State your intention
2. Invoke the aid of the gods
3. Cleanse the tool
4. Purify the tool
5. State your success
6. Immediately use the tool

Typically, a consecration is done in a cast circle, so you've already done all the ritual preparation needed. (See *Casting a Circle* on page 78.)

Stating Your Intention

You can incorporate this into subsequent steps, or you can simply say:

"This [tool] will now be consecrated for [purpose]."

For example:

*"I now consecrate this athame, that it represent my will
and intention in all things and direct my energies."*
"This pentacle shall be made sacred to serve as a tool upon my altar."

Invoking the Aid of the Gods

Since you're asking the gods for help, you can combine steps one and two:

*"Lord and Lady, lend your aid as I consecrate this wand
to serve as a tool of my will."*

Or, it can be a separate step, first stating your intention and then presenting the tool to the gods (by lifting it before their symbols).

So, after stating your intention, you can lift up the tool and say something like:

"Lord and Lady, lend your power to this consecration."

Other powers can be called upon:

*"By the power of the gods, by the strength of my will,
by the balance of the universe, I do consecrate this sword."*

Cleansing

Cleansing and purifying, together, combine the four elements—the building blocks of the universe—and so leverage the powers of balance and creation.

Cleansing uses saltwater, which combines the elements of Earth and Water. (You will already have mixed a bit of consecrated salt into the consecrated water.) Water cleanses, obviously, and salt is a preservative. Saltwater is the source of life, which emerged from the ocean. Amniotic fluid is primarily saltwater, so our own lives begin in it.

Thoroughly wet the object being consecrated by dipping your fingers into the water dish and transferring the drops to the object. Wet every part of the object. If water would destroy it, wet around it, or wrap it in something protective and wet the wrapping.

If you're consecrating something metal, clean it immediately after the ritual to avoid salt damage.

Say something like:

"By Water and Earth, I cleanse this [tool] that it be consecrated."

Purifying

Passing the object through the burning incense smoke purifies it. The smoke combines the elements of Fire and Air. Again, be sure every part of the object, top to bottom, is touched by the smoke, while you say:

"By Fire and Air, I purify this [tool] that it be consecrated."

You can fold the first two steps into steps three and four like this:

"I do cleanse this [tool] by Water and Earth, that it be [purpose of tool].
Lord and Lady, aid my work!"
"I do purify this [tool] by Fire and Air, that it be [purpose of tool].
Lord and Lady, aid my work!"

State Your Success

In business, this is called "closing the sale." Don't leave the request (or even the demand) for consecration dangling.

"This [tool] is now consecrated. So mote it be!"

"So mote it be" is the traditional Wiccan phrase for "it is done," and it ends many acts of magic. You can use more colloquial language if you prefer.

Immediately Use the Tool

This seals the deal and completes the cycle. If there isn't an obvious use for the tool, you can present it to the gods and the quarters as its first use.

Example: Consecrating an Athame

Clear your mind, take a deep breath, and focus on your intention.
Hold the athame up, and say:

"I do consecrate this athame, that it be a tool of my Will.
Lord and Lady, lend your aid to this work, that my Will be manifest."

Wet the athame with saltwater thoroughly, saying:

"By Water and Earth, I do cleanse and consecrate this tool of my Will."

Pass the athame through the incense smoke, back and forth, thoroughly smoking it, saying:

"By Fire and Air, I do purify and consecrate this tool of my Will."

Lift the athame and say:

"The work is done. So mote it be!"

Draw an invoking pentagram in the air to use the athame.

Altars

People use the word "altar" to mean a wide variety of different things, and that can be confusing. An altar is:

- The physical object (usually a table) upon which magical tools and other things are placed during ritual. Usually, this is set up only for the duration of the ritual. So, you'll hear things like, "My coffee table is my altar."
- The prescribed setup of tools and objects for a ritual. For example, "A Wiccan altar always has an athame on it." Symbolically, the altar in this sense can represent the universe itself, as it contains all magical tools and elements.
- A permanent magical setup for a specific act of worship or reverence. For example, an ancestor altar or an altar to Hecate. People often have one or more such altars in their homes. This is also called a "shrine."
- A permanent magical setup for generic meditation or magic. A spot that's your "go-to" when working at an altar is something you need, as discussed under *Wiccan Practices* on page 71.
- A temporary setup for a specific spell or act of worship. For example, a spell to pass Organic Chemistry might require daily work at an altar, which would be dismantled once you successfully pass.

The Altar Table for Ritual

A working surface is 100% necessary, but a table isn't. If you must, you can lay a cloth on the floor or on the ground. Often, a coffee table doubles as an altar. Currently, my altar and my coffee table are the same piece of furniture, because my apartment is just not big enough for a dedicated ritual space with its own furnishings. Where would I put a coffee table-sized object when not in use? In this place, *nowhere.* It's probably the only significant magical object that just about everyone allows to serve a dual magical/mundane purpose.

The dual purpose can be handled a number of ways. A lot of people have altar cloths—you lay the cloth over the ordinary table, and *voila*! It is no longer ordinary. Some people have different altar cloths for different occasions and/or seasons.

Or, you might have a table runner, and *removing* the cloth signals the difference between magical and mundane.

My current altar is custom-made, fitting exactly the size and shape specifications I wanted, with a bottom shelf for convenience. I designed it for use as an altar to double as a coffee table—not the other way around. It is a beautiful piece of furniture that I'm proud to display, and cleaning it and then setting it up for ritual is all I need to make the needed mental shift.

Most people don't consecrate the altar, but it's fine if you want to do so.

My first altar was very small, which made it impossible to do some of the things I wanted to do—such as use a large vase of flowers or a particularly ornate statue of the Goddess. I loved (and love) that piece of furniture passionately, but eventually I just wanted something more practical.

My recommendations, then, born of long experience: Lay out your tools where you're going to be casting the circle to get a sense of how much space you need. Check for sturdiness—you'll have candles and incense on this piece of furniture, so it should not be wobbly. The shape should not be too rectangular. It doesn't have to be perfectly round or square, but it should fit nicely in your Wiccan circle and not bisect it. If it's twice or three times as long as it is wide, it doesn't feel, to me, like it fits with the symmetry of a circle. If you're working with a group, it should be small enough so that people can reach across, and see each other, and still feel connected even though there's a table between them.[19] Coffee table height (about 18 inches) is correct if you're sitting on the floor or on cushions, full-size table height only works if you use chairs, and not everyone has chairs in the circle. (Chairs are an ability issue—for most of my life, chairs in ritual were unthinkable; we always used cushions on the floor. But as my knee troubles got worse, getting up and down from the floor became my least favorite thing.)

Figure out how to protect your surface. Altar cloths protect the table, but that means you'll be removing melted wax from them. (Melted wax is the bane of every witch's existence.) Cloth isn't fireproof, so adding a fireproof tile for your censer is probably needed. (My first, tiny altar had a tile surface, so I didn't need an extra tile until recently.)

Home Altars

A home altar setup can be very individual. Whole books have been written on the subject. Ancestor altars, devotional altars, meditation altars, elemental altars—each have their own needs. Let's set those aside and talk here about a generic home altar.

When performing Wiccan ritual, you'll prepare the space, get it all set up, and take it all apart afterward. Most of us don't have the luxury of a dedicated ritual room where all that's needed is cleaning.

Having something permanent set aside is helpful, though. I use my altar for all sorts of things:

- Morning meditation—clearing my mind, bringing the Goddess to me as my day begins
- Perhaps refocusing or praying at some point during the day
- Perhaps shielding (I may or may not do this at my altar)
- Impromptu magic

19 This is assuming the altar is in the center. Some people put it in one of the quarters, which changes the requirements.

- Meditation before ritual

When setting up the altar, keep in mind that it has two states, *active* and *passive*. This means it has two purposes: First, to be used (active) in any of the ways mentioned above (plus others, of course), and second, to be a permanent (passive) setup that you can see and stop at, whenever you pass by.

The physical space: My altar's space is defined by a beautiful mirror—everything is on or near it. You might use a tray, a cloth, a cheeseboard, a table, a shelf—anything that defines a small area.

The four elements: There are lots of ways to do this. For a permanent altar, a lit flame, incense, or water aren't practical—flames burn out and water evaporates. You can use these things when you activate your altar, but you want permanent things for its passive state as well. Here are some recommendations:

- *Air:* A feather, a fan, a bell, a piece of pumice stone
- *Fire:* A piece of lava, flint, or tiger's eye, an ornate book of matches
- *Water:* A goblet, a seashell, a piece of aquamarine or quartz crystal
- *Earth:* A dish of salt or rock salt, a dish of soil, a piece of moss agate or granite

The gods: Can be represented by statuettes, pictures, or symbols, as discussed under tools. If you also have a devotional altar, you might not have them here.

Incense and candles: Have these handy for when you activate the altar, as well as a lighter or matches and a candle holder, of course.

Something to activate and deactivate the altar: For example, a bell or rattle, so that a sound signals the beginning and ending of your use of the altar. Sometimes I use a rattle or tambourine throughout my altar work, sometimes just at the beginning and end. You might also use an object that is moved forward and then back, or a cloth cover over a piece of the altar that is removed and then replaced.

Tools of focus and concentration: This can be anything, and you might want more than one thing, to give yourself options. For example, a rosary or prayer beads, a prayer wheel, a rattle, a wand, a stone, or some other object that you hold, etc. Or you can use candle-gazing, since you already have candles.

Decoration: Beautify your altar in any way that feels good and makes it a sacred space to you. I have lovely stones and shells, a fancy candle snuffer, a beautiful dish...the possibilities are endless.

When your altar isn't in active use, be sure to keep it clean so that it pleases you and feels sacred.

Tools from Nature and the Cosmos

The things a Wiccan uses in magic and ritual aren't confined to manufactured tools like wands and brooms. Nature and the cosmos provide their own inherent tools. When we use "natural" tools, we leverage their innate properties.

There are many such tools. We'll cover herbs, crystals/gems, numbers, and colors. But there are many, many others, including planets and other astrological features, foods, metals, trees, weather systems, and more.

Herbs and Plants

Herbs have their own physical properties. Lavender and chamomile are calming. The scent of rosemary is energizing and stimulates memory. Black tea is a stimulant. Willow bark is an analgesic.

Often, the physical property of an herb is associated with its magical properties by analogy. For example, using lavender in a spell to calm someone far away isn't relying on its natural calming properties, which a distant person can't experience. Instead, the biological nature of the plant creates a sympathetic magical nature.

Plant properties that we learn from folklore might be related to their physical properties, to experimentation by ancient peoples, or by analogies. The solar properties of a sunflower, for example, are because of what it looks like, as well as how it faces the sun.

When thinking of the use of a plant and its magical nature, keep in mind that different parts of a plant might have different properties. The leaf, root, stem, flower, and fruit of a plant are all different. In the kitchen, turnip greens are very different from the turnip itself (the root). Similarly, cilantro and coriander are the same plant—cilantro is the leaf and coriander is the seed.

An herbalist might be an expert in all sorts of herbal preparations and their uses, and might also have their own garden, *and* might be skilled in wildcrafting—finding and harvesting wild herbs. But even without a deep knowledge of any of these areas of herbalism, you can still use plants in your witchcraft.

Plant Preparations

Virtually everyone uses plants in their rituals—in the form of incense. But please note that not every plant can be burned. I was once warned to *never ever* burn garlic. The warning was so intense that my curiosity got the better of me, and I have regretted it ever since. The smell was so disgusting, I was tempted to get a hotel room until the house completely aired out.

Many plants that can be burned, especially leafy ones, burn very dry and are gone in a flash. Woody ones, on the other hand, last but are exceptionally smoky. A good incense mix takes a bit of skill to get right and needs binding agents—generally resins like frankincense—to hold it together.

Plants can be used fresh or dried. Fresh or dried herbs can be made into teas, infusions, tinctures, or oils. Creating an essential oil is a specialized skill requiring distillation equipment, but herbs can be added to oils in other ways. Simply leaving fresh herbs sitting in oil for a while will impart the aroma and essence of the herb, and this process can be repeated: Leave the herbs soaking in oil for 24 hours, then squeeze out the oil with a cheesecloth, discarding the herbs, and repeat the whole process with fresh herbs in the already-infused oil.

Using Plants in Ritual and Magic

There are dozens of ways to bring the magical properties of a plant into your ritual. Here are some ideas:

- Use the plant as an ingredient in cooking something that will be eaten as part of a ritual or spell.
- Burn the plant in your incense.
- Use aromatherapy: As a part of a spell, or as a preliminary step, inhale the aroma of a fresh plant or essential oil.
- Add fresh or dried plant parts to wax when making a candle.
- Create a sachet and sleep with it under your pillow for overnight magic.
- Add herbs to a ritual bath.
- Use herb-infused anointing oil.
- Create a magical wash or soak by making a tea from a plant and then washing, painting, or soaking an object or space with the tea.
- Choose wood for magical tools based on the properties of that wood (trees are plants, after all).
- Carry a leaf or seed on your person to bring the properties of that plant.
- Hang fresh or dried plants (such as garlic for protection) in a meaningful place or sprinkle it on the ground.

A Word About Sage

Because "smudging" is popular among white Westerners, white sage is being overharvested to an alarming degree. While not yet officially endangered, it is becoming harder for Native Americans to acquire.

The word "smudge" for the use of a sage bundle is considered inappropriate unless it is being done in a Native American context. There is no need for non-Native people to culturally appropriate this practice, as there are plenty of ways to purify and cleanse yourself without interfering with and contributing to the scarcity of traditional Native practices.

Sage is a powerful herb for healing and purification. I grow some myself, using some in the kitchen (it's so good in soup) and making sage bundles or incense from the rest. What I do not do, and what I can ask you not to do, is buy sage bundles commercially, because that contributes to overharvesting.

Gems, Crystals, and Minerals

The use of crystals in magic and ritual has become increasingly popular over the past couple of decades—it's a practice picked up from the New Age community. Certainly, the occult properties of stones have been known since ancient times and appear in the Bible, but their ritual use is relatively new, yet quite effective.

Much is made of the crystalline structure of various stones, along which vibration is said to travel. Most of the powers of stones, though, can be understood through their color, through their obvious physical properties, and through folklore associated with stones. For example, diamonds are the hardest stone and are associated magically with physical strength—the physical property creates sympathy with the occult property. Rubies are associated with power, just as the color red is.

Using Stones in Ritual and Magic

As with plants, there are many ways to bring the magical properties of a stone into your ritual or magical work. Here are a few ideas:

- Add stones to anything being created for a magical purpose, such as candle wax, poppets, or mojo bags.
- Create "stone water" by soaking a stone in consecrated water and using the water.
- Create magical jewelry from meaningful stones.
- Embed stones in magical tools, such as your wand or the hilt of your athame.
- Create a geometric pattern out of stones and use it as a meditation mandala.
- Place meaningful stones at the four quarters of your ritual space.
- Consecrate yourself with a stone's properties by rubbing it onto your power points, as if you were anointing yourself.
- Add gem chips to the oil when making anointing oil.
- Carry a stone on your person to bring the properties of that stone.
- Use stones on your personal altar(s).
- Hold an appropriate stone while visualizing a desired outcome during a spell.

Colors and Numbers

When we talk about plants and minerals, we are talking about natural substances that grow or develop. But colors and numbers don't grow; they simply are. They are *properties.*

In the case of each, they have inherent qualities as well as qualities that are culturally driven. We can say, for example, that colors have their own vibration—they each have a unique wavelength on the visible spectrum. But many color correspondences are cultural. Associating purple with royalty, for example, is because purple robes were once worn exclusively by kings (because of the rarity of the natural dye).

The story with numbers is similar. Certain numbers have a specific nature that has nothing to do with human culture: One is singular, and things associated with singularity are associated with that number, regardless of whose numerology you study. Yet, other numbers have strong cultural associations. You don't associate four with the seasons of the year, for example, unless you're from someplace that has four seasons.

Color

Color correspondences are found in many magical systems. To name just a few, there are colors associated with the signs and planets of astrology, with alchemy, with the chakras in Hinduism, and with Kabbalah in Judaism (both chakras and Kabbalah are also often used by Western occultists, including Wiccans—some consider this cultural appropriation).

Because color correspondences have such a wide variety of sources, they will sometimes contradict each other. For example, white in the West is largely associated with purity, chastity, and brides. In the East, it is a funeral color and is associated with death. You'll have to look over the correspondences and determine if they're meaningful to you and stick with a specific meaning—white will lose its power for you if sometimes it's purity, sometimes it's death, and sometimes it's ice cream.

There are colors associated with both the Goddess and the God, as well as with many other Pagan deities. Colors can help focus you on the face or aspect of the Goddess or God as well. The Goddess, after all, is both Lady of the Moon and Mother Earth—these have different color associations—while the God is both Death and Rebirth, both agriculture and the hunt. There are also colors associated with each Sabbat.

Using Color in Ritual and Magic

As a general rule, color will be an adornment of, or addition to, something else in your ritual, not the primary focus. For example, if you were making a mojo bag for a magical purpose, you might add stones, herbs, and other objects to the bag—but the color of the bag itself can also be meaningful. You might choose a color based on the astrological sign of the subject of the magic or based on the purpose of the magic.

Some traditions define what color things should be in ritual, but barring that, you can choose the color of candles, robes, and altar cloths to add the magical properties of color to any ritual. In working magic, candles, again, are frequently where color will play a role, but if you paint or decorate any magical object, color is meaningful. Some people add color symbolism to their magical tools as well.

Numbers

There are many different systems of numerology, as well as magic associated with numbers outside of any "system." However, in Western occultism—the area that includes Wicca—there are primarily two. These are Pythagorean numerology, and Hebrew numerology as found in the Kabbalah.

Pythagorean Numbers

Pythagoras was a philosopher who lived around 500 BCE. Part of his numerological system corresponded numbers to letters. In this way, words have numeric values. But keep in mind that Pythagoras was Greek, so originally the letters were not the Latin ones used in English.

The numeric value of a word is derived by *arithmetic reduction*: This is easiest to teach by example, so we'll start with my name, DEBORAH. In Pythagorean numerology, D=4, E=5, B=2, O=6, R=9, A=1, H=8. So, you add these numbers together: 4+5+2+6+9+1+8=35

Recursive reduction means that you continue this process until you reach a single digit, or one of the master numbers (11, 22, or 33), which are not reduced. So, 4+5+2+6+9+1+8=35, then take 35 and reduce it further: 3+5=8. My name number is 8. Now, I can analyze the number 8 to learn more about my name.

Kabbalistic Numbers

Hebrew numerology is a vast mystical system rooted in the Hebrew alphabet. As such, it doesn't translate to English-language use. Numerology based on Kabbalah can be called "Hebrew," since Kabbalah begins in Judaism and the Hebrew language, but it is much simpler. Because so much Hermetic Kabbalah exists in English, it. is also usable by English-speakers.

Astrological Numbers

There are numbers associated with astrology, although it's not a numerological system. It's straightforward: Aries is the first sign, and the signs are numbered in order. The signs *do* have a relationship with their numbers: One is singularity and leadership, and Aries, as a sign, is a leader. The second sign, Taurus, is deeply concerned with relationships, associating it with the "couples" aspect of the number two. Three is a number of flux, and the third sign, Gemini, is a sign in constant flux.

Using Numbers in Ritual and Magic

There are innumerable (teehee) ways of using numbers in ritual and magic because everything in your ritual exists in a quantity.

Wiccan ritual already leverages numbers: There are four elements, two deities, four quarters, one altar—number symbolism permeates ritual. But you can add numbers to ritual and magic in ways limited only by your imagination:

- Use numerology when choosing a magical name. If you like a name but don't like its numeric resonance, change the spelling. People spell my name DEBORAH, DEBORA, or DEBRA. Consonants can be doubled. Double consonants can be made single. There's lots of ways to manipulate the numerology of a name.
- If you wear a beaded necklace or other beaded item in ritual it can have a number of stones, and multiple numbers can be used. Using the *Gems and Minerals: Reference Table* on pages 63-65. you can choose to make a necklace balanced in the four elements by using a stone of each element. You can then choose a different number for each stone so that each individual number has meaning, and the reduced total has meaning.
- When doing a spell using candles, *how many* candles do you use?

- When chanting or reciting a rhyme during ritual or spellwork, *how many* repetitions do you use?
- When dancing in ritual, *how many times* do you circle the altar?
- When creating an incense, *how many* ingredients does it have?
- When creating a mojo bag, *how many* items are added to the bag?
- Some spells are repeated over *a number* of days.
- Dates and times are numbers and scheduling can leverage numerology. This is almost impossible in a group, when real world schedules take precedence, but is very doable for a solitary.

Reference Tables

The following tables will help you easily find the information you need in regard to the various tools we've discussed.

Wiccan Tools			
Tool	**Priority**	**How It's Used**	**Substitutions**
Athame	Highest	• Directs, concentrates, and focuses energy • Cuts energy • Casts the circle • Commands spirits	Sword, wand, your hand
Wand	Highest	• Directing energy • Summoning spirits • Inviting deity	Athame, staff, your hand
Cup	Highest	• Receiving blessings by drinking • Communion with the gods	None
Pentacle	Highest	• Receiving blessings through food • Gateway to other worlds	None

Wiccan Tools			
Tool	**Priority**	**How It's Used**	**Substitutions**
Book of Shadows	Extremely high	• Writing spells, rituals, invocations, etc. that are then used • Keeping notes on rituals that have been performed (journaling) • Notes on dreams, trances, and other mystical experiences • Receiving a handed-down tradition, or passing such a tradition on	None
Censer	High	Holding burning incense	An incense stick holder or dish
Sword	Medium	Same as the athame	Athame, wand, staff
Broom	Medium	• Riding • Cleansing • Handfasting	Riding pole or staff (for riding only)
White-handled knife/sickle/boline	Medium	Cutting anything used for magic	A non-magical knife
Staff	Low	Can replace the wand, sword, or riding pole	Wand, sword, riding pole, broom
Aspergillum	Low	Sprinkling water	Your hand or a bundle of herbs
Cauldron	Low	Holding fire, water, or food	A firepit, a large bowl
Crystal	Low	• Gathering energy • Focal point for meditation • Symbolizing spirit • Substituting for athame or wand	Fire can be a focal point; pentacle can gather energy
Bell	Low	• Summon spirits with sound • Signaling beginnings and endings	Your voice, hand claps, or another instrument

The following table focuses on easily found plants and those I find exceptionally useful. It is meant as a start and is not comprehensive.

Herbs and Plants			
Plant	**Magical Properties**	**Element**	**Planet**
Alfalfa	Prosperity, money	Earth	Venus
Allspice	Money, luck, healing	Fire	Mars
Anise	Protection, purification	Air	Jupiter
Basil	Love, wealth, protection, luck	Fire	Mars
Bay	Protection, purification, psychic powers, healing	Fire	Sun
Birch	Protection, purification, exorcism	Water	Venus
Cardamon	Love, lust	Water	Venus
Cedar	Healing, purification, protection, money	Fire	Sun
Chamomile	Sleep, meditation, love, purification	Water	Sun
Cinnamon	Love, lust, healing, psychic powers, money	Fire	Sun
Comfrey	Travel, money	Water	Saturn
Cumin	Protection, fidelity, exorcism, anti-theft	Fire	Mars
Dragon's blood	Love, protection, exorcism, sexual potency	Fire	Mars
Fennel	Protection, healing, purification	Fire	Mercury
Frankincense	Protection, exorcism, spirituality	Fire	Sun
Hemp (marijuana)	Healing, love, meditation	Water	Saturn
Lavender	Love, protection, sleep, longevity, purification, happiness, peace	Air	Mercury
Marjoram	Protection, love, happiness, healing, money	Air	Mercury
Mint (garden mint)	Money, lust, healing, travel, exorcism, protection	Air	Mercury
Mugwort	Psychic power, dreams, protection, healing, astral travel	Earth	Venus

Herbs and Plants			
Plant	**Magical Properties**	**Element**	**Planet**
Myrrh	Protection, exorcism, healing, spirituality	Water	Moon
Patchouli	Money, fertility, lust	Earth	Saturn
Rose	Love, psychic power, healing, luck, protection	Water	Venus
Rosemary	Protection, love, lust, exorcism, purification, healing, sleep	Fire	Sun
Rue	Healing, exorcism, love	Fire	Mars
Sandalwood	Protection, healing, exorcism, spirituality	Water	Moon
Sunflower	Fertility, wisdom	Fire	Sun
Tea	Wealth, courage, strength	Fire	Sun
Thyme	Healing, sleep, psychic power, love, purification, courage	Water	Venus

Some of the stones listed here are precious gems, but others are commonly found in nature or easy to purchase. Some you may already have in your home.

You'll do well with a visual guide, a book, or an app that lets you know what stone you have in your hand. (See *Recommended Reading* on page 351.)

Gems and Minerals			
Stone	**Magical Properties**	**Element**	**Planet**
Agate, Green	Fertility, healing, courage, protection	Earth	Mercury
Agate, Moss	Gardening, healing, wealth, longevity, strength	Earth	Mercury
Agate, Red (blood agate)	Strength, courage, healing, peace, protection	Fire	Mercury
Amber	Healing, strength, fertility, protection, magical power, anti-hexing	Fire	Sun
Aquamarine	Travel protection (travel by water), purification, communication, psychic power, peace	Water	Moon

Gems and Minerals			
Stone	**Magical Properties**	**Element**	**Planet**
Aventurine	Luck, eyesight, creativity, perception, peace	Air	Mercury
Bloodstone	Healing, strength, courage, wealth	Fire	Mars
Coral	Protection, healing, wisdom, peace, sleep, anti-hexing, anti-depressant	Water	Venus
Diamond	Strength, courage, sexuality, spirituality	Fire	Sun
Emerald	Love, money, knowledge, memory, protection	Earth	Venus
Flint	Protection	Fire	Mars
Garnet	Protection, healing (skin, inflammation, heart), strength	Fire	Mars
Granite	Grounding, focus, healing, courage, detoxification	Earth	Moon
Hematite	Grounding, healing, divination	Fire	Saturn
Jade	Love, healing (kidney, heart, stomach), gardening, money, protection	Water	Venus
Jet	Protection, health, luck, divination	Earth	Saturn
Lapis Lazuli	Healing, love, psychic powers, fidelity, protection	Water	Venus
Moonstone	Love, sleep, gardening, travel protection, psychic powers	Water	Moon
Opal	Luck, psychic powers, beauty, power	Water	Venus
Opal, Fire	Money	Fire	Mercury
Pearl	Love, money, protection (against fire)	Water	Moon
Pumice	Banishment, protection	Air	Mercury
Quartz, clear	Psychic power, magic, healing, lactation	Water	Moon
Quartz, rose	Love	Water	Moon
Quartz, smoky	Anti-depression, grounding	Fire	Sun
Ruby	Energy, protection, wealth	Fire	Mars
Salt	Purification, grounding, money	Earth	Moon
Sapphire	Love, peace, protection, healing	Water	Moon
Sodalite	Peace, healing	Water	Venus

Gems and Minerals			
Stone	**Magical Properties**	**Element**	**Planet**
Topaz	Peace, anti-hexing, money, love	Fire	Sun

Elemental Colors				
	Air	**Fire**	**Water**	**Earth**
Alchemical Color	Yellow	Red	Blue	Green
Additional Color Correspondences	White, sky blue	Orange	Sea green, silver	Black, brown

Astrological Colors and Numbers			
Sign	**Number**	**Standard Color(s)**[20]	**Golden Dawn Color(s)**[21]
Aries	1	Red	Scarlet
Taurus	2	Emerald green, pastel green, pastels generally	Red-orange
Gemini	3	Turquoise, iridescent colors, silver	Orange
Cancer	4	Silver, pale blue	Amber
Leo	5	Gold, orange, yellow	Greenish yellow
Virgo	6	Brown, gray, white	Yellowish green
Libra	7	Blue	Emerald
Scorpio	8	Dark red	Greenish blue
Sagittarius	9	Purple	Blue
Capricorn	10	Black	Indigo
Aquarius	11	Electric blue, rainbow	Purple
Pisces	12	Sea green, violet, indigo	Crimson

Planetary Colors		
Planet	**Standard Colors**	**Golden Dawn Color(s)**
Sun	Yellow, gold	Orange
Moon	Silver, blue, white	Blue
Mars	Red	Red
Mercury	Yellow, gray	Yellow

20 Per Larousse Encyclopedia

21 Per Regardie.

Planetary Colors		
Planet	**Standard Colors**	**Golden Dawn Color(s)**
Venus	Emerald, pink	Green
Jupiter	Blue	Violet
Saturn	Black, brown	Indigo
Uranus	Sky blue	
Neptune	Violet	
Pluto	Dark red	

Pythagorean Numbers			
Number	**Letters**	**Planet**	**Meaning**
1	A, J, S	Sun	Leadership, beginning, strength, independence, courage, self-sufficiency, egotism, ambition, dominance, selfish
2	B, K, T	Moon	Partnership, diplomacy, gentle, charm, supportive, relationship, cooperation, timid
3	C, L, U	Venus	Optimism, creative, social, spontaneous, imaginative, lazy, communicator, artistic
4	D, M, V	Saturn and Uranus	Practical, determined, builder, doer, traditional, security, earthy, poor health
5	E, N, W	Mercury	Progress, freedom, adventure, sensual, curious, resourceful, procrastination, aimless
6	F, O, X	Jupiter	Service, domestic, careful, teacher, reliable, unselfish, nervous
7	G, P, Y	Neptune	Investigator, loner, eccentric, analysis, inner exploration, rigid, spirituality
8	H, Q, Z	Saturn	Power, control, strength, problem solving, money, organizer, judge, impatient, vanity
9	I, R	Mars	Universe, generalist, teacher, humanitarian, healer, old soul, occult, generosity, moody
11		Neptune	Intuition, inspiration, prophecy, nervous, impractical
22		Uranus	Materialism, spiritual mastery, negative magic
33			Spiritual, need for guidance, honesty, transformation

Colors and Numbers in Kabbalah				
Sephirah	**Planet**	**Color[22]**	**Number**	**Qualities**
Keter	The "cosmic swirl"	White	1	Potential, creativity, the cosmos
Chokmah	The zodiac	Gray	2	Force, energy, motion, the Father
Binah	Saturn	Black	3	Form, shape, limitation, the Mother
Chesed	Jupiter	Blue	4	Compassion, forgiveness, loving kindness
Gevurah	Mars	Red	5	Law, judgment, limits
Tipheret	Sun	Yellow	6	Harmony, rebirth
Netzach	Venus	Green	7	Connection, kindness, passion, generosity
Hod	Mercury	Orange	8	Communication, self-actualization, ego, rationality
Yesod	Moon	Purple	9	Dreams, imagination, trance
Malkut	Earth	Citrine, Olive, Russet, and Black (seen as a quartered circle)	10	Reality

Color Qualities for Magic		
Color	**Qualities[23]**	**Chaos Magic[24]**
Red	Blood, so the body and healing, war, strength, power	War magic: conflict, defense, protection
Orange	Ego, materialism, pride, self-confidence, courage, money[25]	Thinking magic: responsibility, strategy, travel, gambling, risk-taking
Yellow	Logic, philosophy, education	Ego magic: knowledge, success, illumination, illusions
Green	Agriculture, plants, creativity, beauty, art	Partnership magic: developing or maintaining relationships, including with plants and animals

22 There are multiple color scales used in Kabbalah. Most commonly used is this one, the "Queen Scale."

23 Adapted from Bonewits.

24 Per Forge.

25 Many people associated green with money, but that is specifically American, and not in the nature of the color. Of course, if it works for you, go for it.

Color Qualities for Magic		
Color	**Qualities[23]**	**Chaos Magic[24]**
Blue	Emotions, religion, psychic phenomenon, the unconscious, divination	Wealth magic: money, prosperity
Indigo	Rain, weather, the sky, space, time	
Purple	Violence, passion, love,[26] lust, hate, fear, royalty, power, politics	Sex magic: also including creation, creativity, and fertility
Brown	The woods, animals, hunting[27]	
Black		Death magic: necromancy, mediumship, vampirism

Sabbat Colors	
Sabbat	**Colors**
Beltane	Green, brown, any floral color
Midsummer	Green, blue
Lammas	Yellow, brown, orange, gold
Fall Equinox	Brown, orange, red
Samhain	Black, orange, red
Yule	Green, red, white, gold
Candlemas	White, yellow
Spring Equinox	Pastels of all kinds

Deity Colors	
Deity	**Color**
Earth Mother	Brown, green
Lady of the Moon	Indigo, silver
Lady of the Ocean	Blue, seafoam green, coral pink
God of the Hunt	Black, red
Lord of the Underworld	Black

26 Both violence and lust are also often associated with red.

27 Also often associated with red.

Deity Colors	
Deity	**Color**
Sun Lord	Gold, yellow
God of the Crops	Green, gold (like wheat)

Chapter Six:

WICCAN PRACTICES

We've spent a lot of time on theoretical stuff—what Wicca is and isn't, and what kind of ideas and beliefs accompany Wicca. But it's time to get real—what do Wiccans actually *do*?

Well, we do a lot, both formally and informally, and how much we do and how we do it, is often a matter of personal preference. Some people honor every full moon and are happy with a once-a-month practice, while others add new moons. Some also have a daily practice.

In mainstream religions, you might go to weekly worship services without fail, you might only do so occasionally, or you might not go at all. You might pray every day, or only in times of great need. You might socialize with other people in your religious circle, or you might find the deepest moments of spirituality in private and have no wish for community. Wicca is no different in this regard and shows a similar range of expression and affiliation.

Nonetheless, there are specific ritual forms and traditions, as well as a host of additional practices, so let's dig in.

Who and How

When we talk about the "who" of your practice, there are three options:

- You practice alone (usually referred to as "solitary")
- You practice in a closed or semi-closed group (a coven, grove, or circle)
- You practice with an open or public group of some kind.

Let's look at each.

Solitary

The vast majority of Wiccans practice alone, whether by preference or necessity. There are both advantages and disadvantages. Full disclosure: I strongly prefer practicing in a group. I will try not to let my bias show, but it may be unavoidable.

Advantages of Solitary Practice

- Many people find it inhibiting to practice around others; they only truly let go in private. Maybe you love to sing, but you're embarrassed about the quality of your voice, and only truly sing out alone. Or perhaps drumming or dancing enhances your ritual, but also makes you feel shy. Maybe you want to practice skyclad but feel self-conscious about nudity around other people.

- You don't have to coordinate travel or schedules when setting up time for ritual.
- You can practice exactly as you like, not worrying if others in a group want to do what you feel like doing. You can build a ritual using Shakespeare, rock and roll, or silence, without concern about how others in a group will respond to that. Groups often run on consensus—magical energy is best when everyone is in harmony. If one person in a group absolutely hates a piece of poetry, for example, that can be a real needle scratch to the energy of the group. So, the group will almost certainly not use that piece, even if everyone else loves it. You don't have to accommodate the ability level and preferences of other people if you're solitary.
- You may just like being alone and feel most spiritual when you're alone.

Disadvantages of Solitary Practice

- You have only your own skills to draw on. In a group, there are some people who are musical, some who are crafty, some who like to do research, etc., and rituals can benefit from each of these. Alone, you have fewer resources.
- Having other people depend on you can keep you honest and focused. As a solitary, if you don't feel like doing ritual, you can blow it off, whereas if someone is waiting for you to show up so that you can do ritual together, you're more likely to follow through.
- You incur all the expenses and effort alone. In my group, one person brings cakes, one brings flowers for the altar, and one brings wine. No one is overburdened. Alone, it's all on you.
- You have to learn on your own, without others to learn from or learn with. In Wicca, we talk about "elders"—people with years of experience and knowledge to share, who help us gain our own wisdom. Culturally, we value this a lot less than we used to: Zoomers and Millennials are more comfortable learning on their own than Gen X or Boomers. But as great as social media is for sharing knowledge in an egalitarian way, it's also great for sharing disinformation. Solitary practice requires you to figure out how to do everything, maybe reinventing the wheel, maybe not knowing which sources are reliable and which are nonsense, which books are great, and which are crap.

Covens and Other Closed Groups

A "closed group" is private, for members or invited guests only. They generally meet at someone's home. You might go through a formal application or interview process to be invited to such a group.

As a rule, initiatory groups aren't inviting you to be initiated if they invite you to join their group. Rather, they have some kind of "outer" or training group, and if things work out, you'll be initiated. In some traditions, the training group is essentially a class, and initiation is the graduation ceremony upon successfully completing that class. In other traditions, initiation might or might not happen because it is based not just on accomplishments but on intuition or psychic information, which is to say, the group or group leaders have to feel or know it's right. Some traditions have a formal "dedicant" level prior to initiation—there's a lot of variation. The point is that meeting with a closed group is often a first step, and that works both ways. You're screening them as much as they're screening you.

Practicing in a closed group requires finding such a group and being accepted as a member. This may not be easy. You might also be moved to start a group, and that's *also* not easy. Let's skip over all that for now and look at why you might, or might not, *want* to do so.

To a certain extent, you can look at the advantages and disadvantages of solitary work and flip them around. Where feeling less inhibited is an advantage of solitary work, feeling observed and, therefore, inhibited is a disadvantage of group work—in each case listed above, that's true. But it's not the whole picture.

Advantages of Closed Group Practice

- Empowerment and reinforcement: This is a big one. The other members believe in you even when you don't believe in yourself, and this can be transformative. Standing in circle with a group, you can see yourself as the others see you—as a powerful and talented witch. Sometimes, it can be awfully hard to see that in the mirror, but as you hold up a mirror to one another, things change. You know your fellow coven members are full of self-doubt, and you see how unnecessary it is, how awesome they are. Seeing that makes it easier to reverse that knowledge and see yourself as they see you and set self-doubt aside.
- A coven often forms a kind of group mind, and this is a powerful magical and spiritual experience.
- "Love and trust:" This phrase is often heard in association with Wicca. A loving, trusting connection with another human is considered sacred in Wicca, and having such connections in ritual is, itself, an act of worship.
- Community: During the pandemic shutdown, we all became accustomed to being alone in ways that would previously have been considered abnormal and even unhealthy. Interconnection is a human need, and losing it increases depression, anxiety, and unhealthy habits. A 2020 study suggests that attending religious services regularly has a significant positive impact on health.[28] A coven can be a chosen family and a community.
- The whole is greater than the sum of its parts: It's not just that other people have skills you lack (as mentioned under solitary practice), it's that a group can combine its skills and styles in unique and unexpected ways.
- Accountability: This was also mentioned under solitary practice. I find this true for myself in myriad ways. Yes, I am more likely to have ritual when people show up at my home for ritual, but it's more than that. We know what's going on with one another, we do magic for one another, and we help each other with whatever we're working on. So, if we all do a spell for Jane to get a job, we'll naturally ask Jane how it's going, and Jane will naturally be more conscientious about holding up her end—following up on interviews and so on.
- It's wonderful to have experienced teachers, and finding a group like that is ideal. But even a group of beginners, learning together, can bounce things off one another and help with exploration and experimentation.

28 Chen, King, and VanderWeele.

- Many hands make light work when it comes to preparing for and cleaning up after ritual.
- Power is easier to raise in a group. Think of the energy of a cheering crowd at a concert or sporting event—groups get on a shared wavelength, which can build to a huge crescendo, and a big part of working magic is *using* that crescendo. You can certainly raise power as an individual, but there are peaks that are generally achieved only in groups.

Disadvantages of Closed Group Practice

- Just as a positive group can be a chosen family, a negative group can be a dysfunctional family, with all sorts of drama. Many people choose to be solitary for precisely this reason.
- Leadership and hierarchy—in groups that have them—can become toxic. A hierarchical group has an inherent power imbalance that can be abused. While I've never experienced this in any group I've been a part of, I know lots of people who have.
- Consensus, on the other hand, can be time-consuming and drain the fun out of new ideas, which have to be discussed endlessly and then agreed on or dropped.
- Traveling to and from group meetings can be a chore. Ritual can take a lot out of you, and driving afterwards can be risky. I ultimately took to sleeping on the high priestess's couch when I was in my first group, after a couple of scary experiences behind the wheel. I am generally in no shape to drive after ritual. This is a significant barrier for some people.

Finding a Group

Social media, of course, is the biggest resource for seekers. Attending public events (see the next section) is also a great way to connect with people who are associated with covens or other closed groups, as, very often, they are the people leading public rituals or teaching public classes.

When reaching out to a group, be patient and polite. You are requesting an invitation to someone's home, so demanding admittance won't get you far.

There are a number of websites with group listings, but the listings get old. Be willing to chat in various online spaces and ask questions, so that you can find current information.

Red Flags and Green Flags

Groups can be great or awful or anywhere in between. People can form groups because they're sincere and passionate about Wicca, or because they're manipulative assholes. Pay attention.

Red Flags

- No legitimate Wiccan tradition requires you to participate in sex for initiation or anything else. If this is suggested to you, it is a huge red flag—get out!
- Taking money for Wicca is frowned upon and forbidden in most traditions. It is okay to charge for publicly offered services such as classes or readings, and it is okay to ask for contributions for normal expenses (incense costs money, after all). It is not okay, in Wicca, to charge for attending a ritual or to pay anything for initiation. If you are asked to pay for these,

it's a red flag. *This has no bearing on other traditions.* I've seen Wiccans criticize other Pagan or polytheistic religions for charging money, but others aren't obligated to follow our rules.

- Your bodily and personal autonomy are sacred, and any group that interferes with that is suspect, to say the least. Groups that tell you who you're allowed to date, who you're allowed to socialize with, or what you're allowed to read are probably not okay. A lot of groups might steer you away from some books for a variety of reasons, but "please don't read that" and "you're forbidden to read that" are very different things.
- In my group, you are not allowed to attend the rituals of another group without clearing it with group leadership (me) first. There are lots of good reasons for this. I can steer you away from toxic groups, help you avoid a hornet's nest of gossip and drama, and keep an eye on your ritual experiences as I train you. But it's a red flag to completely forbid you from interacting with the wider Wiccan and Pagan community. Isolation is a tool of abuse!
- Sadly, there are groups that are homophobic, transphobic, and/or racist. Some of those groups claim (falsely) that this is "traditional." Ask questions!

Green Flags

- Do you feel comfortable with the people you meet? Do you have a good connection? Do they make you laugh? Remember that if it works out, you'll be forming a family-like relationship—you should *like* them.
- Are they respectful of your time? Do they apologize when they make mistakes? Do they ask questions that let you know your values are important to them?

Whether we're talking about red flags or green flags, it primarily comes down to trusting your gut.

Forming a Group

One option is to form a group of beginners for joint study. Don't sell yourself as a teacher or leader if you're a beginner, but being an organizer is great.

Don't expect people to be beating down your doors—if you find three like-minded people, that's a lot.

You might start as a study group, book discussion group, or something along those lines. Book discussion can be one of the best ways to learn together, especially books with exercises.

Groups like this do best where you are likely to find other interested beginners, like campuses, but *Meetup.com* and the like can be great ways of starting as well.

Start with some kind of agenda for meetings and some kind of organizing principles. Are you democratic? Anarchic? Consensus-based? Private? Open to the public? These decisions shape the future of the group.

Public/Open Groups and Events

Throughout North America, and indeed, throughout much of the world, Pagan gatherings of various kinds are held. Some are specifically Wiccan, but most are not. They range from one-day fairs and Pagan Pride events to weekends at hotels, to week-long camping festivals, and everything in between. Witches' Balls are popular around Halloween, but open circles might happen at any time—often in the summer, when outdoor spaces are most enjoyable. Although uncommon, there are groups in many locations that host regular public rituals open to all.

For some people, attending such events is the entirety of their group practice, and allows them to enjoy solitary practice while also having some connection with other Pagans. For others, they are part of a group but also enjoy connecting with the larger community. For still others, events like this are a great way of networking and perhaps finding a group.

The high priestess who trained me strongly encouraged us to attend as many public gatherings as possible. She wanted us to connect to our community, attend classes and workshops so we could bring our newfound knowledge back to the group, learn new chants to use in ritual, and so on. Vendors allowed us to buy magical tools and other things we couldn't necessarily find at home. These events were an enormous part of my education and growth as a Pagan and witch.

I attended my first Pagan weekend at the age of twenty-two. At various stages of life, I was pregnant, nursing, the mother of a toddler, and of a teen, at Pagan events. I met my daughter's late father at a festival in Massachusetts, and, a dozen years later, asked him for a divorce at a different festival. I met Professor Spouse at a Pagan Pride in Kentucky. My connection to the larger community is part of what has made my practice sustainable throughout life.

Ritual

When discussing the defining characteristics of Wicca, I mentioned several ritual acts: Casting the circle, calling the quarters, marking lunar events, and following the Wheel of the Year.

This raises the question: How are these things done? What is meant by "casting the circle?" Are there rules about the performance of ritual?

Rules, of course, are based in the tradition you follow. For every rule, there's someone out there who doesn't follow it. Nonetheless, there are "best practices," good ideas, and ideas that aren't so good.

Some things you learn from experience. There are rules I was taught that I decided to throw out the window, and only after did I realize those rules really were the best practice.

What I will present in the following pages are *my* rules. I am *not* teaching you a specific tradition, but I am saving you from having to reinvent the wheel. I'm here to help you do things that are time-tested as effective and meaningful, as well as avoid foolishness.

Preliminaries

Having some preliminaries helps put you in a frame of mind conducive to magic and to making the connections that are the goal of ritual.

For a small act of magic—lighting a candle to focus on a goal, or saying a brief, private prayer, my preliminaries are few. I take some deep breaths, clear my mind, visualize what's next, see myself as ready, and then begin. That's a minimum.

More ritual means more prep. Some preparation is built into the ritual itself—the structure of a Wiccan circle is designed to gradually build you toward a peak and then bring you down. But preparation in advance is also helpful.

Necessary Preparation

It is absolutely necessary to create an atmosphere of privacy and focus. This means turning off phones, locking doors, and clearing the schedule.

Before beginning, I make sure the pets are fed so they're not clamoring for my attention. Back in the day, I made sure the baby was asleep. If I have something urgent to do (a call to make, a bill to pay), I do it before ritual, not after, so that it's not on my mind. While it's possible to have plans for after ritual, they should be loose enough, or far enough away, that the thought of ending "on time" is not a distraction. In fact, I cover all visible clocks so that time itself disappears for the duration of ritual.

Set up the space for your ritual, making sure it is clean and clear of obstacles (remember you'll be walking by candlelight!). Different traditions have different placements for the altar. I put mine in the center, facing North (so that I stand in the South).

Optional Preparation: The Body

Almost everyone will do some of the following, but most people don't do all of it.

- Putting on ritual robes, or stripping naked
- Putting on ritual jewelry
- Removing non-ritual jewelry
- Taking a ritual bath
- Anointing

Optional Preparation: The Mind

Preparing your mind is absolutely necessary, but there are many ways to do so.

They include:

- Deep breathing
- Meditation
- Drumming, singing, chanting, toning, etc.
- Yoga poses
- Prayer

How Much Structure?

Some people perform ritual according to a set of rules and guidelines, and for some ritual is entirely freeform; either written anew each time or done spontaneously in the moment.

When I began seeking Wicca, I was hungry for rules. Some of that is just my personality, but some of it was looking for something I didn't already have. I felt the power in my body, I felt the magic of nature, but I didn't know what to *do* with that power, that magic. I had no patience for someone telling me to just "do what you feel," because that hadn't gotten me very far on my own.

In time, I found many, many circumstances where doing what I felt was exactly the right thing to do, and I became increasingly comfortable with doing so. Paradoxically, it was structure that gave me that comfort.

Talented musicians with great skills at improvisation are, first, talented musicians. Improv actors first know how to act. Learning some rules and structures helps you feel free to improvise—it's the net that catches you when you fall.

Here's an example. When someone is bereaved, it's easy to freeze because we don't know what to say. But we can say, "I am sorry for your loss." Knowing the formulaic statement isn't empty, it's a tool through which we can communicate when our own thoughts fail us. Perhaps once we've said that, our tongues are loosened enough to add personal words of support. Ritual structure gives many such formulas that we can step through and also loosen up inside.

You absolutely can make up a ritual in the moment, if you're comfortable with that, and you feel you know what you're doing. Indeed, in my personal rituals, as highly structured as they are, there is always room for spontaneity—there are always blank spots in the script for just that reason, and there are always moments when we find it right to deviate from the script when the circumstance calls for it. (Again, all of that is preceded by knowing what we're doing.)

You also absolutely can write new rituals, and I have done so many times. But no one wants to feel they have to reinvent the wheel every month!

It's true that "formulaic" can sometimes equal "boring." But creativity can happen within a structure—like improv within a play. You have the outline, and you fill in the details creatively or spontaneously, if that's what suits you.

Or just go by the words you are given. Sometimes the power is most palpable when you forget about the script and just pour your energy into the moment. And sometimes that happens only because the script is already there, a given, just waiting to be imbued with that energy.

Casting a Circle

A Wiccan circle is an enclosure that holds ritual energy. Gerald Gardner wrote numerous times that the primary purpose of a circle was to hold energy in, not protection or to keep negativity out.[29] The Wiccan attitude toward natural and supernatural forces is primarily welcoming.

There's a lot you *do* want to keep out of the circle—mundane concerns, negative thoughts, and self-doubt are good examples. I have, over the years, encountered negative (one might say

---

29 For example, *Witchcraft Today*, page 17: "It is necessary to distinguish [the Witches' Circle] clearly from the work of the magician or sorcerer, who draws a circle...and summons...spirits and demons to do his bidding, the circle being to prevent them from doing him harm...The Witches' Circle, on the other hand, is to *keep in* the power which...they raise from their own bodies and to prevent it from being dissipated before they can mould it to their own will."

"demonic") entities, and it's nice that a circle keeps them out, but they're rare and I don't worry about them all that much.

But keeping the power *in*, that's a really powerful thing. When boiling water, a lid on the pot keeps the steam in, and the water boils faster and more efficiently. The cast circle is similar—it makes the space a pressure cooker, filling with magic that builds and builds until consciously released by the practitioner.

The *Steps for Casting and Closing a Circle* on page 79 form a basic ritual structure that can be used at any time. This is the structure for a full moon, for a holiday, for a funeral—for anything. By learning a basic structure, you have confidence that any ritual can be created and experienced in a satisfying way.

As we've discussed, you may want a loose, freeform, spontaneous experience, or you may want something formal, ornate, and baroque. In either case, though, you're empowered by knowing more or less what you're doing, and your creativity is freest when you don't have to start from scratch every time.

Steps for Casting and Closing a Circle

Here I'll step you through the process of casting the circle, with suggested words for each step. If you're in a group, these steps can be divided among multiple people. For quarters, one person can do all four, or four different people can do them.

See *The Meaning of Each Step* on page 89 for explanations about what you're doing and why. Here, we'll just step through everything.

It is common in Wicca for roles to be gendered, as an expression of polarity. I will mention that here, but you can also perform this ritual without regard to gender or entirely alone.

Tools Needed

(See *Wiccan "Things:" Magical Tools* on page 35 for details.)

- A sword, athame, or wand
- Representatives of the four elements, typically loose incense (Air), a lit charcoal on a censer (Fire), a dish of water (Water), and a dish of salt (Earth)
- An altar table on which to place everything
- A candle at each of the four cardinal points (East, South, West, North)
- Two altar candles on the altar (optional)
- Representations of the Goddess and God
- Cakes or bread
- Wine, ale, cider, or a fermented drink
- A libation bowl (if the ritual is indoors)
- Flowers for the altar

Before You Begin

Do a final run-through of your preliminaries, making sure the doors are locked and phones are off.

The quarter candles and altar candles are lit before the circle begins.

When everyone is gathered, a brief guided meditation or some deep breathing helps center everyone. This can be long and thorough, or very brief. I'll give you a brief example here, and a slightly longer one for Sabbats.

> *Take a deep, cleansing breath. Hold it. Let it out.*
> *Now another. Hold it. Let it out.*
> *Now another breath. Hold it. Let it out with a sigh.*
> *Become aware of your body. Notice your feet on the ground/floor.*[30] *Notice your legs. Notice your hips, pelvis, and genitals. Notice your belly. Notice your chest. Notice your arms and your hands. Become aware of your shoulders. Become aware of your neck. Notice your head and your jaw. Notice your face. Notice your crown.*
> *Notice that, head to toe, you are here, present, and alive.*
> *Become aware of your center.*
> *Take another deep breath and hold it at your center.*
> *Exhale from your center.*
> *Gather your energy to your center as you inhale.*
> *Hold it, knowing you are centered, and let it go with a sigh.*
> *We are ready to begin.*

1. Declaration of Opening

Start by saying your purpose and intention. For example:

> *"We are here to worship by the light of the moon. The circle will now be cast."*

2. Consecrations

Your tools are already consecrated (see *Consecrating Tools* on page 49), but you'll typically consecrate the four elements each time.

Place your athame into the dish of incense and say:

> *"In the names of the Lady and Lord,*
> *I consecrate Air that it bring mindfulness to my circle."*

Place incense onto the lit charcoal so that smoke begins to rise. Place your athame into the smoke and say:

> *"In the names of the Lady and Lord,*
> *I consecrate Fire that it bring passion to my circle."*

---

30 Use whichever word is appropriate.

Place your athame into the dish of water and say:

"In the names of the Lady and Lord,
I consecrate Water that it bring feeling to my circle."[31]

Place your athame into the dish of salt and say:

"In the names of the Lady and Lord,
I consecrate Earth that it bring commitment to my circle."

Place three pinches of salt into the water. Say:

"So mote it be."

3. Cast the Circle Three Times

Different traditions have different ways of doing this, and cast a different number of times, but this is the way I have found to be most powerful.

The first time around is the actual casting, done with your will and your words, using a magical tool. This is usually a sword or athame, although some people use a wand or staff.

Take your tool to the East, point it to the spot on the ground that defines the boundary of the circle, and begin walking from East to South to West to North and then back to your starting point. Focus on sending energy from the tip of the tool to the line drawn on the ground, such that the line glows, growing into an egg shape that encloses the circle around, above, and below.

Say:

"Round and about, round and about, power stay in, world stay out."

Repeat these words over and over until you've returned to the East. Then walk silently back to the altar.

The second casting is with Water and Earth. Pick up the dish of saltwater and return to the East. Wet your fingers and flick drops around the circle, East to East, sprinkling the entire perimeter, saying:

"Round and about, by Water and Earth, I cleanse this circle."

Repeat these words over and over until you've returned to the East. Then walk silently back to the altar.

The final casting is with Fire and Air. Pick up the censer. If it's not very smoky, add some more incense and stir it up a bit. Return to the East. Move the censer around so that you're

31 Dry the athame on your robe or the altar cloth immediately so as not to damage the blade.

censing (with smoke) the perimeter, as you walk again around the circle, East to East, sprinkling the entire perimeter, saying:

"Round and about, by Fire and Air, I purify this circle."

Repeat these words over and over until you've returned to the East. Then walk silently back to the altar.

4. Call the Quarters

There are a few physical options here:

- Most people walk to the quarter, face it, and invoke, using the athame. If there are others in the circle with you, everyone faces the quarter during the invocation.
- You can stand at the altar and face the quarter without walking there—in a large outdoor space, this can be preferable.
- You can bring a tool or symbol of the element corresponding to the quarter to that quarter, placing that energy in the quarter as part of the invocation. (Such as the water and salt dishes, incense, and a candle.)
- Conversely, you can set up the circle with such a symbol at each quarter and bring it to the altar after the invocation—symbolizing that its energy is now part of the circle.

Here I'm assuming that you are walking to each quarter and invoking with your athame.

In the East, face out, point your athame and draw an invoking pentagram, starting at the top and moving to the bottom left, saying:

Invoking Pentagram

"I invoke the Guardian of East, the Guardian of Air
Bring sweet winds and beautiful flights to us
Bring wisdom to our circle and protect us from harm

Honor the Lady and Lord with us
Welcome, Guardian! Blessed be."

All repeat: *"Blessed be."*
Walk *deosil* (clockwise) back to your place.
In the South, face out, point your athame and draw an invoking pentagram, saying:

"I invoke the Guardian of South, the Guardian of Fire
Bring warm days and healing fire to us
Bring strong will to our circle and protect us from harm
Honor the Lady and Lord with us
Welcome, Guardian! Blessed be."

All repeat: *"Blessed be."*
Walk deosil back to your place.
In the West, face out, point your athame and draw an invoking pentagram, saying:

"I invoke the Guardian of West, the Guardian of Water
Bring flowing streams and lovely moonlight to us
Bring deep love to our circle and protect us from harm
Honor the Lady and Lord with us
Welcome, Guardian! Blessed be."

All repeat: *"Blessed be."*
Walk deosil back to your place.
In the North, face out, point your athame and draw an invoking pentagram, saying:

"I invoke the Guardian of North, the Guardian of Earth
Bring rich soil and good homes to us
Bring stability to our circle and protect us from harm
Honor the Lady and Lord with us
Welcome, Guardian! Blessed be."

All repeat: *"Blessed be."*
Walk deosil back to your place.
Walk back to the East for a final, silent salute. (There's no need to invoke.)

5. Invoking the Gods

The following simple invocations can be replaced by those specific to the deities being invited.

In some traditions, the priestess invokes the Goddess, and the priest invokes the God, because they are representations of themselves. In other traditions, the priestess invokes the God as her beloved, and the priest invokes the Goddess as his beloved—referencing (heterosexual) divine love and partnership. In still other traditions, no gender is assigned to this act.

My former partner and I used to hold up the wand together, both invoking while one at a time spoke. I loved the way the partnership between us invoked the partnership of the Gods, and I loved that each of us was empowering the invocation simultaneously, regardless of who was speaking.

Face North, holding the wand, and say:

"Beloved Lady, Goddess of the Earth and the Moon
Delight of our hearts, Queen of the Witches
Mother of us all
Be here among us! Come to this circle, formed in your honor
Accept our offerings and our love.
Welcome! Blessed be!"

All repeat: *"Blessed be."*

"Beloved Lord, God of Death and Rebirth,
Horned One, Lord of all wild things
King of the harvest
Be here among us! Come to this circle, formed in your honor
Accept our offerings and our love.
Welcome! Blessed be!"

All repeat: *"Blessed be."*

6. Offerings

The step of making offerings to the gods is the most freeform part of the ritual, and could include:

- Singing, chanting, or toning
- Drumming or playing instruments
- Dance
- Recitation
- Performance, including performance specific to the occasion (such as one of the eight solar holidays)
- Incense offered on the censer

Note: This is where some people perform acts of magic. I prefer magic after cakes and wine, because I want to offer to the gods before I ask them for help. But many people have noted that cakes and wine can contribute to relaxing and grounding the energy of ritual, so they place using the energy—magic—before that happens.

7. Cakes and Wine

This is sometimes called "cakes and ale."

Because this represents the loving, sexual, and cosmic union of the Goddess and God, it is typically performed with a priestess holding the cup and a priest holding the athame. The two face each other, holding the cup and athame as described.

For a solitary ritual, hold the cup for the first part, then place it on the altar and hold the athame. Holding one in each hand is an invitation to spill wine everywhere.

Start by saying:

"The Gods have accepted our offering.
Let us now receive their blessings in return."

Hold the cup and say:

"The cup, the Goddess, the blood of life
Our Lady blesses us with all good things
She offers herself to us
She offers herself to the God."

Hold the athame over the cup and say:

"The blade, the God, the force of life
Our Lord blesses us with all good things
He offers himself to us
He offers himself to the Goddess."

Plunge the athame into the cup and say:

"Blessed be."

Consecrate the cakes by dipping the athame into the wine and sprinkling drops onto the cakes, forming an invoking pentagram. Say:

"Lady and Lord, you bless us with abundance
The Earth gives us all we need
We thank you.
Blessed be."

Take a cake or a portion of whatever food is on the plate and place it in the libation bowl.

Lift the cup and speak from the heart. It can be as simple as "to the Gods," or it can be detailed. End with "Blessed be." Then, make an offering to the gods by pouring a bit of wine into the libation bowl. Drink only after offering.

If multiple people are present, each in turn offers, pours, and drinks. Each offering ends with "Blessed be," and everyone responds by saying "Blessed be."

If people are concerned about sharing a cup (germs are icky), pour from the main cup into each person's individual cup before drinking. Then, each offers, pours, and drinks in turn.

After the cup goes around, or while the cup is on its way around, pass the cakes. The single cake offered is an offering for all, having people take bits of their food and put that in the libation bowl tends to make a mess.

After the ritual is over, the contents of the libation bowl should be poured out onto the Earth. If the ritual is outdoors, then libations are poured directly onto the Earth, and a bowl is not needed.

8. Acts of Magic, Rites of Passage, or Celebrations of Season

Depending on the ritual, this could include:

- Spells for healing, protection, or anything else
- Celebration of one of the eight solar holidays
- Rites of passage, such as a handfasting, baby blessing, coming of age ritual, initiation, or funeral
- Group meditative journeys
- Scrying or divination
- Teaching

9. Closing the Circle

Face North, raise the wand, and say:

"Beloved Lady,
Moonlight and fertile Earth,
You have enriched us with your presence.
Thank you, and farewell!"

All repeat: *"Farewell!"*

"Beloved Lord,
Death and Rebirth,
You have enriched us with your presence.
Thank you, and farewell!"

All repeat: *"Farewell!"*

Go to the East, draw a banishing pentagram, and say:

"We thank you, Guardian of the East, Guardian of Air
For protecting this rite
Thank you, and farewell!"

All repeat: *"Farewell!"*

Go to the South, draw a banishing pentagram, and say:

Banishing Pentagram

"We thank you, Guardian of the South, Guardian of Fire
For protecting this rite
Thank you, and farewell!"

All repeat: *"Farewell!"*
Go to the West, draw a banishing pentagram, and say:

"We thank you, Guardian of the West, Guardian of Water
For protecting this rite
Thank you, and farewell!"

All repeat: *"Farewell!"*
Go to the North, draw a banishing pentagram, and say:

"We thank you, Guardian of the North, Guardian of Earth
For protecting this rite
Thank you, and farewell!"

All repeat: *"Farewell!"*
Facing the center, say:

"The circle is open but unbroken, the rites are ended.
Merry meet, merry part, and merry meet again!"

All repeat: *"Merry meet, merry part, and merry meet again!"*

Modifications for the Occasion

You can take the basic structure found in the *Steps for Casting and Closing a Circle* above and turn it into any ritual you want or need.

In addition to the changes below, changes to language can make the ritual simpler or more complex, more or less formal, more or less verbal, and so on. I've done rituals entirely in silence, rituals entirely sung, rituals for hundreds of people in public spaces, and each of these was a variation on basically the same structure.

The many rituals in this book—esbats, sabbats, and rites of life—have variations that you can experiment with and enjoy, and can also serve as an example for you of how to create your own rituals.

Before You Begin

Decorations make a big difference. Some people have different altar cloths for different occasions, or different altar candles or candle colors. Seasonal decorations enhance seasonal holidays. Autumn leaves, spring flowers, dancing Santa figurines—the sky's the limit! Some people also use different deity icons for different ritual occasions: Your full moon statuette may not be the same as the one you use at new moons, for example.

1. Declaration of Opening

State the purpose of the ritual, such as:

- We gather to celebrate the full moon.
- Tonight, I cast a circle in memory of my mother.
- On this Yule night, we celebrate the turning of the wheel.

...And so on.

Consecrations and Circle Casting are generally the same each time and are not modified for the occasion so I won't go into them here.

4. Call the Quarters

It's traditional to tell the Guardians what they're guarding. For example, when invoking the Guardian of Air, I used:

"Bring wisdom to our circle and protect us from harm."

Here you can instead say:

"Bring wisdom to our Yule circle and protect us from harm."

Fill in the blank—where I say "Yule," say whatever is appropriate.

Some people rewrite the entire quarter callings for the occasion rather than just inserting a word or two.

5. Invoking the Gods

Here, we might use specific deity names, or we might invoke them by aspects appropriate to the occasion, or we simply tell them why they are coming. I will offer examples of this for each holiday under the *Sabbats: Wheel of the Year* on page 108.

6. Offerings

Offerings are often the part most specific to the work being done (yep, holidays are "work"—we are "turning the wheel").

Cakes and Wine is generally the same each time and not modified for the occasion.

8. Acts of Magic, Rites of Passage, or Celebrations of Season

This is often the meat of the "special occasion"—it's the section of ritual set aside for the purpose of the rite. However, as you've seen, the entire ritual has built toward this moment, so that by the time, for example, you're here and ready to celebrate Samhain, you've seen altar decorations appropriate to Samhain, heard the Guardians being invited to guard and protect Samhain, and heard invocations specific to Samhain. So now that you're here, you're geared up and ready to go!

9. Closing the Circle

If you've invited specific deities, or deities with specific titles, use those same names/titles here when saying farewell.

The Meaning of Each Step

In my book *The Elements of Ritual*, I explore, in great detail, what each step of ritual means, why it is done, why it is done *in that order*, and variations on how, why, and when each step can be done. Here, I'm keeping it much simpler, but you still need an explanation.

1. Declaration of Opening

Sometimes life is a big mush. Days run into each other, nothing feels special. Ritual is, in part, a way to create meaning in our lives by marking separation. We mark phases of the moon, the turning of the wheel, and special occasions, awakening us to the uniqueness and beauty of each day. We declare when a ritual begins and ends as part of this.

It also just helps. We need to "get into" the ritual. We need to alter consciousness toward the magical and sacred. We do all sorts of things to separate ritual time from mundane time—

we anoint or bathe, we wear special robes and jewelry, we use a different name. Part of that separation is stating it aloud: *Now, we begin.*

2. Consecrations

The four elements are the building blocks of the universe.[32] They are found throughout Western occultism, and Wicca is no exception. When we create a circle—a world between the worlds—we start at the beginning, building this microcosm of the universe from its basic pieces—the elements.

3. Cast the Circle Three Times

Three is a magical number. You cast first with your will, using a tool that symbolizes and expresses your will, and with your word.

Then you cleanse the circle with Water and Earth.

In Wicca, we begin at the East, with Air, and then move to the South/Fire, the West/Water, and finally the North/Earth. Why, then, do we use Water and Earth before Air and Fire? Simply because cleansing must precede purification. I like to say that you shower first, *then* put on your perfume. That's basically what is happening here.

First, create the circle. Then cleanse it, then purify it with Fire and Air. We've used three steps, four elements, and our declaration. With these steps, the circle is well and truly made.

4. Call the Quarters

Calling the quarters brings the concept of "direction"—where am I?—to the metaphysical space you've created. It grounds and solidifies the circle. It also invites Guardians—one for each direction—to watch over the circle. Most people correspond the quarters with the elements, and I have done so here.

5. Invoking the Gods

In ADF,[33] we used to open rituals with "We are here to honor the Gods." I love that simplicity and directness. If we are, indeed, here to honor the Gods, we should invite them. We should create a beautiful and sacred space that is a fit place for them, and we should make them welcome. Invocations are how we invite gods.

Invocations work best when they are heartfelt and specific. We can invite specific deities by referencing their qualities, what we love about them, their stories, and characteristics like Brigid's flaming hair, Thor's mighty hammer, or Hera's peacocks. Invocations should also include words of invitation and welcome.

---

32 My book *The Way of Four* explores the four elements in depth.

33 ADF is Ár nDraíocht Féin: A Druid Fellowship, founded by Isaac Bonewits.

6. Offerings

I believe that an invocation of gods must always be followed by an offering to them. It's just polite. You have invited gods into your space, a sacred space that you have created in their honor. The right thing to do is to immediately make some kind of offering to them. After all, if you invited a friend into your home, especially if they were coming by to do you a favor, you would immediately offer them a glass of water or lemonade, a comfy chair, or a snack. You'd hang up their coat. You'd *make them feel welcome*, and that is what you should do with the gods.

Even if you are performing non-Wiccan witchcraft, where the purpose of the circle is not necessarily in honor of the gods, if you invoke them, the same rules of courtesy and respect apply. If you want the gods to help you with your witchcraft, the least you can do is be nice to them.

Under this step in the script, all I did was offer bullet points. This is always a freeform moment in my circles, regardless of the level of formality. Sure, I often plan it in advance, but it is not set in stone, and it is not rigidly defined. Offerings should come from the heart; they can be passionate or contemplative, verbal or physical, quiet or loud, but you should always *mean it.*

As a beginner, I learned a handful of offerings that could easily be plugged into any ritual, as described below.

Tip: Offer until you really feel it. If one chant doesn't make you feel a connection to the energy, do another, or add an incense offering, or just howl at the moon. You're going to open the next step by saying that the gods have accepted your offerings—you should *believe* that.

Incense Offering

One at a time, everyone comes to the altar, takes a pinch of incense, makes an offering—aloud or silently—and places it on the censer. This is best in a small group of three to six people. Solitary, it won't feel like enough, and in a large group, it's both time-consuming and very smoky.

Immanence Offering

Here, we offer to the gods as seen in one another.

The priestess, typically standing to the right of the altar, turns to the priest, typically on her left, and says:

"[Name], you are the God. I see the God in you in [quality]."

For example:

"Sage, you are the God. I see the God in you in your empathy and kindness."

Then, the priest does the same for the person on his left, and so on, all the way around the circle, the last person completing the loop by speaking to the priestess.

This is usually gendered, with the God being seen in men and the Goddess being seen in women. You are free to adapt this, of course.

Obviously, this isn't a great option for a solitary, but using a mirror and speaking to it can be very powerful indeed.

Song or Music Offering

This is accessible to any number of people, from solitary to a big crowd. Simply say something like:

"Let us now offer our joyous song to the Gods."[34]

Saying this creates important context—you're doing it as an offering, not as a power-raising or for fun.

A group, over time, builds up a repertoire of chants and songs that can be used in ritual. The internet is a great repository for finding such chants—there are dozens, if not hundreds.[35] You can also just drum or play musical instruments.

I'll note here that it's ideal for there to be a distinction between this step and step 8 (acts of magic, etc.). If you use the same chant both times, for example, it will feel repetitive and dull. Be creative and make each part of ritual unique and distinctive.

Because there *are* so many chants out there, you can find ones with words unique to each part of ritual. During offerings, you can find ones about the gods, about nature, about the cycle of the seasons, etc. During magic, find ones about power, healing, energy, or the like. Often, I will choose a chant with an elemental relationship to the work being done, for example, "The Ocean is the Beginning of the Earth,"[36] for work related to water.

7. Cakes and Wine

The rite of "Cakes and Wine" is the spiritual and mystical center of Wiccan ritual. It is where we are blessed by the Gods, where we enact their blessings and their relationship to each other in a reciprocal communion. It is a rite of polarity, union, fertility, and love.

We say, in Cakes and Wine, that we are receiving the blessings of the Gods, but first we, ourselves, take on the roles of the Gods and impart those blessings. Then, blessing the wine *as* the Gods, we use the wine to bless the cakes. Then, before eating or drinking, we again make an offering—back and forth, giving and receiving, enacting and being acted upon—we are flowing in a cycle of blessing the entire time. Finally, we eat and drink, filling our bodies and spirits with blessing.

Traditionally, this is enacted heterosexually, with the Goddess represented by the priestess and the God by the priest. Keep in mind that, if this is uncomfortable or unavailable to you, the tools themselves—the cup and athame—are consecrated and have polarity with each other. Bringing them together enacts the loving, fertile, and polar union of Goddess and God.

---

34 For a solitary, "I now offer my joyous song to the Gods."

35 For example, chantarchive.com

36 By Delaney Johnson and Starhawk from the album *Chants: Ritual Music*

I give myself fully to this part of the ritual, regardless of my real-life relationship with my partner. Over the years, I have done this rite with romantic partners of all genders, with an ex-lover, with both gay and straight male friends, with a straight female friend, and with an asexual friend. The sexual/romantic context is present in the relationship between Lady and Lord being enacted. It can be made more accessible if there's a similar romance between the humans involved, but it's not necessary (which is why solitary ritual also works well). When working with a partner, make eye contact and establish emotional intimacy in the moment, but don't believe that a romantic partner is required for the rite.

8. Acts of Magic, Rites of Passage, or Celebrations of Season

When we are full of the blessings of the Lady and Lord, we are fully empowered to use those blessings for a variety of purposes. As with making an offering, it is my experience that this step of the ritual is different every time.

Tip: Eating can be very grounding, and your energy can drop. If you're going to do magic or something else where you want your energy high, just take a symbolic nibble of cakes, and save the snacking for after your work.

9. Closing the Circle

The important thing to know here is that the powers invoked do not simply dissipate and leaving them hanging around can have unintended consequences. In a cast circle, where energy is contained, having elemental and other powers present is great, but having them hang around your apartment or campsite is another matter entirely.

When I first became Wiccan my focus was spiritual, and I wasn't sure I believed in all the magical, "woo" stuff. But I learned, sometimes the hard way, that what we do is very real, and, therefore, it should be done cautiously. For this reason, the common phrase, "Stay if you will, go if you must," is absolutely banned in my circles. You do *not* want elemental powers to stay if they will, trust me.

Use "last in, first out" for closing the circle, which is to say, reverse the order. The last invitation you issued was to the gods, so thank them first and say, "Farewell." Saying goodbye is a polite way of telling them to go. (It works with houseguests, too. Here's your hat, what's your hurry?) Then, thank the Guardians.

Some people physically uncast the circle, going around, perhaps with the sword, and "picking it up." However, we are taught that a circle is a sealed space that should not be broken, so, once you've ended the circle, walking about willy-nilly effectively breaks it.

Some people close using widdershins (counterclockwise) movement, but you'll see here that I do not. I use widdershins only for specific purposes related to death, negativity, banishing, and the like. I want my circle to end harmoniously, not harshly.

In truth, it's easy to close the circle, which is why the statements are all shorter. Our minds naturally veer toward the ordinary. It's an effort to place ourselves in a magical state, and very little effort to slip out of that state. Nonetheless, it's important to close, both to seal off all the energies and to create boundaries, just as we did at opening.

Ritual Behavior and Etiquette

Certain behaviors are expected in Wiccan ritual. Some are just customary, some are there for a reason. Knowing them will be helpful if you attend public ritual, or are a guest at someone's circle, and they're good habits to build even when working as a solitary.

Respecting the Circle

The most important customs regard respect for the circle itself. The circle, once cast, is considered an enclosure. If you were doing something very serious, you might not want to leave the circle at all until it was over, lest energy "leak" out. But even under more ordinary circumstances, you should be respectful of its boundaries.

Know where it is: Whether or not you are the one who cast the circle, know where it is exactly so that you don't accidentally violate its boundaries by sticking your foot or an elbow through its walls. Some people cast to the walls of the room they're in to prevent this from happening. I don't generally like to do that, because I feel like the circle stays more firmly in mind when I am visualizing its shape around me, but if you do cast to the walls, do so intentionally and consciously. If you're not the one who cast the circle, make sure you know where it is. Generally, if someone is casting to the walls, they'll say so in advance, and if not, *watch*.

Don't casually enter and leave: Only leave the circle if you must—use the bathroom before ritual starts, have everything you need before you begin, and so on, to prevent unnecessary traffic.

Create a door by which to leave and return: To exit a circle, use your athame to cut a door-shaped space, step through, and seal it behind you with three slashes (we used to call this the "mark of Zorro") and an invoking pentagram. Some people leave their athame on the floor at the spot where they exited. Then return with the same technique.

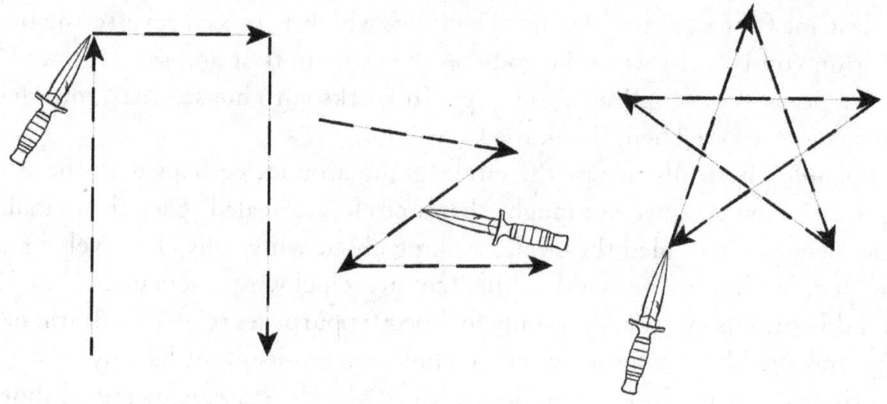

1. Cut a door, 2. Seal, 3. Invoking Pentagram

Stay Focused

It's easy for your mind to wander in circle and drift away from the magical into the mundane. Paying attention to the circle and the energy helps a lot. Another trick is to use a magical posture. The "god position" or "Osiris position"—standing with arms crossed, with your left hand at your right shoulder, and your right hand at your left shoulder—is a traditional posture for maintaining your energy and concentration.

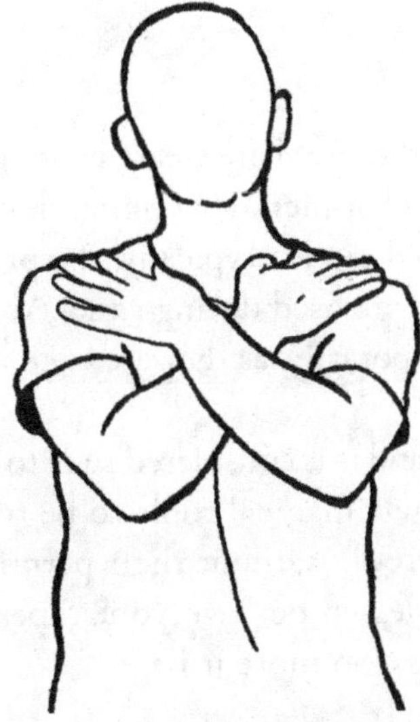

Osiris Position

Some rituals set aside time for conversation, but that conversation should not drift into the ordinary. Don't talk about work, traffic, television, or anything that pulls your focus away from the sacred.

Some rituals (including my own) ban time entirely. Not only do we avoid talking about timebound things (anything from what time it is, or schedules, to what will happen X days from now), but we don't allow watches or time in the circle. We cover wall clocks and turn off our phones. Time is a distraction that pulls us relentlessly into the ordinary world and away from sacred space.

Movement

Always move deosil, or clockwise, in the circle. This is also called "sunwise" and is the direction the sun appears to move in the sky.[37] This movement is representative of nature and natural cycles. If you're sensitive to energy, you can feel a quiet clockwise swirling of energy throughout the ritual.

When I'm South of the altar, I walk *all the way around*, West to North to East, before I begin casting the circle. Each time I return to the East I do this, even though I could just cut across from the South to the East. I am respecting the deosil flow of energy and not disrupting it.

37 This is true in both the Northern and Southern Hemispheres.

Some traditions are more or less strict about this. In my circle, if someone wants to hand something to the person to their immediate right, they'd instead hand it to the person on their left, and send it all the way around, so that it moves only deosil. (Usually, there's an exception for those directly behind the altar.)

Widdershins, counterclockwise, or anti-sunwise movement is considered to unwind or destroy. It can be used to consciously dismantle something, but shouldn't be a part of ordinary ritual.

Courtesy and Custom

In some traditions, the leaders of the ritual are treated with great respect, as they are representatives of the gods. This isn't a social or hierarchal thing—it only applies during the ritual—but it's a meaningful part of the sacred circle. Typically, the priest and priestess have titles such as "my Lady" or "my Lord," which are used during ritual. You would also ask their permission before leaving the circle, even temporarily, as they are energetically responsible for the space.

People often have magical names, and it is considered rude to use their ordinary names in ritual.

Some people do not want their magical tools to be touched by others. Never pick up someone's athame (or any other tool) without their permission.

In ritual, if someone says, "Blessed be," everyone repeats "Blessed be." If someone says, "So mote it be," everyone repeats, "So mote it be."

Creating Ritual

This book offers quite a number of rituals: For moons, for Sabbats, and for special occasions. At some point, though, you'll want a ritual that isn't in here. So, here's some guidance on how to create meaningful rituals that work for you.

Have a template: The *Steps for Casting and Closing a Circle* (page 79) and *Modifications for the Occasion* (page 88) are designed to give you a framework into which you can insert your own creative and meaningful details.

When I write a book, I know there will be an introduction, a central thesis, examples and perhaps exercises, and a conclusion. With that frame in mind, I write an outline. Once the outline is done, I begin writing the details. As the details emerge and inspire me, I might change the outline.

When I make soup, I know there will be stock, vegetables, and a base (chicken, lentils, whatever). The specific ingredients make vastly different dishes, hardly even the same except they're served in a bowl and with a spoon, yet I know what "soup" is. This lets me invent recipes or just come up with substitutions—I know what I'm doing.

Ritual is a delicious soup, with steps for your stock, you can add whatever ingredients please you.

Know what will change: The framework has "holes" in it, places where you can plug in your ritual variations.

You can also tweak the frame itself, which you'll see in the Sabbats and Rites of Life. All these rituals use the same template, but components such as the opening statement and calling the quarters can be changed to suit the situation.

Choose a tone: Ritual can be formal, relaxed, playful, solemn, experimental, soothing.... The words and actions used serve to set a mood.

Balance the ritual: If a ritual is all words, people get bored. If it's all action, people get confused. Find a balance between different ways of performing ritual—speaking, moving around, singing, using props—all of these work, and all create different atmospheres. Explore what you like best. Try different things and don't be afraid to fail.

Adapt: I have been to public rituals of fifty-plus people where the leaders did pretty much exactly what they do at home. The problem is, if everyone comes to the altar one at a time at home, that takes *forever* with fifty people. Adapt the ritual to the people and the situation. If you're outdoors on rough terrain, running around the circle like you do in your living room might not work. Number of people, location, physical abilities, level of intimacy (do these people know each other?), weather—any and all of these aspects may require you to make changes to your ritual. Because you have a template that you can rely on, you're empowered to adapt within that framework.

Have fun!

Chapter Seven:

THE WICCAN YEAR

Because Wicca venerates nature and the cycles of nature, it is not surprising that celebrations occur in accordance with those cycles. Wicca has no commemorative holidays—there's no big bash on Gerald Gardner's birthday or what have you. Instead, celebrations are attuned to nature: moon phases and sun cycles, including agricultural cycles.

Esbats are lunar celebrations that are considered "routine." They are the ordinary work of a coven or an individual, much like Sunday mass is the ordinary work of a Catholic.

Sabbats are the eight solar holidays known as the "Wheel of the Year." They are the *quarter days* of *Beltane* (May 1), *Lammas/Lughnasadh*[38] (August 1), *Samhain*[39]*/Halloween* (October 31), and *Imbolc/Oimelc/Candlemas* (February 1), and the *cross-quarter days* of *Spring Equinox* (March 21), *Summer Solstice/Midsummer* (June 21), *Fall Equinox/Harvest Home*[40] (September 21), and *Winter Solstice/Yule* (December 21).[41]

By celebrating the eight sabbats, we are doing the magical and spiritual work of "turning the wheel." That is, we are causing appropriate seasonal change to come into being. Of course, as modern, scientifically oriented people, we know that seasonal change has to do with the Earth's rotation and the climate more than with ritual, but as Wiccans, we know that literal truth is not the only truth. In this time of global climate crisis, turning the wheel can be seen as our most important magical work.

History

Each of the eight holidays has been celebrated by some European Pagan cultures somewhere, but there isn't an ancient tradition of celebrating all eight by any single ancient version of Paganism. The use of all eight, spaced approximately evenly around the year, is a modern invention.

Gardner taught his coven that ancient Pagans either celebrated the quarters or cross-quarters and asked them to choose which set to use. Being party animals, they chose both—why not have twice as many parties? Gardner was wrong about the history here; Pagan cultures were much less rigid, and any locality might have had five or six of these celebrations, as well as others. But the die was cast, and Wicca now celebrates these eight.

38 Pronounced "LOO-nuh-sah"

39 Pronounced "SOW-when"

40 The names "Ostara" for Spring Equinox, "Litha" for Summer Solstice, and "Mabon" for Fall Equinox were coined in 1974 by Aidan Kelly. Although they are widespread today, they are not used by traditional Wiccans (nor by me).

41 Dates in the Southern Hemisphere are Beltane, October 31; Lammas, February 1; Fall Equinox, March 21; Samhain, May 1; Yule, June 21; Imbolc, August 1; and Spring Equinox, September 21.

The sabbats, as celebrated by early Wiccans, seemed designed for fleshing out. Over the years, Wiccans and other Pagans have done an enormous amount of research into the European folklore and customs surrounding each holiday, and an explosion of ritual creativity has led to many wonderful Pagan celebrations. While Wicca is a distinct path within Paganism, the holiday celebrations of Wiccans and other Pagans often don't look very different from one another, because the research that was done was shared by all. A circle is cast in a Wiccan manner, but otherwise, a Wiccan festival itself will tend to resemble any other Pagan celebration of that festival (the exception being rituals specific to a tradition).

Interconnection

Many people have attempted to turn the eight holidays into a single, continuous story[42]. That's very logical—and very modern. It's simply not necessary. We can worship our gods in cycles and have holidays that tell stories connected to other holidays, as we'll see, without needing a Grand Unification Theory of Holidays.

There is a unifying factor: *you*. Your connection to nature is part of what's being celebrated here. Each sabbat connects to the one immediately before, the one immediately after, and the one directly opposite on the wheel. Each sabbat also connects to other celebrations of that sabbat—both in other years, and in other places.

So, when I celebrate Samhain, I am connected to Fall Equinox, to Yule, to Beltane, to last year's Samhain, to next year's Samhain, and to Samhain festivals being held all over the Northern hemisphere.[43]

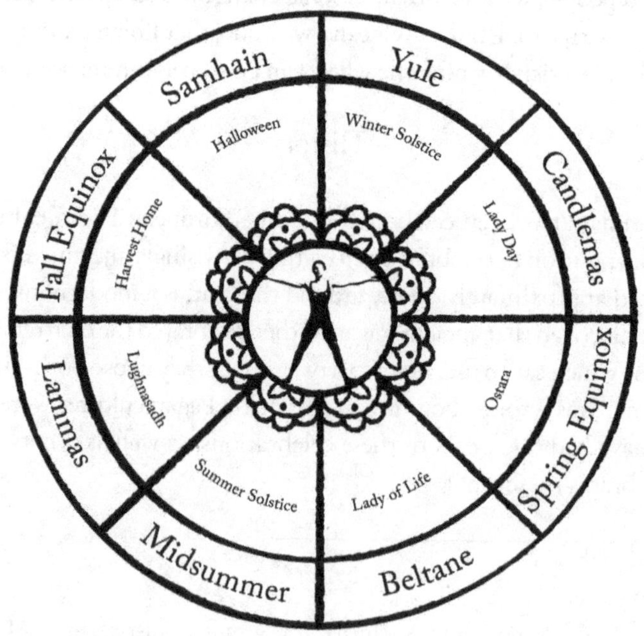

42 For example, Janet and Stewart Farrar in *Eight Sabbats for Witches*.

43 Meanwhile, Beltane is being celebrated in the Southern hemisphere.

Scheduling

Many people believe that it is vital to meet on the exact date of a holiday or the moon.

Lunar energies are powerful and measurable. We know that everything from crime rates to surgical outcomes to animal reproduction changes during the period of the full moon (which is three days: from the day before full to the day after). It makes little sense to celebrate "the full moon" when the moon isn't full.

Similarly, the astrological and astronomical qualities of each holiday are meaningful.

On the other hand, we have jobs and obligations. Regular ritual, forming that vital connection to the gods (and one another if we meet in a group) in a reliable way, has a profound impact on us. An infrequent and unpredictable spiritual practice will simply not have the same life-altering impact as one that you can count on, one that you do when you say you will do it, regardless of convenience.

Each group and individual will make their own decisions on this. My own practice is to meet on Saturday nights. Because I've worked in corporate 9-to-5 environments my whole life, this is the time that is most workable for me. I place esbats on the calendar as close to the full moon as possible, and when it's not possible, we get together and worship without the full moon portion of our ceremony. *The Charge* tells us to gather "once in the month, and better it be when the moon is full." Sometimes "better" is not available, but I understand "once in the month" to be the higher priority.

As far as holidays go, our ancestors who celebrated agricultural festivals did so according to the crops, not the calendar. Harvest was celebrated when the harvest was brought in, even if the calendar suggested a few days earlier or later. If you're an agricultural Pagan, you bring in the harvest and you have, as a result, a ton of food to prepare, preserve, and eat. Party time! The cycle of work determines the cycle of celebration, not the other way around.

In that spirit, I think it's totally legitimate to celebrate holidays in accordance with my modern, urban cycle of work. I celebrate when I have a day off rather than taking a day off to celebrate (unless I'm traveling to a Pagan event—those require days off and are *totally* worth it).

One caveat, though, is that the energy of a season is deeply present as a holiday approaches and dissipates once the holiday passes. If you can't celebrate Samhain on October 31, celebrate the week prior. By early November, it is well and truly passed, and I think you can *feel* that.

Meaning

How do we understand the meaning of these holidays? I expect it changes for all of us as time passes. As a young Wiccan, I just wanted to absorb the folklore, the community, and the celebration. I wasn't all that concerned with applying it to my personal life. But I could and did *observe* my personal life in the context of the holidays.

One of the first things I remember noticing was how my own ideas about work and life tend to change with the seasons. Some of the best humor I've written was done over the course of a summer: As the weather gets colder, I get more introspective and tend more toward serious subjects.

As I learned to ground my Paganism in my own life, I started paying attention to all the little things: The way that sunlight affected my commute (for many years, I drove due East each morning, and as the time of sunrise changed throughout the year, it had a big impact), the way that secular holiday celebrations resonated with Pagan ideas (everything from trick-or-treating, to Christmas lights, to local spring fairs), the way that weather-related ordinances coincided with Pagan holidays (my town had parking laws that changed for snow removal, the annual dates were Beltane and Samhain).

If we're urban or suburban, we can most directly find meaning in the solar aspects of holidays rather than the agricultural ones. It can be hard for urban and suburban people to relate to the meaning derived from the growing season, but we certainly experience differences in light. When it starts getting dark earlier, we all feel that, even if we don't have Seasonal Affective Disorder. Sunlight affects mood, it impacts behavior, and it changes how we interact with the world.

It really helps to grow a garden. I haven't always done so: I just have hydroponics now, as mentioned earlier. Gardening has so many lessons to teach us, especially if we struggle to understand our connection to our agricultural ancestors and how they understood Paganism. Going for a walk in nature is beautiful, but it's not the same as the interdependence you experience as a gardener.

Even if you do grow a garden or are a farmer, you will often experience the holidays in a metaphorical manner, and that is completely okay. Sometimes, planting seeds is about goals, dreams, money, or love, not about corn. Sometimes, it's our heart, not our soil, that needs to thaw. These stories—cycles of growth and diminishment, hope for the future, and embracing the results of the present—are meaningful in so many different aspects of our lives. They are about career, creativity, family, and love. They never stop informing us of their meaning.

So, if meaning isn't agricultural for you, that doesn't mean you're doing Wicca wrong. Even if you're entirely urban, I recommend using agricultural experience—even just a houseplant—to help you connect to the truths that the eight holidays have for you.

Esbats

An esbat can be:

- A full moon ritual
- A new moon ritual
- A "working" ritual where you or your group cast a circle at some other time of the month to worship and work magic
- An emergency magical ritual (I've had several of these over the years; Wiccans gathering to work magic when one of our own has been in an accident or fallen ill.)

For the ordinary or extraordinary working ritual, use the *Steps for Casting and Closing a Circle* (page 79), with no modification (except as you desire) until you get to step 8. Here, you'll insert your emergency spell, your teaching or study, or whatever.

For moons, you'd create a variant, building upon what you know about casting a circle.

Ritual for the Full Moon

Preparation

Prepare as usual, with the following adjustments:

- For the full moon rite, some people like "moon cakes"—cakes or cookies cut into crescents. Or decorate your cakes with lunar symbols.
- The goddess on the altar should be associated with the moon.
- The ritual should not begin until after dark.
- If you are working indoors, try to go outside and *see* the moon before the rite, so that the enchanting experience of moonlight can be brought indoors and influence your circle.
- The ritual is basically the same for a solitary or a group. Change "we/us" to "I/me" as appropriate. Where a little more change is needed, it is noted.

Declaration of Opening

"We gather at the full moon[44] *to worship in Her fullness."*

Consecrations and Circle Casting are unchanged from *Steps for Casting and Closing a Circle.*

Quarters

In the East, face out, point your athame, and draw an invoking pentagram.

"I invoke the Guardian of East, the Guardian of Air
Bring sweet winds and beautiful flights to us
Bring wisdom to our Full Moon circle and protect us from harm
Honor the Lady and Lord with us
Welcome, Guardian! Blessed be."

All repeat: *"Blessed be."*
In the South, face out, point your athame, and draw an invoking pentagram, saying:

"I invoke the Guardian of South, the Guardian of Fire
Bring warm days and healing fire to us
Bring strong will to our Full Moon circle and protect us from harm
Honor the Lady and Lord with us
Welcome, Guardian! Blessed be."

All repeat: *"Blessed be."*
In the West, face out, point your athame, and draw an invoking pentagram, saying:

44 For a solitary: "I cast the circle of the full moon."

"I invoke the Guardian of West, the Guardian of Water
Bring flowing streams and lovely moonlight to us
Bring deep love to our Full Moon circle and protect us from harm
Honor the Lady and Lord with us
Welcome, Guardian! Blessed be."

All repeat: "*Blessed be.*"

In the North, face out, point your athame, and draw an invoking pentagram, saying:

"I invoke the Guardian of North, the Guardian of Earth
Bring rich soil and good homes to us
Bring stability to our Full Moon circle and protect us from harm
Honor the Lady and Lord with us
Welcome, Guardian! Blessed be."

All repeat: "*Blessed be.*"

Walk back to the East for a final, silent salute. (There's no need to invoke.)

Invoking the Gods

Face North, holding the wand, and say:

"Beloved Lady, Goddess of the Moon
Shining light, ruler of tides
Delight of our hearts, Queen of the Night, Queen of the Witches
Mother of us all
Be here among us![45] *Come to this circle, formed in your honor at your sacred time*
Accept our offerings and our love.
Welcome! Blessed be!"

All repeat: "*Blessed be.*"

"Beloved Lord, God of Death and Rebirth,
Horned One, Lord of all wild things
King of the harvest
Beloved of the Lady,
Be here among us! Come to this full moon circle,
Receive our worship and worship the Goddess with us
Accept our offerings and our love.
Welcome! Blessed be!"

All repeat: "*Blessed be.*"

45 For a solitary: Be here with me!

Offerings

Any offerings are appropriate here. Poetry to the moon, songs and chants about the moon or about the goddess, songs or chants about the ocean or tides, drumming, or incense offerings—any of these can be part of a full moon ritual.

Full moons tend more toward ecstasy—song, dance, and drumming—rather than contemplative offerings—but this is up to you.

It is common to start with praise—often a song or poem—dedicated specifically to the full moon. This can be written for the occasion, or can be part of a tradition, or could be something from literature you particularly like. I offer an original poem here. It can be recited by one person, or someone can recite each line, and all repeat it. In either case, all repeat "Blessed be" at the end.

"Lady shining upon us,
Lady transforming us with your light,
Queen of the Tides,
Queen of the Depths,
Queen of our Dreams,
Mother of Night, we adore you!
Mother of Fullness, we bow before you!
Mother of Witches, we implore you
Be among us
Bless us
Accept all we offer
Blessed be!"

Cakes and Wine

Start by saying:

"The Gods have accepted our offering. Let us now receive their blessings in return."

Hold the cup and say:

"The cup, the Goddess, the blood of life
Our Lady blesses us with all good things
She offers herself to us
She offers herself to the God."

Hold the athame over the cup and say:

"The blade, the God, the force of life
Our Lord blesses us with all good things
He offers himself to us
He offers himself to the Goddess."

Plunge the athame into the cup and say:

"Blessed be."

Consecrate the cakes by dipping the athame into the wine and sprinkling drops onto the cakes, forming an invoking pentagram. Say:

"Lady and Lord, you bless us with abundance
The Earth gives us all we need
We thank you.
Blessed be."

Take a cake or a portion of whatever food is on the plate and place it in the libation bowl.

Lift the cup and speak from the heart. It can be as simple as "to the Gods," or it can be detailed. End with "Blessed be." Then make an offering to the gods by pouring a bit of wine into the libation bowl. Drink only after offering.

If multiple people are present, each in turn offers, pours, and drinks. Each offering ends with "Blessed be," and everyone responds by saying "Blessed be."

Or pour from the main cup into each person's individual cup before drinking. Then, each offers, pours, and drinks in turn.

After the cup goes around, or while the cup is on its way around, pass the cakes.

After the ritual is over, the contents of the libation bowl should be poured out onto the Earth. If the ritual is outdoors, then libations are poured directly onto the Earth, and a bowl is not needed.

After Cakes and Wine

The full moon is the ideal time for acts of magic oriented toward growth, love, or fullness, such as healing, finding a lover, a partner, members for a coven, a job, etc.

Of course, if there is an emergency need for magic of some other kind, it can always be done.

The ritual can also be for worship alone, offering dance, feasting, and celebration for the full moon.

Closing the Circle

Face North, raise the wand, and say:

"Beloved Lady,
Moonlight in fullness
Fertile Earth,
You have enriched us with your presence.
Thank you, and farewell!"

All repeat: "*Farewell!*"

"Beloved Lord,
Death and rebirth,
You have enriched us with your presence.
Thank you, and farewell!"

All repeat: "*Farewell!*"
Go to the East, draw a banishing pentagram, and say:

"We thank you, Guardian of the East, Guardian of Air
For protecting this Full Moon rite
Thank you, and farewell!"

All repeat: "*Farewell!*"
Go to the South, draw a banishing pentagram, and say:

"We thank you, Guardian of the South, Guardian of Fire
For protecting this Full Moon rite
Thank you, and farewell!"

All repeat: "*Farewell!*"
Go to the West, draw a banishing pentagram, and say:

"We thank you, Guardian of the West, Guardian of Water
For protecting this Full Moon rite
Thank you, and farewell!"

All repeat: "*Farewell!*"
Go to the North, draw a banishing pentagram, and say:

"We thank you, Guardian of the North, Guardian of Earth
For protecting this Full Moon rite
Thank you, and farewell!"

All repeat: "*Farewell!*"
Facing the center, say:

"The circle is open but unbroken, the rites are ended.
Merry meet, merry part, and merry meet again!"

All repeat: "*Merry meet, merry part, and merry meet again!*"

Sabbats: The Wheel of the Year

In *Casting a Circle* (page 78), we learned how to take a set of basic steps and build a specific ritual around it. Let's use that skill now to create rituals for each Sabbat.

For each Sabbat, we'll discuss its meaning, including how it might relate to other Sabbats. This will be followed by how it is celebrated publicly, such as at open Pagan events, festivals, and the like. After that, there will be two ritual scripts: One for a group and one for a solitary Wiccan.

As ever, modify these scripts as you like. The structure is consistent with Wiccan ritual and tradition, but the wording and the specifics are up to you. You might want language that is more flowery and formal, or more laid back and natural. You might need to adapt to mobility or other concerns. These scripts allow you to worship, celebrate, learn, and grow within a Wiccan framework, but they shouldn't suppress your creativity.

Opening Meditation for Sabbats

In a group, one person reads. A solitary can record the meditation to play back during ritual, or memorize it.

Close your eyes.

Take a deep, cleansing breath, and let it out.
Take another breath and let it out with a sound.
Take another breath and let it out with a tone.
Feel your feet on the ground and know you are solid, planted, and upon the Earth.
Feel the Earth Mother supporting you, holding you up.
Feel the energy at your center. Send your energy into the Earth, from your center, to the base of your spine, down through the soles of your feet, like roots of a tree. Feel the Mother returning your energy, like the sap feeding a tree. You receive her energy and are fully alive and connected to her.
Again, feel your center. Feel the energy moving up, through your upper body, and out through the top of your head, like the branches of a tree. Feel the sky above you, returning your energy, giving you the infinite possibility that is the cosmos. Feel Sun and Moon sending energy down to you, through your branches, back into your center.
Take another breath.
Feel the calm that sits at your center and find the energies of sky and Earth converging.
[Notice the people in the circle with you. Notice that they, too, are connected to Earth and sky. Find, now, that you are connected to each other by the circle that you share.][46]
Take another deep, cleansing breath, and as you let it out, open your eyes.
We[47] *are ready to begin.*

---

46 This paragraph is omitted for solitaries.

47 Use "You" for a solitary.

Beltane

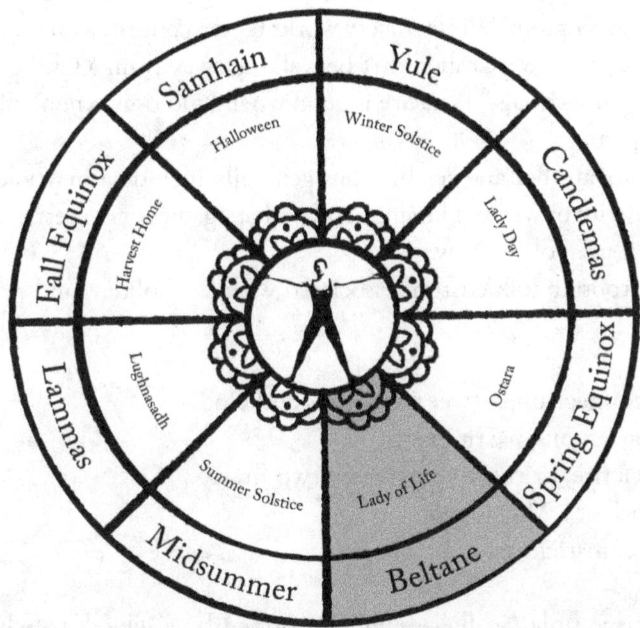

Beltane is seen as the beginning of the Goddess half of the year. It's when the Goddess rules the fertile Earth. It is contrasted with Samhain, directly opposite on the wheel, when the God takes over rulership of the Earth. The May Queen, Lady of Life, contrasts with the Lord of Death at Samhain. Beltane is the dawn of the year, and Samhain is the sunset.

"Hooray, hooray, it's the first of May.
Outdoor fucking begins today."

Beltane is a holiday of licentiousness, of sexual freedom, fertility, and celebrating pleasure. All of this can and should happen in an environment of respect and enthusiastic consent.

A lot of Pagan and Wiccan rituals in the 1970s, 1980s, and 1990s involved random kissing and touching in ways that were playful and sexy, and most people, most of the time, understood how to treat others appropriately. But it also served as cover for people who had no intention of being respectful, which is to say, while everyone else was having a good time, predators were able to hide in plain sight.

As society generally has become more conscious of "yes means yes," the Pagan community has embraced consent culture. Which is to say, there are far fewer public rituals where one might be encouraged to kiss strangers—even on the cheek. While I don't think Pagan events have more or fewer, "me too" moments than any other kind of event, I think it's correct that we are conscientious in our efforts to prevent them.

But figuring out ways of celebrating pleasure without running roughshod over consent, and without being rigidly heteronormative, is important. Pagan culture has served, in part, as a counterpoint to prudish religions. While society works hard to punish women (it's always women) for having sexual desire at all, Wicca shouldn't be walking away from a Charge that says, "all acts of love and pleasure are my rituals." Pleasure is good when (and only when) all parties agree that pleasure is what's happening.

Public and large private Beltane celebrations generally include a maypole (with or without kissing), a spiral dance (with or without kissing), and perhaps games or contests, which might consist of electing a King and Queen of the May.

Rituals often incorporate folk custom associated with the holiday, and might enact (among other things):

- A romantic connection between Goddess and God
- Romantic play among participants
- Leaping over a fire, or running between two fires
- The appearance of a May Queen
- Riding on broomsticks or hobby horses

A maypole is a large pole (10 feet or more) topped by a wheel, to which long ribbons are tied. The maypole dance weaves the ribbons around the pole. The pole and wheel are seen as a symbolic sexual joining (not unlike the athame and cup), and the dance is an act of energy-raising, with the ribbons wrapping and binding the fertile energy for the coming year, working to manifest good crops, good weather, and abundance. It's a joyful and lighthearted affair, full of optimism for the coming season.

How to Do the Maypole Dance

You need an even number of people, but you will always find that some people want to drop out partway through, and can step out and join the drumming or just watch, letting someone else step in. Drumming and song help! Recorded music could also be used.

Everyone holds a ribbon, half the people facing clockwise (the ones in the illustration) and half facing counterclockwise (the twos). When the dance begins, as each one-two pair meets, the ones lift their ribbon up, and the twos duck under. When the next pair meets, the twos lift their ribbons up, and the ones duck under. So, the ones proceed, up/down/up/down, and the twos proceed, down/up/down/up. As each pair meets, they can kiss if everyone is comfortable with that. (Which should be a quick peck if it's a large maypole because otherwise you're slowing everything down!)

Over the years, I have attended more and more maypoles and other events with other Wiccans whom I've known for a long, long time. There's no cutesy kissing strangers when you know everyone, and their partners, and their kids. Instead of kissing, when pairs meet, they smile, laugh, make eye contact, or pass a cute remark, all of which can be as intimate—or more so—than a kiss.

As the dance proceeds, the pole gets wrapped up, and the ribbon you're holding gets shorter and shorter, making the dance tighter and funnier. Finally, the last people run around the pole and wrap up the base.

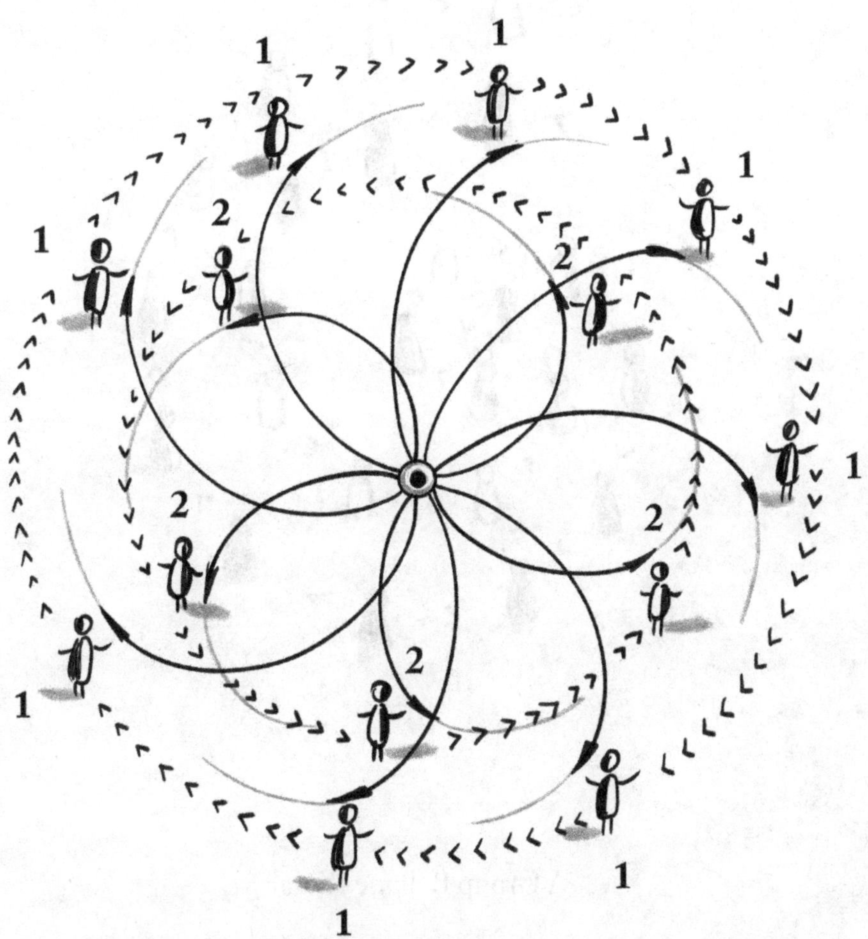

The Spiral Dance

The spiral dance is almost like a maypole dance without the pole. It can be raucous and wild, or slow and stately.

Everyone holds hands and moves in a spiral to the center. As the first person reaches the center, they turn and start spiraling outward in the opposite direction. This brings them into eye contact with the people behind them, one at a time. This is where kissing might happen, or, more typically, just eye contact, which can be loving and very beautiful. When the last person has spiraled to the center and all the way out, the dance ends.

A modified spiral dance is offered in the ritual below.

A Group Beltane Ritual

The script (indeed, any of the group scripts in this book) can be divided up among as many people as you like, with different people doing consecrations, calling each quarter, etc. If there's a group leader, that is the person who declares opening, casts the circle with sword or athame, and declares closing.

Tools Needed

In addition to the usual tools, for Beltane, you need:

- Extra flowers as decoration
- Materials for a maypole, if you're having one
- Materials for creating and extinguishing a fire, if outdoors
- A cauldron with sand in the bottom and a bunch of candles for an indoor fire (and a fire extinguisher)

- A headdress for the Queen of the May
  Important: The headdress will be burned at Midsummer, so it should be made from things that can be burned: Paper, string, yarn, flowers, wood, and so on. Metals or metallic paper, or paper with toxic coatings, are a bad idea.
- A taper candle for the May Queen to carry

Before You Begin

- If you're having a maypole dance, that will happen before the ritual begins.
- Choose a May Queen or have a game of skill or chance in which the winner is the May Queen.
- If you're outdoors, get the fire going at the center of the circle.
- If you're indoors, place the candles in the cauldron and light them.

Begin with the opening meditation found in *Sabbats: The Wheel of the Year* (page 108).

1. Declaration of Opening

The leader says:

"We are gathered to welcome the May!
We give welcome to fruitfulness and plentiful life!
Winter is passed and we rejoice in the glorious love between Lady and Lord.
Beloved Gods, brighten our days with your abundance
as we worship You on this sacred day."

2. Consecrations

Place your athame into the dish of incense and say:

"In the names of the Lady and Lord,
I consecrate Air that it bring mindfulness to my circle."

Place incense onto the lit charcoal so that smoke begins to rise. Place your athame into the smoke and say:

"In the names of the Lady and Lord,
I consecrate Fire that it bring passion to my circle."

Place your athame into the dish of water and say:

"In the names of the Lady and Lord
I consecrate Water that it bring feeling to my circle."

Place your athame into the dish of salt and say:

"In the names of the Lady and Lord,
I consecrate Earth that it bring commitment to my circle."

Place three pinches of salt into the water and stir.
Say:

"So mote it be."

3. Cast the Circle

With your athame or sword, go to the East, directing energy to the circle as you say:

"Round and about, round and about, power stay in, world stay out."

Repeat these words over and over until you've returned to the East. Then walk silently back to the altar.

Pick up the dish of saltwater and return to the East. Wet your fingers and flick drops all the way around the circle, East to East, sprinkling the entire perimeter, saying:

"Round and about, by Water and Earth, I cleanse this circle."

Repeat these words over and over until you've returned to the East. Before finishing, *sprinkle a few drops into the fire*. Then, walk silently back to the altar.

Pick up the censer, stirring it up to get it smoky if needed. Return to the East. Cense the perimeter, as you walk again around the circle, East to East, saying:

"Round and about, by Fire and Air, I purify this circle."

Repeat these words over and over until you've returned to the East. After completing the circuit, take a pinch of incense and *place it into the fire*. Then, walk silently back to the altar.

4. Call the Quarters

In the East, face out, point your athame, and draw an invoking pentagram, saying:

"I invoke the Guardian of East, the Guardian of Air
Bring sweet winds and beautiful flights to us
Bring wisdom to our circle and protect us from harm
Honor the Lady and Lord with us
On this Beltane night
Welcome, Guardian! Blessed be."

All repeat: *"Blessed be."*
Walk deosil back to your place.
In the South, face out, point your athame, and draw an invoking pentagram, saying:

"I invoke the Guardian of South, the Guardian of Fire
Bring warm days and healing fire to us
Bring strong will to our circle and protect us from harm
Honor the Lady and Lord with us
On this Beltane night
Welcome, Guardian! Blessed be."

All repeat: *"Blessed be."*
Walk deosil back to your place.
In the West, face out, point your athame, and draw an invoking pentagram, saying:

"I invoke the Guardian of West, the Guardian of Water
Bring flowing streams and lovely moonlight to us
Bring deep love to our circle and protect us from harm
Honor the Lady and Lord with us
On this Beltane night
Welcome, Guardian! Blessed be."

All repeat: *"Blessed be."*
Walk deosil back to your place.
In the North, face out, point your athame, and draw an invoking pentagram, saying:

"I invoke the Guardian of North, the Guardian of Earth
Bring rich soil and good homes to us
Bring stability to our circle and protect us from harm
Honor the Lady and Lord with us
On this Beltane night
Welcome, Guardian! Blessed be."

All repeat: *"Blessed be."*
Walk deosil back to your place.
Walk back to the East for a final, silent salute. (There's no need to invoke.)

5. Invoking the Gods

All join hands.
The leader says:

"Lord and Lady, come to us with joy and mirth
Gracious Goddess of the Spring, bring rebirth

Be here Lady as flowers bloom
Be here Lord, and drive away gloom
Lighten our hearts in our sacred rite
Bring easy days and thrilling nights
Come among us on this day
Join us on this first of May.
Welcome! Blessed be!"

All repeat: *"Blessed be."*

6. Offerings/Seasonal Celebration

The leader (presumably the priestess) releases the hand of the person to their right. She stands in front of the person to her left (still holding hands). They make eye contact, and can kiss, nod, smile—whatever is comfortable.

The priestess now moves one person over, so that two people are now facing in, and these two greet the people they face. They then move one person over, with three now facing in, etc. (See illustration below.) Whether there are three people or thirteen, the process is repeated until all have made eye contact and returned to their place.

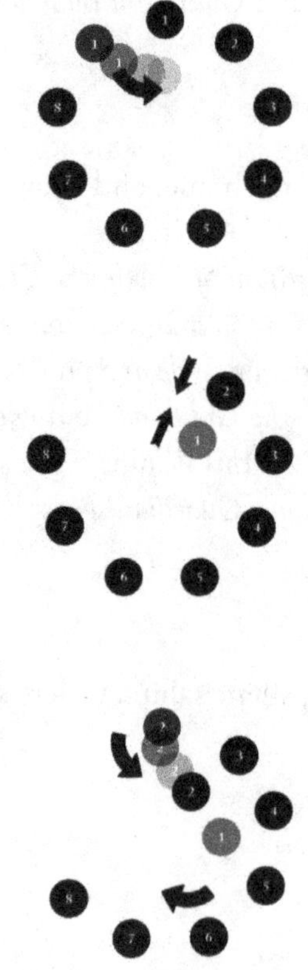

Beltane Group Ritual Diagram

Leader says:[48]

"Let us greet the May Queen!"

The May Queen steps forward and puts on the headdress, saying:

"I am here to bring joy and blessing. I am here to represent the Lady on Earth."

The May Queen picks up the taper and lights it from the fire. She brings it to her third eye, and then her heart, blessing herself.

She then goes to the priestess[49] and repeats the motion—third eye and heart—saying:

"Be blessed by the sacred fire of Beltane. Let all good come with the spring."

She repeats this process for each person.

She now puts the taper out, and everyone again joins hands as the May Queen leads a dance around the fire.

7. Cakes and Wine

Say:

"It is time to receive the blessings of vine and Earth!"

Hold the cup and say:

"The cup, the Goddess, the blood of life
Our Lady blesses us with all good things
She offers herself to us
She offers herself to the God."

Hold the athame over the cup and say:

"The blade, the God, the force of life
Our Lord blesses us with all good things
He offers himself to us
He offers himself to the Goddess."

Plunge the athame into the cup and say:

"Blessed be."

48 If the leader is also the May Queen, someone else should say this.

49 Or the first person to the left of the priestess, if the May Queen and the priestess are the same person.

Consecrate the cakes by dipping the athame into the wine and sprinkling drops onto the cakes, forming an invoking pentagram. Say:

"Lady and Lord, you bless us with abundance
The Earth gives us all we need
We thank you.
Blessed be."

Take a cake and place it in the libation bowl. If you are outdoors, the cake goes directly into the fire.

Lift the cup and speak from the heart. It can be as simple as "to the Gods," or it can be detailed. End with "Blessed be." Then, make an offering to the gods by pouring a bit of wine into the libation bowl. Drink only after offering.

Each person in turn offers, pours, and drinks. Each offering ends with "Blessed be," and everyone responds by saying "Blessed be."

Or pour from the main cup into each person's individual cup before drinking. Then, each offers, pours, and drinks in turn.

After the cup goes around, or while the cup is on its way around, pass the cakes.

After the ritual is over, the contents of the libation bowl should be poured out onto the Earth. If the ritual is outdoors, then libations are poured directly onto the Earth.

8. Celebration of Season

The primary seasonal rite has been performed as an offering. After cakes and wine, traditional activities on Beltane include games, divination, song, and dance. Cakes and wine can continue to be enjoyed during this activity.

9. Closing the Circle

Face North, raise the wand, and say:

"Beloved Lady,
Moonlight and fertile Earth,
You have enriched us with your presence at our Beltane rite.
Thank you, and farewell!"

All repeat: *"Farewell!"*

"Beloved Lord,
Death and Rebirth,
You have enriched us with your presence at our Beltane rite.
Thank you, and farewell!"

All repeat: *"Farewell!"*
Go to the East, draw a banishing pentagram, and say:

"We thank you, Guardian of the East, Guardian of Air
For protecting this Beltane rite
Thank you, and farewell!"

All repeat: *"Farewell!"*
Go to the South, draw a banishing pentagram, and say:

"We thank you, Guardian of the South, Guardian of Fire
For protecting this Beltane rite
Thank you, and farewell!"

All repeat: *"Farewell!"*
Go to the West, draw a banishing pentagram, and say:

"We thank you, Guardian of the West, Guardian of Water
For protecting this Beltane rite
Thank you, and farewell!"

All repeat: *"Farewell!"*
Go to the North, draw a banishing pentagram, and say:

"We thank you, Guardian of the North, Guardian of Earth
For protecting this Beltane rite
Thank you, and farewell!"

All repeat: *"Farewell!"*
Facing the center, say:

"The circle is open but unbroken, the rites are ended.
Merry meet, merry part, and merry meet again!"

All repeat: *"Merry meet, merry part, and merry meet again!"*

A Solitary Beltane Ritual

Tools Needed

In addition to the usual tools, for Beltane, you need:

- Extra flowers as decoration
- Materials for creating and extinguishing a fire, if outdoors

- A cauldron with sand in the bottom and a bunch of candles for an indoor fire (and a fire extinguisher)
- A headdress for the Queen of the May
  Important: The headdress will be burned at Midsummer, so it should be made from things that can be burned: Paper, string, yarn, flowers, wood, and so on. Metals or metallic paper, or paper with toxic coatings, are a bad idea.
- A taper candle for the May Queen to carry

Before You Begin

- If you're outdoors, get the fire going at the center of the circle.
- If you're indoors, place the candles in the cauldron and light them.

Begin with the opening meditation found in *Sabbats: The Wheel of the Year* on page 108.

1. Declaration of Opening

"I am here to welcome the May!
I give welcome to fruitfulness and plentiful life!
Winter is passed, and I rejoice in the glorious love between Lady and Lord.
Beloved gods, brighten my days with your abundance as I worship you on this sacred day."

2. Consecrations

Place your athame into the dish of incense and say:

"In the names of the Lady and Lord,
I consecrate Air that it bring mindfulness to my circle."

Place incense onto the lit charcoal so that smoke begins to rise. Place your athame into the smoke and say:

"In the names of the Lady and Lord,
I consecrate Fire that it bring passion to my circle."

Place your athame into the dish of water and say:

"In the names of the Lady and Lord,
I consecrate Water that it bring feeling to my circle."

Place your athame into the dish of salt and say:

"In the names of the Lady and Lord,
I consecrate Earth that it bring commitment to my circle."

Place three pinches of salt into the water.
Say:

"So mote it be."

3. Cast the Circle

With your athame or sword, go to the East, directing energy to the circle as you say:

"Round and about, round and about, power stay in, world stay out."

Repeat these words over and over until you've returned to the East. Then walk silently back to the altar.

Pick up the dish of saltwater and return to the East. Wet your fingers and flick drops all the way around the circle, East to East, sprinkling the entire perimeter, saying:

"Round and about, by Water and Earth, I cleanse this circle."

Repeat these words over and over until you've returned to the East. Before finishing, *sprinkle a few drops into the fire.* Then walk silently back to the altar.

Pick up the censer, stirring it up if needed. Return to the East. Cense the perimeter, as you walk again around the circle, East to East, saying:

"Round and about, by Fire and Air, I purify this circle."

Repeat these words over and over until you've returned to the East. After completing the circuit, take a pinch of incense and *place it into the fire.* Then walk silently back to the altar.

4. Call the Quarters

In the East, face out, point your athame, and draw an invoking pentagram, saying:

"I invoke the Guardian of East, the Guardian of Air
Bring sweet winds and beautiful flights to me
Bring wisdom to my circle and protect me from harm
Honor the Lady and Lord with me
On this Beltane night
Welcome, Guardian! Blessed be."

In the South, face out, point your athame and draw an invoking pentagram, saying:

"I invoke the Guardian of South, the Guardian of Fire
Bring warm days and healing fire to me
Bring strong will to my circle and protect me from harm

Honor the Lady and Lord with me
On this Beltane night
Welcome, Guardian! Blessed be."

In the West, face out, point your athame, and draw an invoking pentagram, saying:

"I invoke the Guardian of West, the Guardian of Water
Bring flowing streams and lovely moonlight to me
Bring deep love to my circle and protect me from harm
Honor the Lady and Lord with me
On this Beltane night
Welcome, Guardian! Blessed be."

In the North, face out, point your athame, and draw an invoking pentagram, saying:

"I invoke the Guardian of North, the Guardian of Earth
Bring rich soil and good homes to me
Bring stability to my circle and protect me from harm
Honor the Lady and Lord with me
On this Beltane night
Welcome, Guardian! Blessed be."

Walk back to the East for a final, silent salute.

5. Invoking the Gods

Begin slowly clapping your hands, and say the invocation in rhythm with your beat:

"Lord and Lady, come to me with joy and mirth
Gracious Goddess of the Spring, bring rebirth
Be here Lady as flowers bloom
Be here Lord, and drive away gloom
Lighten my heart in this sacred rite
Bring easy days and thrilling nights
Come to my rite on this day
Join me on this first of May.
Welcome! Blessed be!"

6. Offering

Pick up the headdress and hold it above your head, but don't put it on. Walk slowly deosil, once around the circle, repeating:

"The Queen is coming!"

Change the walk to a dance step the second time around.
The third time around, dance or walk rapidly, still repeating:

"The Queen is coming!"

After the third round, say:

"The Queen is here!"

Place the headdress on your head.
Say:

"I am here to bring joy and blessing. I am here to represent the Lady on Earth."

Pick up the taper and light it from the fire. Bring it to your third eye, and then your heart, blessing yourself.
Say:

"I am blessed by the sacred fire of Beltane. Let all good come with the spring."

Put out the taper and dance around the fire. End by removing the headdress.

7. Cakes and Wine

Say:

"It is time to receive the blessings of vine and Earth!"

Hold the cup and say:

"The cup, the Goddess, the blood of life
My Lady blesses me with all good things
She offers herself to her children
She offers herself to the God."

Hold the athame over the cup and say:

"The blade, the God, the force of life
Our Lord blesses me with all good things
He offers himself to his children
He offers himself to the Goddess."

Plunge the athame into the cup and say:

"Blessed be."

Consecrate the cakes by dipping the athame into the wine and sprinkling drops onto the cakes, forming an invoking pentagram. Say:

"Lady and Lord, you bless me with abundance
The Earth gives me all I need
Thank you.
Blessed be."

Take a cake and place it in the libation bowl. If you are outdoors, the offering can go directly into the fire.

Lift the cup and speak from the heart. It can be as simple as "to the Gods," or it can be detailed. End with "Blessed be." Then, make an offering to the gods by pouring a bit of wine into the libation bowl. Drink only after offering and then eat a cake.

After the ritual is over, the contents of the libation bowl should be poured out onto the Earth. If the ritual is outdoors, then libations are poured directly onto the Earth.

8. Celebration of Season

You can continue to dance and sing in celebration, or do a reading for the coming season, or just meditate on the Goddess and the gifts she has brought.

9. Closing the Circle

Face North, raise the wand, and say:

"Beloved Lady,
Moonlight and fertile Earth,
You have enriched me with your presence at this Beltane rite.
Thank you, and farewell!
Beloved Lord,
Death and Rebirth,
You have enriched me with your presence at this Beltane rite.
Thank you, and farewell!"

Go to the East, draw a banishing pentagram, and say:

"I thank you, Guardian of the East, Guardian of Air
For protecting this Beltane rite
Thank you, and farewell!"

Go to the South, draw a banishing pentagram, and say:

"I thank you, Guardian of the South, Guardian of Fire
For protecting this Beltane rite
Thank you, and farewell!"

Go to the West, draw a banishing pentagram, and say:

"I thank you, Guardian of the West, Guardian of Water
For protecting this Beltane rite
Thank you, and farewell!"

Go to the North, draw a banishing pentagram, and say:

"I thank you, Guardian of the North, Guardian of Earth
For protecting this Beltane rite
Thank you, and farewell!"

Facing the center, say:

"The circle is open but unbroken, the rites are ended.
Merry meet, merry part, and merry meet again!"[50]

Midsummer

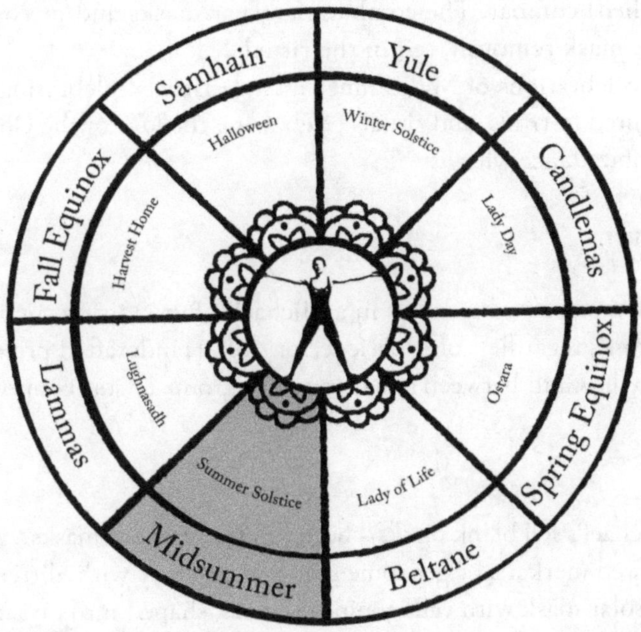

50 "Meeting" and "parting" may not seem right to you for a solitary ritual, although you may think of it as meeting the gods. You can leave this line out.

Summer Solstice is the longest day of the year—the 24-hour period with the most daylight. It contrasts with Winter Solstice, the shortest day of the year. The solstices are seen as the lifecycle of the Sun God.

In Wicca, the goddess is generally seen as immortal: Like the moon, she waxes and wanes, going through a lifecycle of youth (waxing moon), maturity (full moon), and old age (waning moon), but never truly dying. Even at the dark of the moon, she is darkness; although invisible, she remains with us.

By contrast, the god is seen as eternally dying and resurrecting. He is seen in the crops that are cut down and the animals that are hunted or herded—all sacrificing their lives to feed us. He is also the sun, the daylight. We could, I suppose, see the sun as immortal, just as the goddess is, but we relate the waxing and waning of the sun to the waxing and waning of crops and animals, and so, we see death and rebirth rather than eternal, constant life.

The death and birth of the sun are characterized as old age and youth (as in Father Time and the Baby New Year, seen at the Winter Solstice), or as combat between vigorous gods, which is typical of the Summer Solstice. Often, these gods are seen as vying for the affection of the Goddess, who will choose one over the other each solstice.

There is a kind of spiritual paradox here; the peak of the sun's power is when it begins to die, just as the sun's weakest moment is when it is born.

So, in the glory of summer sun, the waxing god (the Oak King or Bull God) is slain by the waning god (the Holly King or Stag God), and as we enjoy our summer fun, it's the god of the waning year who rules.

I've participated in wonderful, large Pagan rituals where two men represent the gods in ritual (choreographed) combat. The combatants wear masks and/or costumes so that one can "die" and then, mask removed, rejoin the ritual.

Less elaborate celebrations of Midsummer include rituals celebrating the ocean, bonfire dances, flower-oriented festivals, and rituals celebrating the love of the Goddess and the God, as they share their abundance with us.

Crafting Midsummer

I love crafting. I am a person who drools in a Michael's. But crafting simple ritual supplies is within reach of anyone, regardless of experience or skill. Handcrafted projects are a great way to stay connected to the Craft between rituals, and in a group, to stay connected to one another.

Masks

Craft stores like Michael's sell blank masks—both full face and eye masks. A blank mask can be decorated with colored markers, or get some glue and go crazy with glitter, paper, yarn, etc. I once finished off a solar mask with yellow pipe cleaners, shaped into rays, and stapled around the outside.

For a pair of God masks, contrast is key. One can be bright yellow or gold for the sun, the other black. Decorations can include oak, stag, and sun motifs for the bright year, and holly, bull, and night motifs for the dark year. They can be simple or elaborate, as long as they are easily recognizable.

Another option is a crown or headband, with a cloth face-covering attached. A thin fabric might be see-through, or eye holes can be cut.

Robes or Cloaks

Despite my love of crafts, I have no sewing skills, but I've done it for ritual from time to time. A *tabard* is the easiest robe in the world—it's just a rectangle with a hole for the head—the sides remain open. If you have a little skill, you can trim it, hem it, and make a matching belt, but you can also just cut a vaguely correct shape and use a rope for a belt.

A cloak is slightly more complicated, but easy patterns are available online.

By starting with two distinct colors for these costumes, you've created the contrast you need. The rest of the decoration is just to beautify and celebrate. You can use trim, fabric paint, or appliqué with appropriate themes.

A Group Midsummer Ritual

The ritual requires a minimum of three people. Typically, roles are divided by gender, with a woman as the Goddess and men as the gods. This may or may not work for you and has not been specified in the script.

Divide the script up as you like, with the leader (if there is one) declaring the opening and closing and casting the circle.

Let's change up the quarter callings this time. Why? Just for fun! If you prefer the ones here, you can use them at any sabbat or esbat (removing the reference to Midsummer, of course).

Tools Needed

In addition to the usual tools, for this ritual, you need:

- Seasonal decorations
- The May Queen headdress from Beltane
- Masks or robes for the Stag/Bright God and the Bull/Dark God

- Materials for creating and extinguishing a fire, if outdoors
- A cauldron with sand in the bottom and a bunch of candles for an indoor fire (and a fire extinguisher)
- Drums, rattles, or other rhythm instruments

Before You Begin

- Determine who will play the roles of Goddess, Oak King, and Holly King.
- If you're outdoors, get the fire going at the center of the circle.
- If you're indoors, place the candles in the cauldron and light them.

Begin with the opening meditation found in *Sabbats: The Wheel of the Year* on page 108.

1. Declaration of Opening

The leader says:

"Welcome to the longest day! The Sun Lord is at his peak,
but at the top of every mountain, the descent begins.
The Dark Lord is at his weakest—but he has nowhere to go but up!
Darkness and Light, we worship you and the Lady of the fertile Earth!"

2. Consecrations

Place your athame into the dish of incense and say:

"In the names of the Lady and Lord,
I consecrate Air that it bring mindfulness to my circle."

Place incense onto the lit charcoal so that smoke begins to rise. Place your athame into the smoke and say:

"In the names of the Lady and Lord,
I consecrate Fire that it bring passion to my circle."

Place your athame into the dish of water and say:

"In the names of the Lady and Lord,
I consecrate Water that it bring feeling to my circle."

Place your athame into the dish of salt and say:

"In the names of the Lady and Lord,
I consecrate Earth that it bring commitment to my circle."

Place three pinches of salt into the water and stir.
Say:

"So mote it be."

3. Cast the Circle

With your athame or sword, go to the East, directing energy to the circle as you say:

"Round and about, round and about, power stay in, world stay out."

Repeat these words over and over until you've returned to the East. Then walk silently back to the altar.

Pick up the dish of saltwater and return to the East. Wet your fingers and flick drops all the way around the circle, East to East, sprinkling the entire perimeter, saying:

"Round and about, by Water and Earth, I cleanse this circle."

Repeat these words over and over until you've returned to the East. Then walk silently back to the altar.

Pick up the censer, stirring it up if needed. Return to the East. Cense the perimeter, as you walk again around the circle, East to East, saying:

"Round and about, by Fire and Air, I purify this circle."

Repeat these words over and over until you've returned to the East. Then walk silently back to the altar.

4. Call the Quarters

In the East, face out, point your athame, and draw an invoking pentagram, saying:

"Come to us, Air!
Guard us in the East!
Come to us, wind
Come to us, intelligence
Come on eagle's wings
Guard our Midsummer rite!
Welcome, O Air! Blessed be."

All repeat: *"Blessed be."*
Walk deosil back to your place.
In the South, face out, point your athame, and draw an invoking pentagram, saying:

"Come to us, Fire!
Guard us in the South!
Come to us, heat
Come to us, passion
Come with a lion's roar
Guard our Midsummer rite!
Welcome, O Fire! Blessed be."

All repeat: *"Blessed be."*
Walk deosil back to your place.
In the West, face out, point your athame, and draw an invoking pentagram, saying:

"Come to us, Water!
Guard us in the West!
Come to us, oceans
Come to us, love
Come riding on dolphins
Guard our Midsummer rite!
Welcome, O Water! Blessed be."

All repeat: *"Blessed be."*
Walk deosil back to your place.
In the North, face out, point your athame, and draw an invoking pentagram, saying:

"Come to us, Earth!
Guard us in the North!
Come to us, soil
Come to us, commitment
Come with mighty hooves
Guard our Midsummer rite!
Welcome, O Earth! Blessed be."

All repeat: *"Blessed be."*
Walk back to the East for a final, silent salute.

5. Invoking the Gods

This invocation could be split among different people: The person who will play the Goddess invokes the Gods, and one of the Gods invokes the Lady, or they invoke her in unison:

Raise your wand into the air and invoke:

"Lord of the Sun, glory of light and growth
Come on the longest day to be adored
Lord of the Sun, summer's peak

Come and dance with us!
Lord Who is Two, join us!
Lady of the Sea, Lady of the Flowers
Lady of the Fertile Earth
Lover of the God
The Sun dies and is reborn, but You are eternal
Your lover dies, Your lover is born, Your love is eternal.
Welcome and blessed be."

All repeat: *"Blessed be."*

6. Offerings/Seasonal Celebration

The person representing the Goddess steps to the spot between the altar and the fire and dons the May Queen headdress, saying:

"I am the summer queen. Who will be my lover?"

The person representing the Bright God puts on their mask and/or robe and stands in the West.

The Goddess goes to the West and takes the hand of the Bright God. They dance, skip, or walk one full circuit around. Then the Goddess takes off the headdress and throws it into the fire if outdoors. (If indoors, take a small piece of the headdress, such as a flower or leaf, and toss it into the fire. Place the rest of the headdress on the floor next to the cauldron—it can be burned outdoors after the ceremony is over.) When this happens, the Bright God, in the East, sits down and covers their face with their hands or with a cloak.

The Goddess repeats:

"I am the summer queen. Who will be my lover?"

The person representing the Dark God puts on their mask and/or robe and stands in the East.

The Goddess goes to the East and takes the hand of the Dark God. They dance, skip, or walk one full circuit around. Then they stand in front of the fire and raise their hands together, saying:

"Blessed be the turning of the wheel!"

All repeat: *"Blessed be."*

Both Gods remove their masks/robes and return to being ordinary members of the circle.

7. Cakes and Wine

Say:

"It is time to receive the blessings of vine and Earth!"

Hold the cup and say:

"The cup, the Goddess, the blood of life
Our Lady blesses us with all good things
She offers herself to us
She offers herself to the God."

Hold the athame over the cup and say:

"The blade, the God, the force of life
Our Lord blesses us with all good things
He offers himself to us
He offers himself to the Goddess."

Plunge the athame into the cup and say:

"Blessed be."

Consecrate the cakes by dipping the athame into the wine and sprinkling drops onto the cakes, forming an invoking pentagram. Say:

"Lady and Lord, you bless us with abundance
The Earth gives us all we need
We thank you.
Blessed be."

Take a cake and place it in the libation bowl. If you are outdoors, the cake goes directly into the fire.

Lift the cup and speak from the heart. It can be as simple as "to the Gods," or it can be detailed. End with "Blessed be." Then make an offering to the gods by pouring a bit of wine into the libation bowl. Drink only after offering.

Each person in turn offers, pours and drinks. Each offering ends with "Blessed be," and everyone responds by saying "Blessed be."

Or pour from the main cup into each person's individual cup before drinking. Then, each offers, pours, and drinks in turn. After the cup goes around, or while the cup is on its way around, pass the cakes.

After the ritual is over, the contents of the libation bowl should be poured out onto the Earth. If the ritual is outdoors, then libations are poured directly onto the Earth, and a libation bowl is not needed.

8. Celebration of Season

The primary seasonal rite has been performed as an offering. After cakes and wine, traditional activities on Midsummer include song and dance. You already have instruments, so enjoy them!

You can continue to eat and drink during this part of the rite.

9. Closing the Circle

Face North, raise the wand, and say:

"Beloved Lady,
Lover and beloved, Earth and Sky,
Your passion has blessed our Midsummer rite.
Thank you, and farewell!"

All repeat: *"Farewell!"*

"Beloved Lord,
Brightness and Darkness
Stag and Bull
The Sun at its peak and the Sun waning
You have blessed our Midsummer rite.
Thank you, and farewell!"

All repeat: *"Farewell!"*
Go to the East, draw a banishing pentagram, and say:

"We thank you, Guardian of the East, Guardian of Air
For protecting this Midsummer rite
Thank you, and farewell!"

All repeat: *"Farewell!"*
Go to the South, draw a banishing pentagram, and say:

"We thank you, Guardian of the South, Guardian of Fire
For protecting this Midsummer rite
Thank you, and farewell!"

All repeat: *"Farewell!"*
Go to the West, draw a banishing pentagram, and say:

"We thank you, Guardian of the West, Guardian of Water
For protecting this Midsummer rite
Thank you, and farewell!"

All repeat: *"Farewell!"*
Go to the North, draw a banishing pentagram, and say:

"We thank you, Guardian of the North, Guardian of Earth
For protecting this Midsummer rite
Thank you, and farewell!"

All repeat: *"Farewell!"*
Facing the center, say:

"The circle is open but unbroken, the rites are ended.
Merry meet, merry part, and merry meet again!"

All repeat: *"Merry meet, merry part, and merry meet again!"*

A Solitary Midsummer Ritual

While robes were an option as a costume for the group rite, you'll be playing all roles as a solitary: Taking off and putting on masks is probably a lot easier than doing so with robes, so masks are specified.

Tools Needed

In addition to the usual tools, for this ritual, you need:

- Seasonal decorations
- The May Queen headdress from Beltane
- Masks for the Stag/Bright God and the Bull/Dark God
- Materials for creating and extinguishing a fire, if outdoors
- A cauldron with sand in the bottom and a bunch of candles for an indoor fire (and a fire extinguisher)
- A drum, rattle, or other rhythm instrument

Before You Begin

- If you're outdoors, get the fire going at the center of the circle.
- If you're indoors, place the candles in the cauldron and light them.

Begin with the opening meditation found in *Sabbats: The Wheel of the Year* on page 108.

1. Declaration of Opening

Say:

"Today is the longest day! The Sun Lord is at his peak,
but at the top of every mountain, the descent begins.

The Dark Lord is at his weakest—but he has nowhere to go but up!
Darkness and Light, I worship you and the Lady of the fertile Earth!"

2. Consecrations

Place your athame into the dish of incense and say:

"In the names of the Lady and Lord,
I consecrate Air that it bring mindfulness to my circle."

Place incense onto the lit charcoal so that smoke begins to rise. Place your athame into the smoke and say:

"In the names of the Lady and Lord,
I consecrate Fire that it bring passion to my circle."

Place your athame into the dish of water and say:

"In the names of the Lady and Lord,
I consecrate Water that it bring feeling to my circle."

Place your athame into the dish of salt and say:

"In the names of the Lady and Lord,
I consecrate Earth that it bring commitment to my circle."

Place three pinches of salt into the water and stir.
Say:

"So mote it be."

3. Cast the Circle

With your athame or sword, go to the East, directing energy to the circle as you say:

"Round and about, round and about, power stay in, world stay out."

Repeat these words over and over until you've returned to the East. Then walk silently back to the altar.

Pick up the dish of saltwater and return to the East. Wet your fingers and flick drops all the way around the circle, East to East, sprinkling the entire perimeter, saying:

"Round and about, by Water and Earth, I cleanse this circle."

Repeat these words over and over until you've returned to the East. Then walk silently back to the altar.

Pick up the censer, stirring it up if needed. Return to the East. Cense the perimeter, as you walk again around the circle, East to East, saying:

"Round and about, by Fire and Air, I purify this circle."

Repeat these words over and over until you've returned to the East. Then walk silently back to the altar.

4. Call the Quarters

In the East, face out, point your athame, and draw an invoking pentagram, saying:

"Come to me, Air!
Guard my circle in the East!
Come to me, wind
Come to me, intelligence
Come on eagle's wings
Guard my Midsummer rite!
Welcome, O Air! Blessed be."

In the South, face out, point your athame, and draw an invoking pentagram, saying:

"Come to me, Fire!
Guard my circle in the South!
Come to me, heat
Come to me, passion
Come with a lion's roar
Guard my Midsummer rite!
Welcome, O Fire! Blessed be."

In the West, face out, point your athame, and draw an invoking pentagram, saying:

"Come to me, Water!
Guard my circle in the West!
Come to me, oceans
Come to me, love
Come riding on dolphins
Guard my Midsummer rite!
Welcome, O Water! Blessed be."

In the North, face out, point your athame, and draw an invoking pentagram, saying:

"Come to me, Earth!
Guard my circle in the North!
Come to me, soil
Come to me, commitment
Come with mighty hooves
Guard my Midsummer rite!
Welcome, O Earth! Blessed be."

Walk back to the East for a final, silent salute.

5. Invoking the Gods

Raise your wand into the air and invoke:

"Lord of the Sun, glory of light and growth
Come on the longest day to be adored
Lord of the Sun, summer's peak
Come and dance with me!
Lord Who is Two, join me!
Lady of the Sea, Lady of the Flowers
Lady of the Fertile Earth
Lover of the God
The Sun dies and is reborn, but You are eternal
Your lover dies, Your lover is born, Your love is eternal.
Welcome and blessed be."

6. Offerings/Seasonal Celebration

Put on the Bright God mask and visualize the energy of the summer and sunshine entering you.

Say:

"I am the Sun and the Stag. Today is My day. My energies brighten the world."

Dance once around the circle.

Return to the altar, remove the Bright God mask, and put on the May Queen headdress, allowing the energy of the Goddess to enter you. Dance once around the circle and throw the headdress into the fire. (If indoors, take a small piece of the headdress, such as a flower or leaf, and toss it into the fire. Place the rest of the headdress on the floor next to the cauldron—it can be burned outdoors after the ceremony is over.)

Put on the Dark God mask, allowing the energy of night and winter to enter you.

Say:

"I am the Night and the Bull. Tonight is My night. I whisper secrets to the world."

Dance once around the circle.
Take off the mask and say:

"But now it is summer, and the love of the Goddess is everywhere on the Earth.
Blessed be the turning of the wheel!"

7. Cakes and Wine

Say:

"It is time to receive the blessings of vine and Earth!"

Hold the cup and say:

"The cup, the Goddess, the blood of life
Our Lady blesses us with all good things
She offers herself to us
She offers herself to the God."

Hold the athame over the cup and say:

"The blade, the God, the force of life
Our Lord blesses us with all good things
He offers himself to us
He offers himself to the Goddess."

Plunge the athame into the cup and say:

"Blessed be."

Consecrate the cakes by dipping the athame into the wine and sprinkling drops onto the cakes, forming an invoking pentagram. Say:

"Lady and Lord, you bless us with abundance
The Earth gives us all we need
We thank you.
Blessed be."

Take a cake and place it in the libation bowl. If you are outdoors, the cake goes directly into the fire.

Lift the cup and speak from the heart. It can be as simple as "to the Gods," or it can be detailed. End with "Blessed be." Then make an offering to the gods by pouring a bit of wine into the libation bowl. Drink only after offering. After you drink, eat a cake.

After the ritual is over, the contents of the libation bowl should be poured out onto the Earth. If the ritual is outdoors, then libations are poured directly onto the Earth, and the bowl is not needed.

8. Celebration of Season

The primary seasonal rite has been performed as an offering. After cakes and wine, traditional activities on Midsummer include song and dance. You can continue to eat and drink as well.

9. Closing the Circle

Face North, raise the wand, and say:

"Beloved Lady,
Lover and beloved, Earth and Sky,
Your passion has blessed my Midsummer rite.
Thank you, and farewell!
Beloved Lord,
Brightness and Darkness
Stag and Bull
The Sun at its peak and the Sun waning
You have blessed my Midsummer rite.
Thank you, and farewell!"

Go to the East, draw a banishing pentagram, and say:

"We thank you, Guardian of the East, Guardian of Air
For protecting this Midsummer rite
Thank you, and farewell!"

Go to the South, draw a banishing pentagram, and say:

"We thank you, Guardian of the South, Guardian of Fire
For protecting this Midsummer rite
Thank you, and farewell!"

Go to the West, draw a banishing pentagram, and say:

"We thank you, Guardian of the West, Guardian of Water
For protecting this Midsummer rite
Thank you, and farewell!"

Go to the North, draw a banishing pentagram, and say:

"We thank you, Guardian of the North, Guardian of Earth

For protecting this Midsummer rite
Thank you, and farewell!"

Facing the center, say:

"The circle is open but unbroken, the rites are ended.
Merry meet, merry part, and merry meet again!"

Lammas

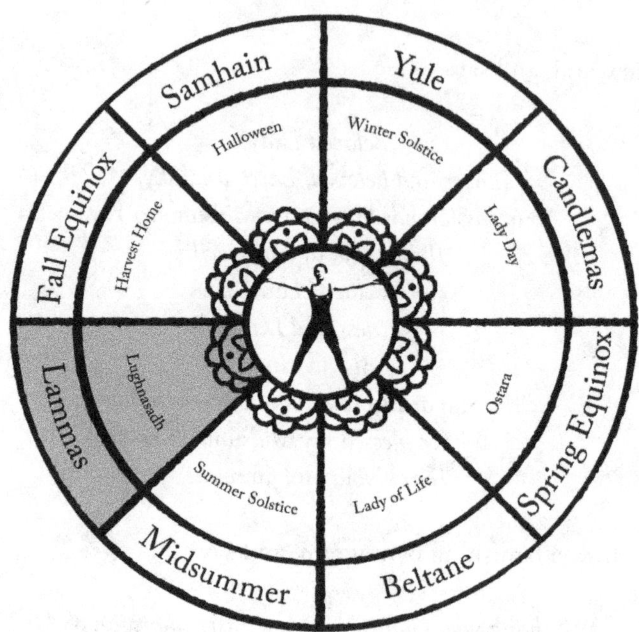

The holiday known as August Eve, Lammas, or Lughnasadh is the first of three harvest festivals.

At the height of summer's heat, we pay attention to the darkness of winter that will come, as we venerate the God's sacrifice. Just so, at Candlemas, the depth of winter's cold, we will pay attention to the brightness of spring that is to come. These holidays look across the wheel at one another.

Marking sacred time through agricultural cycles is an ancient tradition, but we tend to romanticize agricultural life, as if that's the "real" Paganism. Pagans were always both rural and urban, and today, Wiccans are urban, suburban, and rural in about the same mix as everyone else. There is absolutely nothing wrong with being an urban witch! I've lived in the country, the suburbs, and the city at various times in my life, and I assure you, the sacred is everywhere.

Nonetheless, all of us are affected by agricultural cycles. I go to a local farmer's market in my city and can see the seasonal cycles in the availability of different foods. (My favorite vegetables, fiddlehead ferns, are only available for about three weeks each spring.) Most of us will never starve, and the availability or unavailability of a particular crop will not cause us undue anxiety.

But harvest is also about the metaphorical fruits of our labor—we plant seeds (like sending out query letters) that we hope to harvest (a publisher picking up our book).

Moreover, we may think of food as something that comes in a package, but all food is part of the sacred cycle of life sustaining life. Plants and animals are alive and die—cut down or slaughtered—that we may live, and are reborn in us.

Lammas (literally "loaf mass") is the celebration of the sacredness of bread. The god who is the embodiment of grain, John Barleycorn, is cut down, but lives again as bread and whiskey. (I should note that, because John Barleycorn is specifically associated with whiskey, some people in recovery might be uncomfortable with that name and might use a different god-name in ritual.)

Rituals for this holiday often involve bread and/or the enactment of sacrifice. I've attended a large bread-baking ritual, where bread was baked all day in open ovens while people socialized and celebrated, followed by an evening ritual where the bread was consumed.

Home-baked bread for ritual is very special. Baking bread involves living yeast, it involves something pounded down and rising up, rhythmically, over a period of time—the act of making bread is almost a microcosm of the entire festival season.

I've attended "Wicker Man" celebrations, where a larger-than-life wicker man was created and filled with loaves of bread, and then sacrificed (usually burned).

In my group, we've often constructed a man of bread. Members bake (or sometimes buy) bread and bring it to the festival. With a little creativity and toothpicks to hold everything together, various loaves form the head, body, arms, legs, and phallus of our bread-man. We then crown him king and fete him before he is sacrificed (often quite dramatically) in the evening ritual.

I'd say a wicker man or bread man ritual like the ones described requires a minimum of ten people, so the ritual offered here is scaled down.

This holiday is also known as Lughnasadh, a gathering for the Celtic god Lugh (god of all skills) and his mother Tailtiu, goddess of the grain harvest. Traditionally, it was a huge gathering of multiple tribes for games, contests, trade, and socializing—not unlike a modern Pagan festival.

A Group Lammas Ritual

The ritual here is a little more elaborate than previous ones. There's a real beauty in doing a more theatrical ritual. Theater, after all, was invented by the Greeks for ritual purposes.

This ritual requires two people who will embody the Goddess and God. They will be referred to as the priestess and priest, but how you work that out is up to you.

Because we changed up the quarter callings at Midsummer, this time we can change up the circle casting, just to give you more options.

Tools Needed

In addition to the usual tools, for Lammas, you need:

- Seasonal decorations such as corn, corn husks, and wheat

- One or more loaves of bread, covered by a cloth
- A crown for the priest
- Materials for creating and extinguishing a fire, if outdoors (optional)
- Drums and/or musical instruments

Before You Begin

- Baking bread prior to ritual can be part of preparation, and indeed, part of celebration. If you choose, bake an extra loaf and freeze it (wrapping it with extra care so that it will not get freezer burn). You can then defrost it as part of your Candlemas celebration.
- Place the crown on top of the covered bread. The bread and crown are placed in the West.
- If you're outdoors, get the fire going at the center of the circle.

Begin with the opening meditation found in *Sabbats: The Wheel of the Year* on page 108.

1. Declaration of Opening

The leader says:

"We are gathered to celebrate the Grain God,
he who is born, rises in the Earth, dies, and is reborn in the loaf.
We are gathered to celebrate the Mother, in whom the God is born, and dies, and is reborn.
We are gathered to celebrate the circle in which all life occurs."

2. Consecrations

Place your athame into the dish of incense and say:

"In the names of the Lady and Lord
I consecrate Air that it bring mindfulness to my circle."

Place incense onto the lit charcoal so that smoke begins to rise. Place your athame into the smoke and say:

"In the names of the Lady and Lord,
I consecrate Fire that it bring passion to my circle."

Place your athame into the dish of water and say:

"In the names of the Lady and Lord,
I consecrate Water that it bring feeling to my circle."

Place your athame into the dish of salt and say:

"In the names of the Lady and Lord,
I consecrate Earth that it bring commitment to my circle."

Place three pinches of salt into the water and stir.
Say: *"So mote it be."*

3. Cast the Circle

With your athame or sword, go to the East, directing energy to the circle as you say:

"I consecrate this circle, and charge it, that it will be a fit place for us to meet the Gods. O circle, be a boundary between the world of humankind and the world of the Gods, that we may meet them in the middle. Keep us safe in our rites. So mote it be!"

Finish as you return to the East: If you finish early, don't say "so mote it be" until you've returned to the East. If you haven't finished when you return to the East, stand there as you finish.
All repeat: *"So mote it be!"*

Pick up the dish of saltwater and return to the East. Wet your fingers and flick drops all the way around the circle, East to East, sprinkling the entire perimeter, saying:

"I cleanse this circle by Water and Earth.
O circle, you are cleansed. So mote it be!"

All repeat: *"So mote it be!"*

Return to the altar.
Pick up the censer, stirring it up if needed. Return to the East. Cense the perimeter, as you walk again around the circle, East to East, saying:

"I purify this circle by Fire and Air. O circle, you are purified. So mote it be!"

All repeat: *"So mote it be!"*

Return to the altar.

4. Call the Quarters

(These are the quarter callings from Midsummer. You can use these, the ones from Beltane, or ones you've written yourself.)
In the East, face out, point your athame, and draw an invoking pentagram, saying:

"Come to us, Air!
Guard us in the East!

Come to us, wind
Come to us, intelligence
Come on eagle's wings
Guard our Lammas rite!
Welcome, O Air! Blessed be."

All repeat: *"Blessed be."*
Walk deosil back to your place.
In the South, face out, point your athame, and draw an invoking pentagram, saying:

"Come to us, Fire!
Guard us in the South!
Come to us, heat
Come to us, passion
Come with a lion's roar
Guard our Lammas rite!
Welcome, O Fire! Blessed be."

All repeat: *"Blessed be."*
Walk deosil back to your place.
In the West, face out, point your athame, and draw an invoking pentagram, saying:

"Come to us Water!
Guard us in the West!
Come to us, oceans
Come to us, love
Come riding on dolphins
Guard our Lammas rite!
Welcome, O Water! Blessed be."

All repeat: *"Blessed be."*
Walk deosil back to your place.
In the North, face out, point your athame, and draw an invoking pentagram, saying:

"Come to us, Earth!
Guard us in the North!
Come to us, soil
Come to us, commitment
Come with mighty hooves
Guard our Lammas rite!
Welcome, O Earth! Blessed be."

All repeat: *"Blessed be."*
Walk back to the East for a final, silent salute.

5. Invoking the Gods

The priest raises the wand and points to the North, saying:

> *"Gracious and beloved Goddess of the Earth, Ceres of the grain, Lady of all seasons, be here among us! Honor us with your presence as we worship you this August Eve."*

The priestess raises the pentacle towards the North, saying:

> *"Mighty and beloved God of the harvest, John Barleycorn of the fields, two-faced God of resurrection, be here among us! Honor us with your presence as we worship you this August Eve."*

Both together:

"Welcome and blessed be."

All repeat: *"Blessed be."*

6. Offerings/Seasonal Celebration

The priest now touches the priestess on the third eye with the wand and places the wand back on the altar.

The priestess touches the priest on the third eye with the pentacle and places the pentacle back on the altar.

Priest and priestess now move to the center of the circle, in front of the altar. They hold hands and face each other.

Priestess: *"Life is a cycle, and the wheel turns."*

Priest: *"Life is a cycle, and the wheel turns."*

Priestess: *"The wheel turns, and summer will end."*

Priest: *"Summer will end, and the wheel turns."*

Priestess: *"The god rises like grain and falls like the harvest."*

Priest: *"I rise like the grain and fall like the harvest."*
The priest now kneels before the priestess.

Priestess: *"The wheat rose in the summer."*

Priest: *"The wheat rose, and I am here."*

Priestess: "*The wheat has been cut down.*"

Priest: "*The wheat has been cut, and I am here.*"

Priestess: "*From the wheat, the bread has been baked.*"

Priest: "*The bread is baked, and I am here.*"

Priestess: "*Who are you?*"

Priest (standing): "*I am the Dark Lord, the Winter King, and I will take my crown.*"

The priestess signals that drumming, clapping, or other music can now begin. The priest marches slowly from the center of the circle to the East and then to the West. In the West, he picks up the loaf of bread and brings it to the center, presenting it to the priestess. While the priestess holds the bread, the priest takes the crown and places it on his own head. Then, the priestess places the bread on the floor/ground between them and removes the cover from the bread. The music stops.

7. Cakes and Wine

This should be done standing over the loaf of bread. An assistant can bring the wine and cup to the priestess and priest.

Say:

"It is time to receive the blessings of vine and Earth!"

Hold the cup and say:

"The cup, the Goddess, the blood of life
Our Lady blesses us with all good things
She offers herself to us
She offers herself to the God."

Hold the athame over the cup and say:

"The blade, the God, the force of life
Our Lord blesses us with all good things
He offers himself to us
He offers himself to the Goddess."

Plunge the athame into the cup and say:

"Blessed be."

Consecrate the bread while standing over it, by dipping the athame into the wine and sprinkling drops onto the bread, forming an invoking pentagram.

Say:

"Lady and Lord, you bless us with abundance
The Earth gives us all we need
We thank you.
Blessed be."

Take a bit of bread and place it in the libation bowl. If you are outdoors, the offering can go directly into the fire.

Lift the cup and speak from the heart. It can be as simple as "to the Gods," or it can be detailed. End with "Blessed be." Then make an offering to the gods by pouring a bit of wine into the libation bowl. Drink only after offering.

Each person in turn offers, pours, and drinks. Each offering ends with "Blessed be," and everyone responds by saying "Blessed be."

Or pour from the main cup into each person's individual cup before drinking. Then, each offers, pours, and drinks in turn.

After the cup goes around, or while the cup is on its way around, pass the cakes.

After the ritual is over, the contents of the libation bowl should be poured out onto the Earth. If the ritual is outdoors, then libations are poured directly onto the Earth, and a libation bowl is not needed.

8. Celebration of Season

The primary seasonal rite has been performed as an invocation and offering. After cakes and wine, traditional activities on Lammas are games and contests of all kinds. This depends on the available space, but could include chase games, guessing games—anything you like. Losers often get a silly punishment, such as a slap on the behind, having to kiss everyone on the hand, reciting "I'm a Little Teapot," or something of the sort. This gets everyone laughing but has a ritual purpose: It's a symbol of John Barleycorn's sacrifice.

During this part, you can continue to eat and drink.

9. Closing the Circle

The priest faces North, raises the wand, and says:

"Beloved Lady,
Goddess of the Earth, Ceres of the grain,
Your love has blessed our Lammas rite.
Thank you, and farewell!"
*(*The priest now touches the priestess with the wand.*)*

All repeat: *"Farewell!"*

The priestess faces North, raises the pentacle, and says:

"Beloved Lord,
Two-faced God of the harvest
John Barleycorn of the fields
Your sacrifice has blessed our Lammas rite.
Thank you, and farewell!"
(The priestess now touches the priest with the pentacle.)

All repeat: *"Farewell!"*
Go to the East, draw a banishing pentagram, and say:

"We thank you, Guardian of the East, Guardian of Air
For protecting this Lammas rite
Thank you, and farewell!"

All repeat: *"Farewell!"*
Go to the South, draw a banishing pentagram, and say:

"We thank you, Guardian of the South, Guardian of Fire
For protecting this Lammas rite
Thank you, and farewell!"

All repeat: *"Farewell!"*
Go to the West, draw a banishing pentagram, and say:

"We thank you, Guardian of the West, Guardian of Water
For protecting this Lammas rite
Thank you, and farewell!"

All repeat: *"Farewell!"*
Go to the North, draw a banishing pentagram, and say:

"We thank you, Guardian of the North, Guardian of Earth
For protecting this Lammas rite
Thank you, and farewell!"

All repeat: *"Farewell!"*
Facing the center, say:

"The circle is open but unbroken, the rites are ended.
Merry meet, merry part, and merry meet again!"

All repeat: *"Merry meet, merry part, and merry meet again!"*

A Solitary Lammas Ritual

The solitary version of this rite is more meditative but still has theatrical elements. You perform for an audience consisting of yourself and the Gods.

Tools Needed

In addition to the usual tools, for Lammas, you need:

- Seasonal decorations such as corn, corn husks, and wheat
- A loaf of bread, covered by a cloth
- A crown
- Materials for creating and extinguishing a fire, if outdoors (optional)

Before You Begin

- Baking bread prior to ritual can be part of preparation, and indeed, part of celebration. If you choose, bake an extra loaf and freeze it (wrapping it with extra care so that it will not get freezer burn). You can then defrost it as part of your Candlemas celebration.
- Place the crown on top of the covered bread. The bread and crown are placed in the West.
- If you're outdoors, get the fire going at the center of the circle.

Begin with the opening meditation found in *Sabbats: The Wheel of the Year* on page 108.

1. Declaration of Opening

Say:

"Tonight, I celebrate the Grain God, he who is born,
rises in the earth, dies, and is reborn in the loaf.
Tonight, I celebrate the Mother, in whom the God is born, and dies, and is reborn.
Tonight, I celebrate the circle in which all life occurs."

2. Consecrations

Place your athame into the dish of incense and say:

"In the names of the Lady and Lord,
I consecrate Air that it bring mindfulness to my circle."

Place incense onto the lit charcoal so that smoke begins to rise. Place your athame into the smoke and say:

"In the names of the Lady and Lord, I consecrate Fire that it bring passion to my circle."

Place your athame into the dish of water and say:

"In the names of the Lady and Lord,
I consecrate Water that it bring feeling to my circle."

Place your athame into the dish of salt and say:

"In the names of the Lady and Lord,
I consecrate Earth that it bring commitment to my circle."

Place three pinches of salt into the water and stir.
Say:

"So mote it be."

3. Cast the Circle

With your athame or sword, go to the East, directing energy to the circle as you say:

"I consecrate this circle, and charge it, that it will be a fit place for me to meet the Gods. O circle, be a boundary between the world of humankind and the world of the Gods, that I may meet them in the middle. Keep me safe in my rites. So mote it be!"

Finish as you return to the East: If you finish early, don't say "so mote it be" until you've returned to the East. If you haven't finished when you return to the East, stand there as you finish.

Return to the altar.

Pick up the dish of saltwater and return to the East. Wet your fingers and flick drops all the way around the circle, East to East, sprinkling the entire perimeter, saying:

"I cleanse this circle by Water and Earth.
O circle, you are cleansed. So mote it be!"

Return to the altar.

Pick up the censer, stirring it up if needed to make it smoky. Return to the East. Cense the perimeter, as you walk again around the circle, East to East, saying:

"I purify this circle by Fire and Air. O circle, you are purified. So mote it be!"

Return to the altar.

4. Call the Quarters

(These are the quarter callings from Midsummer. You can use these, the ones from Beltane, or ones you've written yourself.)

In the East, face out, point your athame, and draw an invoking pentagram, saying:

"Come to me, Air!
Guard my circle in the East!
Come to me, wind
Come to me, intelligence
Come on eagle's wings
Guard my Lammas rite!
Welcome, O Air! Blessed be."

In the South, face out, point your athame, and draw an invoking pentagram, saying:

"Come to me, Fire!
Guard my circle in the South!
Come to me, heat
Come to me, passion
Come with a lion's roar
Guard my Lammas rite!
Welcome, O Fire! Blessed be."

In the West, face out, point your athame, and draw an invoking pentagram, saying:

"Come to me, Water!
Guard my circle in the West!
Come to me, oceans
Come to me, love
Come riding on dolphins
Guard my Lammas rite!
Welcome, O Water! Blessed be."

In the North, face out, point your athame, and draw an invoking pentagram, saying:

"Come to me, Earth!
Guard my circle in the North!
Come to me, soil
Come to me, commitment
Come with mighty hooves
Guard my Lammas rite!
Welcome, O Earth! Blessed be."

Walk back to the East for a final, silent salute.

5. Invoking the Gods

Raise the wand and point to the North, saying:

"Gracious and beloved Goddess of the Earth, Ceres of the grain, Lady of all seasons, be here with me!
Honor me with your presence as I worship you this August Eve.
Mighty and beloved God of the harvest, John Barleycorn of the fields,
two-faced God of resurrection, be here with me!
Honor me with your presence as I worship you this August Eve.
Welcome and blessed be."

6. Offerings/Seasonal Celebration

Say:

"Life is a cycle, and the wheel turns
The wheel turns, and summer will end
Summer will end, and the wheel will turn
The God rises like grain, and falls like the harvest
The wheat rose in the summer, and the God is here
The wheat has been cut down, and the God is here
From the wheat, the bread has been baked, and the God is here
The Sun God has fallen, and the Dark Lord is here."

Meditate on the meaning of bread. It is the root of civilization, it is sacrifice, and it is rebirth.
Say:

"This is the funeral of John Barleycorn. The God has been cut down."

Carry the tray three times around the circle. Return to the altar. Place the crown upon your own head, or upon the altar—whichever feels right to you.[51] Remove the cloth.
Say:

"John Barleycorn is reborn!"

7. Cakes and Wine

Hold the wine directly over the loaf of bread.
Say:

51 The priest wears the crown. Female-identified people should decide if they're comfortable in that role, or if they prefer to have the crown on the altar and enact only the role of the priestess.

"It is time to receive the blessings of vine and Earth!"

Hold the cup and say:

"The cup, the Goddess, the blood of life
Our Lady blesses us with all good things
She offers herself to us
She offers herself to the God."

Hold the athame over the cup and say:

"The blade, the God, the force of life
Our Lord blesses us with all good things
He offers himself to us
He offers himself to the Goddess."

Plunge the athame into the cup and say:

"Blessed be."

Consecrate the bread while standing over it, by dipping the athame into the wine and sprinkling drops onto the bread, forming an invoking pentagram.

Say:

"Lady and Lord, you bless us with abundance
The Earth gives us all we need
We thank you.
Blessed be."

Take a bit of bread and place it in the libation bowl. If you are outdoors, the offering can go directly into the fire.

Lift the cup and speak from the heart. It can be as simple as "to the Gods," or it can be detailed. End with "Blessed be." Then make an offering to the gods by pouring a bit of wine into the libation bowl. Drink only after offering, then eat some bread.

After the ritual is over, the contents of the libation bowl should be poured out onto the Earth. If the ritual is outdoors, then libations are poured directly onto the Earth, and a libation bowl is not needed.

8. Celebration of Season

The primary seasonal rite has been performed as an invocation and offering. Enjoy your bread and wine and meditate on the changing seasons.

9. Closing the Circle

Face North, raise the wand, and say:

"Beloved Lady,
Goddess of the Earth, Ceres of the grain,
Your love has blessed my Lammas rite.
Thank you, and farewell!
Beloved Lord,
Two-faced God of the harvest
John Barleycorn of the fields
Your sacrifice has blessed my Lammas rite.
Thank you, and farewell!"

If you are wearing the crown, remove it and place it on the altar.
Go to the East, draw a banishing pentagram, and say:

"I thank you, Guardian of the East, Guardian of Air
For protecting this Lammas rite
Thank you, and farewell!"

Go to the South, draw a banishing pentagram, and say:

"I thank you, Guardian of the South, Guardian of Fire
For protecting this Lammas rite
Thank you, and farewell!"

Go to the West, draw a banishing pentagram, and say:

"I thank you, Guardian of the West, Guardian of Water
For protecting this Lammas rite
Thank you, and farewell!"

Go to the North, draw a banishing pentagram, and say:

"I thank you, Guardian of the North, Guardian of Earth
For protecting this Lammas rite
Thank you, and farewell!"

Facing the center, say:

"The circle is open but unbroken, the rites are ended.
Merry meet, merry part, and merry meet again!"

Fall Equinox

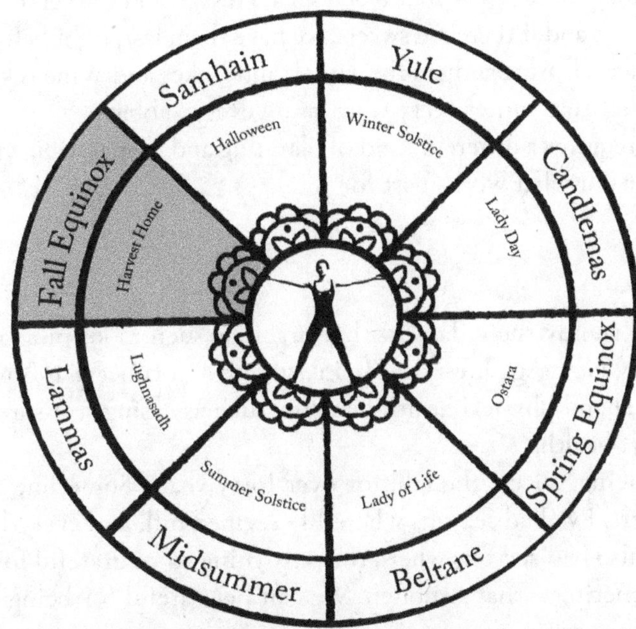

Fall Equinox, sometimes called "Harvest Home," is the second of three harvest festivals, often thought of as a Wiccan Thanksgiving. In many ways, it is the most laid-back of the harvests: Lammas is often a major celebration, a time to gather together. It can even be the time when solitaries and small groups choose to gather for major festivities. It's also a time in which the cycle of the seasons dominates: The God dies and is reborn, so it's pretty dramatic.

Samhain, the final harvest, is focused on death, as we'll be discussing. It can be a time of anxiety.

In between is Fall Equinox. The equinoxes, of course, are times of balance—day and night are exactly equal. They are times of stasis, and some occultists will avoid any important magic at this time, believing that the universe itself is in stasis and no transformation can occur. Some traditions, for example, never do initiations on the equinoxes.

In a temperate climate, the Fall Equinox is when we start noticing the change of weather—it's the beginning of sweater season. You begin to draw in, moving your focus indoors. We can see summer ending, perhaps leaves are turning, and we start to turn our thoughts toward the cooler days to come.

Feasting

Eating together is an ancient way of creating community. In Wicca, we break bread both figuratively and literally—ripping off a bit of unsliced loaf is typically how we eat consecrated bread in ritual.

Feasting in the context of ritual can take many forms and varies from group to group. The coven I was trained in treated Cakes and Wine as dessert; we ate beforehand (together or separately), and our cakes were sweet—cupcakes or cookies.

I probably practiced that way for ten years or more, but eventually I discovered that sweets aren't really compatible with magic—your blood sugar crashes, and you get too grounded. So, cakes in my circles are savory, and if there are sweets, we have them last, right before closing.

Some covens have a feast together after ritual, and Cakes and Wine is kind of an appetizer. Other covens feast *in* ritual, either every time, or on every Sabbat.

Each approach requires a different kind of planning and preparation, and you may want to experiment to figure out what works best for you.

Gratitude

Gratitude is almost trendy these days, with a practice, such as keeping a gratitude journal, being a part of many New Age lifestyles. Thanksgiving as a concept is obviously much older. Gratitude has mental and physical health benefits, such as easing stress, reducing depression, and supporting heart health.

I've been practicing Wicca, though, for over forty years. Sometimes, gratitude is more accessible than others. I've had seasons where life seemed full, and everything felt like it was going my way. I've also had seasons where the only thing to be grateful for was the ability to gather in ritual. Sometimes, that's enough. We can be grateful for being alive, in the hopes that things will get better.

The gratitude of Fall Equinox balances the grief of Samhain. As the wheel turns, we move through all stages and all experiences.

A Group Fall Equinox Ritual

Like Lammas, this ritual has some back-and-forth interplay between two people: Presumably a priestess and priest, although it is less elaborate.

The ritual also calls for feasting, as it is a celebration of abundance and thanks. To that end, prepare the ritual space for a feast.

Our change to the basic script this time is to the consecrations. The elements to be consecrated are at the quarters—a different person can be responsible for bringing each element to the altar, and that person can consecrate that element.

Tools Needed

In addition to the usual tools, for Fall Equinox, you need:

- Seasonal decorations such as gourds
- Loose incense and charcoal: Even if you normally use stick incense, the ritual calls for dropping an offering onto the charcoal[52]
- Setup for a feast

52 Incense offerings like this can get very smoky, especially with something resinous like frankincense. Some people unplug their smoke alarms for the duration of ritual.

Before You Begin

- This is ideally a potluck, with everyone contributing to the feast.
- Have the food in the circle, but off to the side, so that it's not in the way prior to Cakes and Wine. Make sure to have serving utensils, napkins—everything you'd need for a dinner but might not think of for ritual.
- For this variation of the consecrations, have each ritual item in its corresponding quarter—the dish of incense in the East, the censer in the South, the dish of water in the West, and the dish of salt in the North.

Begin with the opening meditation found in *Sabbats: The Wheel of the Year* on page 108.

1. Declaration of Opening

The leader says:

"We are gathered to celebrate the Fall Equinox, the time of balance.
We are gathered to thank the Gods for the abundance they have brought to us."

2. Consecrations

Go to the East. Pick up the dish of incense and bring it to the altar. Place your athame into it and say:

"I bring Air from the East. Air, be consecrated for our rite."

Go to the South. Pick up the censer and bring it to the altar. Place incense onto the lit charcoal so that smoke begins to rise. Place your athame into the smoke and say:

"I bring Fire from the South. Fire, be consecrated for our rite."

Go to the West. Pick up the dish of water and bring it to the altar. Place your athame into it and say:

"I bring Water from the West. Water, be consecrated for our rite."

Go to the North. Pick up the dish of salt and bring it to the altar. Place your athame into it and say:

"I bring Earth from the North. Earth, be consecrated for our rite."

Place three pinches of salt into the water and stir.
Say:

"So mote it be."

3. Cast the Circle

(This is the circle casting from Lammas. You can use this, the one from Midsummer, or one you've written yourself.)

With your athame or sword, go to the East, directing energy to the circle as you say:

"I consecrate this circle, and charge it, that it will be a fit place for us to meet the Gods. O circle, be a boundary between the world of humankind and the world of the Gods, that we may meet them in the middle. Keep us safe in our rites. So mote it be!"

Finish as you return to the East: If you finish early, don't say "so mote it be" until you've returned to the East. If you haven't finished when you return to the East, stand there as you finish.

All repeat: *"So mote it be!"*

Pick up the dish of saltwater and return to the East. Wet your fingers and flick drops all the way around the circle, East to East, sprinkling the entire perimeter, saying:

"I cleanse this circle by Water and Earth.
O circle, you are cleansed. So mote it be!"

All repeat: *"So mote it be!"*

Return to the altar.

Pick up the censer, stirring it up if needed. Return to the East. Cense the perimeter, as you walk again around the circle, East to East, saying:

"I purify this circle by Fire and Air. O circle, you are purified. So mote it be!"

All repeat: *"So mote it be!"*

Return to the altar.

4. Call the Quarters

In the East, face out, point your athame, and draw an invoking pentagram, saying:

"Come to us, Air!
Guard us in the East!
Come to us, wind
Come to us, intelligence

Come on eagle's wings
Guard our Fall Equinox rite!
Welcome, O Air! Blessed be."

All repeat: "*Blessed be.*"
Walk deosil back to your place.
In the South, face out, point your athame, and draw an invoking pentagram, saying:

"Come to us, Fire!
Guard us in the South!
Come to us, heat
Come to us, passion
Come with a lion's roar
Guard our Fall Equinox rite!
Welcome, O Fire! Blessed be."

All repeat: "*Blessed be.*"
Walk deosil back to your place.
In the West, face out, point your athame, and draw an invoking pentagram, saying:

"Come to us, Water!
Guard us in the West!
Come to us, oceans
Come to us, love
Come riding on dolphins
Guard our Fall Equinox rite!
Welcome, O Water! Blessed be."

All repeat: "*Blessed be.*"
Walk deosil back to your place.
In the North, face out, point your athame, and draw an invoking pentagram, saying:

"Come to us, Earth!
Guard us in the North!
Come to us, soil
Come to us, commitment
Come with mighty hooves
Guard our Fall Equinox rite!
Welcome, O Earth! Blessed be."

All repeat: "*Blessed be.*"
Walk back to the East for a final, silent salute.

5. Invoking the Gods

The priest and priestess hold the wand together, facing North.

Priestess:

"Lady of the harvest, join us tonight!
Lady of grain, hear our call
Be here in the scent of new-mown hay
In the early twilight, which brings the shadows of Samhain
In the crisp bite of autumn air
You who teach us to pause and reflect on the season
Welcome, and blessed be."

Priest:

"Lord of growing things, join us tonight!
Lord of the harvest, hear our call
Be here in the scent of fallen apples
In warmth of firelight, gathering inward with those we cherish
In the bounty of your sacrifice
You who teach us to be thankful for all we receive
Welcome, and blessed be."

All repeat: *"Blessed be."*

6. Offerings/Seasonal Celebration

One person begins a slow chant, such as Hoof and Horn,[53] while everyone takes a pinch of incense and, incense in hand, slow dances or walks around the circle.

Priestess: "*Take a moment to contemplate your life as it is today. What are you thankful for? Where have you been given abundance?*"

Priest: "*We harvest rebirth. We give thanks to the Earth.*"

Priestess: "*We harvest rebirth. We give thanks to the Earth.*"

Both together: "*We harvest rebirth. We give thanks to the Earth.*"

Priestess: "*Now it's time to make an offer of thanks. Come to the altar and place your incense on the*

53 A popular Pagan chant by Ian Corrigan. Here's one link: youtu.be/GkPcqAoqyB8?si=yH6R27mWC8egaUHw

censer. You can say aloud whatever you are thankful for, or, if you wish to keep it private, simply say, 'I give thanks to the Earth.'"

One by one, beginning with the priestess,[54] people come to the altar and place their incense on the censer, speaking as moved. After each offering, all say, "*Blessed be.*" The priestess and priest can embrace each person.

The priest gives the last offering and says: "*For all we have, we know the future brings new gifts. We give thanks for unknown blessings to come.*"

Priestess: "*We give thanks for unknown blessings to come.*"

Both together: "*We give thanks for unknown blessings to come.*"

7. Cakes and Wine

Bring the cup of wine and athame to the setup for the feast and perform the wine consecration over the feast. Say:

"*It is time to receive the blessings of vine and Earth!*"

Hold the cup and say:

"*The cup, the Goddess, the blood of life*
Our Lady blesses us with all good things
She offers herself to us
She offers herself to the God."

Hold the athame over the cup and say:

"*The blade, the God, the force of life*
Our Lord blesses us with all good things
He offers himself to us
He offers himself to the Goddess."

Plunge the athame into the cup and say:

"*Blessed be.*"

Consecrate the entire feast, by dipping the athame into the wine and sprinkling drops

54 The priestess has an opportunity to set the tone. In a small group—six or fewer people—you can choose to give thanks at length. In a larger group, that will drag on, so it's better to be brief. If the priestess begins with something brief like, "I give thanks for my chosen family," most people will follow suit, whereas if they give more detail, others will feel free to do so as well.

onto the whole thing, being sure to get at least a drop on every dish,[55] forming an invoking pentagram.

Say:

"Lady and Lord, you bless us with abundance
The Earth gives us all we need
We thank you.
Blessed be."

Prepare the libation bowl with a bit of each dish.

Lift the cup and speak from the heart. It can be as simple as "to the Gods," or it can be detailed. End with "Blessed be." Then make an offering to the gods by pouring a bit of wine into the libation bowl. Drink only after offering.

Each person in turn offers, pours, and drinks. Each offering ends with "Blessed be," and everyone responds by saying "Blessed be."

Or pour from the main cup into each person's individual cup before drinking. Then each offers, pours, and drinks in turn.

After the ritual is over, the contents of the libation bowl should be poured out onto the Earth. If the ritual is outdoors, then libations are poured directly onto the Earth.

8. Celebration of Season

Now is the time to sit down and feast! Appropriate topics of conversation can include gratitude and plans for the coming season. Have a good time!

9. Closing the Circle

Priest and priestess together hold the wand, facing North.

Priestess:

"Lady of the harvest, Lady of grain
Thank you for joining us tonight
Thank you for the feast
Farewell!"

All repeat: *"Farewell!"*

Priest:

"Lord of growing things
Lord of the harvest

---

55 If you use wine, but have an alcoholic in the group, symbolize consecration by touching the dish with the athame, or touching the plate, but not the food, with the wine.

Thank you for joining us tonight
Thank you for the feast
Farewell!"

All repeat: "*Farewell!*"
Go to the East, draw a banishing pentagram, and say:

"We thank you, Guardian of the East, Guardian of Air
For protecting this Lammas rite
Thank you, and farewell!"

All repeat: "*Farewell!*"
Go to the South, draw a banishing pentagram, and say:

"We thank you, Guardian of the South, Guardian of Fire
For protecting this Lammas rite
Thank you, and farewell!"

All repeat: "*Farewell!*"
Go to the West, draw a banishing pentagram, and say:

"We thank you, Guardian of the West, Guardian of Water
For protecting this Lammas rite
Thank you, and farewell!"

All repeat: "*Farewell!*"
Go to the North, draw a banishing pentagram, and say:

"We thank you, Guardian of the North, Guardian of Earth
For protecting this Lammas rite
Thank you, and farewell!"

All repeat: "*Farewell!*"
Facing the center, say:

"The circle is open but unbroken, the rites are ended.
Merry meet, merry part, and merry meet again!"

All repeat: "*Merry meet, merry part, and merry meet again!*"

A Solitary Fall Equinox Ritual

There are times that being a solitary Wiccan is an absolute joy, and times it is not. When the group ritual is a feast, the solitary ritual can feel lonely. If you find it doesn't feel good to feast alone:

- Have a solitary ritual and invite friends or family for a feast to take place afterwards.
- Bring a feast to a homeless shelter after your ritual.
- Bring the ingredients for a feast to a food bank after your ritual.
- Cut out the ritual entirely and simply host a feast.

Tools Needed

In addition to the usual tools, for Fall Equinox, you need:

- Seasonal decorations such as gourds
- Loose incense and charcoal: Even if you normally use stick incense, the ritual calls for dropping an offering onto the charcoal
- Setup for a feast

Before You Begin

- Have the food in the circle, but off to the side, so that it's not in the way prior to Cakes and Wine. Make sure to have serving utensils, napkins—everything you'd need for a dinner but might not think of for ritual.
- For this variation of the consecrations, have each ritual item in its corresponding quarter—the dish of incense in the East, the censer in the South, the dish of water in the West, and the dish of salt in the North.

Begin with the opening meditation found in *Sabbats: The Wheel of the Year* on page 108.

1. Declaration of Opening

Say:

"Tonight, I celebrate the Fall Equinox, the time of balance.
Tonight, I thank the Gods for the abundance they have brought to me."

2. Consecrations

Go to the East. Pick up the dish of incense and bring it to the altar. Place your athame into it and say:

"I bring Air from the East. Air, be consecrated for our rite."

Go to the South. Pick up the censer and bring it to the altar. Place incense onto the lit charcoal so that smoke begins to rise. Place your athame into the smoke and say:

"I bring Fire from the South. Fire, be consecrated for our rite."

Go to the West. Pick up the dish of water and bring it to the altar. Place your athame into it and say:

"I bring Water from the West. Water, be consecrated for our rite."

Go to the North. Pick up the dish of salt and bring it to the altar. Place your athame into it and say:

"I bring Earth from the North. Earth, be consecrated for our rite."

Place three pinches of salt into the water and stir.

Say:

"So mote it be."

3. Cast the Circle

(This is the circle casting from Lammas. You can use this, the one from Midsummer, or one you've written yourself.)

With your athame or sword, go to the East, directing energy to the circle as you say:

"I consecrate this circle, and charge it, that it will be a fit place for me to meet the Gods. O circle, be a boundary between the world of humankind and the world of the Gods, that I may meet them in the middle. Keep me safe in my rites. So mote it be!"

Finish as you return to the East: If you finish early, don't say "so mote it be" until you've returned to the East. If you haven't finished when you return to the East, stand there as you finish.

Pick up the dish of saltwater and return to the East. Wet your fingers and flick drops all the way around the circle, East to East, sprinkling the entire perimeter, saying:

"I cleanse this circle by Water and Earth.
O circle, you are cleansed. So mote it be!"

Return to the altar.

Pick up the censer, stirring it up if needed. Return to the East. Cense the perimeter, as you walk again around the circle, East to East, saying:

"I purify this circle by Fire and Air. O circle, you are purified. So mote it be!"

Return to the altar.

4. Call the Quarters

In the East, face out, point your athame, and draw an invoking pentagram, saying:

"Come to me Air!
Guard my circle in the East!
Come to me, wind
Come to me, intelligence
Come on eagle's wings
Guard my Fall Equinox rite!
Welcome, O Air! Blessed be."

In the South, face out, point your athame, and draw an invoking pentagram, saying:

"Come to me, Fire!
Guard my circle in the South!
Come to me, heat
Come to me, passion
Come with a lion's roar
Guard my Fall Equinox rite!
Welcome, O Fire! Blessed be."

In the West, face out, point your athame, and draw an invoking pentagram, saying:

"Come to me, Water!
Guard my circle in the West!
Come to me, oceans
Come to me, love
Come riding on dolphins
Guard my Fall Equinox rite!
Welcome, O Water! Blessed be."

In the North, face out, point your athame, and draw an invoking pentagram, saying:

"Come to me, Earth!
Guard my circle in the North!
Come to me, soil
Come to me, commitment
Come with mighty hooves
Guard my Fall Equinox rite!
Welcome, O Earth! Blessed be."

Walk back to the East for a final, silent salute.

5. Invoking the Gods

Hold the wand, face North, and say:

"Lady of the harvest, join me tonight!
Lady of grain, hear my call
Be here in the scent of new-mown hay
In the early twilight, which brings the shadows of Samhain
In the crisp bite of autumn air
You who teach me to pause and reflect on the season
Welcome, and blessed be.
Lord of growing things, join me tonight!
Lord of the harvest, hear my call
Be here in the scent of fallen apples
In warmth of firelight, gathering inward with those I cherish
In the bounty of your sacrifice
You who teach me to be thankful for all I receive
Welcome, and blessed be."

6. Offerings/Seasonal Celebration

Begin a slow chant, such as Hoof and Horn.[56] Take a pinch of incense and, incense in hand, slow dance around the circle.

After one to three rounds of dance, say:

"Now I pause, to contemplate my life as it is today. Now I find that which I am thankful for. Now I discover where I have you been given abundance.
I harvest rebirth. I give thanks to the Earth." (repeat three times)

Meditate for a moment on what you are thankful for, on what abundance you wish to thank the gods for. Placing your incense offering on the altar, thank the gods specifically, and out loud.

Say:

"For all I have, I know the future brings new gifts.
I give thanks for unknown blessings to come." (repeat three times)

7. Cakes and Wine

Bring the cup of wine and athame to the setup for the feast, and perform the wine consecration over the feast.

Say:

"It is time to receive the blessings of vine and Earth!"

Hold the cup and say:

56 See note on page 160

"The cup, the Goddess, the blood of life
The Lady blesses me with all good things
She offers herself to me
She offers herself to the God."

Hold the athame over the cup and say:

"The blade, the God, the force of life
The Lord blesses me with all good things
He offers himself to me
He offers himself to the Goddess."

Plunge the athame into the cup and say:

"Blessed be."

Consecrate the entire feast by dipping the athame into the wine and sprinkling drops onto the whole thing, being sure to get at least a drop on every dish, forming an invoking pentagram.

Say:

"Lady and Lord, you bless me with abundance
The Earth gives me all I need
I thank you.
Blessed be."

Prepare the libation bowl with a bit of each dish.

Lift the cup and speak from the heart. It can be as simple as "to the Gods," or it can be detailed. End with "Blessed be." Then make an offering to the gods by pouring a bit of wine into the libation bowl. Drink only after offering.

After the ritual is over, the contents of the libation bowl should be poured out onto the Earth. If the ritual is outdoors, then libations are poured directly onto the Earth, and a bowl is not needed.

8. Celebration of Season

Now is the time to sit down and feast, meditating on the rich symbolism of feasting, knowing that the abundance on your plate represents the abundance of your life, and more goodness to come.

9. Closing the Circle

Hold the wand, facing North, and say:

"Lady of the harvest, Lady of grain
Thank you for joining me tonight
Thank you for the feast
Farewell!
Lord of growing things
Lord of the harvest
Thank you for joining me tonight
Thank you for the feast
Farewell!"

Go to the East, draw a banishing pentagram, and say:

"I thank you, Guardian of the East, Guardian of Air
For protecting this Equinox rite
Thank you, and farewell!"

Go to the South, draw a banishing pentagram, and say:

"I thank you, Guardian of the South, Guardian of Fire
For protecting this Equinox rite
Thank you, and farewell!"

Go to the West, draw a banishing pentagram, and say:

"I thank you, Guardian of the West, Guardian of Water
For protecting this Equinox rite
Thank you, and farewell!"

Go to the North, draw a banishing pentagram, and say:

"I thank you, Guardian of the North, Guardian of Earth
For protecting this Equinox rite
Thank you, and farewell!"

Facing the center, say:

"The circle is open but unbroken, the rites are ended.
Merry meet, merry part, and merry meet again!"

Samhain

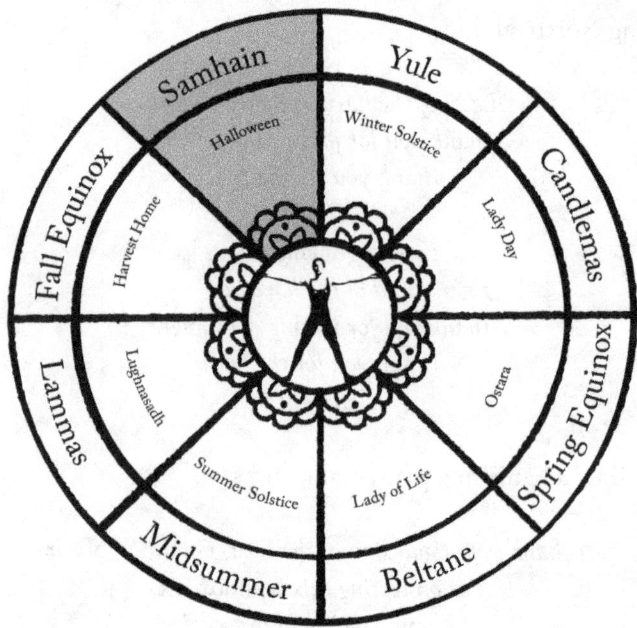

Halloween, or Samhain, is probably the most popular Wiccan celebration. Certainly, it's the most popular time for the outside world to take an interest in us! But it can't be denied that most witches really love the spooky, dark vibe of the season. Where does it come from?

In agriculture, the last harvest is fraught with tension. This is where you find out if there's enough food to get you through the winter. This is also when animals are slaughtered, which is a delicate decision. Slaughter too few, and your feed won't last, but slaughter too many, and you won't have sufficient breeding stock when spring comes. Tension and fear regarding death, and life-and-death decisions are probably the origins of Samhain being the day we honor the dead.

At the great sabbats of Beltane and Samhain, the veil between this world and the next is thin; we understand our communication with "the other side" to be easiest on these two days. Folklore associated with Beltane is rich in stories of encounters with the fairy folk, sometimes with dire consequences, while the stories of Samhain tend toward encounters with the dead. It's said that the dead wait for Samhain before crossing over, hanging around between the worlds until the veil thins and they can pass.

One mythic version of Samhain is that the Goddess leaves the Earth at this time and joins her beloved in the Underworld. and her leaving "opens the door," which is why we can commune with the dead. In this, she is analogous to Persephone, who, in Greek myth, lived in the Underworld with Hades during the winter months and on Earth with her mother, Demeter, during the growing season.

So, the two central motifs of this Sabbat are the last harvest and honoring the dead. Public Pagan gatherings tend toward the latter, with a focus on those who have died since last Samhain. This might be a large celebration, a "dumb supper," a feast of some kind, a recitation of the names of the dead, or some combination of all of these.

For a small gathering of just a few people, you can remember all your dead, not just the ones who passed this year, whereas with huge public gatherings, if names are recited, they're usually confined to those who have passed since last Samhain; otherwise, you'd never finish.

A Group Samhain Ritual

Last Sabbat—the Fall Equinox—we gathered to feast with one another. This Sabbat, we feast with our dead. A literal feast is optional, but the idea is to share the evening with our beloved dead. We will name them, remember them, and honor them.

While our personal focus is on our beloved dead, our spiritual focus is on the God as Lord of the Dead, ruler of the Underworld.

When you bring your ancestors to ritual, remember that you get to choose who you will honor: you never have to honor an abuser. People don't get a clean slate just because they died. Conversely, I'd consider it improper to celebrate any death, even that of a truly evil person, in this ritual. Just leave them out. Also, remember that you're not confined to relatives or even people you knew personally. Often, the death of someone famous can be inexplicably moving, and it is okay to honor the connection you feel. Our beloved dead are also not always human; many pets have been honored in my circles.

Tools Needed

In addition to the usual tools, for Samhain, you need:

- An apple, and a knife to slice it
- An ancestor altar—a separate small table is usually appropriate—in the West. Set it up with a nice altar cloth and an unlit candle
- Setup for a feast, if you're having one
- Drums or other rhythm instruments

Before You Begin

- In advance of the ritual, ask everyone to bring remembrances for the ancestor altar. These can be pictures, mementos, I've even had ashes—whatever people choose to bring.
- Before the ritual starts, set up the ancestor altar so that everyone's contributions have a place.
- It's best that everyone be given instructions in advance regarding the drumming/chanting of names.
- Because there's already something extra in one quarter, I'm reverting to the consecrations we used in previous rituals, not the one introduced for Fall Equinox, but that's up to you.

Begin with the opening meditation found in *Sabbats: The Wheel of the Year* on page 108.

1. Declaration of Opening

The leader says:

"At this time when the veil is thin, when shadows draw near, we know the God as Lord of the Underworld. We know the Lady as Persephone, his beloved.
Tonight, we honor our beloved dead, and make merry with them, and worship the gods of the world beyond."

2. Consecrations

Place your athame into the dish of incense and say:

"In the names of the Lady and Lord,
I consecrate Air that it bring mindfulness to my circle."

Place incense onto the lit charcoal so that smoke begins to rise. Place your athame into the smoke and say:

"In the names of the Lady and Lord,
I consecrate Fire that it bring passion to my circle."

Place your athame into the dish of water and say:

"In the names of the Lady and Lord,
I consecrate Water that it bring feeling to my circle."

Place your athame into the dish of salt and say:

"In the names of the Lady and Lord,
I consecrate Earth that it bring commitment to my circle."

Place three pinches of salt into the water and stir.
Say:

"So mote it be."

3. Cast the Circle

With your athame or sword, go to the East, directing energy to the circle as you say:

"I consecrate this circle, and charge it, that it will be a fit place for us to meet the Gods. O circle, be a boundary between the world of humankind and the world of the Gods, that we may meet them in the middle.

Keep us safe in our rites. So mote it be!"

Finish as you return to the East: If you finish early, don't say "so mote it be" until you've returned to the East. If you haven't finished when you return to the East, stand there as you finish.

All repeat: "*So mote it be!*"

Pick up the dish of saltwater and return to the East. Wet your fingers and flick drops all the way around the circle, East to East, sprinkling the entire perimeter, saying:

"I cleanse this circle by Water and Earth. O circle, you are cleansed. So mote it be!"

All repeat: "*So mote it be!*"

Return to the altar.

Pick up the censer, stirring it up if needed. Return to the East. Cense the perimeter, as you walk again around the circle, East to East, saying:

"I purify this circle by Fire and Air. O circle, you are purified. So mote it be!"

All repeat: "*So mote it be!*"

Return to the altar.

4. Call the Quarters

In the East, face out, point your athame, and draw an invoking pentagram, saying:

"Come to us, Air!
Guard us in the East!
Come to us, wind
Come to us, intelligence
Come on eagle's wings
Guard our Samhain rite!
Welcome, O Air! Blessed be."

All repeat: "*Blessed be.*"

Walk deosil back to your place.

In the South, face out, point your athame, and draw an invoking pentagram, saying:

"Come to us, Fire!
Guard us in the South!
Come to us, heat
Come to us, passion
Come with a lion's roar
Guard our Samhain rite!
Welcome, O Fire! Blessed be."

All repeat: *"Blessed be."*
Walk deosil back to your place.
In the West, face out, point your athame, and draw an invoking pentagram, saying:

"Come to us, Water!
Guard us in the West!
Come to us, oceans
Come to us, love
Come riding on dolphins
Guard our Samhain rite!
Welcome, O Water! Blessed be."

All repeat: *"Blessed be."*
Walk deosil back to your place.
In the North, face out, point your athame, and draw an invoking pentagram, saying:

"Come to us, Earth!
Guard us in the North!
Come to us, soil
Come to us, commitment
Come with mighty hooves
Guard our Samhain rite!
Welcome, O Earth! Blessed be."

All repeat: *"Blessed be."*
Walk back to the East for a final, silent salute.

5. Invoking the Gods

Point the wand to the North and say:

"Mighty Horned One, Lord of Death and Lord of Rebirth.
Be here among us.
Beloved Lady, though you leave the Earth tonight, still we worship you.
Be here among us.
Lord, we know the crops will return.
Lady, we know your footsteps will again be heard upon the Earth.
Join us, beloved gods.
Welcome, and blessed be."

All repeat: *"Blessed be."*

6. Offerings/Seasonal Celebration

Begin a slow, quiet drumbeat.

Speak rhythmically, in time with the drum, saying:[57]

"Tonight, we call to the dead.
Tonight, they hear us.
Tonight, we give love to the dead.
Tonight, they hear us.
Tonight, we call their names.
Tonight, they hear us.
Tonight, they hear us.
Tonight, they join us.
We will speak their names.
Tonight, they join us.
We will repeat their names.
Tonight, they join us.
We will chant their names.
Tonight, they join us.
We will drum their names.
Tonight, they join us."

The leader can start, saying a name that everyone will repeat. As the group chants the name, the person who said that name can say more.

For example:

Mourner: "*Nana.*"

Everyone: "*Nana! Nana! Nana!*"

Mourner: "*Jean Goldberger, Nana.*"

Everyone: "*Nana! Nana! Nana!*"

In this way, the rhythm is maintained by the group, while the individual mourner can give the multiple names a person was known by in life, so that the invocation is complete.

There is no need to take turns. People can feel free to call names out spontaneously. I have done this ritual year after year for over thirty years, in groups as small as five and as large as several hundred. Even though the description on the page seems chaotic, it always works. Names are called, and chanted, and as a chant dies down, the next name is called.

57 One person can say this, or two people can alternate lines, as you prefer.

The chanting goes on as long as everyone continues to give names, or until it drops off spontaneously. Sometimes it dies down quietly. Often, the chanting and rhythm become joyful, more a celebration of the dead than grief.

7. Cakes and Wine

Normally, the wine goes around once, with everyone making an offering to the gods. On Samhain, the wine goes around many times. The first offering is to the gods, but at least one more round is needed so that people can offer to their beloved dead.

If there is to be a feast, the remaining "rounds" will be during the feast; otherwise, the rounds continue after the consecration of the food, and you can pass the food during the rounds.

If there is to be a feast, bring the cakes, wine, and apple to the feast table before proceeding.

Say:

"It is time to receive the blessings of vine and Earth!

Hold the cup and say:

"The cup, the Goddess, the blood of life
Our Lady blesses us with all good things
She offers herself to us
She offers herself to the God."

Hold the athame over the cup and say:

"The blade, the God, the force of life
Our Lord blesses us with all good things
He offers himself to us
He offers himself to the Goddess."

Plunge the athame into the cup and say:

"Blessed be."

Slice the apple in half horizontally, revealing the Goddess hidden within. Say:

"Lady, we know you are with us because you have left us this sign."

Hold up the sliced apple for all to see.

Now proceed with consecrating the rest of the food. If you're feasting, consecrate the entire feast by dipping the athame into the wine and sprinkling drops onto the whole thing, being sure to get at least a drop on every dish, forming an invoking pentagram.

Say:

"Lady and Lord, you bless us with abundance
The Earth gives us all we need
We thank you.
Blessed be."

Prepare the libation bowl with a bit of each dish.

Lift the cup and speak from the heart. It can be as simple as "to the Gods," or it can be detailed. End with "Blessed be." Then make an offering to the gods by pouring a bit of wine into the libation bowl. Drink only after offering.

Each person in turn offers, pours, and drinks. Each offering ends with "Blessed be," and everyone responds by saying "Blessed be."

Or pour from the main cup into each person's individual cup before drinking. Then each offers, pours, and drinks in turn.

Now, the wine goes around again, this time for people to pour to their honored dead.

After the ritual is over, the contents of the libation bowl should be poured out onto the Earth. If the ritual is outdoors, then libations are poured directly onto the Earth.

8. Celebration of Season

Continue to pour offerings to the dead. (The libation bowl tends to be especially full after a Samhain rite!) Share stories of the dead and enjoy their company. Tears are okay, and so is laughter. This is a celebration!

9. Closing the Circle

Face West, raising your arms in the air, and say:

"We thank you, beloved dead, for joining us this night.
We love and honor you. Farewell!"

All repeat: *"Farewell!"*

Lift the wand, face North, and say:

"Lord of Death and Rebirth
Thank you for joining us tonight
Farewell!"

All repeat: *"Farewell!"*

"Lady who walks above and below
Thank you for joining us tonight
Farewell!"

All repeat: *"Farewell!"*
Go to the East, draw a banishing pentagram, and say:

"We thank you, Guardian of the East, Guardian of Air
For protecting this Samhain rite
Thank you, and farewell!"

All repeat: *"Farewell!"*
Go to the South, draw a banishing pentagram, and say:

"We thank you, Guardian of the South, Guardian of Fire
For protecting this Samhain rite
Thank you, and farewell!"

All repeat: *"Farewell!"*
Go to the West, draw a banishing pentagram, and say:

"We thank you, Guardian of the West, Guardian of Water
For protecting this Samhain rite
Thank you, and farewell!"

All repeat: *"Farewell!"*
Go to the North, draw a banishing pentagram, and say:

"We thank you, Guardian of the North, Guardian of Earth
For protecting this Samhain rite
Thank you, and farewell!"

All repeat: *"Farewell!"*
Facing the center, say:

"The circle is open but unbroken, the rites are ended.
Merry meet, merry part, and merry meet again!"

All repeat: *"Merry meet, merry part, and merry meet again!"*

A Solitary Samhain Ritual

While the feast of Fall Equinox might have felt lonely, the Samhain feast, if you choose to have one, can feel like exactly the right amount of company. You are feasting with your beloved dead, which can be an exceptionally beautiful experience as a solitary Wiccan.

Your personal focus is on your beloved dead, people (and animals) whom you choose to welcome into your circle. Ancestors who were abusive do not deserve your honor.

The spiritual focus of this rite is on the God as Lord of the Dead, ruler of the Underworld. There is comparatively less focus on the Goddess at Samhain.

Tools Needed

In addition to the usual tools, for Samhain, you need:

- An apple, and a knife to slice it
- An ancestor altar—a separate small table is usually appropriate—in the West. Set it up with a nice altar cloth and an unlit candle
- Setup for a feast, if you're having one
- Anything specific a particular ancestor would like
- A drum, rattle, or other rhythm instrument

Before You Begin

- Prepare remembrances for the ancestor altar. This can be pictures, mementos, ashes—whatever you choose.
- Before the ritual starts, set up the ancestor altar.
- Because there's already something extra in one quarter, I'm reverting to the consecrations we used in previous rituals, not the one introduced for Fall Equinox, but that's up to you.

Begin with the opening meditation found in *Sabbats: The Wheel of the Year* on page 108.

1. Declaration of Opening

Say:

"At this time, when the veil is thin, when shadows draw near, the God is known as Lord of the Underworld. The Lady is known as Persephone, his beloved.
Tonight, I honor my beloved dead, and make merry with them, and worship the gods of the world beyond."

2. Consecrations

Place your athame into the dish of incense and say:

"In the names of the Lady and Lord,
I consecrate Air that it bring mindfulness to my circle."

Place incense onto the lit charcoal so that smoke begins to rise. Place your athame into the smoke and say:

"In the names of the Lady and Lord,
I consecrate Fire that it bring passion to my circle."

Place your athame into the dish of water and say:

"In the names of the Lady and Lord,
I consecrate Water that it bring feeling to my circle."

Place your athame into the dish of salt and say:

"In the names of the Lady and Lord,
I consecrate Earth that it bring commitment to my circle."

Place three pinches of salt into the water and stir.
Say:

"So mote it be."

3. Cast the Circle

With your athame or sword, go to the East, directing energy to the circle as you say:

"I consecrate this circle, and charge it, that it will be a fit place for me to meet the Gods. O circle, be a boundary between the world of humankind and the world of the Gods, that I may meet them in the middle. Keep me safe in my rites. So mote it be!"

Finish as you return to the East: If you finish early, don't say "so mote it be" until you've returned to the East. If you haven't finished when you return to the East, stand there as you finish.

Pick up the dish of saltwater and return to the East. Wet your fingers and flick drops all the way around the circle, East to East, sprinkling the entire perimeter, saying:

"I cleanse this circle by Water and Earth.
O circle, you are cleansed. So mote it be!"

Return to the altar.

Pick up the censer, stirring it up if needed. Return to the East. Cense the perimeter, as you walk again around the circle, East to East, saying:

"I purify this circle by Fire and Air. O circle, you are purified. So mote it be!"

Return to the altar.

4. Call the Quarters

In the East, face out, point your athame, and draw an invoking pentagram, saying:

"Come to me, Air!

Guard my circle in the East!
Come to me, wind
Come to me, intelligence
Come on eagle's wings
Guard my Samhain rite!
Welcome, O Air! Blessed be."

In the South, face out, point your athame, and draw an invoking pentagram, saying:

"Come to me, Fire!
Guard my circle in the South!
Come to me, heat
Come to me, passion
Come with a lion's roar
Guard my Samhain rite!
Welcome, O Fire! Blessed be."

In the West, face out, point your athame, and draw an invoking pentagram, saying:

"Come to me Water!
Guard my circle in the West!
Come to me, oceans
Come to me, love
Come riding on dolphins
Guard my Samhain rite!
Welcome, O Water! Blessed be."

In the North, face out, point your athame, and draw an invoking pentagram, saying:

"Come to me, Earth!
Guard my circle in the North!
Come to me, soil
Come to me, commitment
Come with mighty hooves
Guard my Samhain rite!
Welcome, O Earth! Blessed be."

Walk back to the East for a final, silent salute.

5. Invoking the Gods

Point the wand to the North and say:

"Mighty Horned One, Lord of Death and Lord of Rebirth.
Be here with me tonight.
Beloved Lady, though you leave the Earth tonight, still I worship you.
Be here with me tonight.
Lord, I know the crops will return.
Lady, I know your footsteps will again be heard upon the earth.
Join me in my rite, beloved gods.
Welcome, and blessed be."

6. Offerings/Seasonal Celebration

Begin a slow rhythm on the drum or rattle. Allow the rhythm to shift your thoughts towards your beloved dead.

"Tonight, I call to the dead.
Tonight, they hear me.
Tonight, I give love to the dead.
Tonight, they hear me.
Tonight, I speak their names.
Tonight, they hear me.
Tonight, they hear me.
Tonight, they join me.
I will speak their names.
Tonight, they join me."

Go to the West and light the candles on the ancestor altar. Speak aloud the name of each person represented on your altar. Speak freely to them. Think about, and express, why you choose to honor them. It's okay to cry, and it's also okay to be happy—this is a reunion.

You might choose to honor a particular ancestor in a special way. My Nana loved when I shared whatever I was working on with her, so, in this ritual, I have read my latest writing to her. My step-father deeply valued his Judaism, so, in this ritual, I said the *shema* for him. When my ex-husband passed, I toasted him with his favorite whiskey. The correct thing for your beloved dead is something only you can know.

7. Cakes and Wine

If there is to be a feast, bring the cakes, wine, and apple to the feast table before proceeding.

Say:

"It is time to receive the blessings of vine and Earth!"

Hold the cup and say:

"The cup, the Goddess, the blood of life

My Lady blesses me with all good things
She offers herself to me
She offers herself to the God."

Hold the athame over the cup and say:

"The blade, the God, the force of life
My Lord blesses me with all good things
He offers himself to me
He offers himself to the Goddess."

Plunge the athame into the cup and say:

"Blessed be."

Slice the apple in half horizontally, revealing the Goddess hidden within. Say:

"Lady, I know you are with me because you have left me this sign."

Now proceed with consecrating the rest of the food. If you're feasting, consecrate the entire feast by dipping the athame into the wine and sprinkling drops onto the whole thing, being sure to get at least a drop on every dish, forming an invoking pentagram. Say:

"Lady and Lord, you bless me with abundance
The Earth gives me all I need
I thank you.
Blessed be."

Prepare the libation bowl with a bit of each dish.

Lift the cup and speak from the heart. It can be as simple as "to the Gods," or it can be detailed. End with "Blessed be." Then make an offering to the gods by pouring a bit of wine into the libation bowl. Drink only after offering and then eat some of the feast.

Now offer again, this time to your honored dead, and drink again.

After the ritual is over, the contents of the libation bowl should be poured out onto the Earth. If the ritual is outdoors, then libations are poured directly onto the Earth.

8. Celebration of Season

Continue to pour offerings to the dead. (The libation bowl tends to be especially full after a Samhain rite!) You may think of others you wish to honor who are not on your ancestor altar. Include them, name them, and offer to them. Continue to enjoy the feast and share it with your dead.

9. Closing the Circle

Face West, raising your arms in the air, and say:

"I thank you, beloved dead, for joining me this night. I love and honor you. Farewell!"

Lift the wand, face North, and say:

"Lord of Death and Rebirth
Thank you for joining me tonight
Farewell!
Lady who walks above and below
Thank you for joining me tonight
Farewell!"

Go to the East, draw a banishing pentagram, and say:

"I thank you, Guardian of the East, Guardian of Air
For protecting this Samhain rite
Thank you, and farewell!"

Go to the South, draw a banishing pentagram, and say:

"I thank you, Guardian of the South, Guardian of Fire
For protecting this Samhain rite
Thank you, and farewell!"

Go to the West, draw a banishing pentagram, and say:

"I thank you, Guardian of the West, Guardian of Water
For protecting this Samhain rite
Thank you, and farewell!"

Go to the North, draw a banishing pentagram, and say:

"I thank you, Guardian of the North, Guardian of Earth
For protecting this Samhain rite
Thank you, and farewell!"

Facing the center, say:

"The circle is open but unbroken, the rites are ended.
Merry meet, merry part, and merry meet again!"

Yule

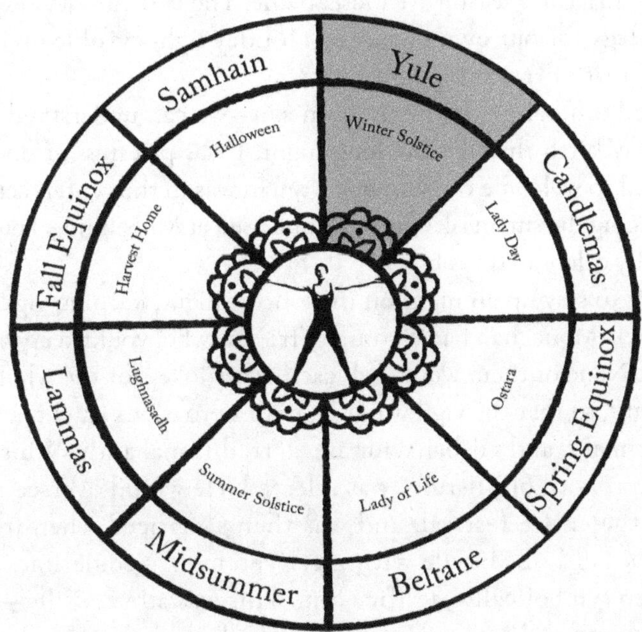

In the Northern Hemisphere, Yule—the Winter Solstice—corresponds with the Christmas season. Ancient Pagan celebrations of the season include Anglo-Saxon and Germanic Yule festivities and the Roman Saturnalia. Many modern Pagan customs, and indeed, many Christmas customs, derive from these. Ancient Pagans decorated trees (but did not bring them indoors), gave gifts, sang seasonal songs, burned the Yule log, and partied hard. The Pagan god Odin rode Slepnir—his eight-legged horse—through the night sky at Yule and brought gifts to good children.

Some kind of celebration of light is nearly universal as night grows longer. Chanukah—the Jewish festival of light—takes place sometime in November or December, while Diwali, the Hindu festival of light, is in October or November. There is great power in venerating light in the face of darkness.

Notice the way we're alternating lightness and darkness in the Wheel. Lammas was dark, venerating the sacrifice of John Barleycorn, then Fall Equinox was a joyous feast, then Samhain was about death and the Underworld. Now, we're back to light. (This pattern doesn't hold for the entire year, but it is interesting nonetheless.)

The Winter Solstice is directly opposite Midsummer on the Wheel of the year and is another festival of the conflict between two gods who are really one, the two-faced God of the waxing and waning year. Some people[58] do the equal-and-opposite enactment: essentially the same battle as at Midsummer, with a different victor. However, if you're in the Northern

58 For example, Janet and Stewart Farrar in *Eight Sabbats for Witches*.

Hemisphere, it makes sense to ride the enormous cultural wave that is the "Holiday season," and celebrate Yule as the birth of a baby God while the old year (Father Time, if you will) fades and dies.

I have never been Christian, but I am American, and the songs, imagery, stories, and decorations of the Christmas season are inescapable. They are full of energy, and as Wiccans, we can use that energy for our own purposes. Holiday lights visible on the streets can feed the deeply Pagan spirit of returning light.

Because the God is a baby—the newly born sun—we can understand the Goddess as the Great Mother, giving birth through the long night. I was priestess at one memorable ritual where, as we chanted to welcome the sun, one woman was in the center, acting out labor pains and ultimately bringing the sun mask (the same one used at Midsummer) out from between her legs. We then joyfully celebrated his birth.

One tradition is to stay up all night on the longest night, keeping vigil for the sun's birth. My late friend Patricia Monaghan had a group of friends who would keep vigil together, telling jokes all night long. None of them would tell each other jokes for the whole year, saving all of them up for one night, so that the vigil was a night of uproarious laughter.

Laughter, merriment, and misbehavior are all traditional at the Winter Solstice. During Roman Saturnalia, a "Lord of Misrule" was selected. He would oversee merry pranks, lead the festivities for the entire festival, and was then sacrificed when it ended. In my old group, we'd select a Lord of Misrule with great ceremony—sometimes by lot, sometimes by voting—and then symbolically sacrifice him. This was all very silly—we'd tie him up in holiday wrapping paper and garlands so that he looked like a ridiculous mummy, crown him Lord of Misrule, and then unwrap him. He'd rule the post-ritual party, serving drinks, telling jokes, and generally making a fool of himself in the best possible way. One year, the Lord of Misrule decided pranks were necessary, and the next morning, I discovered all the drawers in my bedroom had been switched, and I couldn't find my clothes.

These are the themes you'll see over and over in Pagan and Wiccan celebrations of the Winter Solstice: Returning light—often enacted through fires, darkness, or fires lit in the darkness—the two-faced God and some kind of exchange or combat between them, the Mother giving birth, and vigil for the birth of the Sun, as well as Santa-themed celebrations, gift-giving, and mischief.

I long ago came to understand Yule as a holiday of faith. At the darkest moment, we believe that light will return. While it is certainly scientific to understand how solstices and orbiting the sun work, it is also a fundamental act of faith that serves as a metaphor for all the darkness we experience in our lives. Somehow, even though we can't see it, light will return.

The Yule Log

Ancient Pagan tradition says the Yule log is made from a tree or piece of wood that fell naturally on your property or was given to you as a gift. Among my friends, we've developed a tradition of keeping a piece of the maypole (drying it, so that it doesn't rot) and using that as our Yule log.

However you acquire it, three holes are fashioned into the log to form a triple candelabra. The three candles are given different attributions by different people: You can see them as the

Mother Goddess, the Waxing (baby) God, and the Waning God (Father Time). All three candles can be white, to represent the season of snow, or you can use gold for the new god, red for the mother, and black for the old god.

A bonfire is traditional at this time, and the Yule log can be burned in the fire after the ceremony is over. You're probably celebrating indoors: If you do have an all-night vigil, that could be outdoors, at a fire, after the circle has been closed.

A Group Yule Ritual

This ritual is different from, but parallel to, the Summer Solstice rite. Like that one, this one calls for a minimum of three people, in the roles of Goddess, Dark God, and Light God, and is traditionally gendered. In this ritual, if there are only two people, the person playing the God can change costumes.

The variant to our script that I've added to this ritual is in the Cakes and Wine. The back-and-forth it introduces works well with the back-and-forth of this sabbat. I have written it for two partners, presumably (but not necessarily) priestess and priest.

The script assumes an indoor circle. For an outdoor circle, build the bonfire at the North end of the circle.

Tools Needed

In addition to the usual tools, for this ritual, you need:

- Seasonal decorations, especially holly, mistletoe, and yew
- The masks or robes from Midsummer used for the Stag/Bright God and the Bull/Dark God
- A cauldron with sand in the bottom that will be filled with candles (and a fire extinguisher)
- A candle for each person
- Drums, rattles, or other rhythm instruments

Before You Begin

- Determine who will play the roles of Goddess, Dark God, and Bright God.
- The person who will represent the Goddess needs matches or a lighter at hand.

Begin with the opening meditation found in *Sabbats: The Wheel of the Year* on page 108.

1. Declaration of Opening

The leader says:

> *"In the season of darkness, we celebrate light.*

Welcome, all who come to greet the birth of the Sun!"

2. Consecrations

Place your athame into the dish of incense and say:

"In the names of the Lady and Lord,
I consecrate Air that it bring mindfulness to my circle."

Place incense onto the lit charcoal so that smoke begins to rise. Place your athame into the smoke and say:

"In the names of the Lady and Lord,
I consecrate Fire that it bring passion to my circle."

Place your athame into the dish of water and say:

"In the names of the Lady and Lord,
I consecrate Water that it bring feeling to my circle."

Place your athame into the dish of salt and say:

"In the names of the Lady and Lord,
I consecrate Earth that it bring commitment to my circle."

Place three pinches of salt into the water and stir.
Say:

"So mote it be."

3. Cast the Circle

With your athame or sword, go to the East, directing energy to the circle as you say:

"I consecrate this circle, and charge it, that it will be a fit place for us to meet the Gods. O circle, be a boundary between the world of humankind and the world of the Gods, that we may meet them in the middle. Keep us safe in our rites. So mote it be!"

Finish as you return to the East: If you finish early, don't say "so mote it be" until you've returned to the East. If you haven't finished when you return to the East, stand there as you finish.
All repeat: *"So mote it be!"*

Pick up the dish of saltwater and return to the East. Wet your fingers and flick drops all the way around the circle, East to East, sprinkling the entire perimeter, saying:

"I cleanse this circle by Water and Earth.
O circle, you are cleansed. So mote it be!"

All repeat: *"So mote it be!"*

Return to the altar.

Pick up the censer, stirring it up if needed. Return to the East. Cense the perimeter, as you walk again around the circle, East to East, saying:

"I purify this circle by Fire and Air. O circle, you are purified. So mote it be!"

All repeat: *"So mote it be!"*

Return to the altar.

4. Call the Quarters

In the East, face out, point your athame, and draw an invoking pentagram, saying:

"Come to us, Air!
Guard us in the East!
Come to us, wind
Come to us, intelligence
Come on eagle's wings
Guard our Yule rite!
Welcome, O Air! Blessed be."

All repeat: *"Blessed be."*

Walk deosil back to your place.

In the South, face out, point your athame, and draw an invoking pentagram, saying:

"Come to us, Fire!
Guard us in the South!
Come to us, heat
Come to us, passion
Come with a lion's roar
Guard our Yule rite!
Welcome, O Fire! Blessed be."

All repeat: *"Blessed be."*

Walk deosil back to your place.

In the West, face out, point your athame, and draw an invoking pentagram, saying:

"Come to us, Water!

Guard us in the West!
Come to us, oceans
Come to us, love
Come riding on dolphins
Guard our Yule rite!
Welcome, O Water! Blessed be."

All repeat: *"Blessed be."*
Walk deosil back to your place.
In the North, face out, point your athame, and draw an invoking pentagram, saying:

"Come to us, Earth!
Guard us in the North!
Come to us, soil
Come to us, commitment
Come with mighty hooves
Guard our Yule rite!
Welcome, O Earth! Blessed be."

All repeat: *"Blessed be."*
Walk back to the East for a final, silent salute.

5. Invoking the Gods

Say:

"Beloved Lady, be here among us
Mother of the night sky, be here in a thousand twinkling lights
Mother of all gods, be here tonight to give birth to the Sun,
that we may again know his warmth
Lady of the wheel, we adore you
Join us!
Welcome and blessed be."

All repeat: *"Blessed be."*
Say:

"Mighty Lord, god of darkness and light, be here among us
God of the sun, and father of time, come to us and be born
Bring your light, your warmth, and your promise
God of beginnings and endings, we adore you
Join us!
Welcome and blessed be."

All repeat: *"Blessed be."*

6. Offerings/Seasonal Celebration

The person representing the Dark God enters (or is already in the circle and puts on their costume). They step to the center of the circle and begin speaking as they slowly walk around the circle, clockwise:[59]

"I have ruled the waning year, and my rule has been good.
I have brought darkness."
(put out the altar candles)
"In darkness, you have learned the secrets of night."
(put out the East quarter candle)
"I have taken away brightness, though your passions burn."
(put out the South quarter candle)
"All things sleep, like seeds beneath the Earth, and I have enshrouded your dreams."
(put out the West quarter candle)
"The seeds of sleep will return, but now it is my turn to fade."
(put out the North quarter candle)

The circle is now completely dark.
The leader shouts:

"Mother! Bring forth the light!"

The leader now begins a slow chant.[60] The person representing the Goddess lights a candle and holds it up high. Chanting continues.

The Goddess relights each candle, starting at the altar, then East, South, West, and North, as chanting continues. When the Goddess reaches the North, all are signaled to silence.

In silence, the Goddess goes to the person representing the Bright God (who was already in the circle but has put on his costume—it can be the same person who represented the Dark God) and brings him into the center of the circle.

The leader shouts:

"The light has returned!"

The Bright God now goes around the circle and hands everyone an unlit candle.

---

59 Why clockwise? Because this is a natural and normal cycle, not an unwinding or anti-cycle.

60 Options include "Solstice Chant" by Anne Bearheart, "We Are One with the Infinite Sun" (Sioux traditional), or "Let it Begin Now" by Starhawk.

Now begin a joyful, upbeat chant.[61]

The Bright God lights his own candle from the Goddess's, then lights everyone's candle, one at a time, as chanting continues. Together, the two lead everyone to the cauldron, where, one at a time, they place their candles in the cauldron.[62]

Each person who has placed their candle in the cauldron now has their hands free and can pick up a musical instrument. Dancing, drumming, and singing can continue around the fire for as long as everyone wants. It is a merry night!

7. Cakes and Wine

Say:

"It is time to receive the blessings of vine and Earth!"

The priest holds the athame, the priestess holds the cup.[63]

Priestess: *"The sky to the Earth."*

Priest: *"The twilight to the dawn."*

Priestess: *"Energy to matter."*

Priest: *"Lord to Lady."*

The priest plunges the athame into the cup and says:

"Blessed be."

Consecrate the cakes by dipping the athame into the wine and sprinkling drops onto the cakes, forming an invoking pentagram.

Say:

Priest: *"Sun to the flowers."*

Priestess: *"Rain to the soil."*

Priest: *"Blessings to the body. Blessed be."*

---

61 My favorite is "Light is Returning" by Charlie Murphy.

62 If there are more than a few people, it is very important that the first people place their candles in the center, so that the later people can place candles around the perimeter of the cauldron without burning themselves.

63 Or a gender-variant version is done.

Take a cake and place it in the libation bowl.

Lift the cup and speak from the heart. It can be as simple as "to the Gods," or it can be detailed. End with "Blessed be." Then make an offering to the gods by pouring a bit of wine into the libation bowl. Drink only after offering.

Each person in turn offers, pours, and drinks. Each offering ends with "Blessed be," and everyone responds by saying "Blessed be."

Or pour from the main cup into each person's individual cup before drinking. Then, each offers, pours, and drinks in turn.

After the cup goes around, or while the cup is on its way around, pass the cakes.

After the ritual is over, the contents of the libation bowl should be poured out onto the Earth.

8. Celebration of Season

The primary seasonal rite has been performed as an offering. After cakes and wine, traditional activities include storytelling and caroling. There are lots of "Paganized" versions of Christmas carols out there, and quite a few that need no rewrite to be understood as Pagan. Continue to eat and drink while enjoying the season.

9. Closing the Circle

Face North, raise the wand, and say:

"Beloved Lady,
Mother of the night sky,
You have given birth to the Sun in all our hearts
Thank you, and farewell!"

All repeat: *"Farewell!"*

"Beloved Lord,
Brightness and darkness
You have brought back the light and the warmth
Thank you, and farewell!"

All repeat: *"Farewell!"*

Go to the East, draw a banishing pentagram, and say:

"We thank you, Guardian of the East, Guardian of Air
For protecting this Yule rite
Thank you, and farewell!"

All repeat: *"Farewell!"*

Go to the South, draw a banishing pentagram, and say:

"We thank you, Guardian of the South, Guardian of Fire
For protecting this Yule rite
Thank you, and farewell!"

All repeat: *"Farewell!"*

Go to the West, draw a banishing pentagram, and say:

"We thank you, Guardian of the West, Guardian of Water
For protecting this Yule rite
Thank you, and farewell!"

All repeat: *"Farewell!"*

Go to the North, draw a banishing pentagram, and say:

"We thank you, Guardian of the North, Guardian of Earth
For protecting this Yule rite
Thank you, and farewell!"

All repeat: *"Farewell!"*

Facing the center, say:

"The circle is open but unbroken, the rites are ended.
Merry meet, merry part, and merry meet again!"

All repeat: *"Merry meet, merry part, and merry meet again!"*

A Solitary Yule Ritual

This ritual is different from, but parallel to, the Summer Solstice rite. You'll reuse the masks that you created at that time.

The script assumes an indoor circle. For an outdoor circle, build the bonfire at the North end of the circle.

Tools Needed

In addition to the usual tools, for this ritual, you need:

- Seasonal decorations, especially holly, mistletoe, and yew
- The masks from Midsummer used for the Stag/Bright God and the Bull/Dark God
- A large white candle
- A cauldron with sand in the bottom, in which you will place a white candle (and a fire extinguisher)
- A drum, rattle, or other rhythm instrument

Before You Begin

- Have matches or a lighter at hand—you won't want to fumble around in the dark.

Begin with the opening meditation found in *Sabbats: The Wheel of the Year* on page 108.

1. Declaration of Opening

Say:

"In the season of darkness, I celebrate light. Tonight, I greet the birth of the Sun!"

2. Consecrations

Place your athame into the dish of incense and say:

"In the names of the Lady and Lord,
I consecrate Air that it bring mindfulness to my circle."

Place incense onto the lit charcoal so that smoke begins to rise. Place your athame into the smoke and say:

"In the names of the Lady and Lord,
I consecrate Fire that it bring passion to my circle."

Place your athame into the dish of water and say:

"In the names of the Lady and Lord,
I consecrate Water that it bring feeling to my circle."

Place your athame into the dish of salt and say:

"In the names of the Lady and Lord,
I consecrate Earth that it bring commitment to my circle."

Place three pinches of salt into the water and stir.
Say:

"So mote it be."

3. Cast the Circle

With your athame or sword, go to the East, directing energy to the circle as you say:

"I consecrate this circle, and charge it, that it will be a fit place for me to meet the Gods. O circle, be a boundary between the world of humankind and the world of the Gods, that I may meet them in the middle. Keep me safe in my rites. So mote it be!"

Finish as you return to the East: If you finish early, don't say "so mote it be" until you've returned to the East. If you haven't finished when you return to the East, stand there as you finish.

Pick up the dish of saltwater and return to the East. Wet your fingers and flick drops all the way around the circle, East to East, sprinkling the entire perimeter, saying:

"I cleanse this circle by Water and Earth. O circle, you are cleansed. So mote it be!"

Return to the altar.

Pick up the censer, stirring it up if needed. Return to the East. Cense the perimeter, as you walk again around the circle, East to East, saying:

"I purify this circle by Fire and Air. O circle, you are purified. So mote it be!"

Return to the altar.

4. Call the Quarters

In the East, face out, point your athame, and draw an invoking pentagram, saying:

"Come to me, Air!
Guard my circle in the East!
Come to me, wind
Come to me, intelligence
Come on eagle's wings
Guard my Solstice rite!
Welcome, O Air! Blessed be."

In the South, face out, point your athame, and draw an invoking pentagram, saying:

"Come to me, Fire!
Guard my circle in the South!
Come to me, heat
Come to me, passion
Come with a lion's roar
Guard my Solstice rite!
Welcome, O Fire! Blessed be."

In the West, face out, point your athame, and draw an invoking pentagram, saying:

"Come to me, Water!

Guard my circle in the West!
Come to me, oceans
Come to me, love
Come riding on dolphins
Guard my Solstice rite!
Welcome, O Water! Blessed be."

In the North, face out, point your athame, and draw an invoking pentagram, saying:

"Come to me, Earth!
Guard my circle in the North!
Come to me, soil
Come to me, commitment
Come with mighty hooves
Guard my Solstice rite!
Welcome, O Earth! Blessed be."

Walk back to the East for a final, silent salute.

5. Invoking the Gods

Say:

"Beloved Lady, be here with me
Mother of the night sky, be here in a thousand twinkling lights
Mother of all gods, be here tonight to give birth to the Sun,
that I may again know his warmth
Lady of the wheel, I adore you
Join me!
Welcome and blessed be.
Mighty Lord, god of darkness and light, be here with me
God of the sun, father of time, come to me and be born
Bring your light, your warmth, and your promise
God of beginnings and endings, I adore you
Join me!
Welcome and blessed be."

6. Offerings/Seasonal Celebration

Say:

"All is dark, as days have grown shorter and shorter."

Put on the mask of the Dark God. Step to the center of the circle and begin speaking as you walk slowly around, so that your speech is timed with the dousing of the candles.

"The Dark God has banished light."
(put out the altar candles)
"In darkness, I have learned the secrets of night."
(put out the East quarter candle)
"Even without light, my passions still burn."
(put out the South quarter candle)
"All things sleep, like seeds beneath the Earth. The Dark God has enshrouded my dreams."
(put out the West quarter candle)
"The seeds of sleep will return, but now is the time even darkness will fade."
(put out the North quarter candle)

The circle is now completely dark.
Remove the mask of the Dark God and shout:

"The Goddess will bring forth light!"

Light the white candle and hold it up high.
Begin a slow chant or *om.*[64] Relight each candle, starting at the altar, then East, South, West, and North, all while chanting. When you reach the North, it is time for silence.
Silently put on the mask of the Bright God. Walk one full circuit around the circle in silence and return to the center.
Shout:

"The light has returned!"

Now, begin a joyful, upbeat chant or song. Dance at least three times around the cauldron with your candle, then place the candle in the cauldron.
You can now pick up an instrument and continue dancing and singing as joyfully as you like, for as long as you like.

7. Cakes and Wine

Say:

"It is time to receive the blessings of vine and Earth!"

Hold the athame over the cup and say:

"The sky to the Earth

64 See the group ritual for chant suggestions.

The twilight to the dawn
Movement to stillness
Lord to Lady."

Plunge the athame into the cup and say:

"Blessed be."

Consecrate the cakes by dipping the athame into the wine and sprinkling drops onto the cakes, forming an invoking pentagram. Say:

"Sun to the flowers
Rain to the soil
Blessings to the body.
Blessed be."

Take a cake and place it in the libation bowl.

Lift the cup and speak from the heart. It can be as simple as "to the Gods," or it can be detailed. End with "Blessed be." Then, make an offering to the gods by pouring a bit of wine into the libation bowl. Drink only after offering and enjoy a cake.

After the ritual is over, the contents of the libation bowl should be poured out onto the Earth.

8. Celebration of Season

The primary seasonal rite has been performed as an offering. After cakes and wine, you can enjoy seasonal songs and foods. There are lots of "Paganized" versions of Christmas carols out there, and quite a few that need no rewrite to be understood as Pagan.

9. Closing the Circle

Face North, raise the wand, and say:

"Beloved Lady,
Mother of the night sky,
You have given birth to the Sun within my heart
Thank you, and farewell!
Beloved Lord,
Brightness and darkness
You have brought back the light and the warmth
Thank you, and farewell!"

Go to the East, draw a banishing pentagram, and say:

"I thank you, Guardian of the East, Guardian of Air
For protecting this Yule rite

Thank you, and farewell!"

Go to the South, draw a banishing pentagram, and say:

"I thank you, Guardian of the South, Guardian of Fire
For protecting this Yule rite
Thank you, and farewell!"

Go to the West, draw a banishing pentagram, and say:

"I thank you, Guardian of the West, Guardian of Water
For protecting this Yule rite
Thank you, and farewell!"

Go to the North, draw a banishing pentagram, and say:

"I thank you, Guardian of the North, Guardian of Earth
For protecting this Yule rite
Thank you, and farewell!"

Facing the center, say:

"The circle is open but unbroken, the rites are ended.
Merry meet, merry part, and merry meet again!"

Candlemas

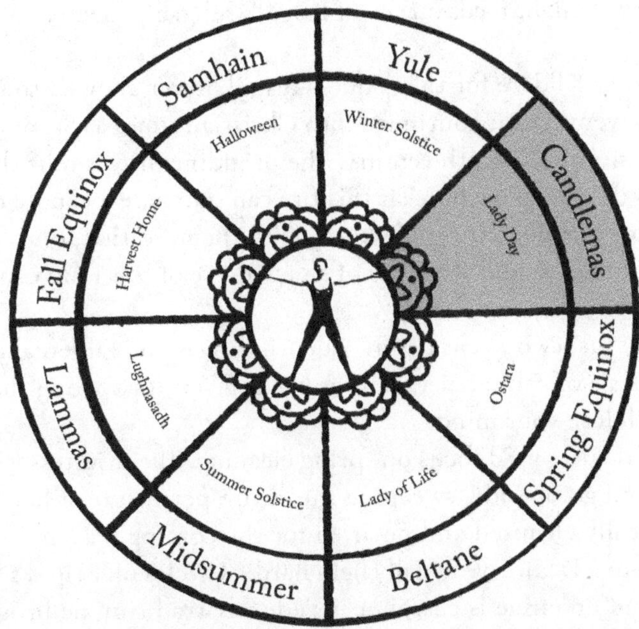

The holiday that falls on February 1 or 2 is varied in its names and in the types of ritual one might find to celebrate it. The name Candlemas is from Catholicism, but many of the Catholic themes and customs are cognate with Pagan ones (and of course, the date is the same—February 2).

Most often, this holiday is associated with preparing for the coming spring. The name *Imbolg* probably comes from "in the belly" and refers to pregnant sheep, while the name *Oimelc* means "with milk" and also refers to pregnant sheep. It is at this time of year that sheep begin to lactate, showing, in the darkness of winter, that spring and new birth are on the way. Groundhog Day (also February 2) is actually part of this. The whole "groundhog sees its shadow" thing sounds nonsensical until you realize that it's weather lore—a rainy or cloudy day on February 2 predicts early spring, but sunshine (wherein the groundhog can see its shadow) means winter will continue for six weeks (until Spring Equinox). Ignore Punxsutawney Phil and just look outside. Groundhogs are a North American creature, so the weather lore may be associated with European Paganism, but the specific animal is not.

Opposite on the Wheel of the Year to Lammas, Candlemas sees springtime and light in the heart of winter, while Lammas sees darkness and winter in the depth of summer.

Purification is an important theme for this holiday, which is associated with spring cleaning, ritual cleansing of all kinds, and preparing for the change of seasons. It is a folk custom in many places to bless candles for use in the coming year, and this is part of Catholic ritual as well.

Another name for this holiday is Brigid,[65] or Brigid's Day. Just as Lammas is a festival of the Irish God Lugh, Candlemas is a festival for the Irish Goddess Brigid. Brigid is a deeply loved goddess, ruler of the three fires: Fire of the body (she is a goddess of healing, and the life force associated with healing is understood as fire), fire of the forge (she is the goddess of smithcraft),

65 Also spelled "Brigit" or "Brid."

and fire of the head (she is the goddess of poetry, and the inspiration to create poetry is also understood as fire). She is also associated with milk and domesticated animals. Celebrations of Brigid's Day (or "Lady Day") might focus on any of Brigid's rulership: poetry and song, healing, fire generally, and so on.

A sacred fire burned in Kildare for the goddess Brigid, never allowed to go out. No one knows how far back this went, but it continued into Christian times as St. Brigid's fire, until it was put out, probably in the sixteenth century. The Brigidine Sisters relit this fire in 1993, and it is guarded to this day. People who visit this fire can purchase a candle that is lit from the sacred fire, then bring the doused candle home with them, so that, on returning home, they can light their own fire of Brigid. The idea of a sacred fire of this kind can also be incorporated into Candlemas rituals.

Finally, this holiday is just two weeks before Valentine's Day and Lupercalia. I often think of these holidays as festivals of cabin fever. Winter has gone on for so long that if you don't celebrate *something*, you'll lose your mind.

In the group I trained with, we'd focus on spring cleaning. The priestess would leave the circle with her broom and go outside, sweeping the entire perimeter of her house, so that everything was symbolically cleansed and purified for the coming season.

When I was married to a Druid, we usually held Bardic Circles on Brigid's Day. This isn't a Wiccan ritual at all, and no circle is cast, but it's a lovely tradition he brought with him from California that honors Brigid by offering poetry, song, and performance of all kinds.

Like I said, there's a huge variety. At Beltane, you can almost guarantee a maypole, but Candlemas is different almost everywhere you celebrate it. Partly, that's because there are few, if any, large Pagan gatherings in the depths of winter, so we're all kind of on our own. But the diversity is beautiful.

A Group Candlemas Ritual

This ritual incorporates a few different aspects of the holiday: The idea of blessing candles, the idea of cleaning and purification, and the idea of performance as an offering.

The ritual assumes a priestess and priest are leading the rite. As ever, modify as appropriate for your group.

The Cakes and Wine this time is based on Kabbalah. It also assumes a priestess and priest are present but can be changed as needed. Kabbalah might not be to your taste, but I thought a more occult variation would be interesting. If you're passionate about Kabbalah, you might consider Kabbalistic variations of consecrations, quarter callings, and other language as well.

Tools Needed

In addition to the usual tools, for this ritual, you need:

- Seasonal decorations can include a Brigid's cross, cow or sheep imagery, wheat imagery, extra altar candles,[66] and/or a white altar cloth

- A broom
- Extra candles—one fresh white candle per person, on a tray or plate

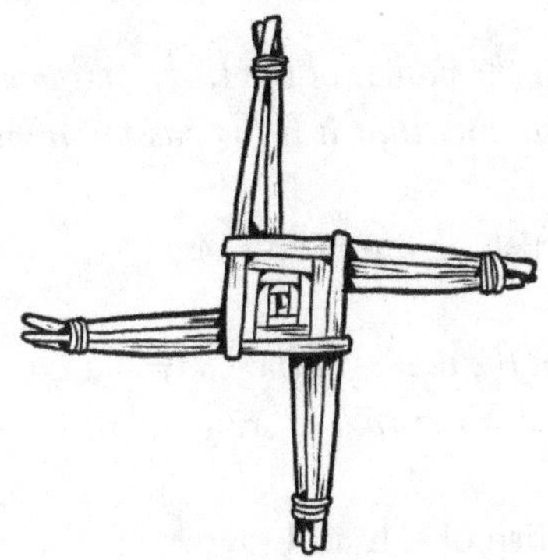

Brigid's Cross

Before You Begin

- If you froze a loaf of bread at Lammas, defrost it and make bread pudding from it. This ties the two opposite festivals together and incorporates milk, which is associated with this festival. The bread pudding can be your cakes for cakes and wine.
- Instruct everyone on how the broom passing will be done.
- Let everyone know in advance that performance will be a part of the ritual so that they have time to prepare.

Begin with the opening meditation found in *Sabbats: The Wheel of the Year* on page 108.

1. Declaration of Opening

The leader says:

"We gather to purify ourselves for the coming spring,
to prepare and renew ourselves on this Candlemas."

2. Consecrations

Place your athame into the dish of incense and say:

"In the names of the Lady and Lord,

66 Because three is a sacred number, and is specifically sacred to Brigid, you can have three altar candles, representing Brigid's three fires, or three additional candles beside the usual two.

I consecrate Air that it bring mindfulness to my circle."

Place incense onto the lit charcoal so that smoke begins to rise. Place your athame into the smoke and say:

"In the names of the Lady and Lord,
I consecrate Fire that it bring passion to my circle."

Place your athame into the dish of water and say:

"In the names of the Lady and Lord,
I consecrate Water that it bring feeling to my circle."

Place your athame into the dish of salt and say:

"In the names of the Lady and Lord,
I consecrate Earth that it bring commitment to my circle."

Place three pinches of salt into the water and stir.
Say:

"So mote it be."

3. Cast the Circle

With your athame or sword, go to the East, directing energy to the circle as you say:

"I consecrate this circle, and charge it, that it will be a fit place for us to meet the Gods. O circle, be a boundary between the world of humankind and the world of the Gods, that we may meet them in the middle.
Keep us safe in our rites. So mote it be!"

Finish as you return to the East: If you finish early, don't say "so mote it be" until you've returned to the East. If you haven't finished when you return to the East, stand there as you finish.
All repeat: *"So mote it be!"*

Pick up the dish of saltwater and return to the East. Wet your fingers and flick drops all the way around the circle, East to East, sprinkling the entire perimeter, saying:

"I cleanse this circle by Water and Earth. O circle,
you are cleansed. So mote it be!"

All repeat: *"So mote it be!"*
Return to the altar.

Pick up the censer, stirring it up if needed. Return to the East. Cense the perimeter, as you walk again around the circle, East to East, saying:

"I purify this circle by Fire and Air. O circle, you are purified. So mote it be!"

All repeat: *"So mote it be!"*
Return to the altar.

4. Call the Quarters

In the East, face out, point your athame, and draw an invoking pentagram, saying:

"Come to us, Air!
Guard us in the East!
Come to us, wind
Come to us, intelligence
Come on eagle's wings
Guard our Candlemas rite!
Welcome, O Air! Blessed be."

All repeat: *"Blessed be."*
Walk deosil back to your place.
In the South, face out, point your athame, and draw an invoking pentagram, saying:

"Come to us, Fire!
Guard us in the South!
Come to us, heat
Come to us, passion
Come with a lion's roar
Guard our Candlemas rite!
Welcome, O Fire! Blessed be."

All repeat: *"Blessed be."*

Walk deosil back to your place.
In the West, face out, point your athame, and draw an invoking pentagram, saying:

"Come to us, Water!
Guard us in the West!
Come to us, oceans
Come to us, love
Come riding on dolphins
Guard our Candlemas rite!
Welcome, O Water! Blessed be."

All repeat: *"Blessed be."*
Walk deosil back to your place.
In the North, face out, point your athame, and draw an invoking pentagram, saying:

"Come to us, Earth!
Guard us in the North!
Come to us, soil
Come to us, commitment
Come with mighty hooves
Guard our Candlemas rite!
Welcome, O Earth! Blessed be."

All repeat: *"Blessed be."*
Walk back to the East for a final, silent salute.

5. Invoking the Gods

Raise the wand and point to the North, saying:

"Gracious and benevolent Goddess of birth and rebirth,
be here among us on this holy day.
Mighty Horned One, God of cold and of warmth,
be here among us on this holy day.
Beloved Lady and Lord, join us in winter's dark
to prepare a bed in which spring may be born.
Welcome and blessed be."

All repeat: *"Blessed be."*

6. Offerings/Seasonal Celebration

Priestess: *"On Candlemas, we make pure our space and ourselves, ready for the coming spring."*

Priest: *"We sweep away darkness, we bring renewal."*

Priestess: *"Sweep away darkness!"*

She hands the broom to the person to her left, repeating:

"Sweep away darkness!"

The person holding the broom hands it to the person on their left, repeating:

"Sweep away darkness!"

This process repeats all the way around the circle until the broom is returned to the priestess. The priestess now goes to the East and begins sweeping the entire circle, deosil, while everyone chants, "Sweep away darkness," while clapping rhythmically.

When the sweeping is finished, the priestess returns to the altar and raises the broom above their head. Everyone falls silent, and the broom is put down.

Priest: *"As the groundhog awakens and looks to his shadow, we awaken and look to our own shadows."*

Priestess: *"Look within now and find your own shadow. Find the shadow that stops your own renewal. Find the cloud that covers your rebirth. What stops you? What holds you back? What shadow must be lifted and burned away by pure, holy sunlight?"*

Priest (lifts up the tray of candles): *"We bless and consecrate these candles that they are pure and can burn away shadows."*

The priestess sprinkles the candles with consecrated saltwater (avoiding the wicks), saying:

"By Water and Earth, we purify these candles."

The priest hands the tray to the priestess and picks up the censer. The priest censes the candles so that each is touched by the smoke, saying:

"By Fire and Air, we purify these candles."

The tray is now placed on the altar.

The priest hands the first candle to the priestess, saying:

"This holy candle burns away shadows. What is your intention?"

The priestess speaks as she is moved.

The priest says:

"Burn this candle and your will shall be made manifest. So mote it be."

All repeat: *"So mote it be."*

One by one, the priest hands a candle to each person, saying:

"This holy candle burns away shadows. What is your intention?"

Each person speaks as moved, and the priest says:

"Burn this candle and your will shall be made manifest. So mote it be."

All repeat: *"So mote it be."*

At last, the priestess hands a candle to the priest, saying:

"This holy candle burns away shadows. What is your intention?"

The priest speaks as moved, and the priestess says:

"Burn this candle and your will shall be made manifest. So mote it be."

All repeat: *"So mote it be."*

Note: Each person will light their own candle when they get home, repeating the intention stated in ritual, and saying again, "This holy candle burns away shadows." They should then let the candle burn down completely.

7. Cakes and Wine

The priest holds the athame, the priestess holds the cup.[67]

Priestess: *"Force to form."*

Priest: *"Mercy to justice."*

Priestess: *"Wisdom to understanding."*

Priest: *"Lord to Lady."*

The priest plunges the athame into the cup and says:

"Blessed be."

Consecrate the cakes by dipping the athame into the wine and sprinkling drops onto the cakes, forming an invoking pentagram. Say:

Priest: *"Severity to kindness."*

Priestess: *"Victory to splendor."*

Priest: *"Crown to kingdom. Blessed be."*

Take a cake and place it in the libation bowl.

67 Or a gender-variant version is done.

8. Celebration of Season

Libations are done as usual, with everyone pouring an offering into the bowl and having a cake. Then the leader raises their cup and says:

"This is Brigid's Day. On the day of the goddess of poets and bards, it is fitting that we offer poetry or other bardic performance to her. Let us each share a poem, story, or song, as an offering to Holy Brigid."

The leader begins with an offering, ending with: *"To Brigid!"*
All repeat: *"To Brigid!"*

Note: It is not good to applaud in ritual. Applause dissipates energy. Simply say "to Brigid!"
Each person, in turn, offers a poem, story, song, or instrumental, ending with, *"To Brigid!"*
All repeat: *"To Brigid!"*

9. Closing the Circle

Hold the wand, facing North, say:

"We thank you, fiery Brigid, for inspiring us with poetry and song.
Hail to you, great Lady! Farewell!"

All repeat: *"Farewell!"*
Say:

"Lady of the birth and rebirth, Lady of light,
Thank you for joining us tonight
Farewell!"

All repeat: *"Farewell!"*
Say:

"Lord of cold and warmth,
Lord of winter,
Thank you for joining us tonight
Farewell!"

All repeat: *"Farewell!"*
Go to the East, draw a banishing pentagram, and say:

"We thank you, Guardian of the East, Guardian of Air
For protecting this Candlemas rite
Thank you, and farewell!"

All repeat: *"Farewell!"*
Go to the South, draw a banishing pentagram, and say:

"We thank you, Guardian of the South, Guardian of Fire
For protecting this Candlemas rite
Thank you, and farewell!"

All repeat: *"Farewell!"*
Go to the West, draw a banishing pentagram, and say:

"We thank you, Guardian of the West, Guardian of Water
For protecting this Candlemas rite
Thank you, and farewell!"

All repeat: *"Farewell!"*
Go to the North, draw a banishing pentagram, and say:

"We thank you, Guardian of the North, Guardian of Earth
For protecting this Candlemas rite
Thank you, and farewell!"

All repeat: *"Farewell!"*
Facing the center, say:

"The circle is open but unbroken, the rites are ended.
Merry meet, merry part, and merry meet again!"

All repeat: *"Merry meet, merry part, and merry meet again!"*

A Solitary Candlemas Ritual

This ritual incorporates a few different aspects of the holiday: The idea of blessing candles, the idea of cleaning and purification, and the idea of performance as an offering. A solitary performance has the gods as an audience.

Tools Needed

In addition to the usual tools, for this ritual, you need:

- Seasonal decorations can include a Brigid's cross, cow or sheep imagery, wheat imagery, extra altar candles,[68] and/or a white altar cloth.
- A broom

68 See note on page 202.

- One extra white candle

Before You Begin

- If you froze a loaf of bread at Lammas, defrost it and make bread pudding from it. This ties the two opposite festivals together and incorporates milk, which is associated with this festival. The bread pudding can be your cakes for cakes and wine.

Begin with the opening meditation found in *Sabbats: The Wheel of the Year* on page 108.

1. Declaration of Opening

Say:

"I am here tonight to purify myself for the coming spring,
to prepare and renew myself on this Candlemas."

2. Consecrations

Place your athame into the dish of incense and say:

"In the names of the Lady and Lord,
I consecrate Air that it bring mindfulness to my circle."

Place incense onto the lit charcoal so that smoke begins to rise. Place your athame into the smoke and say:

"In the names of the Lady and Lord,
I consecrate Fire that it bring passion to my circle."

Place your athame into the dish of water and say:

"In the names of the Lady and Lord,
I consecrate Water that it bring feeling to my circle."

Place your athame into the dish of salt and say:

"In the names of the Lady and Lord,
I consecrate Earth that it bring commitment to my circle."

Place three pinches of salt into the water and stir.
Say:

"So mote it be."

3. Cast the Circle

With your athame or sword, go to the East, directing energy to the circle as you say:

"I consecrate this circle, and charge it, that it will be a fit place for me to meet the Gods. O circle, be a boundary between the world of humankind and the world of the Gods, that I may meet them in the middle. Keep me safe in my rites. So mote it be!"

Finish as you return to the East: If you finish early, don't say "so mote it be" until you've returned to the East. If you haven't finished when you return to the East, stand there as you finish.

Pick up the dish of saltwater and return to the East. Wet your fingers and flick drops all the way around the circle, East to East, sprinkling the entire perimeter, saying:

"I cleanse this circle by Water and Earth. O circle, you are cleansed. So mote it be!"

Return to the altar.

Pick up the censer, stirring it up if needed to get it smoky. Return to the East. Cense the perimeter, as you walk again around the circle, East to East, saying:

"I purify this circle by Fire and Air. O circle, you are purified. So mote it be!"

Return to the altar.

4. Call the Quarters

In the East, face out, point your athame, and draw an invoking pentagram, saying:

"Come to me, Air!
Guard my circle in the East!
Come to me, wind
Come to me, intelligence
Come on eagle's wings
Guard my Candlemas rite!
Welcome, O Air! Blessed be."

In the South, face out, point your athame, and draw an invoking pentagram, saying:

"Come to me, Fire!
Guard my circle in the South!
Come to me, heat
Come to me, passion
Come with a lion's roar
Guard my Candlemas rite!
Welcome, O Fire! Blessed be."

In the West, face out, point your athame, and draw an invoking pentagram, saying:

"Come to me, Water!
Guard my circle in the West!
Come to me, oceans
Come to me, love
Come riding on dolphins
Guard my Candlemas rite!
Welcome, O Water! Blessed be."

In the North, face out, point your athame, and draw an invoking pentagram, saying:

"Come to me, Earth!
Guard my circle in the North!
Come to me, soil
Come to me, commitment
Come with mighty hooves
Guard my Candlemas rite!
Welcome, O Earth! Blessed be."

Walk back to the East for a final, silent salute.

5. Invoking the Gods

Raise the wand and point to the North, saying:

"Gracious and benevolent Goddess of birth and rebirth, be here with me on this holy day.
Mighty Horned One, God of cold and of warmth,
be here with me on this holy day.
Beloved Lady and Lord, join me in winter's dark
to prepare a bed in which spring may be born.
Welcome and blessed be."

6. Offerings/Seasonal Celebration

Say:

"On Candlemas, I make pure my space and myself, ready for the coming spring.
I sweep away darkness, I bring renewal."

Hold the broom horizontally above your head and walk three times around the circle, repeating:

"Sweep away darkness! Sweep away darkness! Sweep away darkness!"

Then, when you have returned to the altar, go to the East and begin slowly, intently sweeping the entire circle.

Return to the altar and put the broom back in its place.

Say:

"As the groundhog awakens and looks to his shadow,
I awaken and look to my own shadow."

Now you may silently meditate on your own shadow, looking to discover what holds you back, what stops you, what acts as a cloud to cover the sunlight for you.

When you are ready, lift up the new white candle and say:

"I bless and consecrate this candle that it is pure and can burn away shadows."

Sprinkle the candle with consecrated saltwater (avoiding the wick), saying:

"By Water and Earth, I purify this candle."

Now, cense the candle so that it is thoroughly touched by the smoke, saying:

"By Fire and Air, I purify this candle."

Say:

"This holy candle burns away shadows. My intention is [speak as moved]. As I burn this candle, my will shall be made manifest. So mote it be."

Light the candle from the altar candle and place it on the altar.

Note: This candle should be allowed to burn out completely, which means it will still be going after the circle is closed, and might need to be moved to a fire-safe location.

7. Cakes and Wine

Say:

"It is time to receive the blessings of vine and Earth!"

Hold the cup and say:

"Force to form
Mercy to justice

Wisdom to understanding
Lord to Lady."

Plunge the athame into the cup and say:

"Blessed be."

Consecrate the cakes by dipping the athame into the wine and sprinkling drops onto the cakes, forming an invoking pentagram. Say:

"Severity to kindness
Victory to splendor
Crown to kingdom
Blessed be."

Take a cake and place it in the libation bowl.

Lift the cup and speak from the heart. It can be as simple as "to the Gods," or it can be detailed. End with "Blessed be." Then make an offering to the gods by pouring a bit of wine into the libation bowl. Drink only after offering and then enjoy a cake.

After the ritual is over, the contents of the libation bowl should be poured out onto the Earth. If the ritual is outdoors, then libations are poured directly onto the Earth and a bowl is not needed.

8. Celebration of Season

After you've poured your libations, say:

"This is Brigid's Day. On the day of the goddess of poets and bards,
I offer [say what you will offer] to her."

Recite a poem (original or otherwise), sing a song, play music, or whatever kind of performance suits you. Finish with, *"To Brigid!"* Continue performing as long as you are moved—no need to confine yourself to just one song/poem/performance. End each with, *"To Brigid!"*

9. Closing the Circle

Hold the wand, facing North, say:

"I thank you, fiery Brigid, for inspiring me. Hail to you, great Lady! Farewell!
Lady of the birth and rebirth, Lady of light,
Thank you for joining me tonight
Farewell!
Lord of cold and warmth,
Lord of winter,
Thank you for joining me tonight
Farewell!"

Go to the East, draw a banishing pentagram, and say:

"I thank you, Guardian of the East, Guardian of Air
For protecting this Candlemas rite
Thank you, and farewell!"

Go to the South, draw a banishing pentagram, and say:

"I thank you, Guardian of the South, Guardian of Fire
For protecting this Candlemas rite
Thank you, and farewell!"

Go to the West, draw a banishing pentagram, and say:

"I thank you, Guardian of the West, Guardian of Water
For protecting this Candlemas rite
Thank you, and farewell!"

Go to the North, draw a banishing pentagram, and say:

"I thank you, Guardian of the North, Guardian of Earth
For protecting this Candlemas rite
Thank you, and farewell!"

Facing the center, say:

"The circle is open but unbroken, the rites are ended.
Merry meet, merry part, and merry meet again!"

Spring Equinox

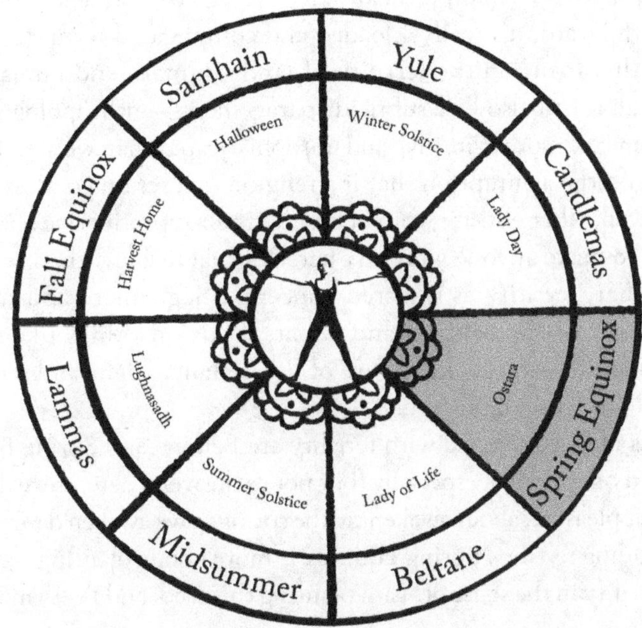

The first thing to discuss about the sabbat of Spring Equinox is its name. Many Wiccans call it Ostara, a name coined by Aidan Kelly in 1974. There was no such name for March 21 prior to that, although it's a fitting name. The historical record indicates that "Ostara" or "Eostre" or "Easter" are Germanic goddess names associated with this time of year (although with April rather than the actual equinox in March). More than that isn't really known. The Christian holiday of Easter wasn't "stolen" from a Pagan "Ostara" holiday, but they have a lot in common.

Eggs and Bunnies

Egg painting is an ancient custom, performed by both Pagan Europeans and early Christians. Eggs (not painted) are also a traditional part of Passover celebrations in Judaism, and Passover also occurs around the Spring Equinox.

The hare, as well, seems to be associated with the goddess Ostara, although the Easter hare leading an egg hunt is a Christian innovation.

Culture is by nature conservative: You keep doing what you've always done. If you painted eggs on the Spring Equinox before Christianity, you keep doing so afterwards—that's not theft or cultural appropriation, that's folk custom, and folk custom is a powerful force. It's also true that European seasonal holidays are all going to be responding to the same reality of early spring, seed germination, and so on.

Eggs and hares (or bunnies) are anciently associated with spring, fertility, and rebirth and are powerful symbols for Pagans and Wiccans.

Fertility

When I was young, it was common to hear Wicca referred to as a "fertility religion." While that sounds straightforward, it's really a loaded and complicated term. "Fertility religion" can mean a religion with a focus on the fertility of land, animals, and humans—a focus on the sacredness of survival. It can also be a subtle disparagement—anthropologists can say "fertility religion" when they mean "more primitive and unsophisticated than we are." It can also be deeply misogynistic, based on the assumption that if a religion focuses on goddesses, it must be about "fertility" because, well, what else are women besides their reproductive ability? And naturally, it can also be a way to make anyone who isn't heterosexual feel less-than.

Despite all of that, fertility as a sacred concept is legitimate and real. But is Wicca a fertility religion? Most of the Sabbats and Esbats focus on things like death and rebirth, and therefore, eternal life—the cyclic nature of life, balance, light and dark, knowledge and enlightenment, and hope for the future.

The two Sabbats most concerned with fertility are Beltane and Spring Equinox. At Beltane, we are heavily focused on sexuality, especially (but not exclusively) heterosexuality. Beltane is about fertility but also about pleasure, about awakening the spring as we awaken desire, and all the delights that can bring—including fertility. Spring Equinox is more about planting seeds. It's directly and specifically about fertility in the sense of "I am planting this seed, and I very much want it to grow."

A Group Spring Equinox Ritual

This ritual is different from, but parallel to, the Fall Equinox rite. In the fall, we gave thanks for "unknown blessings to come." In planting seeds at this time, we are making those unknown blessings real. Where we harvested rebirth in the fall, we plant it today.

Because this is a fertility ritual, it assumes a priestess and priest expressing the fertility of Goddess and God. As always, assign these roles in a way that works in your group.

Tools Needed

In addition to the usual tools, for this ritual, you need:

- Seasonal decorations are more or less the same as Easter decorations—flowers, eggs, and similar imagery. If you have a cute bunny for your altar, that is totally appropriate. It is okay to be ridiculous!
- A bowl with seeds that can be planted at this time of year (mustard, peas, and daisies in temperate zones)
- A transplant pot or small bowl of soil—one per person. All of the pots should be on a tray so that they can be lifted together
- (Optional) Colored eggs to eat during cakes and wine

Before You Begin

- Use the same consecrations as used in Fall Equinox, to emphasize the connection between the two rituals. Remember that you'll have each ritual item in its corresponding quarter—the dish of incense in the East, the censer in the South, the dish of water in the West, and the dish of salt in the North.

Begin with the opening meditation found in *Sabbats: The Wheel of the Year* on page 108.

1. Declaration of Opening

Priestess: "*We gather to celebrate the thawing of the Earth.*"

Priest: "*We gather to honor the God, who fertilizes the seeds of spring.*"

Priestess: "*We gather to honor the Goddess, who sheds the ice and nourishes the seeds of spring.*"

2. Consecrations

Go to the East. Pick up the dish of incense and bring it to the altar. Place your athame into it and say:

"I bring Air from the East. Air, be consecrated for our rite."

Go to the South. Pick up the censer and bring it to the altar. Place incense onto the lit charcoal so that smoke begins to rise. Place your athame into the smoke and say:

"I bring Fire from the South. Fire, be consecrated for our rite."

Go to the West. Pick up the dish of water and bring it to the altar. Place your athame into it and say:

"I bring Water from the West. Water, be consecrated for our rite."

Go to the North. Pick up the dish of salt and bring it to the altar. Place your athame into it and say:

"I bring Earth from the North. Earth, be consecrated for our rite."

Place three pinches of salt into the water and stir.
Say:

"So mote it be."

3. Cast the Circle

With your athame or sword, go to the East, directing energy to the circle as you say:

"I consecrate this circle, and charge it, that it will be a fit place for us to meet the Gods. O circle, be a boundary between the world of humankind and the world of the Gods, that we may meet them in the middle. Keep us safe in our rites. So mote it be!"

Finish as you return to the East: If you finish early, don't say "so mote it be" until you've returned to the East. If you haven't finished when you return to the East, stand there as you finish.

All repeat: *"So mote it be!"*

Pick up the dish of saltwater and return to the East. Wet your fingers and flick drops all the way around the circle, East to East, sprinkling the entire perimeter, saying:

"I cleanse this circle by Water and Earth.
O circle, you are cleansed. So mote it be!"

All repeat: *"So mote it be!"*

Return to the altar.

Pick up the censer, stirring it up if needed. Return to the East. Cense the perimeter, as you walk again around the circle, East to East, saying:

"I purify this circle by Fire and Air. O circle, you are purified. So mote it be!"

All repeat: *"So mote it be!"*

Return to the altar.

4. Call the Quarters

In the East, face out, point your athame, and draw an invoking pentagram, saying:

"Come to us, Air!
Guard us in the East!
Come to us, wind
Come to us, intelligence
Come on eagle's wings
Guard our Spring Equinox rite!
Welcome, O Air! Blessed be."

All repeat: *"Blessed be."*

Walk deosil back to your place.

In the South, face out, point your athame, and draw an invoking pentagram, saying:

"Come to us, Fire!
Guard us in the South!
Come to us, heat
Come to us, passion

Come with a lion's roar
Guard our Spring Equinox rite!
Welcome, O Fire! Blessed be."

All repeat: "*Blessed be.*"
Walk deosil back to your place.
In the West, face out, point your athame, and draw an invoking pentagram, saying:

"Come to us, Water!
Guard us in the West!
Come to us, oceans
Come to us, love
Come riding on dolphins
Guard our Spring Equinox rite!
Welcome, O Water! Blessed be."

All repeat: "*Blessed be.*"
Walk deosil back to your place.
In the North, face out, point your athame, and draw an invoking pentagram, saying:

"Come to us, Earth!
Guard us in the North!
Come to us, soil
Come to us, commitment
Come with mighty hooves
Guard our Spring Equinox rite!
Welcome, O Earth! Blessed be."

All repeat: "*Blessed be.*"
Walk back to the East for a final, silent salute.

5. Invoking the Gods

The priestess and priest hold the wand together, pointing to the North.

Priestess:

"Glorious Maiden of Earth, Lady of new life, be here among us!
Fair one, bringer of joy and renewal, hear our call
Like a crocus springing forth, join us and break the winter's silence
Welcome, and blessed be."

Priest:

"Laughing God of the greenwood, be here among us!

Shepherd of creatures wild and free, hear our call
Dance here with your cloven hooves. Let life be born anew!
Welcome and blessed be."

All repeat: "*Blessed be.*"

6. Offerings/Seasonal Celebration

One person begins an appropriate chant[69] as all dance around the circle (as able). As the energy builds, send it into the seeds.

At the peak of energy, the priest lifts his athame and plunges it into the seeds, saying:

"Thus does the God fertilize the Earth!"

The priestess lifts the tray of soil and says:

"Thus does the Goddess nourish his seeds."

She takes a seed (or a few seeds—check the planting instructions) and plants it in a pot, saying:

"The Earth receives the blessings of the Lord and Lady. My intentions grow with this seed."

As she speaks, she focuses on her intentions, knowing they will grow with the seedling.

All respond: "*So mote it be.*"

Each person comes to the altar, one at a time. The priest holds the bowl of seeds, and the priestess holds the tray of plants (if it's too heavy or awkward, she can lift one pot at a time).

Each person takes a seed from the priest and plants it in the pot held by the priestess. Each time, the priestess says:

"The Earth receives the blessings of the Lord and Lady.
May your intentions grow with this seed."

All respond: "*So mote it be.*"

After the ritual, everyone will take their seed pots home to plant. Depending on the climate, you may want to germinate them indoors before transplanting them outdoors. Because I live in an apartment these days, I sometimes do this kind of magic by planting at my Mom's house, or you can send the seeds home with someone who has a big yard, or you can plant the seeds on public land where they can grow discreetly.

---

69 I like "The Lady's Bransle" by Gwydion Pendderwen. There's also a very nice song called "Ostara" by Lisa Thiel (both available on YouTube at last check). For a full-length song like Ostara, you might prefer to just use the chorus so that a group can chant together. There are *so many* chants on YouTube and elsewhere it hardly seems worthwhile to list them.

7. Cakes and Wine

Say:

"It is time to receive the blessings of vine and Earth!"

Hold the cup and say:

"The cup, the Goddess, the blood of life
Our Lady blesses us with all good things
She offers herself to us
She offers herself to the God."

Hold the athame over the cup and say:

"The blade, the God, the force of life
Our Lord blesses us with all good things
He offers himself to us
He offers himself to the Goddess."

Plunge the athame into the cup and say:

"Blessed be."

Consecrate the cakes by dipping the athame into the wine and sprinkling drops onto the cakes, forming an invoking pentagram. Say:

"Lady and Lord, you bless us with abundance
The Earth gives us all we need
We thank you.
Blessed be."

Take a cake and place it in the libation bowl.

Lift the cup and speak from the heart. It can be as simple as "to the Gods," or it can be detailed. End with "Blessed be." Then, make an offering to the gods by pouring a bit of wine into the libation bowl. Drink only after offering.

Each person in turn offers, pours, and drinks. Each offering ends with "Blessed be," and everyone responds by saying "Blessed be."

Or pour from the main cup into each person's individual cup before drinking. Then each offers, pours, and drinks in turn.

After the cup goes around, or while the cup is on its way around, pass the cakes.

After the ritual is over, the contents of the libation bowl should be poured out onto the Earth.

8. Celebration of Season

The primary seasonal rite has been performed as an offering. After cakes and wine, you can discuss your plans for the coming season, and what you want to "grow" or "fertilize" this year. You can continue to eat and drink during this.

9. Closing the Circle

The priestess and priest face North, raising the wand together.

Priestess:

"Beloved Maiden,
Lady of new life,
We thank you for joining us and blessing our seeds.
Thank you, and farewell!"

All repeat: *"Farewell!"*

Priest:

"Beloved Lord,
Shepherd of the green
We thank you for joining us and blessing our seeds.
Thank you, and farewell!"

All repeat: *"Farewell!"*

Go to the East, draw a banishing pentagram, and say:

"We thank you, Guardian of the East, Guardian of Air
For protecting this Spring Equinox rite
Thank you, and farewell!"

All repeat: *"Farewell!"*

Go to the South, draw a banishing pentagram, and say:

"We thank you, Guardian of the South, Guardian of Fire
For protecting this Spring Equinox rite
Thank you, and farewell!"

All repeat: *"Farewell!"*

Go to the West, draw a banishing pentagram, and say:

"We thank you, Guardian of the West, Guardian of Water
For protecting this Spring Equinox rite
Thank you, and farewell!"

All repeat: *"Farewell!"*
Go to the North, draw a banishing pentagram, and say:

"We thank you, Guardian of the North, Guardian of Earth
For protecting this Spring Equinox rite
Thank you, and farewell!"

All repeat: *"Farewell!"*
Facing the center, say:

"The circle is open but unbroken, the rites are ended.
Merry meet, merry part, and merry meet again!"

All repeat: *"Merry meet, merry part, and merry meet again!"*

A Solitary Spring Equinox Rite

This ritual is different from, but parallel to, the Fall Equinox rite. In the fall, we gave thanks for "unknown blessings to come." In planting seeds at this time, we are making those unknown blessings real. Where we harvested rebirth in the fall, we plant it today.

Tools Needed

In addition to the usual tools, for this ritual, you need:

- Seasonal decorations are more or less the same as Easter decorations—flowers, eggs, and similar imagery. If you have a cute bunny for your altar, that is totally appropriate. It is okay to be ridiculous!
- A bowl with seeds that can be planted at this time of year (mustard, peas, and daisies in temperate zones)
- A transplant pot or small bowl of soil
- **(Optional)** Colored eggs to eat during cakes and wine

Before You Begin

- Use the same consecrations as used in Fall Equinox, to emphasize the connection between the two rituals. Remember that you'll have each ritual item in its corresponding quarter—the dish of incense in the East, the censer in the South, the dish of water in the West, and the dish of salt in the North.

Begin with the opening meditation found in *Sabbats: The Wheel of the Year* on page 108.

1. Declaration of Opening

Say:

"Tonight, I celebrate the thawing of the Earth.
I honor the God, who fertilizes the seeds of spring.
I honor the Goddess, who sheds the ice and nourishes the seeds of spring."

2. Consecrations

Go to the East. Pick up the dish of incense and bring it to the altar. Place your athame into it and say:

"I bring Air from the East. Air, be consecrated for this rite."

Go to the South. Pick up the censer and bring it to the altar. Place incense onto the lit charcoal so that smoke begins to rise. Place your athame into the smoke and say:

"I bring Fire from the South. Fire, be consecrated for this rite."

Go to the West. Pick up the dish of water and bring it to the altar. Place your athame into it and say:

"I bring Water from the West. Water, be consecrated for this rite."

Go to the North. Pick up the dish of salt and bring it to the altar. Place your athame into it and say:

"I bring Earth from the North. Earth, be consecrated for this rite."

Place three pinches of salt into the water and stir.
Say:

"So mote it be."

3. Cast the Circle

With your athame or sword, go to the East, directing energy to the circle as you say:

"I consecrate this circle, and charge it, that it will be a fit place for me to meet the Gods. O circle, be a boundary between the world of humankind and the world of the Gods, that I may meet them in the middle. Keep me safe in my rites. So mote it be!"

Finish as you return to the East: If you finish early, don't say "so mote it be" until you've returned to the East. If you haven't finished when you return to the East, stand there as you finish.

Return to the altar.

Pick up the dish of saltwater and return to the East. Wet your fingers and flick drops all the way around the circle, East to East, sprinkling the entire perimeter, saying:

"I cleanse this circle by Water and Earth.
O circle, you are cleansed. So mote it be!"

Return to the altar.

Pick up the censer, stirring it up if needed to get it smoky. Return to the East. Cense the perimeter, as you walk again around the circle, East to East, saying:

"I purify this circle by Fire and Air. O circle, you are purified. So mote it be!"

Return to the altar.

4. Call the Quarters

In the East, face out, point your athame, and draw an invoking pentagram, saying:

"Come to me, Air!
Guard my circle in the East!
Come to me, wind
Come to me, intelligence
Come on eagle's wings
Guard my Spring Equinox rite!
Welcome, O Air! Blessed be."

In the South, face out, point your athame, and draw an invoking pentagram, saying:

"Come to me, Fire!
Guard my circle in the South!
Come to me, heat
Come to me, passion
Come with a lion's roar
Guard my Spring Equinox rite!
Welcome, O Fire! Blessed be."

In the West, face out, point your athame, and draw an invoking pentagram, saying:

"Come to me, Water!
Guard my circle in the West!
Come to me, oceans
Come to me, love
Come riding on dolphins

Guard my Spring Equinox rite!
Welcome, O Water! Blessed be."

In the North, face out, point your athame and draw an invoking pentagram, saying:

"Come to me, Earth!
Guard my circle in the North!
Come to me, soil
Come to me, commitment
Come with mighty hooves
Guard my Spring Equinox rite!
Welcome, O Earth! Blessed be."

Walk back to the East for a final, silent salute.

5. Invoking the Gods

Hold the wand, pointing to the North, and say:

"Glorious Maiden of Earth, Lady of new life, join me now!
Fair one, bringer of joy and renewal, hear my call
Like a crocus springing forth, join me and break the winter's silence
Welcome, and blessed be.
Laughing God of the greenwood, join me now!
Shepherd of creatures wild and free, hear my call
Dance here with your cloven hooves. Let life be born anew!
Welcome and blessed be."

6. Offerings/Seasonal Celebration

Begin an appropriate chant[70] and dance three times around the circle while chanting. As your energy builds, send it into the seeds.

When you feel the peak of energy, lift your athame and plunge it into the seeds, saying:

"Thus does the God fertilize the Earth!"

Lift the bowl or pot of soil high and say:

"Thus does the Goddess nourish his seeds."

Take a seed (or a few seeds—check the planting instructions) and plant it in the pot or bowl, saying:

---

70 See the note for the group ritual.

"The Earth receives the blessings of the Lord and Lady.
My intentions grow with this seed."

As you speak, focus on your intentions, knowing they will grow with the seedling.

After the ritual, you'll have a seedling to grow. Depending on the climate, you may want to germinate it indoors before transplanting it outdoors. Since I live in an apartment these days, I sometimes do this kind of magic by planting at my Mom's house, or you can plant the seeds on public land where they can grow discreetly.

7. Cakes and Wine

Say:

"It is time to receive the blessings of vine and Earth!"

Hold the cup and say:

"The cup, the Goddess, the blood of life
My Lady blesses me with all good things
She offers herself to me
She offers herself to the God."

Hold the athame over the cup and say:

"The blade, the God, the force of life
My Lord blesses me with all good things
He offers himself to me
He offers himself to the Goddess."

Plunge the athame into the cup and say:

"Blessed be."

Now, consecrate the cakes by dipping the athame into the wine and sprinkling drops onto the cakes, forming an invoking pentagram. Say:

"Lady and Lord, you bless me with abundance
The Earth gives me all I need
I thank you.
Blessed be."

Take a cake and place it in the libation bowl.

Lift the cup and speak from the heart. It can be as simple as "to the Gods," or it can be detailed. End with "Blessed be." Then, make an offering to the gods by pouring a bit of wine into the libation bowl. Drink only after offering and have a cake.

After the ritual is over, the contents of the libation bowl should be poured out onto the Earth.

8. Celebration of Season

The primary seasonal rite has been performed as an offering. After cakes and wine, meditate on your plans for the coming season, and what you want to "grow" or "fertilize" this year.

9. Closing the Circle

Hold the wand, facing North, say:

"Beloved Maiden,
Lady of new life,
I thank you for joining me and blessing my seeds.
Thank you, and farewell!
Beloved Lord,
Shepherd of the green
I thank you for joining me and blessing my seeds.
Thank you, and farewell!"

Go to the East, draw a banishing pentagram, and say:

"I thank you, Guardian of the East, Guardian of Air
For protecting this Spring Equinox rite
Thank you, and farewell!"

Go to the South, draw a banishing pentagram, and say:

"I thank you, Guardian of the South, Guardian of Fire
For protecting this Spring Equinox rite
Thank you, and farewell!"

Go to the West, draw a banishing pentagram, and say:

"I thank you, Guardian of the West, Guardian of Water
For protecting this Spring Equinox rite
Thank you, and farewell!"

Go to the North, draw a banishing pentagram, and say:

"I thank you, Guardian of the North, Guardian of Earth
For protecting this Spring Equinox rite
Thank you, and farewell!"

Facing the center, say:

"The circle is open but unbroken, the rites are ended.
Merry meet, merry part, and merry meet again!"

The Moon and the Sun

The moon and sun are integral to Wicca, with the moon having prominence.

Many, many years ago, when my ex-husband (a Druid) and I were first living together, we attended a Pagan festival. The Druids had a sunrise ritual. They went around the campsite, singing, to wake up people who wanted to attend. My ex heard the song and jumped out of bed. I rolled over, grumpy, half-asleep, and entirely uncaffeinated, and snapped, "This is why witches are better than Druids! We have our rituals at a civilized hour!" I went back to sleep. I stand by this statement.

On the other hand, one of my initiates loves Wicca as much as anyone could but struggles to stay up late enough for ritual. I've seen him fall asleep *sitting up in a chair* after ritual was over. I imagine he would not have complained to my ex that long ago day—he'd probably have led the chanting!

Day and night are one of the universe's great polarities, and we all take our energies primarily from one or the other. As individuals, we are mostly a blend of these energies, but Wicca itself draws largely from night.

Sun lore in Wicca is found mostly by a close reading of the Sabbats. Sun lore focuses on the length of days, with the birth of the waxing sun at Yule and his death at Midsummer, when the waning sun takes over.

Many occultists will perform no magic during the equinoxes, because the stasis of this time is seen as counterproductive. The movement of the sun is considered necessary for magic.

Moon lore is more integral to Wiccan ritual practice.

The Full Moon

The influence of the full moon is well known in folklore and myth. Scientific data supports some, but not all, of the beliefs people hold about the effects of a full moon. While Some crime statistics, some mental health data, and a great deal of animal behavior, do bear up statistically.[71]

It's important to note that where data supports a full moon effect, it shows that "the full moon" lasts for three days: effects last from the day before full until the day after full.

In Wicca, the full moon is a sacred time and is considered the most auspicious time to worship the Goddess, although it is certainly not the *only* time. It is considered the time of the Mother. Because it is a time for worship, spells are often not done during the full moon, unless the need is great.

Many people are familiar with the idea of each month's full moon having a unique name, like the Harvest Moon or the Wolf Moon. These names, though, aren't traditional to Wicca at all, and many of them are North American, originating with indigenous American peoples.

71 For example, Brain Health University, Cajochen et al, Lieber, NeuroLaunch, Wayman, and Zimecki.

The Waxing Moon

The waxing moon (from waxing crescent to first quarter, to waxing gibbous) is the moon of growth. It occurs from the first visible sliver following the new moon until the full moon. It is considered the time of the Maiden.

The waxing moon is the time to do any magical or mundane things that promote growth. It's a great time for fertility magic, for money magic, and for healing that has to do with increasing strength, resilience, and energy. It's the best time to plant seeds.

The New Moon

The new moon, or dark moon, is the night opposite the full moon, when the moon is not visible in the sky. It is a void time, a time of meditation, mystery, dream work, and trance exploration. Some people do not perform any ritual at this time, although I have always done so. It is the time of the dark or devouring Mother.

There isn't a lot of lore in Wicca regarding lunar eclipses, but I've done ritual in a lunar eclipse and found the energy very similar to a dark moon.

The Waning Moon

The waning moon (from waning crescent to third quarter, to waning gibbous) is the moon of shrinking and diminishment. It begins as soon as the full moon ends and continues until the new moon. It is the time of the Crone.

The waning moon is the time to do magical and mundane activities related to ending, reduction, or reversal. Healing that shrinks—such as working to shrink a tumor—is best performed at this time, as are banishments and bindings.

Many people prefer to get their hair cut at this time, as it grows back more slowly. It's a good time for weeding as well, for the same reason.

Weather Lore

Folklore regarding weather is highly regional. The folklore I might know here in New Jersey is not the same as what my Wiccan predecessors knew in England, or what you might know in Arizona or Montana. But the moon and the sun are shared by all, and their energies are an important influence on our lives as witches.

Chapter Eight:

RITES OF LIFE

We've explored a range of periodic rituals—things done every month or every year. But, in addition to having "regular" lives, seasons, and tides, we all also experience once-in-a-lifetime events, and these, too, can be marked ritually.

In the course of a lifetime, some or all of these singular events can occur:

- Birth
- Adoption
- Coming of age
- Marriage (handfasting)
- Divorce
- Coming out
- Transition
- Taking a new name
- Dedication (to Wicca or another path)
- Initiation (into Wicca or another path)
- Forming a new coven or Pagan worship group
- Menopause
- Retirement
- Death

Any of these—and more— can be marked ritually.

Birth and adoption can be marked ritually as a passage in the life of the parents. When I gave birth, the midwife did a small (not Wiccan) ritual with me a few days later.

Coming-of-age rituals are often gendered—manhood and menarche rites—but don't have to be.

Rituals where non-Wiccan guests might be invited, such as Wiccaning and handfasting, are often softened up a bit, which is to say, made more accessible to the guests. That's up to you, of course.

It is rare to perform a Wiccan funeral. Mourners are inherently going to be a mixed lot, and the family of the deceased is unlikely to be 100% on board. Rather, when a Wiccan dies, there is typically a funeral decided upon by the immediate family of the deceased (Christian, Jewish, secular, etc.) and then a Wiccan memorial ritual. This ritual would tend to be different if the deceased was a Wiccan, on one hand, or a relative or beloved of a Wiccan, on the other hand. That is, I did different rituals when my initiate died and when my nephew died.

It's outside the scope of this book to offer a ritual for every possible life passage, but we'll see if we can hit the highlights. Check *Recommended Reading* on page 351 for additional suggestions.

Wiccaning

A "Wiccaning" or "Paganing" ceremony doesn't make your baby Wiccan or Pagan. We're all about free choice, and we don't force our religion on our children. But, like any parents, we convey our values and beliefs to our children as a normal part of their upbringing.

Most importantly, we protect and support our children. To that end, we bring them to the attention of the gods and of the community.

I'm a big believer in "it takes a village;" my daughter was raised among other Pagan parents and their kids. The kids would tend to run off like a wolf pack whenever the parents got together, and I think we all loved that. When Professor Spouse and I got married, the "kids' table" at our wedding was those kids, now mostly grown; it was a table of teens and twenties "kids" who had known each other most of their lives.

So, most of the ritual here is designed for a group. The solitary version brings the baby to the attention of the gods and gives the blessings of the year (more on that in a moment), but the blessings of community are absent.

If you're raising the baby with a partner, your partner should be involved in the ritual, even if they aren't normally involved in your Wiccan practice. Parenting is hard, and the consent and participation of your partner in this major life event will lay down a helpful pattern for the future.

There are four major components to this ritual:

- The blessings of the gods
- The blessings of the community: I call this the Sleeping Beauty part of the ritual. In Sleeping Beauty, every fairy but one gives a unique and special gift to the new baby, but the evil fairy is omitted. This ritual includes everyone, and omits no one, so that the baby is showered in blessings.
- The vows of the godparents (if any)
- The blessings of the year: This is something that was created by my best friend Barbara, who is godmother to my daughter. I first experienced it at my daughter's Wiccaning, and I thought it was so beautiful that I have used it ever since.

A Community Wiccaning

This ritual is ideally done when the baby is pretty small because toddlers get restless in ritual. A babe-in-arms is easier to manage. My daughter was about four months old when we did her Wiccaning. My goddaughter was closer to a year.

If your child is older, consider shortening the ceremony to keep them engaged. In that spirit, the quarter callings here are very short and to the point. They have you stand at the altar and just point for all four quarters, which is less dramatic but faster. Additionally, you may want to use your wand as your primary power tool—kids and knives sometimes don't mix.

Go very easy on the incense and choose an incense that isn't very smoky—little ones can be sensitive.

If grandparents or other non-Wiccans are invited, consider dialing down some of the witchier elements of the ritual. Instead of casting a circle, you might just bless the space. Instead of invoking the gods, you might call upon the "powers of the universe," and so on.

Before You Begin

- Each guest should be prepared with a "gift." This isn't a physical gift (Those are nice, too). Rather, it should be a personal quality. Discuss this with everyone in advance so they have time to think it over. For example, as a writer, I could give the baby my way with words. A singer could give a lovely voice. And so on.
- For the offering, find a song or chant (or a few) that feels appropriate to the occasion, such as praising the Mother Goddess. Rehearse the song with the group before the circle is cast. It should be a quieter song, nothing rowdy, in deference to the baby.
- Many parents choose a Pagan name for their baby, just as they choose one for themselves. Have this ready in advance.
- The ritual calls for a single drop of wine to be placed on the baby's lips. If this is uncomfortable for you, use cider instead. If you do use wine, the baby will appreciate it being something sweet.
- The ritual also calls for guests to kiss the baby. Some parents are uncomfortable with this. Decide in advance if kissing will be allowed, and if not, a simple touch on the baby's forehead can replace the kiss.
- If godparents are present, they should be prepared with promises they will give to the child.

Begin with an opening meditation such as the following:

Take a deep, cleansing breath. Hold it. Let it out.

Now another. Hold it. Let it out.

Now another breath. Hold it. Let it out with a sigh.

Become aware of your body. Notice your feet on the ground/floor. Notice your legs. Notice your hips, pelvis, and genitals. Notice your belly. Notice your chest. Notice your arms and your hands. Become aware of your shoulders. Become aware of your neck. Notice your head and your jaw. Notice your face. Notice your crown.

Notice that, head to toe, you are here, present, and alive.

Become aware of your center.

Take another deep breath, and hold it at your center.

Exhale from your center.

Gather your energy to your center as you inhale.

Hold it, knowing you are centered, and let it go with a sigh.
We are ready to begin.

1. Declaration of Opening

The leader says:

"We are gathered for a truly special and sacred occasion,
as we bring [Baby] into our community and the community of the Gods."

2. Consecrations

Place your athame into the dish of incense and say:

"In the names of the Lady and Lord,
I consecrate Air that it bring mindfulness to this rite."

Place incense onto the lit charcoal so that smoke begins to rise. Place your athame into the smoke and say:

"In the names of the Lady and Lord,
I consecrate Fire that it bring passion to this rite."

Place your athame into the dish of water and say:

"In the names of the Lady and Lord,
I consecrate Water that it bring feeling to this rite."

Place your athame into the dish of salt and say:

"In the names of the Lady and Lord,
I consecrate Earth that it bring commitment to this rite."

Place three pinches of salt into the water and stir.
Say:

"So mote it be."

3. Cast the Circle

With your athame or sword, go to the East, directing energy to the circle as you say:

"Round and about, round and about, power stay in, world stay out."

Repeat these words over and over until you've returned to the East. Then, walk silently back to the altar.

Pick up the dish of saltwater and return to the East. Wet your fingers and flick drops all the way around the circle, East to East, sprinkling the entire perimeter, saying:

"Round and about, by Water and Earth, I cleanse this circle."

Repeat these words over and over until you've returned to the East. Then, walk silently back to the altar.

Pick up the censer, stirring it up if needed. Return to the East. Cense the perimeter, as you walk again around the circle, East to East, saying:

"Round and about, by Fire and Air, I purify this circle."

Repeat these words over and over until you've returned to the East. Then, walk silently back to the altar.

4. Call the Quarters

Stand at the altar and face East. Point your athame and draw an invoking pentagram, saying:

"I invoke the Guardian of East, the Guardian of Air
Protect and guard this sacred Wiccaning
Welcome, Guardian! Blessed be."

All repeat: *"Blessed be."*

Turn to face South. Point your athame and draw an invoking pentagram, saying:

"I invoke the Guardian of South, the Guardian of Fire
Protect and guard this sacred Wiccaning
Welcome, Guardian! Blessed be."

All repeat: *"Blessed be."*

Turn to face West. Point your athame and draw an invoking pentagram, saying:

"I invoke the Guardian of West, the Guardian of Water
Protect and guard this sacred Wiccaning
Welcome, Guardian! Blessed be."

All repeat: *"Blessed be."*

Turn to face North. Point your athame and draw an invoking pentagram, saying:

"I invoke the Guardian of North, the Guardian of Earth
Protect and guard this sacred Wiccaning
Welcome, Guardian! Blessed be."

All repeat: *"Blessed be."*
Face East for a final, silent salute. (There's no need to invoke.)

5. Invoking the Gods

All join hands.
The leader says:

"Beloved Mother and Father of us all
Protector of all children
Guardians of the Wicca
Come to this sacred rite and welcome a new child into your care
Beloved Lady
Beloved Lord
Come to us and be glad
Sing with us and be joyful!
Welcome! Blessed be!"

All repeat: *"Blessed be."*

6. Offerings

Still holding hands, begin your song of offering. Sing it until the energy feels wonderful and let it gently fade.

7. Cakes and Wine

Say:

"The Lady and Lord have heard our song of praise and offer their blessings to us."

Hold the cup and say:

"The cup, the Goddess, the blood of life
Our Lady blesses us with all good things

She offers herself to us
She offers herself to the God."

Hold the athame over the cup and say:

"The blade, the God, the force of life
Our Lord blesses us with all good things
He offers himself to us
He offers himself to the Goddess."

Plunge the athame into the cup and say:

"Blessed be."

Consecrate the cakes by dipping the athame into the wine and sprinkling drops onto the cakes, forming an invoking pentagram. Say:

"Lady and Lord, you bless us with abundance
The Earth gives us all we need
We thank you.
Blessed be."

Take a cake or a portion of whatever food is on the plate and place it in the libation bowl.

8. Celebration of the Occasion

Bring the baby up to the altar. Touch your finger to the consecrated wine, and place your finger on the baby's lips, saying:

"The blessings of the Lady and Lord are yours, beautiful [Baby]."

Hold the baby up, saying:

"Great Mother, holy Father, bless this child and watch over them.
Care for them, look upon them as they grow, smooth their path,
and make safe their journey in this world. Blessed be!"

All repeat: *"Blessed be."*

Now each guest, one by one, comes to the altar to offer a gift to the baby. The parent(s) hold the baby while this occurs (the parents don't give gifts—parenthood itself is their gift).

The way this works is that the guest in position one comes to the parents. When they do so, everyone moves forward one position. Guest 1 gives the gift, kisses the baby, and moves to position 7 (which has been left empty). In this way, everyone can comfortably move around the circle. When everyone is back in their original position, this portion of the ritual is done.

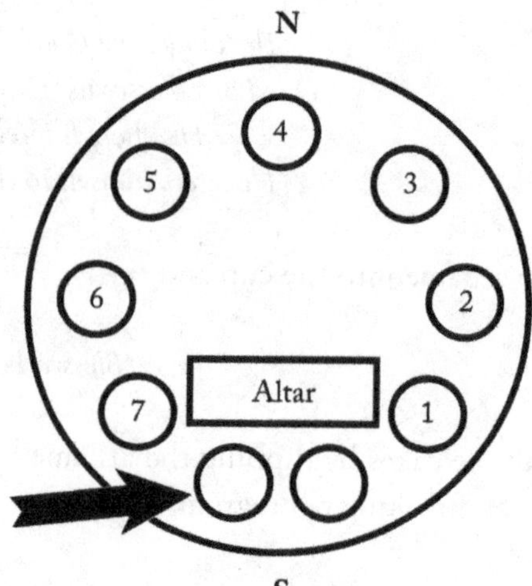

Example:

Guest 1: *"[Baby], I give the gift of strength to face life's challenges. Blessed be."*

All repeat: *"Blessed be."*
Guest 1 kisses baby, moves to position 7.

Guest 2: *"[Baby], I give the gift of song. May your voice always give you pleasure. Blessed be."*
All repeat: *"Blessed be."*
Guest 2 kisses the baby, moves to position seven, while Guest 1 moves to position six.

The leader says:

"The community has blessed this child, but [Baby] will need an additional protector, someone committed to them throughout their life. Is there such a person here?"

Godparent: *"I make that commitment."*

Leader: *"What do you promise to this child?"*

Godparent: *[Gives promise, speaking directly to the child.]*

Leader: *"The Lady and Lord have heard your promise. The community here has heard your promise. May your word be your bond. So mote it be."*

All repeat: "*So mote it be*".

If there is more than one godparent, this is repeated for each.

The godparent now takes the child to the East (if there's more than one, decide in advance who will do this—they can go together, although obviously only one will hold the baby). If there is no godparent present, the priestess or priest can do this.

Godparent: "*Guardian of the East, this is [Baby], blessed of the Lady and the Lord. Bring them knowledge, wisdom, and a strong voice. [Baby], here is springtime, here is a beautiful breeze.*"

Take the child to the South.

Godparent: "*Guardian of the South, this is [Baby], blessed of the Lady and the Lord. Bring them courage, passion, and good health. [Baby], here is summer, here is a sunny day.*"

Take the child to the West.

Godparent: "*Guardian of the West, this is [Baby], blessed of the Lady and the Lord. Bring them love, compassion, and a good heart. [Baby], here is autumn, here are the turning leaves.*"

Take the child to the North.

Godparent: "*Guardian of the North, this is [Baby], blessed of the Lady and the Lord. Bring them strength, commitment, and a powerful body. [Baby], here is winter, here is a snowman, and Santa Claus.*[72] *Here is where all our years end: May that day for you be far, far away.*"

Return to the East.

Godparent: "*But now we return to the East and to Spring. This is how the year is, and soon, you'll learn that for yourself.*"

Leader: "*[Baby] has been blessed by the community and by the gods. [Baby] has received the vows of their godparents and has traveled the wheel of the year. Blessed be [Baby]!*"

All repeat: "*Blessed be [Baby]!*"

9. Closing the Circle

Face North, raise the wand, and say:

"Beloved Lady,
Moonlight and fertile Earth,
You have enriched us with your presence at our Wiccaning rite.
Thank you, and farewell!"

72 In the Northern Hemisphere. Or not at all if you're not into that sort of thing.

All repeat: *"Farewell!"*

"Beloved Lord,
Death and Rebirth,
You have enriched us with your presence at our Wiccaning rite.
Thank you, and farewell!"

All repeat: *"Farewell!"*
Standing at the altar, face the East, draw a banishing pentagram, and say:

"We thank you, Guardian of the East, Guardian of Air
For protecting this Wiccaning rite
Thank you, and farewell!"

All repeat: *"Farewell!"*
Face the South, draw a banishing pentagram, and say:

"We thank you, Guardian of the South, Guardian of Fire
For protecting this Wiccaning rite
Thank you, and farewell!"

All repeat: *"Farewell!"*
Face the West, draw a banishing pentagram, and say:

"We thank you, Guardian of the West, Guardian of Water
For protecting this Wiccaning rite
Thank you, and farewell!"

All repeat: *"Farewell!"*
Face the North, draw a banishing pentagram, and say:

"We thank you, Guardian of the North, Guardian of Earth
For protecting this Wiccaning rite
Thank you, and farewell!"

All repeat: *"Farewell!"*
Face East for a final, silent salute.

Facing the center, say:

"The circle is open but unbroken, the rites are ended.
Merry meet, merry part, and merry meet again!"

All repeat: *"Merry meet, merry part, and merry meet again!"*

A Solitary Wiccaning

If there are two involved parents, it is best if both are a part of this ritual. See the guidance for the community ritual for tips on how to make it baby-friendly.

Before You Begin

- For the offering, find a song or chant (or a few) that feels appropriate to the occasion, such as praising the Mother Goddess. It should be a quieter song, nothing rowdy, in deference to the baby.
- Many parents choose a Pagan name for their baby, just as they choose one for themselves. Have this ready in advance.
- The ritual calls for a single drop of wine to be placed on the baby's lips. If this is uncomfortable for you, use cider instead. If you do use wine, the baby will appreciate it being something sweet.

1. Declaration of Opening

Say:

"This is a special and sacred occasion,
as I bring [Baby] into the community of the Gods."

2. Consecrations

Place your athame into the dish of incense and say:

"In the names of the Lady and Lord,
I consecrate Air that it bring mindfulness to this rite."

Place incense onto the lit charcoal so that smoke begins to rise. Place your athame into the smoke and say:

"In the names of the Lady and Lord,
I consecrate Fire that it bring passion to this rite."

Place your athame into the dish of water and say:

"In the names of the Lady and Lord,
I consecrate Water that it bring feeling to this rite."

Place your athame into the dish of salt and say:

"In the names of the Lady and Lord,
I consecrate Earth that it bring commitment to this rite."

Place three pinches of salt into the water and stir.
Say:

"So mote it be."

3. Cast the Circle

With your athame or sword, go to the East, directing energy to the circle as you say:

"Round and about, round and about, power stay in, world stay out."

Repeat these words over and over until you've returned to the East. Then, walk silently back to the altar.

Pick up the dish of saltwater and return to the East. Wet your fingers and flick drops all the way around the circle, East to East, sprinkling the entire perimeter, saying:

"Round and about, by Water and Earth, I cleanse this circle."

Repeat these words over and over until you've returned to the East. Then, walk silently back to the altar.

Pick up the censer, stirring it up if needed. Return to the East. Cense the perimeter, as you walk again around the circle, East to East, saying:

"Round and about, by Fire and Air, I purify this circle."

Repeat these words over and over until you've returned to the East. Then, walk silently back to the altar.

4. Call the Quarters

Standing at the altar, face East. Point your athame and draw an invoking pentagram, saying:

"I invoke the Guardian of East, the Guardian of Air
Bring sweet winds and beautiful flights
Bring wisdom to my circle and protect us[73] *from harm*
Honor the Lady and Lord with me
At this sacred Wiccaning

73 For solitary rituals, this is normally "me" instead of "us," but here the baby is also in the circle.

Welcome, Guardian! Blessed be."

Turn to face South. Point your athame, and draw an invoking pentagram, saying:

"I invoke the Guardian of South, the Guardian of Fire
Bring warm days and healing fire
Bring strong will to my circle and protect us from harm
Honor the Lady and Lord with me
At this sacred Wiccaning
Welcome, Guardian! Blessed be."

Turn to face West. Point your athame, and draw an invoking pentagram, saying:

"I invoke the Guardian of West, the Guardian of Water
Bring flowing streams and lovely moonlight
Bring deep love to my circle and protect us from harm
Honor the Lady and Lord with me
At this sacred Wiccaning
Welcome, Guardian! Blessed be."

Turn to face North. Point your athame, and draw an invoking pentagram, saying:

"I invoke the Guardian of North, the Guardian of Earth
Bring rich soil and good homes
Bring stability to my circle and protect us from harm
Honor the Lady and Lord with me
At this sacred Wiccaning
Welcome, Guardian! Blessed be."

Turn again to face East for a final, silent salute. (There's no need to invoke.)

5. Invoking the Gods

Say:

"Beloved Mother and Father of us all
Protector of all children
Guardians of the Wicca
Come to this sacred rite and welcome a new child into your care
Beloved Lady
Beloved Lord
Come to us and be glad
Sing with me and be joyful!
Welcome! Blessed be!"

6. Offerings

Begin your song of offering. Sing it until the energy feels wonderful and let it gently fade.

7. Cakes and Wine

Say:

"The Lady and Lord have heard my song of praise and offer their blessings to us."

Hold the cup and say:

"The cup, the Goddess, the blood of life
Our Lady blesses us with all good things
She offers herself to us
She offers herself to the God."

Hold the athame over the cup and say:

"The blade, the God, the force of life
Our Lord blesses us with all good things
He offers himself to us
He offers himself to the Goddess."

Plunge the athame into the cup and say:

"Blessed be."

Consecrate the cakes by dipping the athame into the wine and sprinkling drops onto the cakes, forming an invoking pentagram. Say:

"Lady and Lord, you bless us with abundance
The Earth gives us all we need
We thank you.
Blessed be."

Take a cake or a portion of whatever food is on the plate and place it in the libation bowl.

8. Celebration of the Occasion

Bring the baby up to the altar. Touch your finger to the consecrated wine, and place your finger on the baby's lips, saying:

"The blessings of the Lady and Lord are yours, beautiful [Baby]."

Hold the baby up, saying:

"Great Mother, holy Father, bless this child and watch over them. Care for them, look upon them as they grow, smooth their path, and make safe their journey in this world. Blessed be!"

Take the child to the East.
Say:

"Guardian of the East, this is [Baby], blessed of the Lady and the Lord.
Bring them knowledge, wisdom, and a strong voice
[Baby], here is springtime, here is a beautiful breeze."

Take the child to the South.
Say:

"Guardian of the South, this is [Baby], blessed of the Lady and the Lord. Bring them courage, passion, and good health. [Baby], here is summer, here is a sunny day."

Take the child to the West.
Say:

"Guardian of the West, this is [Baby], blessed of the Lady and the Lord.
Bring them love, compassion, and a good heart.
[Baby], here is autumn, here are the turning leaves."

Take the child to the North.
Say:

"Guardian of the North, this is [Baby], blessed of the Lady and the Lord. Bring them strength, commitment, and a powerful body. [Baby], here is winter, here is a snowman, and Santa Claus.[74] *Here is where all our years end: May that day for you be far, far away."*

Return to the East.
Say:

"But now we return to the East and to Spring.
This is how the year is, and soon, you'll learn that for yourself.
[Baby] has been blessed by the gods. [Baby] has traveled the wheel of the year.
Blessed be [Baby]!"

74 See footnote 73

9. Closing the Circle

Face North, raise the wand, and say:

"Beloved Lady,
Moonlight and fertile Earth,
You have enriched us with your presence at this Wiccaning rite.
Thank you, and farewell!
Beloved Lord,
Death and Rebirth,
You have enriched us with your presence at this Wiccaning rite.
Thank you, and farewell!"

Face the East, draw a banishing pentagram, and say:

"I thank you, Guardian of the East, Guardian of Air
For protecting this Wiccaning rite
Thank you, and farewell!"

Face the South, draw a banishing pentagram, and say:

"I thank you, Guardian of the South, Guardian of Fire
For protecting this Wiccaning rite
Thank you, and farewell!"

Face the West, draw a banishing pentagram, and say:

"I thank you, Guardian of the West, Guardian of Water
For protecting this Wiccaning rite
Thank you, and farewell!"

Face the North, draw a banishing pentagram, and say:

"I thank you, Guardian of the North, Guardian of Earth
For protecting this Wiccaning rite
Thank you, and farewell!"

Face East for a final, silent salute.
Facing the center, say:

"The circle is open but unbroken, the rites are ended.
Merry meet, merry part, and merry meet again!"

Initiation, Dedication, Naming, and Recognition

Many years ago, I was on the phone with Scott Cunningham, and (as we often did) we were poking fun at each other. He was teasing me that, as a Gardnerian, I thought there was no such thing as self-initiation. My retort was that "initiation" just isn't a standalone word. "Initiation into *what*?" I said. "Good point!" he responded.

Scott left this earth in 1993, but his writing remains influential, and largely because of his influence, many people self-initiate. Nonetheless, my question stands.

Words mean things. Isaac Bonewits defined three basic kinds of initiation ceremony: 1) Initiation as a recognition of a status already gained, 2) Initiation as an ordeal of transformation, and 3) Initiation as a method for transferring spiritual knowledge and power.

What does that mean in Wicca? Pretty clearly, the third type requires other people, someone to transfer the knowledge to the initiate. The first type usually requires other people as well. "Recognition" generally means someone else recognizes you. People who perform self-initiation ceremonies sometimes mean this type—they realize they have achieved something and wish to acknowledge it for themselves. Perhaps they are marking an anniversary of time spent practicing Wicca, or they've had a significant spiritual experience they wish to commemorate.

The second type, the ordeal, can happen alone or with others. It can even happen accidentally. This is where you might combine types one and two: You might have been through a traumatic experience that changed you spiritually (ordeal) and wish to mark it ritually thereafter (recognition).

In the 1980s and 1990s, I several times had the experience of meeting someone who had performed a self-initiation (ordeal, recognition, or both). They insisted—sometimes belligerently—that they were therefore entitled to the initiatory knowledge I possessed. Unfortunately, that's not how it works. Fortunately, I don't run into that misapprehension much anymore.

I'll add that there's a fourth type: Initiation as entry into a tradition. This is what you're being initiated *into*. Isaac didn't spell this out because the ceremony itself is still structured around one or more of the other three. You pass through the door of initiation into a tradition either because of the status you've gained or by experiencing an ordeal, or both, and having done so, you are given knowledge unique to that tradition.

I will not be providing a self-initiation ritual for a number of reasons:

- Initiation into a tradition is specific to that tradition, and the only ritual that is meaningful for it is the one performed in the context of that tradition. Some traditions (such as Seax-Wicca) allow for self-initiation, but the ceremony would still be specific, and not something I can write a generic version of.
- Ordeals carry risk, either real or symbolic. I have no intention to send you off alone to do something dangerous. Thank me later.
- Passing of knowledge and power is something that only happens in a group, and those who do the passing will determine when and how to do that—it's not up to me.

Recognition

That leaves recognition—or self-recognition. There are many such ceremonies. Most people don't realize that *b'nai*[75] *mitzvah*—a Jewish coming-of-age ceremony—isn't necessary to the coming-of-age *event*. A Jewish boy is a *bar mitzvah*—a person responsible for keeping the commandments—whether he has the ceremony or not. It happened automatically when he turned thirteen. The ceremony is primarily a recognition of this achievement.

There are many forms of recognition rituals. Indeed, many rites of passage are a recognition of some sort: You are marking that something has changed. Some rites—handfasting, Wiccaning, initiation into a tradition—*effect* the change, but others simply mark that it has already happened. That doesn't mean recognition rituals aren't meaningful. Indeed, it is often true that you don't really *feel* the change until after the ceremony. Recognition in front of a community can be especially powerful, but that isn't available to every Wiccan, many of whom are isolated.

Recognition that you are dedicated to a path, or to the service of the gods, or to the service of a particular deity, is a dedication ceremony.

Recognition of a particular event often has some kind of marker. You might take a new name, or begin wearing a specific piece of jewelry, or get a new tattoo. In the case of the name and the jewelry, you might use them all the time, or just during ritual (you're stuck with the tattoo). Sometimes taking on the marker is all you need—here's my tattoo, my passage has been marked—but sometimes you also want or need a more formal ceremony.

The ceremonies that follow mark significant passages for a group or a solitary. Such ceremonies are deeply personal, and you should change them to suit both you and the specific occasion.

Sometimes ceremonies combine. You could do a naming ceremony or take a new name during a self-dedication ritual, or do a recognition ritual and take a new name during *that*, or add a marker of some kind to your dedication or to your naming or to your recognition... the math of these variations is getting away from me, but there are a *lot*.

What's important here is that these ceremonies are for you and are meant for you to embrace and take ownership of them. This is especially true of a recognition ceremony. There are so many things this could encompass! It could be a new job, graduation, transition, coming out, or completing menopause—too many options to name. Some of these require whole ceremonies—I've been to hugely elaborate menopause rituals, for example—but some can be incorporated into an esbat. So, while I can provide a script for dedication and naming, I'll merely offer a framework that I hope will inspire your creativity for recognition.

The framework for recognition here is for a group ritual. A solitary recognition could be anything. It could be laden with symbolism from beginning to end, or it could be short and sweet. Use the solitary dedication and naming ceremonies to get a feel for a possible structure.

A Group Recognition Ritual

This version of recognition is designed to be a part of a regular group esbat ritual and would be

75 *Bar mitzvah* for a boy, *bat* or *bas mitzvah* for a girl. *B'nai mitzvah* is the plural and is used when more than one person has the ceremony at once—like twins. Many people have begun using *b'nai mitzvah* as a nonbinary formulation—like having they/them pronouns, the plural is the way to make it gender neutral.

done right after cakes and wine. So, for this ritual, we'll just show the "Celebration of the Occasion" part, and you'll fill in the rest from your preferred version of casting and closing the circle.

If your group normally sits and chats as part of cakes and wine, this happens before that. You would start immediately after everyone makes an offering from the cup.

In this ritual, a person is designated as "leader." If the person being recognized is also the leader, someone else leads for this occasion.

The celebrant (the person being recognized) and the group leader(s) should consult in advance about the meaning of the occasion.

You should also examine any symbolism you might want to add to the ceremony.

Simple symbolism can also be powerful. Standing on your toes for part of the ceremony can symbolize rising up, spinning around in a circle can symbolize turning your life around, wearing and then removing a blindfold can symbolize stepping into a new, unknown life. Explore in conversation and meditation what exactly this recognition symbolizes to the celebrant, and how best to express it.

8. Celebration of the Occasion: Recognition

Leader:

"Tonight is a special night. Tonight, we recognize
[name] on the occasion of [reason]. Come before us [name]."

The celebrant comes to the south of the altar, standing with the leader(s).

The leader first speaks about the meaning of this recognition, as planned.

Next, the leader asks the celebrant if they're willing to proceed.

For example:

"Knowing this, Amethyst, do you freely choose
to step into your new life as a part of the LGBTQI community?"

Celebrant: *"I do."*

Leader: *"I call upon the Lady and the Lord to witness and recognize [celebrant] as [new status]."*

The leader and celebrant now proceed with whatever symbolizes the rebirth, transformation, or recognition. Perhaps the celebrant was blindfolded when they first stepped forward, and the leader now spins them around three times and removes the blindfold. Perhaps all join hands and shout a phrase symbolic of the change, three times, and then say, "So mote it be!" Perhaps the celebrant disrobes to enter this new life phase naked as a newborn.

The leader now picks up the censer and censes the person, head to feet and back again.

The leader[76] now picks up the water dish and sprinkles the person with saltwater, flicking

76 If the group is led by a priestess and priest, or any two people, they could each cense and then each sprinkle, or divide it up, one leader doing the censing and one doing the sprinkling.

water drops from their fingers all over the person, head to feet and back again.

The leader says:

"By Air, by Fire, by Water, and by Earth, you are consecrated as [new status]."

The leader now leads the celebrant to the quarters: East, then South, then West, then North, at each quarter saying:

"Hear ye, O Guardian of the [East/South/West/North].
[Celebrant] is now [status]. Blessed be!"

All repeat: *"Blessed be."*
Stop for a silent nod as you return to the East, then go back to the altar.

Leader: "It is done! So mote it be!"

All repeat: *"So mote it be!"*
Hugs all around are appropriate.

Self-Dedication

This is a solitary ritual, but a group could perform a dedication, each individual dedicating themselves.

This ritual assumes dedication to Wicca and to the Lady and Lord. The ritual script here also uses a variation on consecrations and quarter callings, just to give additional options.

Before You Begin

- What does dedication mean to you? Think about this, meditate on it, and journal about it, for at least a full month before performing the ceremony. Are you dedicated to the Lord and Lady? To Wicca? To Paganism? Why? For how long? Under what conditions?
- Go through this script carefully in advance, examining it against the answers you've discovered about your own dedication. It will almost certainly require changes to personalize it.
- For this variation of the consecrations, have each ritual item and its corresponding tool in its quarter—the dish of incense and the athame in the East, the censer and wand in the South, the dish of water and the cup in the West, and the dish of salt and the pentagram in the North.
- This is a celebration! Clean and decorate with special care. Have the nicest flowers you can find on the altar. Have all fresh, new candles, never before used. It would be ideal to have something else new—a new altar cloth or new candle holders, for example.
- If you will have a physical marker for your dedication—such as a piece of jewelry, have it near the altar.

1. Declaration of Opening

Say:

"Tonight, I dedicate myself to the Wicca. May the Lady and Lord bless my path."

2. Consecrations

Go to the East. Pick up the athame in your right[77] hand and the incense in your left, and say:

"By the powers of the East and the powers of my magical tools,
let this Air be consecrated."

Return to the altar and put these items down. Take a pinch of incense to the South. Place the pinch of incense onto the lit charcoal in the South. Pick up the wand in your right hand and the smoking censer in your left, and say:

"By the powers of the South and the powers of my magical tools,
let this Fire be consecrated."

Return to the altar and put these items down. Go to the West. Pick up the cup in your right hand and the water dish in your left, and say:

"By the powers of the West and the powers of my magical tools,
let this Water be consecrated."

Return to the altar and put these items down. Go to the North. Pick up the Pentacle in your right hand and the salt dish in your left, and say:

"By the powers of the North and the powers of my magical tools,
let this Earth be consecrated."

Return to the altar and put these items down. Place a pinch of salt into the water dish and stir it up.

3. Cast the Circle

With your athame or sword, go to the East, directing energy to the circle as you say:

"By Air, Fire, Water, and Earth do I cast this circle. This is a holy space. This is a safe space. This is a space of dedication. By Air, Fire, Water, and Earth do I cast this circle. So mote it be."

77 If you are left-handed, you may wish to switch this for all four tools, holding the tool in the hand with which you normally use it.

Return to the altar.

Pick up the dish of saltwater and return to the East. Wet your fingers and flick drops all the way around the circle, East to East, sprinkling the entire perimeter in silence.

Return to the altar.

Pick up the censer, stirring it up if needed. Return to the East. Cense the perimeter, as you walk again around the circle, East to East, in silence.

Return to the altar.

4. Call the Quarters

In the East, face out, point your athame, and draw an invoking pentagram, saying:

"I invoke the Guardian of East, the Guardian of Air
Guard and watch over me as I dedicate myself in this sacred space.
Welcome, Guardian! Blessed be."

In the South, face out, point your athame, and draw an invoking pentagram, saying:

"I invoke the Guardian of South, the Guardian of Fire
Guard and watch over me as I dedicate myself in this sacred space.
Welcome, Guardian! Blessed be."

In the West, face out, point your athame, and draw an invoking pentagram, saying:

"I invoke the Guardian of West, the Guardian of Water
Guard and watch over me as I dedicate myself in this sacred space.
Welcome, Guardian! Blessed be."

In the North, face out, point your athame, and draw an invoking pentagram, saying:

"I invoke the Guardian of North, the Guardian of Earth
Guard and watch over me as I dedicate myself in this sacred space.
Welcome, Guardian! Blessed be."

Walk back to the East for a final, silent salute. (There's no need to invoke.)

5. Invoking the Gods

Say:

"Beloved Lady and Lord
You who have guided me to this moment
You who are strong, and wise, and hold me in your loving embrace
Be here tonight

Come to this rite
As I dedicate myself to your service and to the Wicca
Mother and Father of us all
Whom I so deeply need
Hear my call and answer me.
Welcome! Blessed be!"

6. Offerings

Add additional incense to the censer, saying:

"Lady and Lord, I offer sweet smoke to you."

Lift up the flowers, saying:

"Lady and Lord, I offer these beautiful flowers to you."

Stand before the altar, open your arms wide in a gesture of giving and say:

"Lady and Lord, I offer myself as a dedicant to you."

Continue to offer as moved—sing, dance, play music as you see fit.

7. Cakes and Wine

Hold the cup and say:

"The cup, the Goddess, the blood of life
Our Lady blesses me with all good things
She offers herself to me
She offers herself to the God."

Hold the athame over the cup and say:

"The blade, the God, the force of life
Our Lord blesses me with all good things
He offers himself to me
He offers himself to the Goddess."
Plunge the athame into the cup and say:
"Blessed be."

Consecrate the cakes by dipping the athame into the wine and sprinkling drops onto the cakes, forming an invoking pentagram. Say:

"Lady and Lord, you bless me with abundance
The Earth gives me all I need
I thank you.
Blessed be."

Take a cake and place it in the libation bowl. If you are outdoors, the cake goes directly into the fire.

Lift the cup and speak from the heart. Speak specifically about your dedication and your journey. The following is an example, but it is important that the words are your own:

"Beloved Lady and Lord, I pour this libation
to you just as I offer myself as a dedicant to you.
Lady and Lord, I thank you for bringing me to this moment."

Pour and then drink.

After the ritual is over, the contents of the libation bowl should be poured out onto the Earth. If the ritual is outdoors, then libations are poured directly onto the Earth, and a libation bowl is not needed.

8. Celebration of the Occasion

Say:

"Lady and Lord, I have received your wine and cake.
My body and heart are full of your blessings.
I offer myself in dedication to your service, as one of the Wicca."

(Here, you should change my words to your own, based on your meditations on what this means to you.)

Optional:

"In token of which, I ..."

Here is where you acknowledge a new piece of jewelry you will wear, or a new name you will take (although that can be a separate ceremony, it can be a part of this ceremony as well), or a new tattoo[78] you have.

Example:

"In token of which, I consecrate this necklace,
which I will wear in all rituals henceforth, as a sign of my dedication."

78 For a new tattoo, don't consecrate it until it has healed. Saltwater on an open wound is no fun.

(Sprinkle the necklace with saltwater.)

"I consecrate this token by Water and Earth."

(Pass the necklace through the incense smoke.)

"I consecrate this token by Fire and Air."

Put on the necklace.

If you are robed, remove the robe. You will do this portion of the ritual skyclad.

Touch your third eye, heart, and hands with saltwater, saying:

"By Water and Earth do I become a dedicant of the Wicca."

Cense your third eye, heart, and hands with incense smoke, saying:

"By Water and Earth do I become a dedicant of the Wicca."

Dip your fingers into the consecrated wine. Touch the wine to your feet, saying:

"I shall walk in the ways of the Wicca."

Touch the wine to your knees, saying:

"I shall kneel at the altar of the Lady and the Lord."

Touch the wine to the top of your pubic bone, saying:

"From the source of life, I dedicate myself to the Wicca."

Touch the wine to your heart, saying:

"I shall love the Lady and the Lord always."

Touch the wine to your lips, saying:

*"I shall speak words of devotion to the Lady and the Lord.
So Mote it Be."*

Go to the East and say:

"Guardians of the East, see before you a new dedicant to the Wicca."

Go to the South and say:

"Guardians of the South, see before you a new dedicant to the Wicca."

Go to the West and say:

"Guardians of the West, see before you a new dedicant to the Wicca."

Go to the North and say:

"Guardians of the North, see before you a new dedicant to the Wicca."

Return to the East for a silent nod before returning to the altar.
At this point, you may want to sit and celebrate for a while before closing the circle.

9. Closing the Circle

Face North, raise the wand, and say:

"Beloved Lady,
Moonlight in fullness
Fertile Earth,
I thank you for all you have given me this night.
Thank you, and farewell!
Beloved Lord,
Death and rebirth,
I thank you for all you have given me this night.
Thank you, and farewell!"

Go to the East, draw a banishing pentagram, and say:

"Thank you, Guardian of the East, Guardian of Air
For protecting this dedication rite
Thank you, and farewell!"

Go to the South, draw a banishing pentagram, and say:

"Thank you, Guardian of the South, Guardian of Fire
For protecting this dedication rite
Thank you, and farewell!"

Go to the West, draw a banishing pentagram, and say:

"Thank you, Guardian of the West, Guardian of Water

For protecting this dedication rite
Thank you, and farewell!"

Go to the North, draw a banishing pentagram, and say:

"Thank you, Guardian of the North, Guardian of Earth
For protecting this dedication rite
Thank you, and farewell!"

Facing the center, say:

"The circle is open but unbroken, the rites are ended.
Merry meet, merry part, and merry meet again!"

Naming

There are lots of reasons to take a new name. It might be the marker used for a dedication or another recognition ritual. Many people take a new name as their entry into Paganism. In my Pagan group, you are not required to take a new name (it takes some people forever to come up with one), but if you have one, you may *only* be referred to in circle by that name. In some groups, giving the new name is part of a ritual of dedication or entry into the group.

Names might be changed for more practical reasons, like to match your gender. Or it might simply be a part of a spiritual transformation—you are no longer the person who had the old name. In any event, it is important that the gods and spirits you meet in ritual know you by the proper name. Names, after all, are considered a vital magical connection to the person who has them. In many traditions worldwide, they're considered a vital component in healing—you cannot heal a person without knowing their name, and naming them connects directly to their life force. (This is one reason that many people keep their Pagan or magical name secret.)

When doing a naming ritual, it's important *not* to put any negative energy onto the old name, if for no other reason than that, from time to time, someone is bound to call you by the wrong name, and you don't want that negativity to redound to you.

How to Choose a New Name

Some people know right away what their new name will be, and some people agonize over it.

A name can be aspirational: It can represent something you are working to achieve, such as a musician taking the name of a musician they admire or taking the name of a god or spirit of music, like Euterpe, the Muse of music and song. An aspirational name can be for a skill such as music, a quality such as beauty or strength, a spiritual condition, or any other quality.

A name can be descriptive: It can be exactly who you are, especially who you are when you feel most powerful, most yourself, or most joyful. It can represent your values, your history, who you are as a person, or who you are as a witch.

A name can be balancing: You can ground and balance yourself with a name that is the opposite of some of your most visible characteristics. I know a very "extra" person who took a very simple magical name as a form of grounding and balance.

Most importantly, when being called that name, it should *feel good.* You should *want* to respond to that particular "hey you."

Sources of Names

There are many places to find a name. For example:

- Mythology
- Nature, including stones, gems, plants, geographic features, places, or weather
- Magical systems such as alchemy, Kabbalah, Tarot, or runes
- Fiction
- Family names
- History
- Numerology (I know someone who simply figured out what he wanted his name to add up to in numerology and then experimented with letter combinations to achieve that until he liked the sound).
- Culture, especially combined with one of the others. So, if you have a particular connection to Ireland, and you love quartz crystals, you could translate "quartz" into Irish Gaelic and take the name *Grianchloch.*

A Group Naming Ritual

Like the group recognition ceremony, this can be incorporated into a regular group esbat rite and would be performed right after cakes and wine. Despite the profound meaning of a new name, the power of the name often exists in *using* it, so it is not an elaborate ceremony.

As with the group recognition, we'll jump straight to the "Celebration of the Occasion" part of the ritual script, and you'll fill in the rest.

This part starts immediately after everyone makes an offering from the cup.

In this ritual, a person is designated as "leader." If the person taking the new name is also the leader, someone else leads for this occasion.

As with most Wiccan rituals, it is traditional for this to be cross-gender, a priestess giving the new name to a man, and a priest renaming a woman. If you are following this tradition, then use the gender of the new name, so that if a trans woman is taking a new name to match her gender (e.g., changing from "John" to "Jane"), you conduct the entire ceremony treating her as a woman, even before she gets the new name.

8. Celebration of the Occasion: A New Name

Leader: *"Is there one among us who is taking a new name?"*[79]

Person taking the name: *"I am."*

Leader: *"Then, come forward and be blessed."*

The person taking the new name comes to the south of the altar, standing with the leader(s).

Leader: *"I call upon the Lady and the Lord to look upon [old name], their beloved worshiper, and bless them with a new name. By what name shall you be known [among us]?"*[80]

Person: *[Gives the new name.]*

Leader: *"I name you [new name]."*

The leader picks up the censer and censes the person, head to feet and back again.

"By Air and Fire, be consecrated in the name [new name]."

The leader picks up the water dish, and sprinkles the person with saltwater, flicking water drops from their fingers all over the person, head to feet and back again.

"By Water and Earth, be consecrated in the name [new name].
Beloved Lady, Mighty Lord, this is [new name].
Bless [new name] and embrace [him/her/them] as your own."

The leader now leads the renamed person to the quarters, East, then South, then West, then North, at each quarter saying:

"Hear ye, O Guardian of the [East/South/West/North].
This is [new name]. Blessed be!"

All repeat: *"Blessed be.*

Stop for a silent nod as you return to the East, then go back to the altar.

Leader: *"I have given you a new name. By Air, Fire, Water, and Earth, you have been consecrated as [new name]. The Lady and Lord and the Guardians of the Elements now recognize you as [new name]. You are [new name]. So mote it be!"*

---

79 If more than one person is taking a name, it is done one at a time and repeated for each person.
80 Here "among us" means "among the Wicca," or "in Pagan ritual" or "in this group." If the name is to be used in all of life, omit these words.

All repeat: *"So mote it be!"*

Hugs all around are appropriate. Each person who hugs the newly named person should call them by the new name.

A Solitary Naming Ritual

While a group naming ritual can be incorporated into your normal esbat, a solitary naming is almost certainly a singular occasion, created from beginning to end for the purpose of taking the new name.

For this ritual, I've added a lot of formality to the language. Some people (me) love "thee" and "thou," while some people find it off-putting. Most of the rituals in this book have used natural, modern language. But it's only right to include one ritual that goes in another direction.

Before You Begin

- Obviously, have the name picked out.
- As with the rite of dedication, this is a personal celebration, so choose an appropriate song or two to sing, or music to play, or a poem to recite, or some other personal, heartfelt offering.
- Beautiful flowers should also be a part of this rite.

1. Declaration of Opening

Say:

> *"Tonight, I will cast the circle as [old name], but I will close the circle with a new name. Blessed be this moment of change!"*

2. Consecrations

Place your athame into the dish of incense and say:

> *"O Air, I do consecrate thee in the names of the Lady and Lord,*
> *that thou bringest mindfulness to this, my circle."*

Place incense onto the lit charcoal so that smoke begins to rise. Place your athame into the smoke and say:

> *"O Fire, I do consecrate thee in the names of the Lady and Lord,*
> *that thou bringest passion to this, my circle."*

Place your athame into the dish of water and say:

"O Water, I do consecrate thee in the names of the Lady and Lord,
that thou bringest love to this, my circle."

Place your athame into the dish of salt and say:

"O Earth, I do consecrate thee in the names of the Lady and Lord,
that thou bringest stability to this, my circle.

Place three pinches of salt into the water and stir.
Say:

"So mote it be."

3. Cast the Circle

With your athame or sword, go to the East, directing energy to the circle as you say:

"O circle, I do cast and consecrate thee, in the names of the Lady and the Lord, that thou beist a holy place, sealed and strong, in which I shall perform my sacred work. O circle, be thou a space between the world of humankind and the worlds of the gods. So mote it be."

Return to the altar.

Pick up the dish of saltwater and return to the East. Wet your fingers and flick drops all the way around the circle, East to East, sprinkling the entire perimeter in silence.

Return to the altar.

Pick up the censer, stirring it up if needed. Return to the East. Cense the perimeter, as you walk again around the circle, East to East, in silence.

Return to the altar.

4. Call the Quarters

In the East, face out, point your athame, and draw an invoking pentagram, saying:

"I invoke thee, O Guardian of East, Guardian of Air
Bring sweet winds and beautiful flights
Bring wisdom to my circle and protect me from harm
Honor the Lady and Lord with me at this naming rite
Welcome, Guardian! Blessed be."

In the South, face out, point your athame, and draw an invoking pentagram, saying:

"I invoke thee, O Guardian of South, Guardian of Fire
Bring warm days and healing fire to me

Bring strong will to my circle and protect me from harm
Honor the Lady and Lord with me at this naming rite
Welcome, Guardian! Blessed be."

In the West, face out, point your athame, and draw an invoking pentagram, saying:

"I invoke thee, O Guardian of West, Guardian of Water
Bring flowing streams and lovely moonlight
Bring deep love to my circle and protect me from harm
Honor the Lady and Lord with me at this naming rite
Welcome, Guardian! Blessed be."

In the North, face out, point your athame, and draw an invoking pentagram, saying:

"I invoke thee, O Guardian of North, Guardian of Earth
Bring rich soil and good homes
Bring stability to my circle and protect me from harm
Honor the Lady and Lord with me at this naming rite
Welcome, Guardian! Blessed be."

Walk back to the East for a final, silent salute.

5. Invoking the Gods

Face North, raise the wand, and say:

"Beloved Lady
Thou who art wise and kind
Thou who art Maiden, Mother, and Crone,
Thou who art the stars in the heavens and the Earth at my feet
Be here tonight
Come to this, my rite, as I take a new name.
Beloved Lord
Thou who art wild and free
Thou who art Death and Rebirth
Thou who art the sky above and bread on my table
Be here tonight
Come to this, my rite, as I take a new name
O Goddess, O God,
Join me!
Welcome! Blessed be!"

6. Offerings

Add additional incense to the censer, saying:

"Lady and Lord, I offer sweet smoke to thee."

Lift up the flowers, saying:

"Lady and Lord, I offer these beautiful flowers to thee."

Continue to offer as moved—sing, dance, play music as you see fit.

7. Cakes and Wine

Hold the cup and say:

"The cup, the Goddess, the blood of life
Our Lady blesses me with all good things
She offers herself to me
She offers herself to the God."

Hold the athame over the cup and say:

"The blade, the God, the force of life
Our Lord blesses me with all good things
He offers himself to me
He offers himself to the Goddess."

Plunge the athame into the cup and say:

"Blessed be."

Consecrate the cakes by dipping the athame into the wine and sprinkling drops onto the cakes, forming an invoking pentagram.

Say:

"Lady and Lord, thou who hast blessed me with abundance
Thy Earth giveth me all I need
I thank thee.
Blessed be."

Take a cake and place it in the libation bowl. If you are outdoors, the cake goes directly into the fire.

Speak from the heart, saying something like:

"Lady and Lord, I thank thee for bringing me to this moment."

Pour and then drink.

After the ritual is over, the contents of the libation bowl should be poured out onto the Earth. If the ritual is outdoors, then libations are poured directly onto the Earth and a bowl is not needed.

8. Celebration of the Occasion: A New Name

Stand before the altar and meditate for a moment, taking several deep, cleansing breaths.

Say:

"Beloved Lady, beloved Lord
I have taken the blessing of thy wine and cake
But there is another blessing that I ask
The blessing of a new name.
From today forward, I shall be known as [name].
Bless me in this new name and let it be a boon to me."

Pick up the censer, and cense yourself, head to feet and back again, saying:

"By Air and Fire, I am consecrated in the name [new name]."

Pick up the water dish, and sprinkle yourself with saltwater, flicking water drops from your fingertips, head to feet and back again, saying:

"By Water and Earth, I am consecrated in the name [new name]."

Now go to the quarters, East, then South, then West, then North, at each quarter saying:

"Hear ye, O Guardian of the [East/South/West/North].
I am now [new name]. Blessed be!"

Stop for a silent nod as you return to the East, then go back to the altar.

Pick up the cup and say:

"I offered to thee and received blessings in my old name. Now I, [new name], offer a libation of thanksgiving to the Lady and the Lord. Blessed be!"

Pour and then drink.

9. Closing the Circle

Face North, raise the wand, and say:

"Beloved Lady, wise and kind
Thou hast blessed me
Thank you and farewell!
Beloved Lord, wild and free
Thou hast blessed me
Thank you and farewell!"

Go to the East, face out, and with your athame, draw a banishing pentagram, saying:

"I thank thee, O Guardian of East, Guardian of Air
For thy protection at this naming rite
Thank you and farewell!"

Go to the South, face out, and with your athame, draw a banishing pentagram, saying:

"I thank thee, O Guardian of South, Guardian of Fire
For thy protection at this naming rite
Thank you and farewell!"

Go to the West, face out, and with your athame, draw a banishing pentagram, saying:

"I thank thee, O Guardian of West, Guardian of Water
For thy protection at this naming rite
Thank you and farewell!"

Go to the North, face out, and with your athame, draw a banishing pentagram, saying:

"I thank thee, O Guardian of North, Guardian of Earth
For thy protection at this naming rite
Thank you and farewell!"

Walk back to the East for a final, silent salute.

Handfasting

Handfasting, generally speaking, is the term for a Pagan or Wiccan wedding. Historically, it might mean an informal wedding (not sanctioned by state authorities), a betrothal, or a temporary marriage. In modern Pagan usage, it almost always means a wedding (the traditionally permanent kind) performed in a Pagan religious setting.

The word "handfast" originally meant a contract sealed by shaking or joining hands. Today, Pagans literally tie their hands together with a cord or ribbon as part of the handfasting ceremony. The cord might be elaborately braided or decorated and kept as a wedding memento.

Weddings, as we all know, can be extravagant or simple, highly orchestrated or thrown together. Handfastings are no exception. They are extremely individual. In preparing to write this section, I have gone through my folder of the many handfastings I have performed or been a part of—each is very different.

Factors That Change a Handfasting

What are the things that make handfastings different from one another? Well, the people. Each person who marries is an individual, but let's look a little more closely:

- The people getting married could be a man and a woman, a same-sex couple, a couple with one or more non-binary people, a polyamorous group, or a couple within a polyamorous group (that is, two people are marrying each other, but one or both already has a spouse).
- The guests could be very familiar with Paganism and Wicca, or completely unfamiliar, or (typically) a mixture of both.
- There could be children of one or more of the betrothed who are involved in the ceremony.
- The handfasting could be a large affair or an intimate one. My handfasting to Professor Spouse had about 120 guests. Professor Spouse's handfasting to her previous wife had about ten guests. Headcount alone makes the ceremonies very different.
- How much of a traditional secular or other religious ceremony do the betrothed wish to incorporate? I was priestess at a handfasting where the bride's father very much wanted to give her away. That's not normally part of a Pagan ritual, but I found a way to incorporate it into the ceremony.

The Steps of a Handfasting

1. If there are non-Pagan guests in attendance, the declaration of opening should include an introduction to what will happen, a sort of quick, "What is Wicca?"
2. The circle is cast and the quarters are called more or less as usual, but with a focus on the occasion.
3. When the gods are invoked, they are usually invoked specifically as gods of love. Often, married pairs of deities are named, drawing on any number of Pagan cultures and stories (such as Dagda and Boyne, Shiva and Parvati, Nuit and Geb, or Odin and Freya). As these pairs are almost always heterosexual, Professor Spouse and I skipped that part.
4. The betrothed are welcomed into the circle. This can be a simple procession or more elaborate. At one handfasting I was a part of, we constructed litters, and the bride and groom were carried in on those litters by their attendants. At another, the groom traveled to the North, East, and South, defeating a ritual combatant in each quarter, until greeting his bride in the West (the quarter associated with love). Professor Spouse and I had a more conventional procession: She walked in first and stood with her best man, then I came in on my adult daughter's arm, followed by my maid of honor.
5. The gods are then evoked onto the betrothed. Again, this is often quite heteronormative. The bride is charged as the Goddess, and the presence of the Goddess is invoked upon her, exalting her. Then the groom is charged as the God and the presence of the God is invoked upon him, exalting him. Each can then be instructed to see the Goddess/God in the other.

A less gender-specific charge can be used instead.

I will offer a "traditional" invocation in the ritual below, with the bride as the Goddess and the groom as the God. If you choose to go a less gender-normative route, you'll still be able to use this as a model.

6. A homily or instruction can now be given to the bride and groom, and other readings can be added.
7. The rings are consecrated.
8. The couple's hands are bound together, and a blessing is said over the couple.
9. Vows and rings are exchanged.
10. They are declared married.
11. Their hands are untied, and the athame and cup are handed to the new couple, who perform the rite of Cakes and Wine.
12. The couple leaves the circle, jumping the broom.
13. The normal circle closing is performed.

Marriage Vows

Your most powerful magical tool is your word. Words are the source of a huge percentage of magic. It is, therefore, incredibly important that witches are careful with their words, especially their promises. When I say, "So mote it be" (or "so be it") in ritual, the power of my word backs the statement, this *shall be done* because *I said so.*

If we promise things casually and inattentively, the power of our word is diminished. If I routinely promise to be on time but I am consistently late, if I promise my friend I'll do her a favor and then renege, if I promise to do the dishes and leave them sitting in the sink, then my word is disempowered. The universe, and my inner self, don't take my word seriously because there is evidence that my word cannot be counted on. For this reason, all practitioners of magic should make an effort to be reliable and to be accountable when they don't keep their word (which is sometimes unavoidable).

If this is true of our word in general, how much weightier is the word we give before the gods, in sacred space! When we ask the gods to be witness to the word we give, we truly must take it seriously.

A marriage vow is a word given in sacred space.

Since we're taking that vow, we should examine it carefully. What am I promising? Will I keep this promise, or be accountable if I break it? Is it meaningful? True vows have consequences when you break them, such that it matters to you to keep them and pay attention to the fact that they exist. When we take such a vow, we aren't guaranteeing our own perfection, but if we break it, we have to clean up the mess we made. We have to atone, ask forgiveness, forgive ourselves, and only then move on.

Here are questions to ask when creating a vow: Does the vow mean something? Does it hold me accountable? Is it specific enough so that it can be kept? Does it have parameters that define it?

Let's look at the best-known wedding vows, from the Book of Common Prayer:[81]

81 There are a lot of variations on this, I've combined them to get the most familiar version.

"I [name] take thee [name] to be my wedded [wife/husband], to live together after God's ordinance in the holy estate of matrimony from this day forward, to love, honor, and cherish, for better or for worse, for richer or for poorer,in sickness and in health, and forsaking all others, keep only unto thee, as long as we both shall live."

Breaking it down:

1. I will live with this person in the state of "matrimony."
2. I will love, honor, and cherish this person.
3. I will do this regardless of health, wealth, or other life factors ("better or worse").
4. I will forsake others (meaning, be sexually exclusive).
5. The duration of this vow is from today until one of us dies.

This vow is specific and bounded. It says what we will and will not do, under what circumstances, and for how long.

I have often seen weddings where the "vows" are things like "You're my best friend; I love you so much." That's not a vow, that's a compliment. It promises nothing. I've also seen wedding vows along the lines of "as long as love shall last," which always sounds to me like "as long as I feel like it."

I understand wanting to take a vow that can be kept, but you still have to promise *something*, otherwise, why get married? I have seen people take the "as long as love shall last" and add to it, maintaining a lifelong commitment to kindness and friendship, for example. This, for some people, is a way to vow fealty while acknowledging that sometimes marriages end.

There's no such thing as marriage without moments where you just don't feel much of anything toward your spouse. No matter how deeply you love each other, those moments come. Love must be understood as more than a mood. I had a coworker who often said, "Love is a verb," and I would ignore it as one of those New Age platitudes. But I came to understand its wisdom: Love isn't what you feel, it's what you *do*. Love is taking actions of love. A vow to love understands love as a verb—it understands that the spouses will *behave* lovingly.

If you use the handfasting script that follows, I assume whoever is getting married will write their own vows, and that the ones included are just a placeholder. When writing your own vows, keep in mind the meaning and importance of a vow.

A Little Handfasting History

Most handfasting rituals you can find share a common ancestor. Ed Fitch, Joseph Wilson, and several others began writing accessible Pagan rituals in the late 1960s. These were distributed informally throughout the small but growing Pagan community of the day and eventually published as *The Rituals of the Pagan Way, A Book of Pagan Rituals* (1974). The rituals were not copyrighted but were placed in the public domain to make them available to as many people as possible. An early handfasting appears in this book.

Ed Fitch, a Gardnerian high priest, compiled and expanded upon these rituals in book form two more times: *Magical Rites from the Crystal Well* in 1984, and *A Grimoire of Shadows: Witchcraft, Paganism, & Magic* in 1996. Fitch passed away in 2024.

A couple of passages in the handfasting below (which I shall note) come straight from Ed Fitch: They are extremely widespread and beloved among Wiccans and Pagans. I have about a dozen scripts in my personal files, and they all contain at least some Fitch material. In addition, it's possible that much of the commonly used format, including the invocation onto the couple, the placing of the rings on the wand, and the couple doing the cakes and wine, might be Ed Fitch's invention. His memory and his contribution to Wicca should not be forgotten.

A Note on Names

Most Wiccans and Pagans have magical names they use in ritual. However, in this ritual, there might also be non-Pagans present. The couple should determine if they want to use their Pagan names, their legal names, or both. Some people have two Pagan names, one that is secret and only used in their covens, and one suitable for a public event like this one.

I have used the "known among us" formula for this circumstance, as in, "We are here to join Alice and Jane, known among us as Amethyst and Yesod." Then you refer to them as Amethyst and Yesod throughout the ritual, until you get to the exchange of vows. If you're doing a legal wedding, you might want to use both names there, as in, "Do you, Alice Margaret Jones, also known as Amethyst, take Jane Smith-Morrison, also known as Yesod?"

A Handfasting Ritual

This ritual assumes that there are non-Pagan guests—people unfamiliar with Wiccan or Pagan ritual. The whole opening explanation is provided so that you can invite your parents and coworkers and have the ceremony be accessible to them.

If there are a lot of people, then you need at least *five* assistants who are not the priestess, priest, or betrothed: one person standing at each of three quarters, and *two* at the quarter where the couple will enter. This allows each quarter to be called without anyone having to walk to their spot (or guests having to wait during that walk).

The couple can enter from the East—the direction of beginnings—and then walk all the way around the circle to approach the altar from the North, or they can enter from the North. Entering from the East has symbolic meaning, but a straight path might be easier to negotiate if there are a lot of people.

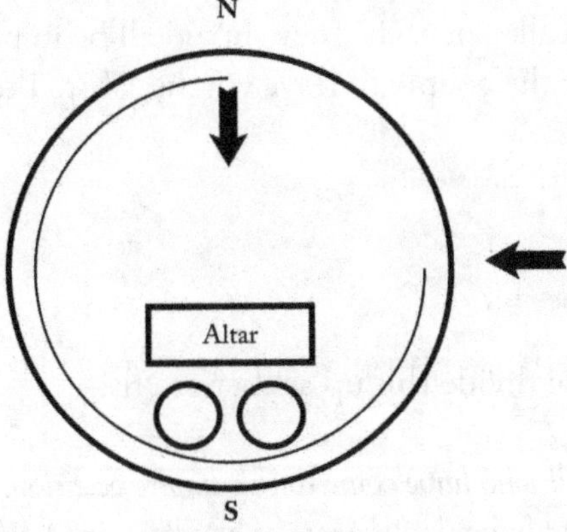

Handfasting Ritual

Roles are divided between priestess and priest in this ritual. This embodies the cooperation and partnership needed for a successful marriage. You may want to adjust the roles, but the partnership should be retained.

Tools Needed

- You might choose to cast the circle with a staff or a wand instead of a sword. Where are you having the ceremony, and is a sword legal to have there?
- Basic altar tools: Cup, athame, wand, pentacle. The wedding rings will be placed on the wand, so check in advance that they fit, and if necessary, get a narrower wand for the occasion
- A large bowl of flower petals. The flower petals will replace salt as the representation of Earth in this ceremony
- A dish of water, a dish of loose incense, and a censer
- A candle at each quarter: For an outdoor ceremony, tiki torches can be used
- Two altar candles (optional)
- Representations of the Goddess and the God
- Wine, ale, cider, or a fermented drink
- A handfasting cord or braid
- A broom
- All five assistants should have their personal athames (or wands) in hand or on their belts
- Flowers for the altar, and as much decoration as you desire for this festive occasion

Before You Begin

- The betrothed will be waiting outside the circle. They can be summoned with a drumbeat or other musical signal, but test this in advance and make sure they can hear from wherever they're waiting.
- Have someone prepared to leave the circle to get them just in case.
- Quarter candles and altar candles are lit before the circle begins.
- There are five assistants: In the quarter where the couple enters, two people with athames act as gatekeepers, one of whom will also be a quarter caller. The other three quarters have one quarter caller in each. They should all be in place.
- It's traditional for the couple to leave via the West. The Western quarter caller should have the broom.

1. Declaration of Opening

The priestess and priest can divide this up as they see fit:

> *"Welcome to all who have come to this happy occasion. We are here to join [name] and [name] in the rite of handfasting: A Wiccan wedding.*

Tonight,[82] we will create a sacred space, balanced in the four elements of Air, Fire, Water, and Earth.
This space is a circle, representing wholeness.
Once the circle has been created, we ask that everyone stay inside.
If you urgently need to step out, one of the people at the quarters will assist you."

(Point out the quarter callers and have them wave so people know who they are.)

"We will invite the Goddess—Mother Earth—and the God—Father of Nature—
to join us in this ceremony and bless our couple.
We will also ask all of you to lend your energy to this sacred rite.
Marriage can be hard. The loving support of friends,
family, and community is one of the things that makes it easier.
So all of you here play an important role, and we thank you for joining us.
So that we can all be fully present, we'll just center ourselves a bit.
Take a deep breath. Hold it. Let it out.
Take another deep breath. Hold it. Let it out with a sound.
Take another deep breath. Hold it. Let it out with a tone.
Now we can begin."

2. Consecrations

The priestess places her athame into the dish of incense and says:

"In the names of the Lady and Lord,
I consecrate Air that it bring mindfulness to our circle."

The priestess places incense onto the lit charcoal so that smoke begins to rise. She places her athame into the smoke and says:

"In the names of the Lady and Lord,
I consecrate Fire that it bring passion to our circle."

The priest places his athame into the dish of water and says:

"In the names of the Lady and Lord,
I consecrate Water that it bring love to our circle."

The priest places his athame into the bowl of flower petals and says:

"In the names of the Lady and Lord,
I consecrate Earth that it bring commitment to our circle."

82 Or "today"—most Wiccan ritual takes place at night, but this could be an exception.

The priest takes the water dish and sprinkles water over the flower petals.

3. Casting the Circle

The priestess takes the staff or sword to the East, directing energy to the circle while saying:[83]

"O circle, you are bound and sealed as a place of love. In the name of the Goddess, in the name of the God, by the powers that surround us, by the love we contain, I create this circle. O circle, be our safeguard from the world as we create the magic of love. This circle is blessed."

She returns to the altar, puts down her staff or sword, and picks up the flower petals. The priest picks up the censer.

The priestess returns to the East with the priest behind her.

Priestess: *"Water and Earth, make sacred this space."*

Priest: *"Fire and Air, make sacred this space."*

She strews the flower petals all around the perimeter of the circle, while he follows, censing. They return to the altar.

Priestess: *"The circle is cast. So mote it be!"*

All repeat: *"So mote it be!"*

4. Calling the Quarters

The quarter caller in the East faces out, pointing their athame and drawing an invoking pentagram, saying:

"I invoke the Guardian of East, the Guardian of Air
O Guardian, be here with your thoughtfulness, and kind words
That your winds blow sweetly into the marriage of [name] and [name]
Blessed be."

All repeat: *"Blessed be."*

The quarter caller in the South faces out, pointing their athame and drawing an invoking pentagram, saying:

"I invoke the Guardian of South, the Guardian of Fire
O Guardian, be here with your passion and your warmth
That your fire stokes the hearth of the marriage of [name] and [name]

83 I made this a little long, assuming a space big enough for a bunch of guests, to give the priestess time to get all the way around.

Blessed be."

All repeat: "*Blessed be.*"

The quarter caller in the West faces out, pointing their athame and drawing an invoking pentagram, saying:

"I invoke the Guardian of West, the Guardian of Water
O Guardian, be here with your love and your dreams
That your feeling flows into the marriage of [name] and [name]
Blessed be."

All repeat: "*Blessed be.*"

The quarter caller in the North faces out, pointing their athame and drawing an invoking pentagram, saying:

"I invoke the Guardian of North, the Guardian of Earth
O Guardian, be here with your stability and your commitment
That your foundation firmly holds the marriage of [name] and [name]
Blessed be."

All repeat: "*Blessed be.*"
The East caller makes a final, silent salute.

5. Invoking the Gods

The priestess and priest lift the wand together, each of their right hands on it, and pointing it to the North.

Priestess: "*Beloved Goddess of the stars, protector of brides, mother of the Earth, bringer of love, we invoke you. Let your wedding gifts be your presence here and your creativity.*"

Priest: "*Beloved Lord of death and rebirth, bringer of understanding, protector of grooms, we invoke you. Let your wedding gifts be your presence here and your energy.*"

Priestess: "*Welcome, and blessed be!*"

All repeat: "*Blessed be.*"
The wand is returned to the altar.

6. Offerings[84]/Celebration of the Occasion: The Handfasting

The priest gestures toward the two people at the quarter where the couple will enter, and says:

"I say to you, open the circle, cut wide the gate,
for two are coming who would be made one!"[85]

The two gatekeepers open a doorway with their athames and form a kind of saber arch under which the wedding party enters.

Forming an entry arch

After the wedding party enters, the gatekeepers close the gate and seal the circle. (See illustration on page 94.)

The couple stands on the North side of the altar, facing the priestess and priest across the altar.

The priestess turns to the bride (if a heterosexual couple[86]) or to one of the couple, saying:

"Do you, [name], known among us as [magical name], come here today, before your gods and your community, in order to tie yourself to [name], known among us as [magical name], in marriage?"

---

84 The handfasting itself is considered an offering, as the gods want us to love each other, so performing this act of love and commitment is an offering to them (among other things).

85 This quote is from Ed Fitch.

86 Keeping the genders separate in a heterosexual wedding—priestess always to bride, priest always to groom—creates a tension released when at last the couple comes together. Same sex couples can decide if they want an alternate means for creating a polarity tension, or if they want to skip it.

(Receives answer.)

The priest turns to the groom/other one of the couple, saying:

"Do you, [name], known among us as [magical name], come here today, before your gods and your community, in order to tie yourself to [name], known among us as [magical name], in marriage?"

(Receives answer.)

Priestess to bride/first person:

"[Magical name], the Goddess is upon you on your wedding day.
You are the green Earth and the blue sea,
You are the shape of the universe and the cup of life
You shall be she who adores and is adored
You shall be lover and beloved
Let the God worship you with his blade."

Priest to groom/second person:

"[Magical name], the God is upon you on your wedding day.
You are the wild hills and the dark underworld,
You are the force of the universe and the sword of energy
You shall be he who adores and is adored
You shall be lover and beloved
Let the Goddess worship you with her cup."

Priestess:

"[Both magical names],
Above you are the stars, below you are the stones.
As time passes, remember...
Like a star should your love be constant,
Like a stone should your love be firm.
Be close, yet not too close.
Possess one another, yet be understanding.
Have patience each with the other,
For storms will come, but they will go quickly.
Be free in giving of affection and warmth
Make love often, and be sensuous to one another.
Have no fear, and let not the ways or the words
Of the unenlightened give you unease.

For the Goddess and the God are with you. Now and always!"[87]

Priest: *"It is time for the blessing of the rings."* (Someone produces rings if they're not already on the altar).

The priest takes the rings and puts them on the wand

Rings on the wand

Priest, priestess, bride, and groom, now put their hands over the rings as the priestess says: *"In the name of the Goddess..."*

Priest: *"In the name of the God..."*

Priestess and priest together: *"We bless these rings with magic and love..."*

Priestess: *"By Air and Fire..."*

Priest: *"By Water and Earth..."*

Priestess and priest together: *"We bless these rings with magic and love. Blessed be!"*

All repeat: *"Blessed be."*

Priestess: *"The handfasting cord represents a contract, an agreement, and so much more. It shows us that these two are bound together, that their hands work in concert. They are two separate people, but they are also one, tied forever more."*

(To bride/first person): *"Do you freely bind yourself to this person?"*

Bride: *[answers]*

Priest to groom/second person: *"Do you freely bind yourself to this person?"*

Groom: *[answers]*

---

87 This entire homily is also by Ed Fitch. It is a part of almost every handfasting I've ever seen. The line beginning "Make love often" is frequently omitted.

The priestess and priest now tie the left hands of the couple together with the cord. They remain tied together throughout the exchange of vows and rings.

Priestess to bride/first person: *"Is it your wish, [full name], known among us as [magical name], to be joined with this man?"*

Bride: *[answers]*

Priestess: *"Then give him your vow and your ring."*

Bride:[88]

"I, [name], vow to you, [name]
To love you, respect you, and care for you
No matter what may come
In good times and bad
For as long as I draw breath."

The bride now puts the ring on the groom's finger.

Priest to groom/second person: *"Is it your wish, [full name], known among us as [magical name], to be joined with this woman?"*

Groom: *[answers]*

Priest: *"Then give her your vow and your ring."*

Groom:

"I, [name], vow to you, [name]
To love you, respect you, and care for you
No matter what may come
In good times and bad
For as long as I draw breath."

The groom now puts the ring on the bride's finger.
Priest turns to the guests and says:

"These two have given their vows in front of a community of family and friends, knowing you would hear them. Do you, family and friends, vow to honor and respect this union, and support its commitments?"

---

88 People who are getting married get nervous. Even if the couple intends to memorize their own vows, the priestess and priest should be prepared to go the "repeat after me" route, just in case.

Guests: *[answer]*

Priestess: *"I now pronounce you (husband and wife/spouses/whatever the couple will go by)!*[89] *You may kiss."*

After the kiss, the priest unbinds the couple by loosening, but not untying, the cords. They slip their hands out through this large opening. Then, the priest holds up the cords so that all can see and pulls the knot tight again. This tied cord becomes a keepsake.

The priest says:

"The cord is removed, but the bond remains."

The priest hands the athame to the groom, saying:

"The knife is for the troubles that lies ahead."

The priestess hands the cup to the bride saying:

"The cup is for the love that conquers them."[90]

7. Cakes and Wine

The bride/person 1 holds the cup and says:[91]

"The cup, the Goddess, the blood of life
Our Lady blesses us with all good things
She offers herself to us
She offers herself to the God."

The groom/person 2 holds the athame over the cup and says:

"The blade, the God, the force of life
Our Lord blesses us with all good things
He offers himself to us
He offers himself to the Goddess."

The groom plunges the athame into the cup.

Both say together:

"Blessed be."

89 By the power of the State of New York or whatever goes here if applicable.

90 This is also from Ed Fitch.

91 As with the vows, memorization can fail when people are nervous. The priestess and priest should be prepared to step in with "repeat after me."

At a handfasting, cakes are often not blessed, as the wedding cake is not necessarily going to fit on the altar. If you want to bless cakes in the ritual, the bride holds the plate while the groom blesses them with the athame:

Groom:

"Lady and Lord, you bless us with abundance
The Earth gives us all we need
We thank you."

Both: *"Blessed be."*

The bride pours a libation, drinks, and gives the cup to the groom, who also pours a libation and drinks.

If cakes have been consecrated, the bride takes one cake and sets it in the libation bowl. Then she takes another cake, splits it in half, feeds half to the groom, and eats the other half.

The priestess now lifts the cup and gestures with the cup to everyone—her libation is on behalf of all.

She says: *"To the gods of love!"*

She pours a libation, then raises the cup again, and says:

"To the happy couple!"

She speaks however she is moved, *does not* pour a libation, and drinks.

Priest: *"The work of love is done but just begun."*

The West assistant now cuts open a gate and places the broom across the threshold of the gate just opened.

The priest and priestess lead all in a chant of "JUMP THE BROOM!"

The couple join hands, run once around the circle, and jump over the broom and out of the circle. The West assistant closes the gate behind them.

8. Closing the Circle

Face North, raise the wand, and say:

"Beloved Lady of the stars,
You have blessed this sacred rite of love.
Thank you, and farewell!"

All repeat: *"Farewell!"*

"Beloved Lord of death and rebirth,
You have blessed this sacred rite of love.
Thank you, and farewell!"

All repeat: *"Farewell!"*
The East caller draws a banishing pentagram and says:

"We thank you, Guardian of the East, Guardian of Air
For protecting this rite
Thank you, and farewell!"

All repeat: *"Farewell!"*
The South caller draws a banishing pentagram and says:

"We thank you, Guardian of the South, Guardian of Fire
For protecting this rite
Thank you, and farewell!"

All repeat: *"Farewell!"*
The West caller draws a banishing pentagram and says:

"We thank you, Guardian of the West, Guardian of Water
For protecting this rite
Thank you, and farewell!"

All repeat: *"Farewell!"*
The North caller draws a banishing pentagram and says:

"We thank you, Guardian of the North, Guardian of Earth
For protecting this rite
Thank you, and farewell!"

All repeat: *"Farewell!"*
Facing the center, say:

"The circle is open but unbroken, the rites are ended.
Merry meet, merry part, and merry meet again!"

All repeat: *"Merry meet, merry part, and merry meet again!"*
Everyone can now cheer and whoop it up!

Handparting and Cutting Ties

The idea of handparting isn't appealing to most people, and yet, we know that most relationships end. The end of a marriage (legal or not) is certainly a life passage, and ritualizing that passage can be meaningful and important, yet most people don't do any ritual at all.

According to Diana Rajchel, author of Divorcing a Real Witch: for Pagans and the People Who Used to Love Them, 76% of respondents to a survey she executed did not perform a hand-parting at the end of their marriage.[92]

There are a zillion reasons for this, and a zillion circumstances that might make a handparting ritual a really good idea, or a really bad one. Let's look at this more closely.

The end of a relationship can be agonizing. Even if you want it to end, even if you're completely sure it's the right thing to do, your body, mind, and heart are flooded with conflicting feelings. A lot of this has to do with brain chemistry and stress response. The loss of a relationship is a stressor, regardless of the circumstances, and the body responds accordingly. Ritual can help to counter these responses. Ritual can ground the deep mind in the knowledge that it's really over, and it's time to move on.

While there are very few published handparting rituals, those that exist often assume that the parting is at least cordial. This isn't necessarily the case. Let's look at different ways that relationships can break up:

1. You're both Wiccan or Pagan. You break up in a friendly or peaceful way. Or you break up with difficulty and some level of anger and accusation, but you're determined to ultimately remain friends, or at least friendly. Perhaps you have children together and you are committed to keeping things as peaceful and kind-hearted as possible for their sake.
2. You are committed to each other as in the first case, but only one of you is Wiccan or Pagan. A partner who was not Pagan may have been willing to be married in a Pagan ceremony but might not be so open to a ritual divorce.
3. You break up badly. You're not on speaking terms.
4. You break up pretty badly. Maybe you're on speaking terms, but you're not ready or able to see each other, or one of you moves far away.
5. There was violence or abuse. You have not merely ended the relationship but escaped from it.

Any of these can be marked by ritual, but each ritual would be very different. The cordial Pagan couple in the first instance might choose to have a handparting ceremony. In all the other cases, the ritual is almost certain to be performed by one partner only (in the case of abuse, this is absolutely necessary—an abuse survivor shouldn't even consider communicating about the ritual with their abuser).

---

92 The Wild Hunt, "A parting of companions around you: Pagans and divorce", Terence P Ward, June 13, 2017, wildhunt.org/2017/06/a-parting-of-companions-around-you-pagans-and-divorce.html (Accessed 2/6/25)

You've probably seen more than one TV show or movie where someone was handed divorce papers to sign by a process server, and it hits them like a ton of bricks. The moment of signing is a fraught and powerful moment. It's a transition. I wonder, what if you cast a circle, brought the papers into the circle, and signed them there? Might that not honor the gravity of the moment?

I like the simplicity of that idea. A breakup ceremony need not be elaborate. It should be calming, in deference to the roiled emotions involved, and it should be clear.

Timing

You probably didn't get married in an overnight whirlwind. The handparting deserves as much planning as the handfasting (probably without the caterer, though).

Is there a significant moment that's coming up? Signing of papers, having the sit-down with the kids, or the one-year anniversary of the breakup? A meaningful time can be chosen.

Don't rush it, though, because at first, you're going to be overwhelmed by all the change, and throwing yourself into planning mode won't help.

If you're still fantasizing about getting back together, you'll be reluctant to do any kind of ritual that finalizes the breakup. It *might* be the best thing for you, but we don't always do the best thing for ourselves. If you're not ready, then you're not. If you're not ready now, it doesn't mean you never will be. Years may go by, and then you're ready to marry your new partner: At that moment, you may find you need to ritually end the last relationship before ritually beginning this one.

Who Does the Handparting

- The couple could do this with the priestess and priest who performed the original handfasting, and no guests, or just one supportive person for each partner. When a couple breaks up within a coven or group, it is often true that one will leave the group. In this case, the departing ex would join with the group, and the ritual would be constructed for them to leave the circle before anyone else.
- It could be done by the couple alone.
- It could be done by one of the former couple alone.
- It could be done by one of the former couple in their group, again, perhaps performed by the priestess and priest who performed the handfasting. In this case, it could be an intimate and solemn affair, or perhaps the person divorcing wants to construct it as a celebration.

Vows

The core of your handfasting was the vows you gave to each other. These were magical words that created a bond, even more so than the handfasting cord. So, a lot depends on exactly what was in your vows, and what you intend to do about them.

There are two things you can do with vows: Break them or redefine them.

Breaking Vows

Just deciding you will no longer be bound by a vow you have taken has spiritual and magical consequences—it reverberates throughout the universe. Yet, some vows can no longer be kept. For this reason, multiple religions in the world have developed procedures for the release from vows.

The procedure is simple enough: In a sacred space, where the gods are present, you ask the gods to release you from your vow. You declare that you now abjure the vow, and that it is null and void. The important part is that you do this before the gods, and with their permission, so that you are not carrying around additional consequences.

This doesn't erase the life experience. It doesn't mean nothing, or that no one was hurt. It doesn't wipe clean the slate of everything you may have done or failed to do. But it does restore the integrity of your word in this regard.

Redefining Vows

When my late ex-husband and I split, we decided we could not break our vows. Instead, we redefined them. This can be done ritually, but it doesn't have to be. Because you're keeping the vows, you can choose not to ritualize a change in how you understand them. Of course, you could still ritualize the entire parting and have the redefinition of the vows be a part of that.

How this works depends entirely on the vows you took, and how you feel you can understand them today.

Here's an example, using the vows from the handfasting ceremony above. Here are those vows:

"I, [name], vow to you, [name]
To love you, respect you, and care for you
No matter what may come
In good times and bad
For as long as I draw breath."

In a parting ritual you could say:

"I vowed to love you and will love you as a friend.
I vowed to respect you and will respect you as a partner in parenting.
I vowed to care for you and will always be a resource for you when you are in need.
I made this vow for as long as I draw breath and will keep this vow for as long as I draw breath:
Friend, partner, and member of my family."

Creating a Handparting Ritual

There are many, many options in creating a handparting ritual—like a handfasting, it is unique to the relationship. Above, I presented five possibilities for who could attend, each of which changes the ritual. But that's really ten possibilities, because each has the option of either releasing the vows or redefining them. And within those ten, there are probably infinite variations. Here are some things to consider:

Tone

What is the tone of the ritual? Will it be solemn and sad, or are you celebrating stepping into the next phase of your life? Incorporate language and action that reflects the feeling you wish the ritual to convey.

The Cords

What will you do with the handfasting cords (assuming you still have them)? If you knotted them during your ceremony (which isn't common), is unknotting them enough? Will you cut them? Will you burn them? (People often burn things in a ceremony like this, which probably means an outdoor ritual with a sizable fire.)

Order of Operations

The obvious first thought here is to simply use the same order as the handfasting, but that doesn't really work.

Recall that, in a ritual, we invoke the Lady and Lord, offer to them, and then perform cakes and wine. Basically, everything before cakes and wine is given *to* the gods, while everything after cakes and wine is a blessing received *from* the gods.

In a handfasting, we are offering the loving relationship and commitment to the gods, while, at the same time, receiving their blessing upon it. When the couple performs the ceremony of cakes and wine, they are pouring the blessing of their offered love into the wine, which is then imbued with the blessings of the Lady and Lord.

That doesn't work in reverse because the handparting, while necessary, doesn't constitute a gift given to the gods. So, the order is something like:

1. The circle is cast, the quarters are called, and the gods are invoked.
2. A suitable offering is given to the gods.
3. Handparting steps begin.
4. Cakes and wine.
5. Handparting is completed.
6. The quarters are dismissed, and the circle is closed.

I put the handparting both before and after the cakes and wine so that the energy stays consistent throughout the ritual, and so that the cakes and wine can act as a climactic moment that seals and completes the rite.

Additional Symbolic Acts

There are many things that people might choose to add to the ceremony, symbols that give meaning and power to the rite. I think that, overall, this ritual should be short and simple, because there's no need to drag it out. Endings are easier to accomplish than beginnings—we see this even in the circle opening and closing. It takes a lot to bring us into sacred space, but ending it takes little more than saying so.

Nonetheless, the people parting should consider how to make this meaningful and honest. Here are some thoughts:

- Return the rings to each other.
- Burn a wedding picture or other symbol of togetherness.
- Enter the circle by stepping back over the broom.
- Sweep the circle with the broom, "sweeping away" the remnants of the past.
- Simply say goodbye to one another while holding hands and then drop hands and turn away.

Handparting: A Ritual for the Couple in a Group

This ritual assumes that both divorcing parties are present, but it can be reworked for just one. It offers a few options regarding vows and cords, but if you are using this ritual, you'll want to make it your own.

This ritual is designed to be outdoors, with a fire going.

I have two leaders, presumably priestess and priest. Where they did much together in the handfasting, here they operate separately in many cases.

Tools Needed

In addition to the usual circle-casting tools, you'll need:

- A broom—preferably the broom jumped at the handfasting
- The handfasting cords
- Any mementos you wish to burn
- Fire-making stuff and a fire extinguisher

Before You Begin

- Get the fire going.
- The couple starts in the circle with everyone else, there is no ceremonial entry.

Begin with the opening meditation found in *Sabbats: The Wheel of the Year* on page 108. It will be especially important that people be grounded.

1. Declaration of Opening

Priestess:
"We are joined tonight with the solemn duty of parting the hands of [name] and [name], in the presence of the Holy Ones."

2. Consecrations

Place the athame into the dish of incense and say:

"In the names of the Lady and Lord,
I consecrate Air that it bring mindfulness to our circle."

Place incense onto the lit charcoal so that smoke begins to rise. With the athame in the smoke, say:

"In the names of the Lady and Lord,
I consecrate Fire that it bring will to our circle."

Place the athame into the dish of water and say:

"In the names of the Lady and Lord,
I consecrate Water that it bring compassion to our circle."

Place the athame into the salt and say:

"In the names of the Lady and Lord,
I consecrate Earth that it bring stability to our circle."

Take three measures of salt, place them into the water, and stir.

3. Casting the Circle

The priestess or leader takes the sword or athame to the East, directing energy to the circle while saying:

"I form this circle between this world and the otherworld, between men and gods, between flesh and spirit, that it be a place of safety and magic. In the names of the ancient Goddess and God, I seal and consecrate this holy circle. So mote it be."

All repeat: *"So mote it be!"*

The priestess/leader returns to the altar, puts down the sword or athame, and picks up the dish of saltwater. She goes to the East, saying:

"Water and Earth, make sacred this space."

She sprinkles the perimeter and returns to the altar.

The priest picks up the censer and goes to the East, saying:

"Fire and Air, make sacred this space."

He censes the perimeter of the circle and returns to the altar.

4. Calling the Quarters

In the East face out, draw an invoking pentagram with the athame, and say:

"I invoke the Guardian of East, the Guardian of Air
O Guardian, be here with your thoughtfulness, and gentle words
Protect the solemn parting of [name] and [name].
Blessed be."

All repeat: "*Blessed be.*
In the South face out, draw an invoking pentagram with the athame, and say:

"I invoke the Guardian of South, the Guardian of Fire
O Guardian, be here with your determination and heat
Protect the solemn parting of [name] and [name].
Blessed be."

All repeat: "*Blessed be.*"
In the West face out, draw an invoking pentagram with the athame, and say:

"I invoke the Guardian of West, the Guardian of Water
O Guardian, be here with your compassion and empathy
Protect the solemn parting of [name] and [name].
Blessed be."

All repeat: "*Blessed be.*"
In the North face out, draw an invoking pentagram with the athame, and say:
"I invoke the Guardian of North, the Guardian of Earth
O Guardian, be here with your pragmatism and your strength
Protect the solemn parting of [name] and [name].
Blessed be."

All repeat: "*Blessed be.*"
In the East, make a final, silent salute.

5. Invoking the Gods

The priestess lifts the pentacle. The priest lifts the wand. Both face North.

Priest:

"Beloved Lady, beloved Lord

You are steadfast with us in darkness and light
Be here tonight for our solemn rite
Join us Lady, protector of all
Join us Lord, overseer of change
Bless this sacred rite.
Welcome, and blessed be!"

All repeat: "*Blessed be.*"
The tools are returned to the altar.

6. Offerings

Each person, one at a time, now steps to the altar, takes a pinch of incense, speaks as moved, and offers the incense to the gods on the censor.

"Speaks as moved" here means as an *offering*. Now is not the time to talk about the end of the relationship. "To the Lady and Lord," or "Thank you for watching over our rite," is truly fine.

If the couple has brought mementos to burn, this can happen here. It could go like this:

Partner 1: "*I offer these [mementos] to the fire. May the positive and joyful energy they once contained be a fit offering to the Lady and the Lord.*"

Partner 2: "*I offer these [mementos] to the fire. May the positive and joyful energy they once contained be a fit offering to the Lady and the Lord.*"

The leader now takes the broom and says:

"*All things change. We sweep away the old that the new may come.*"

They sweep the perimeter of the circle, East to East.

7. Cakes and Wine

Leader:

"*The universe began when the God fell in love with the Goddess:*
They became two so they could become one.
Human love changes, grows, evolves, dies, and is reborn, but the love of the Gods is eternal.
However we love one another, we are always loved by them.
Their embrace sustains us in good times and bad.
Let us celebrate, and receive blessings from,the union of the Lady and the Lord,
that our work may be sacred tonight."

Hold the cup and say:

"The cup, the Goddess, the blood of life
Our Lady blesses us with all good things
She offers herself to us
She offers herself to the God."

Hold the athame over the cup and say:

"The blade, the God, the force of life
Our Lord blesses us with all good things
He offers himself to us
He offers himself to the Goddess."

Consecrate the cakes by dipping the athame into the wine and sprinkling drops onto the cakes, forming an invoking pentagram.

Say:

"Lady and Lord, you bless us with abundance
The Earth gives us all we need
We thank you.
Blessed be."

All repeat: *"Blessed be."*

8. The Handparting

Priestess to Partner 1: *"Do you, [name], wish to be parted from [name], freed of the bonds of handfasting, to be two again where once you were one?"*

Partner 1: *[answers]*

Priest to Partner 2: *"Do you, [name], wish to be parted from [name], freed of the bonds of handfasting, to be two again where once you were one?"*

Partner 2: *[answers]*

Option 1: Release from Vows

Priestess lifts wand and points North, saying:

"Lady and Lord, we ask that you release [name] and [name] from the vows they have taken before you. Let these vows be null and void. Let no harm come to them for breaking them. So mote it be!"

All repeat: *"So mote it be!"*

Priestess holds hands over Partner 1 as they say (from memory or "repeat after me"):

"I, [name], do renounce the vows of handfasting taken with [name].
They bind me no more. So mote it be!"

All repeat: *"So mote it be!"*
Priest holds hands over Partner 2 as they say (from memory or "repeat after me"):

"I, [name], do renounce the vows of handfasting taken with [name].
They bind me no more. So mote it be!"

All repeat: *"So mote it be!"*

Option 2: Redefining Vows

Priestess: *"The vows you took as spouses continue to bind you, but today, we understand them differently. Retake your vows now."*

Priestess holds hands over Partner 1, as they say (from memory or "repeat after me"):

"I vowed to love you and will love you as a friend.
I vowed to respect you and will respect you as a partner in parenting.
I vowed to care for you and will always be a resource for you when you are in need.
I made this vow for as long as I draw breath and will keep this vow for as long as I draw breath:
Friend, partner, and member of my family.
So mote it be!"

All repeat: *"So mote it be!"*
Priest holds hands over Partner 2, as they say (from memory or "repeat after me"):
"I vowed to love you and will love you as a friend.
I vowed to respect you and will respect you as a partner in parenting.
I vowed to care for you and will always be a resource for you when you are in need.
I made this vow for as long as I draw breath and will keep this vow for as long as I draw breath:
Friend, partner, and member of my family.
So mote it be!"

All repeat: *"So mote it be!"*
The priest lifts the handfasting cords. If it was knotted, he unknots it. If it was not knotted, he cuts it with the athame or another knife or scissor and says:

"You are unbound."

He throws the cords into the fire, saying: *"So mote it be!"*
All repeat: *"So mote it be!"*

9. Closing the Circle

Face North, raise the wand, and say:

"Beloved Lord and Lady
Thank you for your presence and blessing at this sacred rite.
Farewell!"

All repeat: *"Farewell!"*
In the East, draw a banishing pentagram and say:

"We thank you, Guardian of the East, Guardian of Air
For protecting this rite
Thank you, and farewell!"

All repeat: *"Farewell!"*
In the South, draw a banishing pentagram and say:

"We thank you, Guardian of the South, Guardian of Fire
For protecting this rite
Thank you, and farewell!"

All repeat: *"Farewell!"*
In the West, draw a banishing pentagram and say:

"We thank you, Guardian of the West, Guardian of Water
For protecting this rite
Thank you, and farewell!"

All repeat: *"Farewell!"*
In the North, draw a banishing pentagram and say:

"We thank you, Guardian of the North, Guardian of Earth
For protecting this rite
Thank you, and farewell!"

All repeat: *"Farewell!"*
Facing the center, say:

"The circle is open but unbroken, the rites are ended.
Merry meet, merry part, and merry meet again!"

All repeat: *"Merry meet, merry part, and merry meet again!"*

A Solitary Handparting Ritual

If you were handfasted, there were other people involved, so a group ritual would make sense for a handparting. But maybe you hired a non-denominational minister of some sort, maybe your wedding wasn't Wiccan or Pagan at all, but you still feel the need to create a Wiccan ceremony for closure.

As with the group ritual, the assumption is that you're outdoors with a fire going. If that's not possible, you could make a small indoor fire in a cauldron, but burning anything sizable should wait until you're outside.

Tools Needed

In addition to the usual circle-casting tools, you'll need:

- A broom—preferably the broom jumped at the handfasting
- The handfasting cords, if you have them
- Any memento you wish to burn
- Fire-making stuff and a fire extinguisher

Before You Begin

- Get the fire going.
- Spend time in advance meditating on what this ending means to you. Journaling helps here. Some people write a letter to their ex: If you're not on speaking terms, reading the letter aloud in ritual space can be healing. This can be done immediately before the sweeping and is then swept away.

Begin with the opening meditation found in *Sabbats: The Wheel of the Year* on page 108.

1. Declaration of Opening

Say:

"Tonight, I part hands with [name] in the presence of the Holy Ones."

2. Consecrations

Place the athame into the dish of incense and say:

"In the names of the Lady and Lord,
I consecrate Air that it bring mindfulness to my circle."

Place incense onto the lit charcoal so that smoke begins to rise. With the athame in the smoke, say:

"In the names of the Lady and Lord,
I consecrate Fire that it bring will to my circle."

Place the athame into the dish of water and say:

"In the names of the Lady and Lord,
I consecrate Water that it bring compassion to my circle."

Place the athame into the salt and say:

"In the names of the Lady and Lord,
I consecrate Earth that it bring stability to my circle."

Take three measures of salt, place them into the water, and stir.

3. Casting the Circle

Take the sword or athame to the East, directing energy to the circle while saying:

"I form this circle between this world and the otherworld, between humans and gods, between flesh and spirit, that it be a place of safety and magic. In the names of the ancient Goddess and God, I seal and consecrate this holy circle. So mote it be."

Return to the altar, put down the sword or athame, and pick up the dish of saltwater. Go to the East, saying:

"Water and Earth, make sacred this space."

Sprinkle the perimeter and return to the altar.
Pick up the censer and return to the East, saying:

"Fire and Air, make sacred this space."

Cense the perimeter of the circle and return to the altar.

4. Calling the Quarters

In the East face out, draw an invoking pentagram with the athame, and say:

"I invoke the Guardian of East, the Guardian of Air
O Guardian, be here with your thoughtfulness, and gentle words
Protect this parting.
Blessed be."

In the South face out, draw an invoking pentagram with the athame, and say:

"I invoke the Guardian of South, the Guardian of Fire
O Guardian, be here with your determination and heat
Protect this parting.
Blessed be."

In the West face out, draw an invoking pentagram with the athame, and say:

"I invoke the Guardian of West, the Guardian of Water
O Guardian, be here with your compassion and empathy
Protect this parting.
Blessed be."

In the North face out, draw an invoking pentagram with the athame, and say:

"I invoke the Guardian of North, the Guardian of Earth
O Guardian, be here with your pragmatism and your strength
Protect this parting.
Blessed be."

In the East, make a final, silent salute.

5. Invoking the Gods

Point the wand to the North and say:

"Beloved Lady, beloved Lord
You are steadfast with me in darkness and light
Be here tonight for my solemn rite
Join me Lady, protector of all
Join me Lord, overseer of change
Bless this sacred rite.
Welcome, and blessed be!"

6. Offerings

Begin by offering something heartfelt to the gods unrelated to the parting. This could be an incense offering, a song, drumming, etc. It is just a gift to them, thanking them for joining you.

Next, you can offer mementos to burn, if you wish, saying:

"I offer these [mementos] to the fire. May the positive and joyful energy they once contained be a fit offering to the Lady and the Lord."

If you have something to read aloud or something else to release, now is the time. It will be swept away by the broom in the next step.

Take the broom and say:

"All things change. I sweep away the old that the new may come."

Sweep the perimeter of the circle, East to East.

7. Cakes and Wine

Say:

"The universe began when the God fell in love with the Goddess:
They became two so they could become one.
Human love changes, grows, evolves, dies, and is reborn,
but the love of the Gods is eternal.
However we love one another, we are always loved by them.
Their embrace sustains us in good times and bad.
I now celebrate and receive blessings from the union of the Lady and the Lord,
that my work may be sacred tonight."

Hold the cup and say:

"The cup, the Goddess, the blood of life
Our Lady blesses me with all good things
She offers herself to me
She offers herself to the God."

Hold the athame over the cup and say:

"The blade, the God, the force of life
Our Lord blesses me with all good things
He offers himself to me
He offers himself to the Goddess."

Consecrate the cakes by dipping the athame into the wine and sprinkling drops onto the cakes, forming an invoking pentagram. Say:

"Lady and Lord, you bless me with abundance
The Earth gives me all I need
I thank you.
Blessed be."

Take a cake and place it in the libation bowl.

Lift the cup and speak from the heart. It can be as simple as "to the Gods," or it can be detailed. End with "Blessed be." Then make an offering to the gods by pouring a bit of wine into the libation bowl. Drink only after offering.

After the ritual is over, the contents of the libation bowl should be poured out onto the Earth. If the ritual is outdoors, libations are poured directly onto the Earth and a bowl is not needed.

8. The Handparting

Option 1: Release from Vows

Lift the wand and point North, saying:

"Lady and Lord, I ask that you release me from the vows to [name]
I have taken before you. Let these vows be null and void.
Let no harm come to me for breaking them. So mote it be!
I, [name], do renounce the vows of handfasting taken with [name].
They bind me no more. So mote it be!"

Option 2: Redefining Vows

Say:

"The vows I took in marriage continue to bind me, but today,
I must understand them differently. I retake me vows now:
I vowed to love [name], and will love them as a friend.
I vowed to respect [name], and will respect them as a partner in parenting.
I vowed to care for [name], and will always be a resource for them when they are in need.
I made this vow for as long as I draw breath, and will keep this vow for as long as I draw breath:
Friend, partner, and member of my family.
So mote it be!"

Lift the handfasting cord. If it was knotted, unknot it. If it was not knotted, cut it with the athame or another knife or scissors, and say:

"I am unbound."

Throw the cord into the fire,[93] saying:

"So mote it be!"

9. Closing the Circle

Face North, raise the wand, and say:

93 If you are indoors, set the cord aside for burning outdoors later.

"Beloved Lord and Lady
Thank you for your presence and blessing at this sacred rite.
Farewell!"

In the East, draw a banishing pentagram and say:

"I thank you, Guardian of the East, Guardian of Air
For protecting this rite
Thank you, and farewell!"

In the South, draw a banishing pentagram and say:

"I thank you, Guardian of the South, Guardian of Fire
For protecting this rite
Thank you, and farewell!"

In the West, draw a banishing pentagram and say:

"I thank you, Guardian of the West, Guardian of Water
For protecting this rite
Thank you, and farewell!"

In the North, draw a banishing pentagram and say:

"I thank you, Guardian of the North, Guardian of Earth
For protecting this rite
Thank you, and farewell!"

Facing the center, say:

"The circle is open but unbroken, the rites are ended.
Merry meet, merry part, and merry meet again!"

Cutting Ties

Cutting ties straddles the space between a rite of passage and a spell. It is something done to formally end a relationship that is toxic and needs to be thoroughly removed from someone's life. Maybe it's over and you want it back, or you are struggling to convince yourself it's really over. Maybe you know it's over, and you know you don't want it back, but you're plagued by thoughts, memories, and feelings.

A toxic relationship could have been emotionally or physically abusive, dishonest, or in any other way harmful. You understand that it wouldn't be healthy to honor the past tie right now, so you have to cut it completely. Maybe, years from now, you can honor it as part of your past, but first you must stop the bleeding—you don't have to worry now about what you'll do with the scar once it's healed.

Cutting ties severs the link between you and another person. It helps you understand that it's really over, it reaches into the realm of the gods to end any ties to your ex that exist there, and it cleanses the aura of connections to your ex. The aura cleansing portion, in my experience, can, and probably should, be repeated several times during the period when you are grieving and recovering from this loss. In this way, it is more of a spell.

A Solitary Rite of Cutting Ties

This ritual should be performed nude. Come into the ritual space completely unbound— even your hair should be loose. Since you are nude, you will almost certainly prefer to be indoors: You can have an indoor fire in a cauldron, but you may want to burn things outdoors after the ritual.

Tools Needed

In addition to the usual circle-casting tools, you'll need:

- Anointing oil[94]
- Any memento you wish to burn
- Fire-making stuff and a fire extinguisher

Before You Begin

- Get the fire going.
- Spend time in advance meditating on what this ending means to you. As with the handparting ritual, journaling helps, and as in that case, you can write a letter to your ex to be read aloud in ritual space.

Begin with the opening meditation found in *Sabbats: The Wheel of the Year* on page 108.

1. Declaration of Opening

Say:

"Tonight, I cut ties with [name] in the presence of the Holy Ones."

2. Consecrations

Place the athame into the dish of incense and say:

94 Create anointing oil with any pure natural oil, such as olive or almond oil. See *Herbs and Plants* on page 62 for ideas on additional ingredients you might add. Then consecrate as you would consecrate a tool (page 49).

"In the names of the Lady and Lord,
I consecrate Air that it bring mindfulness to my circle."

Place incense onto the lit charcoal so that smoke begins to rise. With the athame in the smoke, say:

"In the names of the Lady and Lord,
I consecrate Fire that it bring will to my circle."

Place the athame into the dish of water and say:

"In the names of the Lady and Lord,
I consecrate Water that it bring compassion to my circle."

Place the athame into the salt and say:

"In the names of the Lady and Lord,
I consecrate Earth that it bring stability to my circle."

Take three measures of salt, place them into the water, and stir.

3. Casting the Circle

Take the sword or athame to the East, directing energy to the circle while saying:

"I form this circle between this world and the otherworld, between humans and gods, between flesh and spirit, that it be a place of safety and magic. In the names of the ancient Goddess and God, I seal and consecrate this holy circle. So mote it be."

Return to the altar, put down the sword or athame, and pick up the dish of saltwater. Go to the East, saying:

"Water and Earth, make sacred this space."

Sprinkle the perimeter and return to the altar.

Pick up the censer and return to the East, saying:

"Fire and Air, make sacred this space."

Cense the perimeter of the circle and return to the altar.

4. Calling the Quarters

In the East face out, draw an invoking pentagram with the athame, and say:

"I invoke the Guardian of East, Guardian of Air

O Guardian, be here with your intelligence
Bring new beginnings
Protect this rite.
Blessed be."

In the South face out, draw an invoking pentagram with the athame, and say:

"I invoke the Guardian of South, Guardian of Fire
O Guardian, be here with your determination
Bring firmness of will
Protect this rite.
Blessed be."

In the West face out, draw an invoking pentagram with the athame, and say:

"I invoke the Guardian of West, Guardian of Water
O Guardian, be here with your intuition
Bring transformation
Protect this rite.
Blessed be."

In the North face out, draw an invoking pentagram with the athame, and say:

"I invoke the Guardian of North, Guardian of Earth
O Guardian, be here with your strength
Bring stability
Protect this rite.
Blessed be."

In the East, make a final, silent salute.

5. Invoking the Gods

Point the wand to the North and say:

"Beloved Lady, beloved Lord
You are steadfast with me in darkness and light
Be here tonight for my solemn rite
Join me, Lady, protector of all
Join me, Lord, overseer of change
Bless this sacred rite.
Welcome, and blessed be!"

6. Offerings

Begin by offering something heartfelt to the gods unrelated to the parting. This could be an incense offering, a song, drumming, etc. It is just a gift to them, thanking them for joining you.

Next, you can offer a memento to burn, if you wish, saying:

"I offer this [memento] to the fire. May the positive and joyful energy they once contained be a fit offering to the Lady and the Lord."

If you have something to read aloud, or something else to release and then burn, now is the time.

7. Cakes and Wine

Say:

"The universe began when the God fell in love with the Goddess:
They became two so they could become one.
Human love changes, grows, evolves, dies, and is reborn,
but the love of the Gods is eternal.
However we love one another, we are always loved by them.
Their embrace sustains us in good times and bad.
I now celebrate and receive blessings from the union of the Lady and the Lord,
that my work may be sacred tonight."

Hold the athame over the cup and say:

"The sky to the Earth
The twilight to the dawn
Movement to stillness
Lord to Lady."

Plunge the athame into the cup and say:

"Blessed be."

Consecrate the cakes by dipping the athame into the wine and sprinkling drops onto the cakes, forming an invoking pentagram.

Say:

"Sun to the flowers
Rain to the soil
Blessings to the body.
Blessed be."

Take a cake and place it in the libation bowl.

Lift the cup and speak from the heart. It can be as simple as "to the Gods," or it can be detailed. End with "Blessed be." Then, make an offering to the gods by pouring a bit of wine into the libation bowl. Drink only after offering. Then eat a cake.

After the ritual is over, the contents of the libation bowl should be poured out onto the Earth.

8. Cutting Ties

Stand facing North and say:

"Lady and Lord, assist me in the work of cutting ties with [name]."

Consecrate yourself with incense by censing yourself from feet to head and back again, using your hand to bring the smoke close to your body, saying:

"I consecrate myself by Air and Fire, mind and will ready for this moment."

Consecrate yourself with saltwater by flicking water from your fingertips, all over yourself from feet to head and back again, saying:

"I consecrate myself by Water and Earth, heart and body ready for this moment."

Now lift your athame high, and declare loudly:

"I sever these ties!"

Go over your entire body with your athame, staying about one-half inch to one inch from your skin (not touching your body with the blade), using a cutting motion. It is as if there are threads coming off of you, and you are slicing them.

Get your whole body, back and front, being especially careful to include these significant points:

Chakras: Genitals/perineum, base of the spine, solar plexus, heart, throat, third eye, crown of head.

Additional psychic centers: Soles of feet, palms of hands, base of the skull, back of the neck.

Go as slowly as you need to. Thoroughness is important.

When you are done, say loudly:

"All ties are cut. So mote it be."[95]

95 To repeat this part of the ritual, you don't need a cast circle (although you can do so if you wish). Just do an opening meditation to ground and center, then cense, sprinkle, and cut ties with the athame, ending here.

Now, dip your fingers in the wine and anoint yourself on the feet, knees, genitals (just above the pubic bone), breasts (just above the nipples), throat, lips, and third eye, saying:

"I bless myself with wine."

Repeat the entire process with the oil, saying:

"I bless myself with oil."

Now say:

"I am whole and complete. I am free."

9. Closing the Circle

Face North, raise the wand, and say:

"Beloved Lord and Lady
Thank you for your presence and blessing at this sacred rite.
Farewell!"

In the East, draw a banishing pentagram and say:

"I thank you, Guardian of the East,
Guardian of Air
For protecting this rite
Thank you, and farewell!"

In the South, draw a banishing pentagram and say:

"I thank you, Guardian of the South, Guardian of Fire
For protecting this rite
Thank you, and farewell!"

In the West, draw a banishing pentagram and say:

"I thank you, Guardian of the West, Guardian of Water
For protecting this rite
Thank you, and farewell!"

In the North, draw a banishing pentagram and say:

"I thank you, Guardian of the North, Guardian of Earth

For protecting this rite
Thank you, and farewell!"

Facing the center, say:

"The circle is open but unbroken, the rites are ended.
Merry meet, merry part, and merry meet again!"

Chapter Nine:

DEEPENING PRACTICE

Now that you've got the basics of Wiccan ritual, you may be asking yourself: What *else* do Wiccans do? Maybe you just want the lay of the land, or maybe you want to surround yourself with Wicca all the time, and you're wondering what that looks like.

Daily and Periodic Practice

There's a lot that you can do to deepen your experience of Wicca. Part of this is simply practice—what do you do every day, every week, every month, or once in a while? Part of it is training and learning to be better at the skills used in Wicca.

Requirements

Every religion has its own level of required practice. People are familiar with the idea of going to church in Christianity. In most denominations, you're supposed to go once a week on Sunday, as well as on specific holidays and for certain special occasions (like a baptism). Everything else, such as personal prayer, is optional.

The level of required versus optional participation is enormously variable from religion to religion. Religions with dietary restrictions, such as Islam and Judaism, are essentially asking for perpetual participation; you are constantly aware of religion when everything you eat and drink is affected by that religion.

"Required" is an interesting word, though. Many religions tell you that *not* following the rules will cause some kind of cosmic retribution—you participate because God will bless you if you do, or God will punish you if you do not. Unbaptized children go to Hell.

Not all religions follow that model, so you could argue that, in those cases, *nothing* is required. Release from a punishment-and-reward cycle is liberating, although it can also lead to a kind of ritual laziness. When it's entirely up to you, it's easy to blow off a ritual and watch TV instead.

I speak from experience. One of the reasons I have always had a group is that I am much more motivated when other people depend on me. If I am attending a coven meeting—and especially if people are showing up at my home for a meeting—I am very reliable. If I am casting a solitary circle, I am very *un*reliable. "Know thyself," I guess. I certainly know people with a vibrant and active solitary practice. Solitary motivation must be internal and self-sustaining, and each individual has to find its source. What keeps your practice going?

For me, the interconnection of a community of Wiccans is core to my practice, but I also know that I simply feel better when I have regular ritual in my life. As I've aged, health issues have made group participation a little dicey, and of course, there was the COVID lockdown. After decades of focusing on group practice, I've had to make sure I have plenty of private connections to the Gods.

A less restrictive definition of "required" is the functional rules of a system. It's like playing a game: God doesn't punish you if you violate the rules of Monopoly, but playing without the rules means it's no game at all. Additionally, people have "house rules" for lots of games, rules they've invented that they find make the game better. Once you introduce a house rule, you treat it exactly as seriously as an official rule. Treating rules seriously is a fiction that we implement in our lives because it makes things more fun and satisfying. In Wicca, this is the definition of "required" that we're using.

In Wicca, the ritual requirements are *observe the moons and observe the Sabbats.* That's it.

There are certain additional requirements for specific traditions: For example, to be a member of a tradition, you usually must undergo an initiation ceremony, and there may be additional requirements associated with that. Some traditions have additional rituals, such as a dedication, an elevation to a higher degree, a naming, and so on. Other practices, such as meditation or fasting, may be associated with becoming or being an initiate. But in Wicca as a whole, full moons and the eight holidays are the entirety of the requirement. (If a moon and a holiday fall on the same day, or very close to each other, you generally skip the moon and just perform the holiday.)

Frequency

You may or may not be a person with a knack for creating daily discipline in your life. I know I'm not! Part of putting together a sustaining, enriching practice is to have it be fulfilling, and not a source of blame or shame. If you decide on a daily practice and then beat yourself up when you miss a day, the beating might do more harm than the benefit gained. Don't fall into the trap of considering yourself "not spiritual enough" if your practice is sporadic. We're all different.

There was a period of my life when I had a hyperactive child (baby/toddler/kid as she grew) and a disabled husband. It was *a lot.* There were many days when the idea of a spiritual practice was just out of reach. Eventually, I developed a habit of getting up in the morning and spending about a minute at my altar. Truly, it was just *a minute* of breathing, focusing, and being with the Goddess. That was what I had available in my gas tank—not a minute more. It helped to have that minute but demanding that I do more would have just been unrealistic and painful.

Daily may be out of reach, but "some days" may work for you.

I strongly recommend a weekly practice as well (or instead). The week as a spiritual unit isn't part of Wicca the way it is in many mainstream religions, such as those with Sabbath observance (Friday in Islam, Saturday in Judaism and for Seventh Day Adventists, and Sunday in most Christian denominations). It's inherent, though, in observing moon phases: A week each for new/first quarter, half/second quarter, third quarter, and full/fourth quarter.

During the COVID lockdown, it often felt like every day was the same as every other day, endlessly. I live in a city, so, especially in the early days of mask shortages, leaving the apartment at all felt impossible. It was the only time in my life I really longed for the suburbs. I got very jealous of my mother's big, green, private backyard.

It was during this period that I developed a weekly practice. What it provided was an *end* to the week, and the *beginning* of the next week. Instead of time being an endless slog, I had a reset. It felt cyclic in the positive and nourishing manner of the Wheel of the Year.

Developing a Daily or Periodic Practice

Just because something isn't required doesn't mean you can't do it. There are many practices typical or characteristic of a religion without being required. For Christians, daily prayer or periodic Bible study would be examples of this.

What are the characteristic optional practices of Wicca? I'd say most Wiccans have one, some, or all of these as part of their day-to-day lives:

- Ritual
- Altar practice
- Prayer/worship
- Spellwork
- Meditation
- Mind/body exercises
- Experience in nature
- Shielding
- Journaling
- Divination

Let's look at each of these individually. While none of the following is written to teach you how to do (ritual/altar work/spellwork/etc.), it can show you how to incorporate each into a Wiccan life.

Ritual

There's no rule that says you can *only* do Wiccan ritual on moons and Sabbats. There's no rule that says you have to confine yourself to only *Wiccan* ritual.

A Wiccan can cast a solitary circle whenever they choose. A full circle is, perhaps, more elaborate than you want to commit to daily or weekly, in which case, you could modify normal ritual steps for a quick version. This is also where things like prayer, worship, and altar practice come in.

You might also practice other kinds of ritual. I have a Wiccan friend with a full Hellenistic practice, which has frequent ritual requirements. I know several Wiccans who also do Hindu puja, a Native American Wiccan who maintains both practices, and several who practice ceremonial magic. I am not the only Wiccan I know who attends synagogue regularly—I have a daily Jewish practice as well.

Altar Practice

As discussed under *Altars* (page 52), you may have one or several home altars. Perhaps you have an ancestor altar as well as a generic meditation space. Perhaps you have a devotional altar to a deity with whom you have a special relationship, as well as a more traditionally Wiccan "Lord and Lady" altar.

Part of altar practice is "using" the altar: Grounding and centering there, balancing yourself, and worshiping.

Another part is care and feeding. Altars should be kept clean. Offerings should be renewed. Mere hours ago, as I write this, my daughter and I had a conversation about the ancestor altar she keeps for her late father. She was out of whiskey, and he definitely likes whiskey on his altar! Spirits and entities contacted at our altars become accustomed to the gifts we give them, so there's a commitment there. They have ways of making their wishes known—through dreams, "coincidences," and odd phenomena. (You can put an altar to "sleep" by covering it with a cloth if you want or need, for any reason, to suspend the commitment.)

I really like cleaning my altar and my ritual things. When I do something like polish my metal tools, I focus on the spiritual aspect of cleaning. "Housework" is grounding, it keeps the practice real.

A weekly practice can include things like cleaning the altar, renewing offerings, or bringing fresh flowers.

Sample Altar Work

Here's how I often use my own altar.

I start by standing before it and just looking at it, breathing deeply, calming myself. (It's okay to sit if standing is an issue.) I take in each component.

I ring a small bell to bring myself present to the moment and "declare" a beginning.

I bow before the Goddess.

I light incense and cense myself and the altar.

(Sometimes I skip lighting the incense because my altar is in the bedroom and my spouse has sinus issues. In this case, I touch my third eye with a feather and then a piece of tiger eye, to bring in Air and then Fire.)

I touch each element: Having censed myself, I touch first a seashell (Water), then a piece of granite (Earth), to my third eye.

Sometimes I pick up one of the other objects on the altar—a favorite crystal, perhaps. I hold it and feel its energy. Or I say a small prayer, like, "Beloved Goddess, be with me here at your altar as I worship you." Or I say nothing, and simply breathe, listening for the voice of the Goddess and any messages she may have for me. Or I light a candle, and gaze at the flame, stilling my mind.

I do this until it feels right to stop. I put out the candle if I've lit it (but leave the incense going). I ring the bell to "declare" completion.

Other Altar Practices

My example is a Goddess altar. Yours might be for both Lady and Lord, or a God altar, or an altar to another deity.

Deities are individuals. A devotional altar to Bridget will be very different from one dedicated to Odin. For example, an Aphrodite altar might be replete with seashells, pearls, sparkly things, and makeup. Practice at her altar might include gazing into the mirror with self-love and reciting affirmations of love.

Always *listen* at your altar. It's a place for the small, still voice to be heard. It's a place where the deity or being to whom you are offering can give messages to you, which can include information on how they wish to be worshiped or honored.

An altar might not be dedicated to a deity or other entity at all; it might simply be a place to ground, center, balance, and meditate, or a place to do magic. Or you might have an ancestor altar, which can give honor to the Mighty Dead who were your blood kin or your spiritual kin.

Prayer and Worship

Prayer and worship could be part of your ritual practice, part of your altar practice, or could occur separate from, or in addition to, either of those.

In our first pages, I defined Wicca as "modern Pagan witchcraft." The "Pagan" part is, by definition, religious. While some people understand deities as metaphors, almost every Pagan I've ever met has a religious/spiritual connection to the Gods that is very real to them.

Some people have a practice that includes things like a prayer of thanks before each meal, or prayers before bed. Again, I'm a fan of simplicity. If you want to spend fifteen minutes in deep, contemplative prayer, more power to you. I'm more the type to simply say, "*Thank you, Goddess, for allowing me to open my eyes upon another living day. Blessed be.*"

Here's my advice:

First, use your altar practice to ask the Gods what they *want* of you.

Second, look for the spots of life that feel empty, that look like holes to be filled.

Finally, look to the spots of life that provoke anxiety, dread, or ennui, and ask if the presence of the Gods can alleviate that pain.

During the early days of COVID, there was an enormous amount of attention on handwashing. It became a big source of anxiety for me (as well as for many other people). I began a practice of washing my hands thoroughly first thing each morning and following it with the traditional Jewish prayer for handwashing. This took a source of anxiety and transformed it into a moment of grounding and spiritual connection. When lockdown ended, I maintained the practice.

Spellwork

Again, returning to my opening definition of Wicca, "modern Pagan witchcraft," we can understand that witchcraft is an inherent part of being Wiccan.

I know several Wiccans who maintain a regular healing altar. Here, they focus their energies on any healing requests that have come their way, light a healing candle, and send energy to those in need. Usually, these are family, friends, and friends-of-friends. Some people send healing energy daily, some only at certain moon phases, some on some other schedule.

It's common for healing requests to be an ongoing component of Pagan and Wiccan social media. I respond to healing requests only if I can clearly connect to the subject—connection is a big part of how I do magic. So, if a request is posted without a picture of the person or a description of the illness, or even a name, I don't send energy. This is so common! You see things like "please send healing to my uncle," and these baffle me. Who is your uncle? Where is your uncle? Why does he need energy? What *kind* of energy?

Again, if you find yourself able and willing to respond to such requests, go ahead, but for me, the request is meaningless.

Witchcraft, though, is more than just sending healing energy. Magic and spells can be elaborate or simple, over in a flash, or enacted over a period of days or weeks. Magic can also require prep work, and part of being a witch is often the ongoing mess of herbs and brews in the kitchen, jars being cleaned out, craft projects, or the like.

For myself, I have found that I do less magic as the years go by. Certain things are routine, like placing protection over my home and car, and renewing that from time to time. But by and large, I reserve magic for specific needs: Severe health issues or health issues where the diagnosis is elusive, fertility, protection of someone in danger, job seeking, and other big needs, usually for someone in my immediate circle or someone connected to my immediate circle. For most day-to-day stuff, I don't find magic necessary. But even though I do less than I used to, I still consider it a part of my regular practice, and part of being a witch. (And of course, I'm also doing magic as part of most esbats.)

Meditation

I would venture to say that almost all Wiccans have some kind of meditation practice in their lives. Some meditate daily, some less often, some only as preparation for ritual, but just about everyone does it.

In addition to the well-known mental and physical health benefits of meditation, witchcraft and ritual draw on your ability to calm your mind, focus your thoughts, and access your imagination—all of which are trained in meditation. Ritual asks you to set aside thoughts of the day and be fully present in the moment. Magic asks you to concentrate fixedly on a goal without allowing yourself to become distracted.

A meditation practice requires the ability to carve out uninterrupted stillness. I didn't meditate regularly when I had a toddler. Maybe you can manage ten minutes a day, and deeper meditation once a week, or before ritual. Perhaps a walking meditation will work better for you—getting you physically away from the distractions of your life.

From Hinduism, we have learned the concept of a *mantra*—a repeated phrase used in meditation to help focus the mind, and a *mandala*—an image gazed upon during meditation for the same purpose. (Catholics who recite the rosary are also using a kind of mantra.)

You can easily come up with a mantra that is more specifically Wiccan in nature. I often use a phrase from The Charge: "I am the beauty of the green earth, and the white moon among the stars, and the mystery of the waters, and the desire of the heart of man." As a mandala, you might use an image of the Goddess or God, the moon, an astrological symbol, or a Tree of Life glyph. (While astrology and Kabbalah aren't specifically Wiccan, they are associated with Western occultism, and much more closely related to Wicca than a Hindu or Christian symbol.)

Mind/Body Exercises

Practices like yoga or tai chi, which combine breathing techniques, physical movement, and mental focus, are a part of many people's spiritual path. There is not a specifically Wiccan mind/body practice (except those exclusive to certain traditions), so most people will borrow from other paths. It is not cultural appropriation to borrow, for example, yoga from Hinduism, provided it is done respectfully. Yoga isn't a "closed tradition," and is made available by Hindu teachers to all.

Experience in Nature

Most Wiccans incorporate some kind of connection to nature into their day-to-day lives. How this manifests depends on many factors, including where you live, your physical abilities, and your inclination. Any of the exercises offered under *Nature Exercises* (page 20) can become part of your day-to-day life. For example:

- Simply walking in nature on a regular basis
- Walking in your own neighborhood, even if it's not "nature," and paying attention to the environment: What do you see, hear, and smell? What has changed over time? What is alive?
- Finding a specific tree and regularly connecting to it
- Being outside at night and observing the phase of the moon
- Greeting the moon (I blow a kiss) when you first see it each night
- Greeting the sun each morning
- Gardening

Shielding

Shielding is the act of drawing a psychic shield around oneself for protection. You might consider it a subset of ritual, meditation, or even spellwork. The simplest shield is just visualizing yourself surrounded by a protective egg of white light. Obviously, there's more to it than that, and whole books have been written on the subject (see *Recommended Reading*).

People who consider themselves empaths—people with deep sensitivity to the feelings and thoughts of others—benefit enormously from shielding, which helps to create a barrier between self and other. Shielding also helps when your environment is particularly intense. The environmental energy doesn't have to be *bad* to require shielding; if that energy is wonderful but *a lot*, it's perfectly fine to shield.

For some people, shielding is a regular, daily, or twice-daily activity. For others, it's circumstantial, done only in times of specific need.

Journaling

Many people keep all kinds of journals, for all sorts of reasons, and this can be incorporated into a magical life. A daily diary, a gratitude journal, or a bullet journal aren't particularly Wiccan, but they *are* mindfulness practices.

You can also keep a ritual and/or a spell journal. I note down the date, moon phase, who attended, and what was done. Before menopause, I also noted where I was in my menstrual cycle. (I don't keep other astrological information, but many people do. My late ex-husband kept his notes in an astrological calendar, saving himself the trouble of adding that data.) For spells, I go back with follow-up notes, meaning, if I did a healing spell for someone, I will keep notes on their subsequent health results.

I've also kept dream journals, and this is a powerful way to explore the subconscious mind. For dream journaling, it's crucial to keep the journal near the bed and write immediately upon waking, before the imagery flees. Alarm clocks are disruptive if you're trying to remember dreams, so some people are only able to keep such a journal on their days off.

Finally, many people keep divination journals, which brings us to our next section.

Divination

While divination isn't specifically Wiccan, or even witchcraft, it's nearly universal among witches. Tarot is undoubtedly the most popular divination tool, but there are many others, including runestones, astrology, tea leaf reading, oracle cards, and I Ching.

Divination can be practical, or it can be more psychological. Many people draw a daily Tarot card—a practice so popular that you'll find it called COTD (Card of the Day) on social media. The COTD is meant for insight and wisdom about challenges and opportunities in the day to come. It can be accompanied by journaling—noting the card, insights, and perceptions about what it seems to mean, and end-of-the-day notes about what the actual outcome was.

Mind/Consciousness Work

One thing that is unique about occult religions, as opposed to more mainstream religions, is that you're supposed to be good at it. The ordinary concept of religion doesn't include the idea that religion has any skill involved; you're just supposed to do it. But in Wicca and other occult religions, there's a skill set that makes your rituals more powerful and more satisfying. In fact, this skill set can be applied to mainstream religion as well. When I began to practice Judaism in 2018, I discovered my skill as a Wiccan and as a priestess enabled me to dive in deeply and get value from it that had not been accessible to me as a youngster.

A Wiccan is expected to have skills as a ritualist and as a magician. Some of the ritual skills are creative, some are theatrical, some are interpersonal. But mind and consciousness training is often the root of what we do.

Centering

You will often hear instructions to "ground and center," but these are separate things that are done in tandem, so let's look at them one at a time. Even though people always seem to say "ground and center," they can be done in either order. I usually prefer to center first as I think it makes grounding more effective, but both ways work.

Centering is simply to find your own center and to bring yourself fully to that center. Your "center" is the seat of yourself, the place where the "you" resides. You might see that as your solar plexus, or your heart, or your head, but after a moment's consideration, you'll be able to find it.

The trick is to bring all the parts of yourself that are everywhere *but* your center back home. Most of us are scattered most of the time. We're in the past, either long ago in some memory, or still in the traffic we drove through an hour ago. We're in the future, planning, hoping, worrying, anticipating. We're in different places, with different people. I'm here, but I'm also thinking about my daughter in New York, my mom, my sister's health, my doctor appointment, my job. None of that is conducive to effective ritual. I have to have all of *me* in my rituals, not just for the sake of my Wicca, but to be more present for my daughter, mom, sister, job, etc. Centering is a great ritual skill, but it's also a great life skill.

How to Center

1. Calm yourself.
2. Find your center.
3. Consider all the parts of yourself that are not in your center.
4. Bring them to your center.

Centering Exercise: Birds Fly Home

This is my favorite way to center, and it's what I usually use.

Close your eyes.
Take three slow, deep breaths.
Notice that you have a center. Breathe into that center.
Notice the parts of yourself that are not in your center. Your thoughts and feelings are scattered like birds in the air.
Allow the birds to fly home to the nest that is your center.
Take your concerns of the day and fly home.
Take your concerns about yesterday and fly home.
Take your concerns about tomorrow and fly home.
When all of you has come back to the nest, open your eyes.

Centering Exercise: I Am Here

This one doesn't use any metaphors or imagery and may be more comfortable for some people.

Close your eyes.
Take three slow, deep breaths.
Notice that you have a center. Breathe into that center.
Say (out loud or silently), *"I am here."*
Find the thoughts that are not in your center. Let go of the things you are imagining. Say, *"I am here."*
Let go of the past and breathe into your center, saying, *"I am here."*
Let go of the future and breathe into your center, saying, *"I am here."*
Let go of all the things that are not here, breathing into your center, saying, *"I am here."*
When you are ready, open your eyes.

Grounding

To ground is to connect yourself to your physical reality and the Earth. Grounding alleviates anxiety and is often used to deal with post-traumatic stress.

In Wicca, we use grounding in some specific ways: We don't just "connect to the Earth," we connect to Mother Earth, and we draw on her energy. This prevents us from depleting our own energy in ritual. It also anchors us. Sometimes you see people get incredibly spacey after ritual, or you get a sensation that you are flying away and can't get back to reality after ritual is over. Grounding protects you from that. It allows you to "travel" in ritual while still being able to get back home. Grounding keeps you sane and safe, and it gives you access to the maximum amount of energy you can bring to whatever you do next.

How to Ground

1. Calm yourself.
2. Find your body.
3. Connect your body to the earth.

Grounding Exercise: I Have a Body

This is the technique I use at the beginning of almost all my private meditations. I do this before any other meditation technique or visualization.

Close your eyes. Take three deep, slow breaths.
Notice that you have toes. Breathe in, breathe out.
Notice that you have feet. Breathe in, breathe out.
Notice that you have lower legs. Breathe in, breathe out.
Notice that you have thighs. Breathe in, breathe out.
Notice that you have a butt. Breathe in, breathe out.

Notice that you have genitals. Breathe in, breathe out.
Notice that you have hips and a pelvis. Breathe in, breathe out.
Notice that you have a belly and internal organs. Breathe in, breathe out.
Notice that you have a lower back. Breathe in, breathe out.
Notice that you have a middle back. Breathe in, breathe out.
Notice that you have a chest. Breathe in, breathe out.
Notice that you have an upper back. Breathe in, breathe out.
Notice that you have fingers. Breathe in, breathe out.
Notice that you have hands. Breathe in, breathe out.
Notice that you have forearms. Breathe in, breathe out.
Notice that you have upper arms. Breathe in, breathe out.
Notice that you have shoulders. Breathe in, breathe out.
Notice that you have shoulder blades. Breathe in, breathe out.
Notice that you have a collar bone. Breathe in, breathe out.
Notice that you have a neck. Breathe in, breathe out.
Notice that you have a jaw. Breathe in, breathe out.
Notice that you have a head. Breathe in, breathe out.
Notice that you have a face. Breathe in, breathe out.
Notice that you have a crown. Breathe in, breathe out.
Notice that you have a body. Breathe in, breathe out.
Notice that you are on the Earth in a body. Breathe in, breathe out.
Open your eyes.

A variation on this technique is to clench and relax each body part, instead of simply observing it.

Grounding Exercise: The Tree

Close your eyes. Take three deep, slow breaths.
Find your center.
See, in your center, a glowing ball of energy. Allow this energy to pulse and grow.
See the energy flowing down through your tailbone (if you are seated)/through the soles of your feet (if you are standing), into the earth.
Feel the energy leave you and go through the floor, through the foundation of the building, through concrete, through topsoil, into the deep, cold depths of the earth.
Your energy leaves your body like the roots of a tree, and like the roots of a tree, you find nourishment in the earth.
Allow your roots to be fed by the loving embrace of the Earth Mother. You feel her energy, and she embraces you.
The Earth Mother sends energy up through your roots, up through the earth, into your (soles/spine).
The energy of the Earth fills your legs, fills your torso, fills the entire trunk of the tree that you are.
The energy of the Earth fills your trunk and reaches into your branches.

Notice that your arms and hands are branches, receiving the energy of the Earth.

Notice your head is the top of a tree, receiving the energy of the Earth.

You are touched by the sky, nourished by rain, embraced by wind, and connected to the living Earth.

Reach your branches up to touch the sky.

Feel yourself, from branch to root, energized by the Mother.

When you are ready, open your eyes.

A variation on this technique is to skip the tree imagery entirely but still use the ball of energy that goes into the Earth and feeds your body.

Visualization

People tend to use "visualization" when they mean "imagination." About 80% of people are visual thinkers—they get pictures in their heads. But 20% is a huge minority. If you hear, feel, or imagine in some other way, that is perfectly okay.

Almost always, you can train weak senses. I am not a visual thinker, and in the past, I wasn't able to reliably create pictures in my head, but after a lot of practice, I can do so today. It's a helpful skill. I tend, though, to feel things in my body, and to see words. If you say "rose" to most people, they'll see a rose. I'll see R-O-S-E in my mind's eye, while smelling a rose. But I'm not failing, because I'm bringing forth the rose, and that's what counts.

Visualization/imagination is used all the time in Wicca—you "see" the circle, you "see" the invoking and banishing pentagrams, and, when doing magic, you "see" the target and the goal.

As with any mind skill, practice and training make an enormous difference. Practice with eyes-closed imagery happens during meditation, during grounding and centering, and so on. But it's also important to practice with your eyes open: To see or experience what you choose to see superimposed onto what your optic nerves see.

Imagination Exercise: The Pentagram

With your athame or your fingers, draw an invoking pentagram in the air (see illustration on page 82).

As you do so, see blue electricity come from the tip of your athame/fingers and hang in the air in the shape of the pentagram.

Notice that the electricity crackles and that you can hear it.

Notice that the electricity has a scent and that you can smell it.

Notice that the electricity causes your skin to tingle.

Hold that image.

Now, draw a banishing pentagram in the same spot (page 87) and see the blue electricity absorbed back into your athame/fingers. Notice that the sound, scent, and sensation all withdraw.

Repeat this exercise until each sense, even your weakest ones, helps to create and banish the pentagram.

Stillness

Stillness as a consciousness practice is both ancient and *really damn hard.* It has *always* been hard. Think of stories of monks sitting on mountaintops meditating for decades to achieve true silence. It takes decades because the mind does not like silence.

The "monkey brain"—the endless chatter of thoughts, opinions, memories, and observations—is not you; it is not your spirit or your center. Part of exercising stillness is learning to observe those chattery thoughts and noticing that you are apart from them.

The most difficult kind of stillness meditation is absolute silence, with the goal being no-mind, that is, silencing the monkey. It's possible to have little flickers of that, and even a flicker is astonishing. Instead, most people use some kind of intermediary—candle gazing, reciting a mantra, or looking at a mandala, as mentioned under *Meditation* on page 312.

As you meditate in stillness, your brain will chatter. Your goal is to notice it, let it go, and gently return to your stillness. Often, in the beginning, you'll readily interact with the chatter or criticize it. Your head will go something like this, "I'd love a cup of coffee. Oh, hey, I'm supposed to be meditating, not thinking about coffee. Great, now I'm thinking about my thoughts about coffee, this could go on forever. With hazelnut."

Instead, just observe the thought and release it.

A number of things happen when you practice this as a discipline: First, you get better at releasing unwanted thoughts, which is helpful in ritual. Second, you become familiar with how the voice in your head behaves and its unique method of trying to distract you. Third, thoughts, feelings, and memories that you normally suppress can begin to surface. In this way, you come to know yourself better. As you learn how to let distracting thoughts go, those under-the-surface thoughts come forward. They, too, should be let go during meditation, but later, you can engage with whatever new information you've learned about yourself.

Stillness Exercise: Candle Gazing

Create an atmosphere of privacy and silence. You can use recorded music if that helps you focus. (It's also more pleasant than a timer.)

Light a candle.

Find a comfortable seated position where you feel unbound—that is, your arms and legs are not tight or crossed, and your body is open.

Take some deep breaths.

Center yourself.

Ground yourself.

Look at the candle and allow your mind to go blank.

As thoughts come in, release them. Return to the candle.

In the beginning, just do this for five or ten minutes. Eventually, twenty minutes should be accessible without driving you crazy.

Emotional Focus

Lots of Wiccan teachers (especially early ones) have focused on generating emotion as the most important part of doing magic. Energy is raised, they say, from the passions. To magically heal, *passionately desire* to heal. To magically drive away an enemy, feel the rage and force necessary, the force you'd feel if you were physically driving them away. Thus, generating emotion is another part of training the mind of the witch.

Instead of meditating, the best way to do this is to borrow from Method acting, which has, over more than a century, developed techniques for generating an emotional state in actors to create realistic, compelling performances. The "performance," in our case, is the magical ritual.

Affective memory is finding and bringing to mind a specific memory that generates the desired emotion—something that made you, in these examples, passionate, angry, or forceful. *Emotional recall* takes that memory and brings up the feelings associated with it, and *sense memory* brings in the physical sensations associated with the feeling—rapid breathing when angry, for example. By recalling the memory, emotional feeling, and body sensations, you can generate the emotional state and use that state in ritual.

Famously, Method actors can get lost in the emotions of their characters, and this can negatively impact their lives. Fortunately, you are doing this for an hour or so, not the weeks or months involved with filming a movie or staging a play. Nonetheless, for intense emotional work, ground and center before and after, focusing on calm, steady breathing when you're finished.

Dream Work

Some people are naturally lucid dreamers, but most are not. Some people readily remember their dreams, but many do not.

The dream state is a rich and complex part of life. We spend about one-third of our lives asleep, much of it in the REM state (dreaming). There are a lot of ideas about what dreams are: Nonsensical clearing out of mental synapses, psychological processing of feelings, messages from our higher consciousness or from other spiritual beings, clairvoyance, or none of the above. I tend to think it varies from night to night, from dream to dream. Some dreams are clairvoyant, while most are not. Some are messages, but most don't seem to be.

It is possible to work with our dreams more consciously, to have a better relationship between the waking self and the sleeping self.

Begin by keeping a dream journal. If you have a waking journal, you might want a separate one just for dreams—or not.

Tips for Dream Recall

- Alarm clocks startle you awake and tend to drive away dream recall. If you must wake to an alarm and want to work with dreams, focus on days off or naps as a source of dreams.
- Keep your dream journal and a pen next to you when you sleep or use a voice recorder. Immediate recollection is quite rich, but the longer you're awake without articulating the dream, the more distant the dream becomes.

- If you can't remember your dream, or it starts to run away from you, don't ask yourself, "What was I dreaming?" Instead, ask, "Where was I just now?" or "Who was I just talking with?" Those questions bring you back to the dream state and are much more likely to produce memories.
- Don't worry that you can't. Everyone dreams, and everyone is capable of remembering dreams. This is true of all people, without exception, even if you've never remembered a dream.

Recalling dreams is the first step on a journey of communicating with your dreams in a way that is meaningful and helpful. It opens a pathway without demanding anything on that path.

The next step is to ask questions of your dreams. This can be a form of divination or a form of guidance. It can clarify things that happen in the waking world.

I once had a series of what I can only describe as omens happen, one after another, over the course of a few days. A huge art book fell millimeters from my foot as I was about to pay for it. The next day, a piece of a door jamb fell on my head and drew a bit of blood. (Both of those things could have been much worse.) The next day, I came across a dead bird in my path as I was taking my usual lunchtime walk. I saw a pattern of things falling on me from above, and I wanted to take it seriously.

I do not read Tarot for myself when I consider it important. I want an objective outsider. I got a reading, and it pointed toward a message from a particular goddess. I made a traditional offering to that goddess and then asked for a dream message. (Honestly, a dream message seemed a lot safer than the kind of messages I had been receiving.)

The dream I received seemed to give me certain instructions, which I followed. After a couple of months, I had a very clear dream that this goddess was instructing me to stop—we were done.

I'll be honest here: I have no idea why that goddess was sending me messages, or why she instructed me to stop. It was a strange interlude to be sure. But the dream communications helped.

Things to Ask for in Dreams

- Understanding something happening in waking life
- Guidance on your path
- Messages from a deity you worship
- Messages from the honored dead
- Messages or instructions regarding an upcoming ritual (perhaps just the night before)

How to Ask for a Dream

1. Do not set an alarm for the morning. This should only be done when you can awaken naturally.
2. If you have an altar, ask at your altar, for the desired dream.
3. Otherwise, light a candle and some incense, anoint yourself with saltwater, and say, *"Tonight I will dream X."*
4. Get in bed and say again, *"Tonight I will dream X."*
5. Go immediately to sleep, don't read, play with your phone, have sex, or anything else.
6. Upon waking, immediately journal your dream.

7. Do this every night until you understand yourself to have received an answer (except in the case of the dream work the night before a ritual).

Energy Work

During Wiccan practice, you're often asked to "raise," "feel," or "send" energy, and this can be confusing. You probably have a sense of what this means; you've probably felt energy, but you may be frustrated by the vagueness of it all.

When I was a teenager, I started having some really interesting experiences with energy. There was one time I "massaged" a friend while sitting behind him during a meeting at school—I moved my hands a couple of inches from his head. After the meeting, he said, "That felt amazing, what was that?" My first girlfriend and I would make invisible energy balls and pass them back and forth, shaping the energy with each pass. I desperately wanted to learn what the hell was going on! It was part of what led me to witchcraft in the first place.

What is Energy?

We know what power is, even if we can't define it. It's *oomph*. It can feel tingly, enlivening, like we're full.

Our own bodies have an energy field known as the *aura;* this concept was first popularized in Theosophy. Seven "layers" of aura are defined in Theosophy, and the one that closely hugs the body is the *etheric body*. This field of energy is what I was touching when I massaged my friend. We can easily draw upon it, as my girlfriend and I did long ago.

Energy spills out of us all the time. Think about walking into a room and realizing that the people in it are upset or were just fighting—we feel this before we see people's faces or body language—we just *know*.

The Earth also has energy, which we draw upon when we ground. This protects us from draining our own energy by giving us a power source much greater than ourselves.

Our magical tools are imbued with energy when we consecrate them (page 49), and they gain energy over time, as we use them. This, in turn, allows us to draw on their energy. It's synergistic—we give them energy, then we use them, drawing on their energy, which then increases their power, which we draw on again next time we use them, and so on. Over a period of years, a well-used tool becomes supercharged.

When we cast a circle, we fill it with energy—with our own, with the power of the elements, with power from the Guardians of the quarters, and with power from the gods. There is also, in a group ritual, the power of a group mind—the whole that is greater than the sum of its parts. Group mind can be negative (like mob behavior) or positive (like the joy at a concert). In ritual, we control and elevate group mind energy.

Feeling Energy

By practicing what energy feels like raised from your own body, you will become more skilled with energy—with sensing it, with raising it, and with using it. In magic, we don't want to *just* use our own body's energy, but it's the best place to start learning.

People are individuals. You might feel energy best in your hands (as I do), in your center, in your breath, or in movement. We'll briefly explore each of these.

These exercises are written for you to do alone. However, all of them are great to do with a partner or in a group.

Energy from the Hands

1. Center yourself with three deep breaths.
2. Rub your hands rapidly together until they feel warm.
3. Hold your hands as if you were about to clap them, about an inch apart. Bring them gently in and out, closer and farther, without touching. Do this until you can feel a cushion of energy, heat, or tingling between your hands.

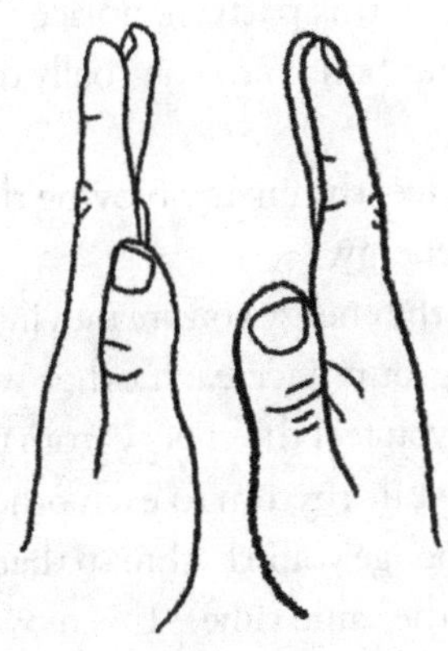

Hands held apart

4. Now gently switch hands. If your left was on top, pull them apart and bring them back to the same position, but with the right on top. Feel the cushion of energy soften and then increase as you do this.
5. Repeat the switch a few times, feeling the energy grow.
6. Experiment with hand movements. What causes the energy to increase? What causes it to decrease? Try a weaving motion with your fingers. Try stretching your hands flat and using only your palms. Try shaping the cushion into a ball.
7. Move your hands in and out to a rhythm, as if clapping to a song (still not touching). What do changes in tempo do to the energy?
8. If you have a partner or a group, bring your hands to another/the other person's hands, again, so they are close but not touching. Feel one another's energy. Move your hands back and forth, feeling each other's energy.
9. With a partner or a group, "send" (push energy out) with one hand while receiving with the other. Then switch.
10. When you're ready to finish, bring your hands to your face (still not touching) and allow the energy to be absorbed back into your body.
11. Now touch your face, touch your hands to each other, and finish with one loud hand clap.

Energy in the Breath

Breathing is a way to access energy from your center, from the heart, or from the breath itself. There are many, many breathing techniques. I am by no means an expert on all or even most of them, but we can start simply.

1. Center yourself with three deep breaths.
2. Inhale deeply through the nose, breathing into your belly, for a count of four. Feel the air move down through you. As you do so, soften your chest and allow the air to push your belly out.
3. Hold for a count of four.
4. Exhale slowly through your mouth, feeling the air moving through you, to a count of four.
5. Hold for a count of four.[96]
6. As you continue to breathe in this pattern, notice the energy moving through your body. Draw the energy through your body into your belly on the inhale. Push the energy out, into your aura, on the exhale.
7. As you continue to breathe, feel the energy moving throughout your body. Pay attention to where you most notice the energy.
8. What do you perceive about the energy you are moving? Does it have a color? A temperature?
9. If you have a partner or a group, face each other while continuing to breathe. Feel one another's energy. Where do you feel the energy from them? Where do they feel it from you? Breathe together, matching your rhythm to each other. How does this change the energy?
10. With a partner or a group, change your rhythm so that one of you is exhaling while the other is inhaling (you will hold at the same time). This moves the energy back and forth between you. How does that feel?
11. When you are ready to finish, take a very deep breath and blow it out hard.

Chanting

Chanting moves the breath and also creates energy through the vibration of sound.

A simple technique is to chant each vowel sound, from the highest to the lowest, on each exhale. Hold the sound through the full exhale.

1. Inhale and then hold as before.
2. On exhale, chant "Ah" (the short A as in "bah").
3. Inhale and hold.
4. On exhale, chant "Eh" (the short E as in "bed").
5. Inhale and hold.
6. On exhale, chant "Ee" (the long E as in "bee").
7. Inhale and hold.
8. On exhale, chant "Oh" (the long O as in "go").
9. Inhale and hold.
10. On exhale, chant "Ooh" (the long U as in "goo").

96 This is sometimes called "square breathing" or "box breathing" because it is 4x4.

Note how the energy changes with each sound. Note that the location of the sound in your body changes with each sound.

Energy in Movement

There are even more movement techniques than breath techniques! All of the following are types of movement that can be used to raise energy:

- Freeform dance
- Simple walking dance steps, like a grapevine or a shuffle
- Swaying back and forth
- Hand clapping
- Foot stomping
- Rhythmic hand movements like patty-cake
- Jumping up and down
- Arm waves

Because movement can be high- or low-intensity, full-body or partial, it is accessible to anyone regardless of physical limitations. Professor Spouse has had four major knee surgeries but has been able to use hand and arm movements when even simple dance was too painful.

Movement works best with musical accompaniment. You can chant or drum (both of which are great sources of energy themselves) or use recorded music. As a solitary, drumming and dancing at once is impractical, but a rattle, tambourine, or other hand-held instrument can be used.

Energy from movement is generated in part from rhythm, which syncs body to brain, in part from the *pleasure* of movement, and in part, like the hand and breath techniques, by expanding your awareness to include your aura (the etheric body), feeling that aura, and enlarging it. Adding music adds the vibration of sound, which is a source of energy as well.

A Movement Experiment

Repeat the chanting exercise while standing (as you are able). Move to each sound. Perhaps you'll lift your arms to the sky on "Ah," and bring your hands to your heart on "Eh." Maybe spin in a circle on "Ee" and sway back and forth on "Oh." Let the feeling of the sound and movement guide you.

These experiments are the beginning of understanding how you can generate and use energy, and how that energy can impact and empower your work as a Wiccan.

Spells

I have identified spellwork as part of the regular practice of Wicca; however, I have not given any information yet on how to do spells.

This is a huge subject. I've written two books[97] on magic and spells, and I can't condense all that here. What I *can* do is give some simple instructions to help you begin your learning journey.

97 *Magical Power for Beginners* and *Magic of the Elements*. See Recommended Reading.

Magic is a lifelong practice. The funny thing about magic is, it's not a matter of getting steadily better as you learn. Most of us have had remarkable early experiences with magic, and most of us have had dry spells where nothing seems to work. Part of magic, I think, is excitement, freshness—when you start thinking of it as easy, you lose your mojo. So, beginners actually have an advantage.

A lot of beginners don't try spells, but doing so is an important part of your practice. You learn by doing, and you build confidence by succeeding. As a beginner, be sure to do things with measurable outcomes, where you know whether or not you've achieved your intention. This is scary, but it's putting your money where your mouth is. You'll learn what went wrong, and what went right, only if you take that risk.

Know What You Want and How to Get It

Believe it or not, this is the hardest part of magic, and the place most people get stuck. We all have vague hopes and wishes, but we're not focusing on achieving them. Magic, by contrast, requires us to be focused and specific.

For the *goal* (what you want to achieve), a beginner is best off with something obvious and real. Willow needs a job. Sage needs an apartment. Troy broke their foot and needs to heal. These are all specific, and you'll know the outcome.

Knowing how to get it is even harder; that's the *target*. For Willow, we might target Willow herself—we might put a "glamour" on her, so that she is attractive to prospective employers. More specifically, we might put a glamour on her résumé. A glamour is not just attraction; it has a "right place at the right time" quality, so that the résumé ends up read by the right person when they're in the right mood. Or we might target a specific employer if she knows where she wants to work. We worked to get Professor Spouse a job by targeting specific schools.

The task is similar for Sage. We can target landlords, locations, or Sage themselves.

For Troy, we can target Troy's foot, and we can look up anatomical illustrations so that we can clearly see exactly what needs to heal. We could also target Troy's doctor. I sometimes target doctors when surgery is involved, to make the surgeon skillful and accurate.

So, step one of every spell has to be figuring out the target and goal. Magic begins with knowing what you're doing.

The Basic Steps of Magic

There are many dozens of ways to do magic, but these steps are enough to get you started.

Focus and Raise Energy

Draw upon the mind skills you've been developing to still your mind, center, ground, and clearly visualize your target and goal.

Draw upon the energy exercises you've been doing. You've learned how to raise energy from your hands, from your breath, from movement, and from rhythm. In a spell, you'll raise energy and send it toward the target while visualizing the goal.

Use Objects to Help You

I just told you to focus on two things at once. How annoying! I split the work up by using a focal object in most of my magic. A picture of Troy's foot gives you a target, while you're visualizing the goal (healthy, dancing Troy) in your mind's eye.

Objects frequently used in spells include:

- Pictures
- Other symbols of a person (perhaps a gift they gave you, or a piece of jewelry) or of an idea (a map for finding a home in a particular location, a payroll check to focus on a job)
- Candles
- Poppets (dolls representing a person)
- Herbs
- Crystals

Send the Energy to the Target

The simplest formula for magic is focus-raise-send. Upon sending the energy, declare success (say, "So Mote it Be") and then release the whole idea. Don't talk about the spell until you are sure it has succeeded or failed.

Some Simple Spells

Here are some sample spells that can guide you toward creating your own spells as needed.

Spells can be done in a cast circle (see *Casting a Circle* on page 78) but that is not required. Be sure you always have the four elements present for consecrations, and your athame, if desired, for focusing and sending energy.

Although there are only three spells, they offer three different techniques and purposes and are a good start for your magical journey.

Chanting Spell for a New Home

In addition to the usual altar setup, have a piece of paper and a pen. It should be fresh, clean paper. You might want to have special paper just for magic. You can also have a rattle or other rhythm instrument.

1. Come up with a short phrase that represents your goal. Because Willow needs a home, it can be as simple as, "*Willow is home and happy.*"

2. Making sure you have quiet and privacy, center and ground yourself.
3. Begin writing your phrase on the paper, saying it aloud each time you do. Fill the paper with your phrase, written over and over.

WILLOW IS HOME AND HAPPY
WILLOW IS HOME AND HAPPY
WILLOW IS HOME AND HAPPY
WILLOW IS HOME AND HAPPY
WILLOW IS HOME AND HAPPY
WILLOW IS HOME AND HAPPY
WILLOW IS HOME AND HAPPY
WILLOW IS HOME AND HAPPY
WILLOW IS HOME AND HAPPY
WILLOW IS HOME AND HAPPY
WILLOW IS HOME AND HAPPY
WILLOW IS HOME AND HAPPY
WILLOW IS HOME AND HAPPY
WILLOW IS HOME AND HAPPY
WILLOW IS HOME AND HAPPY
WILLOW IS HOME AND HAPPY
WILLOW IS HOME AND HAPPY
WILLOW IS HOME AND HAPPY
WILLOW IS HOME AND HAPPY
WILLOW IS HOME AND HAPPY
WILLOW IS HOME AND HAPPY
WILLOW IS HOME AND HAPPY
WILLOW IS HOME AND HAPPY
WILLOW IS HOME AND HAPPY
WILLOW IS HOME AND HAPPY
WILLOW IS HOME AND HAPPY
WILLOW IS HOME AND HAPPY
WILLOW IS HOME AND HAPPY
WILLOW IS HOME AND HAPPY
WILLOW IS HOME AND HAPPY
WILLOW IS HOME AND HAPPY
WILLOW IS HOME AND HAPPY
WILLOW IS HOME AND HAPPY
WILLOW IS HOME AND HAPPY
WILLOW IS HOME AND HAPPY

Chanting Spell

4. When the paper is full, fold it up, over and over, until it's as small as you can get it.
5. Begin raising energy while chanting your phrase. You can use a rattle or other instrument while chanting.
6. When you're ready, send the energy into the paper.
7. Say, *"So mote it be!"*
8. If Willow's intended hometown is nearby, take the paper there and bury it. If Willow is hundreds of miles away, bury the paper at your own home, which will symbolize "home" for Willow as well.

Protection: A Candle Spell

Your friend is traveling to the Middle East and requests protection.

In addition to the usual altar setup, have a yellow candle (yellow is a good color for protection). Use a protective incense, such as frankincense or dragon's blood. Have a fire extinguisher nearby in case of emergency.

1. Carve your friend's name into the candle using a magical tool or your fingernail. If your friend is Pagan and has a Pagan name, use the Pagan name.
2. Make sure you have quiet and privacy, then center and ground yourself.
3. Declare your intention, and ask the gods for help:

"Lady and Lord, look upon me as I protect [person] and lend your aid to this spell. [Person] will be safe in their travels and come home safely. [Person] is protected."

4. Light the candle.
5. Gazing at the flame, begin to raise power through breathing and/or your hands (this isn't a good spell for movement, as you want to continue to gaze at the flame the whole time). While you raise power, visualize a bright yellow shield emanating from the candle and enveloping your friend. Concentrate on how strong and impenetrable that shield is, while continuing to raise energy.
6. When you're ready, send the energy into the candle, visualizing it fully enclosing your friend, and knowing your friend is safe.
7. Say, *"So mote it be!"*
8. Do not blow out the candle. Allow it to burn all the way out.

Healing with a Poppet

1. Create a simple poppet in advance.

   There are a dozen or more ways to do this—craft stores like Michael's often sell blank dolls that you can decorate, as well as doll-making supplies. Or you can create a person-shaped outline and cut two pieces of cloth in that shape, then sew them together. Leave a hole so you can stuff the doll. Finish the part of the body being healed last. A poppet can also be a traditional corn dolly, made from dried corn husks.

Corn dolly

Decorate the poppet so that it resembles the person being healed. Artistry isn't necessary! Hair and eye color make a big difference. You can add the person's astrological sign to the doll with embroidery, appliqué, or a fabric pen. Be attentive to the body part being healed. In our example, make sure that Troy's foot is very detailed.

After stuffing the doll, you can add healing herbs to the targeted body part. Troy's foot might benefit from boneset, arnica, or sage.

2. Make sure you have quiet and privacy, then center and ground yourself.
3. Consecrate the poppet (see *Consecrating Tools* on page 49). Remember that consecrations include a stated purpose. Here, your stated purpose is healing. For example:

> *"I consecrate this poppet to be a tool of healing. This poppet is now Troy, and as I heal it, Troy is healed. Poppet, you are Troy!"*

4. Raise energy using your hands, breath, movement, or rhythm, as you prefer. While raising energy, visualize Troy healthy and happy. Because Troy's foot is the problem, picturing Troy dancing might be just the thing.
5. When you feel you are at peak, send the energy into the foot of the poppet. You can use a throwing or thrusting motion to push the energy into the foot. You can include a shout, such as, *"Be healed!"*
6. Say, *"So mote it be!"*
7. Leave the poppet on your altar.

Chapter Ten:

GODS AND THE SUPERNATURAL

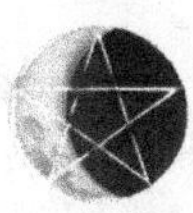

When we talked about the philosophy and ideas of Wicca, naturally, we had to talk about gods, but that conceptual discussion didn't really connect us to them. Now, let's talk about gods and other "supernatural"[98] beings in a more personal and practical way.

Who are the gods and how do we know them? What other supernatural beings can we come to know?

We'll break this down in two ways: First, who are these beings specifically, and second, how do we make vital connections to them?

Gods

Let's begin with "the Goddess" and "the God" of Wicca.

The Goddess

I often talk about goddesses and gods in Paganism and Wicca, but I also talk about The Goddess and The God. I capitalize those words because I am using them as proper nouns.

This can be confusing. Look at it this way: I can be referred to as a woman or as a writer or as many other things, and those are not capitalized. But when I'm called Deborah, that's a proper noun and takes a capital letter. Likewise, a goddess is a deity understood to be female, but The Goddess is the name of the specific goddess of Wicca.

It's a terrible name, though! The thing is, obviously, it's *not* her name. As I mentioned when discussing British Traditional Wicca, her name is considered secret in many traditions, so "The Goddess" is used as a substitute. To be clear, different traditions have different specific names for her, but those various names are all referring to The Goddess.

Who is this Goddess of Wicca? She is magnificent in her complexity. She is simultaneously the Earth Mother, the Lady of the Moon, the Body of the Universe, and the Queen of the Witches.[99]

Finding the Goddess in nature opens us to her Earth Mother side, while worshiping by moonlight opens us to her lunar side, and practicing witchcraft opens us to her aspect as

98 Supernatural is a funny word, isn't it? It implies that gods, elementals, and nature spirits aren't natural, that they're *beyond* nature. I disagree. Maybe "invisible" is a better word, but that can also be confusing. Let's stick with supernatural for now.

99 Jack Chanek's *Queen of All Witcheries* explores her nature in depth.

the queen of witches. But to me, the face that is the universe itself can only be seen when we open ourselves fully, with love and longing, to the vastness of all that is beyond our senses, beyond our knowing. I had a quote by a Hindu saint that I used to keep with me—I wish I could find it. It was something like, "it is wrong to say, 'Mother of the Universe.' I *am* the universe. You cannot fall from my lap." I often think of this when I am having a hard time and find myself reaching out to her—"You cannot fall from my lap." I allow myself to experience being enveloped.

To me, there is a level at which she is all goddesses, not because "they're all one," as if there is no difference, but because part of her nature is infinite.

When I was new to Wicca, I was happy to understand all goddesses as "aspects" of the Goddess. The "Isis, Astarte, Diana" chant made perfect sense to me. Later, I was introduced to a more polytheistic worldview. I began worshiping a multitude of goddesses and gods and came to know them as individuals. These individual beings were not "just" aspects of anyone or anything; they were *themselves*. But then I would turn to the Goddess, and I would find shades of those other deities there, within the galaxies she contains.

I have held that paradox in my worship for decades, and it never explains itself logically to me, but it reveals itself in my rituals, my meditations, and my deepest trances. Kali is Kali, Inanna is Inanna, Demeter is Demeter; they are themselves, specific, and knowable. But these individuals sometimes show themselves in the Goddess, who has a devouring mother face, a warrior queen face, and a nurturing grain mother face.

She is often referred to as Maiden, Mother, and Crone. I think that's a great way to get to know her, but she won't stay put in her three boxes, so let's not force her. Triplicity, though, is one of her defining characteristics, and three is one of her most sacred numbers.

The God

If the Goddess is three, the God is two. We saw this throughout our Wheel of the Year cycle of rituals. At Midsummer, he was both the waxing and waning sun, two mighty gods battling for the affection of the goddess. At Yule, he was again both waxing and waning, this time as old age and infancy. At Beltane, he was vigorous fertility; at Samhain, he was death.

There are many ways to express the duality of the "Two-faced God." He is called the Green God and the Red God, referring to agriculture (green) and the hunt (red). He is death and resurrection. He is the tame and the wild. He is the waxing and waning Sun God. He is the Stag, whose antlers fall off (are "cast") each spring and grow back gradually, reaching full size around the end of summer. The Horned God, then, is more properly the Antlered God—the lifecycle of the antlers is often seen as symbolic of all the various ways the God dies and is reborn.

The God is the Lord of Death, a Hades figure who presides over the Summerland. He guides the dead and comforts the mourners. He is the Lord of Rebirth, present in budding plants showing themselves after being hidden beneath the earth all winter long.

He is wild and untamed—a freedom that includes unrestrained sexuality. This wildness can be madness, ecstasy, drunkenness, and mischief, and he has a trickster aspect. He leads the Wild Hunt, which expresses both his wildness and his association with death.

He is also nurturing: As he is embodied in the grain, he can be seen as the source of all human nourishment, "the staff of life." He sacrifices himself for us at Lammas, offering his own body that we may live.

The Gender of Goddess and God

Culturally, the West has been in a masculine God rut for thousands of years. While Rabbi Danya Ruttenberg says, "God's pronoun is God" (she even sells a T-shirt saying so!), most people, for most of the history of Judaism, Christianity, and Islam, have referred to God as "him." When Wicca first came around, its embrace of the Goddess was groundbreaking. It opened a world of possibilities, of reframing worship and sacredness.

Of course, the initial embrace of the Goddess was colored by the culture from which it emerged. This means that the femaleness of the Goddess has been perceived through deep-seated misogyny, and she's had to pull herself out from under that restraint. One of the serious concerns with defining her as Maiden, Mother, and Crone is that this tends to limit the Goddess to her reproductive capacity—she is defined as virginal, maternal, and menopausal, as if femaleness itself is only what we do with our uteri. Feminist scholarship[100] has applied a more clear-eyed lens to her. We can view her as our mother without treating her capacity for birth as the *sine qua non* of the sacred feminine.

The God is a different story. When a monotheistic God is male, that means that goodness and sacredness are male, and this is very much the history of Western culture. But when a specific, non-monotheistic God is representative of the *sacred masculine*, that means that masculinity is just *one kind* of sacredness, and that's very different. The masculinity of the God is specific.

While misogyny has historically limited our understanding of the Goddess (something that is rapidly changing), the opposite is true of the God. I continue to meet people whose understanding of masculinity is deepened and expanded by connecting to the God. A beloved friend—an effeminate gay man and a powerful high priest of the Craft—shared with me that the God allowed him to understand and appreciate his own masculinity: "If I'm the God, then this" (he said, pointing to himself) "must be masculine." My non-binary spouse (assigned female at birth) has found a deep connection to the God that has allowed her to express her masculine identity. The God, she finds, is at home in her body, even if, she reports, it feels a little amusing to him.

When we understand that femininity as embodied by the Goddess is sacred, and masculinity as embodied by the God is sacred, and that we are vessels in which the Goddess and the God live, it can transform our understanding of, and appreciation of, our own gender(s).

As I said, traditions have names for the Goddess and the God. Individual covens do as well. There is nothing to stop you from using names for them if that works better for you. They will respond to the names you use; they are too great to be confined to a single name anyway. Commonly used names for the Goddess are Isis, Diana, Gaia, and Aradia. For the God, Herne, Pan, Cernunnos, and Lugh are frequently used. These names are of deities that bear the strongest resemblance and historical connection to the Wiccan Goddess and God. On the other hand, if you are a strict hard polytheist, you may not wish to use these names, as they belong to other deities.

In Hinduism, there is a concept of a "*maha*" (great) deity. Lakshmi is specifically the goddess of hearth and home, of prosperity, and the wife of Brahma. But Mahalakshmi—Great

100 See, for example, Firefox.

Lakshmi—is Lakshmi as the universe and all goddesses. Lakshmi, the individual, is a face of Mahalakshmi, and an avenue by which one may know Mahalakshmi (worship Lakshmi and come, ultimately, to the universe). There is a similar relationship between Kali and Mahakali, and between Sarasvati and Mahasarasvati. I see the use of individual names in relation to the Goddess and the God as quite similar. There is an individual goddess named Gaia, and then there is Mahagaia. (But that's just my interpretation.)

A Universe of Deities

There is absolutely nothing in Wicca that confines you to the Goddess and the God. They are central to our rituals, and they are emblematic of what Wicca is, but they are never jealous. You can worship as many deities as you like, and there are a *lot* of them.

Exposure to the world of Pagan deities can come from reading and research, fiction, or attending rituals of other paths. Most of us grow up learning Greek myths in school. Later, we may have heard about Norse mythology or learned a little about Native American traditions. I have had meaningful encounters with Greek, Egyptian, Hindu, Yoruban, Irish, Welsh, and Aztec deities.

Not every deity is going to be comfortable in a Wiccan circle. They are accustomed to their own rituals, performed in the manner of their own traditions. Some deities, for example, are not at home in a skyclad ritual (if that's how you practice).

Meet deities on their own terms. We've already talked about having personal altars: a specific deity altar or shrine allows you to individualize your worship.

Making a Connection

How do we get to know the gods better? How do we feel their presence in our lives?

Ritual

The relationship between ritual and the gods is synergistic—we learn about the gods by performing their rituals, and as we come to know the gods more deeply, we create rituals that reflect that knowledge.

Inherent in ritual is storytelling; there's an implicit story about the gods being told in most rituals. Even if it's as simple as "the Goddess is the Queen of the Witches, the Goddess of Earth and Moon" (as in the invocation used in our esbat ritual)—it's not a story with much *plot*, but it tells us something about her. We'll get back to story in a minute.

Ritual also allows us to be with the gods in a space that is "between the worlds." We aren't encountering them in our ordinary reality, but in a space designed to heighten our access to them. We have placed our circle outside of ordinary time and space, and we have altered our own consciousness to be more receptive. Only then do we invite the gods into the space. We are, in this way, creating authentic and intimate connections with the gods. We ask of them, and we give to them.

The impact of this is immediate. I came to Wicca because I had already felt the presence of the Goddess and meeting her in ritual for the first time blew my mind. Over a period of years, the very familiarity of meeting her in ritual, month after month, helped form connections in unexpected ways. It's a kind of spiritual muscle memory. In my darkest moments, I have not fallen from her lap.

Myth

Humans are storytellers. We've probably been doing it since we were cavepeople, sitting around a fire, keeping each other company. Stories ask questions as much as they give answers, and they have intimacy to them.

I'm a non-fiction writer. As such, it would be easy to write books that are impersonal and factual, but I always include personal experience in my work. In this way, I believe I am forming a connection with you, the reader. This is me, telling a story about me, so that you can find me, and yourself, in what you're reading.

Myths are stories about the gods. In the same manner as me telling a personal story, myths allow you to find both the gods and yourself.

I love reading myths and have quite a few collections on my shelves. When we read myths, we learn facts about the gods, we learn narratives about them, we learn who they are. For example, in *Aradia*, we learn that Aradia is the daughter of the moon and sun, that she is the particular goddess of witches, and that she cares about the oppressed.

This knowledge can also be very practical, as these stories can also tell us what pleases and does not please the gods. For example, Demeter refuses wine and has a barley drink instead—this obviously makes a difference if you're doing a ritual in her honor. Serving wine would be a big *faux pas*! Myths can also be dramatized in ritual, and storytelling time can be set aside in ritual as well, usually during cakes and wine.

Study

For me, myth was the beginning of studying the gods. Learning their stories, though, is only part of learning about them. For many cultures, there is plenty of information available about worship practices. It might be historical information (such as for ancient Greece), or it might be current (such as performing a Hindu *puja*). When working with living traditions, be mindful of cultural appropriation—I use Hinduism as an example specifically because worshiping those gods is not a closed practice.

Studying the gods in this way can inform your private altar practice. If you know that the owl is the sacred animal of Athena, and that votive offerings of pottery were traditional, you might choose to put a ceramic owl on your Athena altar.

Research can teach you traditions regarding:

- Offerings
- Rituals
- Prayers
- Taboos (things *not* to do)
- Times of day/month/year to perform certain rites
- Colors

- Incenses
- Etc.

Meditation

Encountering the gods in meditation is one way for them to reveal their truth to you.

If you're on the Pagan internet for a few minutes, you'll probably encounter the phrase Unverified Personal Gnosis (UPG). This can be a completely neutral expression regarding the source of information, as in "I don't have a source on it, but it came to me in a dream. It's UPG." Or it can be disparaging. "It's *just* UPG."

There is nothing wrong with UPG, provided it's *combined* with study. I have received amazing UPG regarding paleolithic goddesses for whom there is no historical record, and it is consistent with the archeology. The problem with UPG is when people use it instead of research, and they come up with nonsense that contradicts the actual historical record. If someone says, for example, that Oya, the Yoruban goddess of wind and storms, had informed them that her true nature is that of a sun goddess, they'd look pretty ridiculous to the millions of people who worship her in Santeria, Candomble, and other Yoruban religions.

Meeting Them Where They Are

Aradia tells us she is the daughter of the moon and sun and has created the magic circle for us. Meeting her, then, can be accomplished by being in the magic circle, and by paying attention to the sun and to the moon. Any connection to a moon deity can be enhanced by going out on a clear, moonlit night and just being with that experience.

Deities have areas of specialization, and one way of deepening our connection to them is to seek them where they are. Our study of myth and history tells us where to look, and then it's a matter of seeking them out. Gods of the wild woods are found in the wild woods. Deities of the storm are found during storms. Deities of commerce are found in business, and deities of sex are found in sexual situations.

Allow your research to direct you. Your reading tells you that Hecate is a goddess of the crossroads, graves, and boundaries, as well as witchcraft and night. You then learn that traditional offerings include pomegranates, almonds, wine, garlic, and cypress. You note that she is a goddess of triplicity and that three is her sacred number. So, if you want to meet Hecate, you can go to a crossroads, leave an offering of three almonds, and speak with her there.

Art

The last way to meet the gods that we'll discuss is through art and creativity. This can truly be anything: painting, drawing, pottery, singing, drumming—anything. Whatever you do that expresses your creativity, be it cooking, beading, dance, or puzzle design, can be done in dedication to the gods, can be about the gods, and can be a way of encountering them.

Through all these means, you can find relationships with gods, some of which may become lifelong.

Finding a Personal Deity

One of the questions that people ask most often is how to find a personal deity, a patron. (By the way, "patron" means father, and "matron" means mother, but most people understand "patron deity" to apply to any gender deity. I'm not really excited about getting into the linguistic argument.)

First, I want to unhook from the idea that this is necessary, or even important. It has become something of a badge of honor in the Pagan community, and people who have not found a patron sometimes feel less-than. This is completely wrongheaded! My beloved Professor Spouse has been in the Craft for thirty-some-odd years and has never had a patron. For her, the Craft itself is the path, and the Goddess and God are all the patrons she needs. She is as devoted to the gods, and as magically powerful, as anyone I know, and feels no emptiness where a patron "should" go.

If you don't feel the call, you don't, and that's okay. One reason might be that, as with Professor Spouse, Wicca itself is the call. Another is that you might be a generalist by nature, in worship, or in many things. People go to medical school and become orthopedists, podiatrists, or dermatologists, but some people become general practitioners. My doctor is absolutely straightforward with me—go to a specialist for this condition, I don't have the expertise. But having her as my primary physician is valuable to me. I think worship has a similar quality—both the individual relationship *and its absence* have power.

And to be clear, if you don't have a patron, it doesn't mean you don't love the gods you worship, or that you can't form special relationships with them.

I found a patron without asking for one. I was at a Pagan festival, dancing around a fire with a bunch of other people, chanting "Isis, Astarte." At some point, when the name "Kali" was chanted, it seemed to drown out all the other names, then all other sounds, and then, there was Kali, placing her hands on my head and saying, "You belong to me."

Even though it was out of the blue, there were preexisting conditions. Notice that I was in a Pagan space, in an altered state of consciousness, and chanting the names of goddesses. It didn't happen at work or while I was driving. So, here's some advice.

Set Up Preconditions for Success

Deities won't come to you if you have never heard of them. They won't come to you if you're never in an open state where you can hear them. All of the activities discussed under forming a connection to the gods will help: ritual, studying myth, history, and archeology, meditation, meeting them where they are, and connecting through the arts. All of these make you fertile soil in which the gods can choose to plant their seeds.

Experiment

There is nothing wrong with setting up an altar to a deity who is not your patron. There are many reasons you might do so, including curiosity about how that worship relationship will pan out. Again, once you decide to enter into this relationship, even temporarily, do all the ritual, study, etc. needed for it to be an informed and meaningful connection.

How do you choose where to start? Well, whim is okay, but here are some more concrete suggestions:

- Reach out to the gods who have something to offer for a particular experience you're having in life. This might be career, family, or personal. Are you experiencing infertility? Perhaps Eileithyia, the Greek goddess of childbirth, should receive your offerings. Are you a widow? Perhaps Isis, whose husband Osiris was dismembered, could hold your pain. Are you a musician? Consider offering to Apollo or Bridget.
- Explore ethnic connections. The gods are not bigots, and don't require their worshipers to be of any particular ethnicity, but looking into your own ethnic background might be a source of resonance for you. Sometimes the feeling of being "at home" can be a powerful source of energy.
- Is there a specific natural event, feature, or condition where you feel especially empowered? Is the beach your happy place? Or the mountains? Or a thunderstorm? Any of these might lead you to form a special connection with a deity associated with that aspect of nature.
- If you work with a divination system (such as Tarot), a reading might point you in a fertile direction.
- If you work with a magical system that is associated with particular deities, use that to guide you. For example, if you work with Kabbalah, look at what deities are associated with what sephiroth.

Just Ask

In ritual, in meditation, or in dreamwork, ask for your patron deity to make themselves known to you.

A Ritual of Request

Have an extra bouquet of flowers set aside.[101]

1. In a cast circle[102] (see *Steps for Casting and Closing a Circle* on page 79), after cakes and wine, take some deep breaths to ground yourself.
2. Visualize yourself as open. You might sense this openness at the crown of your head, or in your heart, or at the base of your skull, or in some other way.
3. Say: *"I, [name], worship the gods. I open myself to a deeper relationship. I invite my patron to come to me."*
4. Go to the East and say: *"I invite my patron to come to me from the East. I invite my patron to come to me from Air. I invite my patron to come to my mind. I invite my patron to fly to me."*
5. Go to the South and say: *"I invite my patron to come to me from the South. I invite my patron*

101 Your circle will already have a bouquet of flowers for the Goddess, and she shouldn't be short-changed. This is an extra one.

102 You are opening yourself to an unknown entity, so the protection of a cast circle is better than just standing at your altar.

to come to me from Fire. I invite my patron to come to my will. I invite my patron to come to me in a cloud of smoke."

6. Go to the West and say: *"I invite my patron to come to me from the West. I invite my patron to come to me from Water. I invite my patron to come to my heart. I invite my patron to swim to me."*
7. Go to the North and say: *"I invite my patron to come to me from the North. I invite my patron to come to me from Earth. I invite my patron to come to my body. I invite my patron to come to me on foot."*
8. Return to the East and nod in acknowledgment, then return to the altar.
9. Dip your fingers in the saltwater and anoint your forehead, heart, and hands, saying, *"By Water and Earth, I open myself to my patron."*
10. Lift the censer and cense your forehead, heart, and hands, saying, *"By Fire and Air, I open myself to my patron."*
11. Place the flowers on the altar and say, *"I bring an offering to my patron."*
12. Proceed with the rest of the circle. After it is over, place the flowers in a quiet place outdoors (under a tree, in a park, etc.).

Deity Exercises

All of the exercises below can be done specifically for the Goddess and/or the God, for any and all Pagan gods, or can be part of your process of finding a personal deity (if you choose to do that). All of them can be repeated as often as you desire, so that you can do the bibliomancy exercise for the Goddess, and again for finding a personal deity, and so on. One or more might even become a regular part of your Wiccan life.

For ease of explanation, each of them is written as if they are for any and all Pagan gods.

Gods Everywhere

Take a "god walk."

Take three deep, cleansing breaths before you step out your door. Upon leaving your home, what's the first thing you see? What deity does it bring to mind?[103]

For example, if you see a stray cat, that might bring Bast, the Egyptian cat goddess, to mind. The sun might remind you of Helios, the Greek embodiment of the sun. A stray candy wrapper on the ground might recall Tajimamori, the Japanese god of sweets.

Simply walk, staying open, and note what you see. The gods are all around you.

When you return home, you might journal about this experience.

Bibliomancy

Bibliomancy is using books for divination.

Optionally, begin by lighting a candle and some incense, and perhaps anointing yourself with the four elements.

103 Or, how does it relate to the Goddess, or the God?

Take a book off your shelf that is related to Paganism in some way. Take three deep, cleansing breaths and ask your question out loud. It might be, "What does the Goddess have to say to me right now?" Or, "What deity should I be offering to?"

When you're ready, close your eyes and open the book at random. Allow your hands to move over the pages, still with your eyes closed. When you're ready, hold your finger to a spot that feels right, and open your eyes.

What word is your finger on? How does that answer your question?

Again, you could journal about this experience.

The Art of the Story

In advance of this exercise, you need to make two decisions: (1) What myth you wish to work with? And (2) what form of self-expression appeals to you?

Now, you'll make some form of art about a myth. As with bibliomancy, you could first light a candle and some incense and perhaps anoint yourself.

Take three deep cleansing breaths and begin. Here are some examples:[104]

- Make a collage depicting Ra riding his chariot of the Sun.
- Cook a stew that represents the potion of knowledge in the cauldron of Cerridwen.
- Make a beaded necklace that represents Inanna's lapis lazuli necklace, which was taken from her by the guardian of the underworld.
- Paint a picture of the Goddess as Earth and Moon.
- Write a song about the Horned God.

Other Supernatural Beings

Nature is alive. Spirit is everywhere. Maybe you're an animist, someone who believes everything has spirit: stones, trees, car keys, Tarot cards—everything is alive. Even if you're not, the universe has more spirit than just gods and people (and cats).

Elementals

Elementals are the spiritual essence of each element. I've written about them extensively elsewhere,[105] but we can treat them briefly here.

Elementals are uncomplicated beings, in that you and I have all the elements mixed within us. As I sit here writing, my Air is ever-present, as language and thought are associated with Air, but so is my Fire—it takes a stubborn passion to write when there are so many other things to do, and I have a certain egoism about my reputation as an author—Fire rules all of that. Water is present as I allow the words to flow through me, and Earth is here as well—I'm looking toward the final outcome—a finished book, a physical thing.

104 If you don't know these stories, that's more research for you. What fun!

105 In my books, *The Way of Four* and *The Magic of the Elements.*

Elementals, though, have exactly one element always manifest in them. Air elementals do not feel, Fire elementals do not think, and so on.

The elementals were named by the great sixteenth-century alchemist Paracelsus:

- **Sylphs:** The elementals of Air
- **Salamanders:** The elementals of Fire
- **Undines:** The elementals of Water
- **Gnomes:** The elementals of Earth

Some people invoke elementals in the four quarters, rather than the guardians of the quarters (see the next section). Invoking them brings the elemental force to a ritual with definite intensity. On the other hand, elementals can only be exactly themselves—they're not "on your side," they're just Air, Fire, Water, and Earth. The circumstances under which you call them, then, must be carefully controlled, and you must banish them when you're done. I speak from hard-earned experience, and yes, unwanted fire was involved!

A Solitary Elemental Exercise[106]

For this exercise, you'll need an extra dish of water (not saltwater) and a candle. Once you've cast the circle, you'll have mixed elements—Earth and Water together in saltwater, and Air and Fire together in the burning censer. Use these extras for the exercise so that each element is separate.

You'll also need a short piece of recorded music. Use the music as a timer so you don't get too lost in the elemental experience.

1. In a cast circle, look at your altar, noting four elements (incense, a candle, water, and salt) and four elemental tools (athame, wand, cup, and pentacle).
2. Choose the element you will work with.
3. Start the music.
4. Anoint yourself with your chosen element:
    - For Air, cense yourself.
    - For Fire, bring the candle to your third eye and your heart, then put the candle down and wave first your dominant hand, then your other hand, over the flame.
    - For Water, place a drop on your third eye, heart, and each hand.
    - For Earth, touch your third eye with the salt, then take a few grains on your tongue.
5. Hold the tool of your chosen element.
6. Say: *"O [sylphs/salamanders/undines/gnomes], share this circle with me and let me know you."*
7. Allow yourself simply to commune with the elemental. You may be moved to speak out loud the messages the elemental shares with you.
8. When the music ends, you are done. It is *very easy* to get lost with an elemental, so

106 My book *The Way of Four* has numerous elemental exercises, including nature exercises, meditations, and other explorations. This is offered as a first step.

obey your musical cue. Lift your magical tool above you and say: *"Thank you, O [sylphs/salamanders/undines/gnomes], for sharing this time with me. I dismiss you."*

9. Put the tool down forcefully, with the energy of dismissal.
10. Say: *"I am balanced in the four elements. My circle is balanced. I am Air, Fire, Water, and Earth. I am Spirit. So mote it be!"*

Angels and Guardians

Typically, we invoke the guardian of each quarter when calling the quarters. These beings are not elementals; they are intelligent, complex entities who work in service of the gods. They guard the ritual because we ask them to, and because we are also serving the gods, so they align with our purpose.

Some people think the guardians are the same as the archangels, for example:

"In the Craft, the intelligences behind the elements are called the 'Lords of the Outer Spaces,' or the 'Kings of the Elements.' All religions recognize them under different names, the Christians knowing them as the Archangels Raphael, Michael, Gabriel and Auriel."[107]

Are they, though? The four guardians hold sway over a quarter of space each, working jointly to protect the circle. They are not, in my experience, guarding over our lives in any other way. Meeting them is best done in a cast circle, because that is where they are invited to be present, and they understand their purpose to be in that space. Once in circle, we can open our minds to them, meditate on and with them, and commune with them. My experience, though, is they are heavily focused on their "jobs," on protection, and don't much want to hang out.

The earliest literature on the primary archangels seems to define only three, and Uriel (Auriel) was added later to create correspondence with the four elements. However, there are a total of seven archangels, so I wouldn't say the correspondence to the elements is precise.

The guardians are confined to a single location. Angels, by contrast, are all around, all the time. There's a lot of nonsensical angelology out there, as well as solid information.[108] Angels appear in the Hebrew Bible, and are expounded upon and named by Jewish mystics beginning in the first century CE. They are invoked in grimoire magic and the rituals performed by lodge magicians such as the Golden Dawn.

The earliest references to angels refer to them as messengers, but also as parts of ourselves. The silly cartoons showing an angel on one shoulder, and a devil on the other, each whispering in someone's ear, is based on this early understanding of angels—when we are doing good, being our best selves, we create angels that energetically surround us, and when we give in to evil thoughts, we create demonic energies. Personified angels and demons exist in ancient literature side-by-side with this psycho-spiritual concept.

Angels are defined as having specific functions. Raziel, for example, is the angel of secrets, while Arariel is the angel of rivers. In addition, we are each said to have a guardian

107 Crowther, p. 67

108 I've added a good book on angels to the recommended reading to help steer you away from the nonsense.

angel, with a specific interest in being helpful to us. Guardian angels are considered unique beings, or as manifestations of our own higher selves, a sort of avatar we send into the spirit world to watch over ourselves—the cartoon angel on our shoulder, helping us to remain moral, but also a protector.

If you want the help of a guardian angel, simply ask. If that energy is there anyway, for exactly that purpose, why not?

Some Wiccan traditions incorporate angels in their rites, but most do not. Because they originate in the Bible, a lot of people who want to focus on a strictly Pagan practice have no interest in them.

Nature Spirits

The idea of nature spirits overlaps with the concept of animism. If everything has spirit, everything in nature is an obvious subset of that.

Nature spirits are best understood as the specific spirit residing in a single place. So, you might understand Yemaya as the goddess of the ocean, but you might also recognize a spirit in *this particular* ocean at *this particular* beach. Trees, caves, rivers, mountains, and so on all have spirit.

Communing with nature spirits is fairly easy. Be calm and friendly, as well as respectful. Be kind to the land you're on, not littering or damaging anything. Slow your energy to the pace of the spirit you wish to be with—frenetic energy doesn't meet a cave where it is. Bring an offering and just listen.

You might go to a favorite tree, leave a piece of fruit at its roots, and just sit with it, breathing calmly, and see how that goes. Perhaps you'll return to this tree several times, each time with an offering, so that you may get to know each other. It might take those return trips before you start to understand a response. Probably, though, you'll feel a connection right away. It's possible that you'll feel a negative response—something like, "go away." If that happens, respect the boundaries of that spirit just as you would a human's boundaries. While the negative response can happen, it's rare. In all likelihood, you'll make a friend.

Offerings

One of the things that a nature spirit will often communicate is what kind of offerings are acceptable. Place an offering and listen to the inner voice that says, "this is good," or "this is not good," or that says nothing at all. That's the voice that guides you.

Some typical offerings:

- Spring water
- Flowers
- Fruit or nuts
- Grain or flour
- Whiskey
- Coins

The custom of throwing a coin into a well is a vestige of spirit offerings, and indeed, wells are a good place to find a nature spirit hanging around.

The Mighty Dead

Wicca has an annual festival—Samhain—where we love, honor, and make merry with our beloved dead. This tells us that the *concept* of venerating the ancestors is built into Wicca, and many Wiccans make ancestor altars a part of their lives.

There are many reasons one might choose to set up an ancestor altar:

- Simply because it's a part of your practice.
- To connect more deeply with a part of yourself—your family heritage, your artistic predecessors, and so on. I might, for example, include my grandparents, or a writer I admire, or Gerald Gardner as a Wiccan ancestor, or Edie Windsor as a queer ancestor.
- To help process grief.
- To help heal generational trauma.
- Because we've received communication from our beloved dead (that is, they've asked us to).

An ancestor altar is similar to a worship altar: It contains things you might find on any altar, like candles and incense, but it is tailored to the person or people being honored. You'd probably have a picture of them and/or another memento, and you might have a favorite thing of theirs, something they'd enjoy finding on their altar, whether that's a piece of jewelry or a Hershey's kiss. As you commune with them, they'll find ways of letting you know what they'd like to see there.

Set appropriate boundaries with your dead—they can be busybodies just like the living can. Cover the altar when you need privacy, but don't neglect it.

Full disclosure—this section has been very hard to write! I don't have an ancestor altar, and it nags at me. As I mentioned, my daughter does have a practice of ancestor veneration that includes her father, and we've discussed it several times. The good news is that, even after forty years of Paganism and Wicca, I am still growing, still learning, and this is an area where there's room for growth.

Divination Tools

One of the places animism is most visible in the Pagan community is in the use of divination—Tarot, rune stones, pendulums, and other oracular tools. There are many theories as to how divination works, but one theory is that the tool acquires an animating spirit. Some people say that the tool inherently has such a spirit, others say that the spirit enters it as a result of it being used.

At the first ritual I ever attended, my high priestess read my cards. I had some questions about the reading, which led to a second reading overlaid on the first. Then, she handed the cards to me and said, "Now you read me." I was hooked. I've been reading Tarot ever since.[109]

Nonetheless, I've only come around to the idea that my cards and other divination tools have their own spirit in the past several years. Before that, I had a lot of ideas as to how my tools worked, but I didn't ascribe an independent will to them. I've changed my mind on that.

One thing I've learned as a result is to ask my tool what its purpose is. I have one Tarot deck that insists it only be used during magic—it doesn't wish to be a part of ordinary readings. Tarot cards, oracle stones, runes, and all sorts of tools are more than willing to communicate if you just ask them. I even had a Tarot deck tell me a joke once.

Invocation: Calling the Gods

Calling the gods can be simple or complex. The esbats, sabbats, and rites of passage in this book contain a variety of invocations, some of which are just a few words. As you work with various gods and beings, you'll want to understand how to create your own invocations, and what works and does not work. Of course, examples are useful.

Understanding the components of a successful invocation can help.

They are:

1. **Invitation:** You must actually invoke, invite, or ask the being to be present.
2. **Be specific:** *Who* are you inviting?
3. **Be descriptive:** Have you ever seen someone in a crowd yell "Mom!"? Every mother in the place turns her head. Specific and descriptive help you get the right Mom.
4. **Praise:** Everyone likes flattery, even gods.
5. **Need:** *Why* are you inviting them?
6. **Acknowledgment of success:** Assume they have, in fact, responded to your call, and welcome them.

In *Steps for Casting and Closing a Circle* on page 79, the Goddess is invoked like this:

"Beloved Lady, Goddess of the Earth and the Moon
Delight of our hearts, Queen of the Witches
Mother of us all
Be here among us! Come to this circle, formed in your honor
Accept our offerings and our love.
Welcome! Blessed be!"

109 And I have written a book about it: *Tarot Interactions.*

Invitation	Be here among us! Come to this circle
Specific	Lady (Here, "Lady" is the same as "Goddess," a title that substitutes for a name.)
Descriptive	Goddess of the Earth and the Moon Queen of the Witches Mother of us all
Praise	Beloved Delight of our hearts
Need	...formed in your honor Accept our offerings and our love Here, we are saying we need you in the circle *because* it was formed in your honor, we are inviting you *in order to* give offerings and love.
Acknowledgment	Welcome! Blessed be!

Gods generally *want* to be invoked. They like being worshiped, so it isn't rocket science to get them to come to your rituals. But the opposite of any of these components are recipes for failure. In other words, they don't come if you forget to invite them. They don't come if you are so vague that they don't recognize your call. They don't come if you are generic and bland. They don't come for no reason at all.

Invocation isn't all words. The atmosphere of a ritual matters—it's easier to get a deity to come to ritual space than while you're at the office. Things they like matter—music, offerings, incense, candles, colors, and so on. Demeter might be more likely to show up if there's a dish of barley for her. I have often played a recording of sitar music when I worship Kali—it creates an environment that is familiar to her and makes her welcome.

For deities with a strong historical record or a living tradition, using existing invocations keys into that existing energy, drawing on the power of generations of successful invocation.

Invocation of Demeter

Here's an invocation of the Greek goddess Demeter, to provide an additional example.

"Most glorious Demeter, Lady of the Grain
Mother of Persephone, Wanderer of the Earth
Most beautiful, wonderful, and bountiful lady
Be here, join me, receive my offerings
My need is great, glorious goddess
Join my sacred rite.
Welcome! Blessed be!"

Notice that the descriptiveness includes specific known qualities (Mother of Persephone), as well as elements about her known from stories (Wanderer of the Earth). Stories are a wonderful source of descriptions that can make your invocations rich.

Invocation of Odin

"Come to my altar, mighty Odin, mighty All-Father
Odin one-eye, who sacrificed yourself to yourself
Father of the Gods
Who hung on Yggdrassil for nine days
Possessor of wisdom
Come now and share wisdom with me,
O great one, O strong one
Be here that I may share your presence,
That I may stand beside your glory and your knowledge,
Come, I pray.
Welcome! Welcome!"

Look at the above invocation of Odin and see if you can identify the six components.

In this section, we've explored how to develop an intimate relationship with gods and other supernatural beings—where and how to meet them, and where and how to invite them to join you. These explorations can be infinite. They have taken up decades of my life and continue to offer new rewards.

CONCLUSION:

TRAVELING BEYOND THE MAP

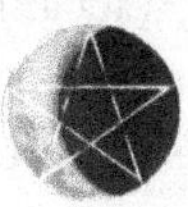

We've come to the end of this book, but not, I hope, the end of your journey. This book is meant for beginners: At some point, you will no longer be a beginner. What's next? How does Wicca become a sustainable life path?

I've dropped hints throughout about my own life journey. The Wicca I practice now is not identical to the Wicca I learned when I was twenty-one, nor should it be. Being willing to adapt, grow, and change is part of what makes the path a sustainable one. Paradoxically, being willing to stay the course is also involved. Over the years, I've learned that if I throw something out because I think it's stupid, boring, or unnecessary, I'll often end up bringing it back sometime later. The lesson for me has been to stick with things and explore them thoroughly before I decide that I'm smarter than some time-worn wisdom that's been around since long before I was born.

For many people who are solitary or eclectic practitioners, initiation becomes a next step. I know several people who had a satisfying practice for *years* before deciding they wanted more, and that the way to get it was to dive into traditional practice. My friend Maggi practiced for four years before becoming initiated in the Gardnerian tradition, which was 25 years ago as of this writing. I started in a traditional training group and quickly became a Gardnerian initiate, and I still practice Gardnerian Wicca. But over the years, I've expanded my practice in many ways. I've joined other groups, explored other ritual forms, and am an initiate of another tradition.

For many solitary practitioners, exploring group practice is part of their growth, while for others, adding solitary work to an existing group practice expands the depth of their witchcraft.

Group work doesn't necessarily mean a coven. Sometimes, it is incredibly enriching to have like-minded people just to hang out with. Some of the deepest learning I've experienced in the Craft has happened by spending time in discussion with other Wiccans. "Why do you suppose we do *this*? Why is it done *that* way? What do you think *that* means?" ...and then spitballing ideas—it's amazing how much you can learn. I think going to Pagan festivals and events is valuable for this among many other reasons. Connecting to a community can help you feel supported, and that allows your path to be lifelong.

Many Wiccans add other magical forms to their work. In addition to developing a magical spellcasting practice, many learn ritual magic, diving into grimoires like the *Key of Solomon*, reading Agrippa, exploring Golden Dawn or Enochian magic, studying Hermetics, or exploring Greek Magical Papyri (PGM). These are all very old forms of magic and are highly structured. But Wicca originated with people who practiced these and other disciplines, so they're quite compatible. Many bring some (or a lot of) ritual magic into their Wiccan circles. Alex Sanders was one such person, and the Alexandrian tradition he founded retains a good deal of that flavor. Or perhaps hoodoo, Chaos magic, or Hellenistic worship is your cup of tea.

A deep dive into disciplines that are associated with Wicca, but that aren't specifically Wicca, is often how people advance their Craft. If you know my other books, you know I've written on the Tarot: Tarot has been a lifelong passion for me, and I use it in many ways. In addition to just doing readings, I use Tarot *with* my Wicca: I do readings before magic to determine if magic should be done, and fine-tune how to do it. I use Tarot as a teaching tool, and we've often explored Tarot games in ritual. Tarot is a personal favorite, but people become herbalists, wildcrafters, gem and crystal experts, astrologers, and more.

You could also bring your Craft into existing disciplines. If you're a painter, try painting on Wiccan themes. If you're a songwriter, a dancer, an instrumentalist: Bring your Craft into your creativity.

I have learned many handcrafts as a result of being Wiccan. I've carved wood to make my own wands, I've made masks, I've sewn robes. I don't love every handcraft I've tried, but it's a fun exploration and a way to be more deeply involved. Plus, you have great homemade things to use in your magic, and lovely gifts to give at Yuletide.

For many of these pursuits, the Recommended Reading that follows is a good place to start.

Over the course of forty years, I've experimented with many things that I've subsequently put down. I've also picked up new things and loved them and incorporated them into my Wicca. Or I've simply allowed these experiences to change me—and a changed person then practices a subtly changed Wicca. Living my life as a Wiccan has sometimes taken me off-road, but the moonlit path remains the one I walk. I hope you find it as fulfilling as I have.

RECOMMENDED READING

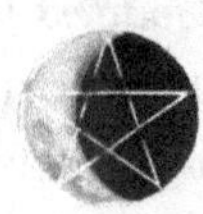

This section is to provide further reading on topics discussed in these pages. Most of these books are favorites of mine. Some are books by favorite authors, and some are recommended by trusted friends who are experts in their subjects. All are meant to help guide you through a sea of often nonsensical books and help you find the good stuff.

78 Degrees of Wisdom: A Tarot Journey to Self-Awareness by Rachel Pollack
One of the true classics in Tarot—nobody knew the subject matter better than Rachel Pollack!
The Angel Code: Your Interactive Guide to Angelic Communication by Chantel Lysette
Aradia or the Gospel of the Witches: A New Translation by Charles Godfrey Leland, Mario Pazzaglini, Ph.D., and Dina Pazzaglini
Astrology: Using the Wisdom of the Stars in Your Everyday Life by Carole Taylor
Bending the Binary: Polarity Magic in a Nonbinary World by Deborah Lipp
The first truly modern book on polarity, it is important for anyone who wants to understand this crucial concept in Wicca without resorting to gender essentialist tropes.
Bonewits's Essential Guide to Witchcraft and Wicca by Isaac Bonewits
Bud, Blossom & Leaf: The Magical Gardener's Handbook by Dorothy Morrison
The Complete Book of Numerology by David A. Phillips Ph.D
A guide to Pythagorean numerology.
Cunningham's Encyclopedia of Magical Herbs by Scott Cunningham
Cunningham's Encyclopedia of Crystal, Gem & Metal Magic by Scott Cunningham
These two are among my absolute favorite reference books; I use them all the time.
The Elements of Ritual: Air, Fire, Water, and Earth in the Wiccan Circle by Deborah Lipp
This is a deep dive into Wiccan ritual for those who want to explore all the nuances of the magic circle.
The Encyclopedia of Goddesses and Heroines by Patricia Monaghan
This thoroughly researched volume is a wonderful resource and can be used in the bibliomancy exercise on page 339.
Jailbreaking the Goddess by LaSara Firefox
The Magic of the Elements by Deborah Lipp
Magical Power for Beginners: How to Raise and Send Energy for Spells that Work
by Deborah Lipp
A detailed breakdown of exactly what magical power is and how to get it. How to construct a spell, and how to make it happen.

The Meaning of Witchcraft by Gerald Gardner

Obviously very dated, but also source material for so much of what we know today.

Meditation: The Complete Guide by Patricia Monaghan and Eleanor G. Viereck

The Pagan Book of Living and Dying: Practical Rituals, Prayers, Blessings, and Meditations on Crossing Over by Starhawk, M. Macha NightMare, and the Reclaiming Collective

Qabalah for Wiccans: Ceremonial Magic on the Pagan Path by Jack Chanek

Queen of All Witcheries: A Biography of the Goddess by Jack Chanek

I truly believe this is one of the most important books on Wicca in the past twenty years. Jack Chanek explores how we understand the goddess in a way that is genuinely a breakthrough. Essential reading.

Queer Rites: A Magickal Grimoire to Honor Your Milestones with Pride by Enfys J. Book

RitualCraft: Creating Rites for Transformation and Celebration by Azrael Arynn K. and Amber K.

Tarot Interactions: Become More Intuitive, Psychic & Skilled at Reading Cards by Deborah Lipp

Throwing the Bones: How to Foretell the Future with Bones, Shells, and Nuts by Catherine Yronwode

Traditional Wicca: A Seeker's Guide by Thorn Mooney

If you decide that Traditional Wicca is your path, this guide is an exceptional resource.

The Way of Four by Deborah Lipp

An in-depth exploration of the four elements, including nature exercises, personal exercises, and (my favorite part), quizzes!

The Witch's Altar: The Craft, Lore & Magick of Sacred Space by Jason Mankey and Laura Tempest Zakroff

The Witch's Shield: Protection Magick and Psychic Self-Defense by Christopher Penczak

GLOSSARY

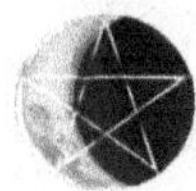

Alexandrian

The Alexandrian tradition of Wicca was founded by Alex and Maxine Sanders in the 1960s. It bears strong similarity to *Gardnerian* Wicca. Alex originally claimed that his Wicca was handed down to him by his grandmother. This was not true and became such a common Wiccan tall tale that the derisive phrase "grandmother story" was coined.

For decades, Alex's Gardnerian initiation was considered by most Gardnerians to be fraudulent or improper. With the emergence of new historical sources, we now know that he was, indeed, a Gardnerian initiate, establishing the through line between the two traditions.

As a general rule, Alexandrian rituals tend to lean more toward ritual magic, incorporating things like the Lesser Banishing Ritual of the Pentagram (a *Golden Dawn* staple), but this varies greatly from coven to coven.

In Europe, Alexandrians and Gardnerians tend to consider each other brethren, while in the United States, they tend to be treated as separate traditions.

Animism

Animism is the belief that everything on earth contains life, all of which is interconnected. In animism, humans, animals, rocks, plants, places, and objects all have animating spirits and can be thought of as beings.

Athame

The athame is considered the quintessential witch's weapon. Traditionally, it is a black-handled, double-edged blade, most closely resembling a boot knife. Many people have non-traditional athames, with other kinds of handles and blades. Some traditions have rules about what kind of athame is proper.

Aura

The aura is an energy field that surrounds the body. Some people can see auras, and the color of an aura is supposed to be informative about the state of mind and physical health of the person. (Animals and objects also have auras.)

In *Theosophy*, the aura is considered to have seven layers, or "bodies." The closest layer to the physical body is the "etheric body," and this is where healing magic and energy work are typically done. The next layers, in order from closest to furthest from the physical form, are emotional body, mental body, astral body, etheric template, celestial body, and Ketheric or causal body.

Book of Shadows

The Book of Shadows (often abbreviated BOS) is a Wiccan's book of spells, rituals, poetry, invocations, and other material. It varies widely from tradition to tradition. For many Wiccans, it is simply where they write down spells, invocations, poetry, and more: It is a personal magical journal. But in some cases, it is a source of handed-down lore and knowledge. Some traditions require every initiate to have a BOS with certain documents in it, and receiving those documents is part of being an initiate. Strictness and rules about how such documents are passed down are different in different traditions.

Ceremonial Magic

Ceremonial magic (sometimes styled "CM") is magic based on texts known as "grimoires" or magic based in lodge systems like the *Golden Dawn*. CM is highly structured, with often elaborate rules on how, for example, one's magical tools are to be constructed, or what time and date a ritual can be performed.

Grimoire magic tends to focus on summoning demons and other supernatural entities to do one's bidding.

Lodge magic tends to focus on *theurgy*, which is to say, doing magic to bring oneself closer to God or the gods—what Aleister Crowley called "knowledge and conversation of the Holy Guardian Angel."

Chakra

Hindu philosophy describes seven chakras—energy centers on the body

They are the root (perineum), sacral (base of the spine), solar plexus, heart, throat, third eye, and crown. Meditating on the chakras and the energy movement between them is a way to open energy flow in the body, find blockages, and deepen understanding of the parts of the self associated with each chakra.

Some people consider it cultural appropriation for Westerners to use Hindu philosophy and systems, such as chakras and yoga. However, these aren't generally reserved for initiates, and most Hindus don't consider it a closed practice and are welcoming of non-Hindus exploring these things.

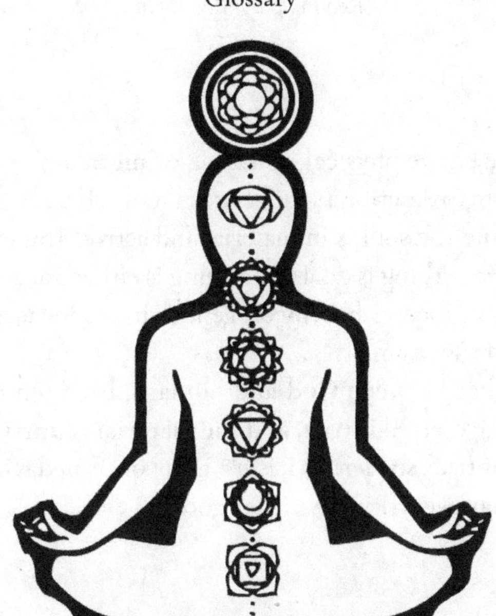

The chakras on the body

Circle

A circle can refer to a ritual, or the group of people in that ritual, or a group of people who meet regularly (or irregularly) for ritual. It can also refer to the round energy field that is "cast" as the core of Wiccan ritual, a boundary "between the worlds."

Coven

A coven, loosely, is a group of witches. It is almost certainly a committed group of people who meet on a regular basis: While a group might get together for a one-off ritual or spell, that would not be considered a coven.

In some traditions of Wicca, only a group of initiates can be called a coven, and other names—such as grove or circle—are used for groups that include non-initiates.

Deosil

Movement in the direction of the sun (clockwise) is called deosil movement. It is pronounced *JEH-sil.* Wiccans use deosil movement for all normal circle-casting activities and all positive magic. Some Wiccans require that only deosil movement is allowed in ritual, meaning that if someone is sitting to your right and you want to hand something to them, you would hand it to the person on your left, and it would be handed all the way around. This is considered to create a vortex of deosil energy that helps to reinforce the power of the circle. (See: *widdershins.*)

Dualism

Dualism is the idea that the entire physical, spiritual, or moral universe is of a dual nature. Plato introduced the idea of dualism to describe a split between soul and nature. In this philosophy, nature is material and passive, while the soul is immaterial and active. This division is meant to describe the nature of the universe: Everything is dual, everything is either nature or soul.

Aristotle, Plato's student, focuses heavily on gender in his ideas about dualism, with nature being defined as female and soul as male.

Hermetic dualism is that between God and humans, between the eternal divine and the ephemeral and material. The eternal is true, and the material is untrue. Thus, body, gender, and the like are fundamentally untrue, so Hermeticism[110] is unconcerned with gender as a dual concept.

Moral dualism adds that everything is either good or evil.

Duotheism

The idea that, to quote Dion Fortune, "all the gods are one god, and all the goddesses are one goddess." That is, all goddesses are ultimately a single Goddess, and all gods are ultimately a single God, and the universe is fundamentally two. Duotheists see reality as binary in nature, although almost all see it as ultimately one—that Goddess and God are part of a single whole.

Esbat

The regular (non-holiday) meetings of a coven or other group of Wiccans are called esbats. These are "working" rituals and are typically held on or near the full moon. (See: *sabbat.*)

Gardnerian

Gardnerian Wiccans are those who have an initiatory lineage directly descending from Gerald Gardner, meaning that Gardner initiated someone, who initiated someone, who initiated someone, and so on, in a direct line. The Gardnerian tradition is the oldest "British Traditional Wicca" tradition, dating from the 1950s.

The term "Gardnerian," coined by Charles Cardell, was originally intended as an insult but is now used proudly by the thousands of Gardnerians all over the world.

The Gardnerian tradition is initiatory, having three degrees of initiation, lineaged, and oathbound.

Golden Dawn

The Hermetic Order of the Golden Dawn ("Golden Dawn" for short) officially existed from 1888 to 1914. It was a magical lodge society that used Hermeticism, Tarot, *Kabbalah*, astrology,

110 To confuse things, an early twentieth-century work, the *Kybalion*, calls itself Hermetic and is deeply concerned with gender, but the Kybalion has no direct connection to the original Hermetic tradition of late Antiquity.

and other magical disciplines. Although short-lived, it was incredibly influential, with many occult luminaries passing through its grades, including Dion Fortune, Aleister Crowley, and Arthur Edward Waite. Through the subsequent organizations founded by former members, and the dissemination of their teaching and concepts, the Golden Dawn remains a huge influence on the occult, including on Wicca. Wiccan concepts regarding circle structure, magical tools, and polarity can all be said to have originated with the Golden Dawn.

Handfasting

The term "handfasting" originally meant a marriage contract, but nowadays, people actually tie ("fast") hands together during a handfasting ceremony. Handfasting can simply be a term for a Wiccan or Pagan wedding. It can also mean a trial marriage—typically one lasting a year and a day.

Kabbalah

Kabbalah is a form of Jewish mysticism that may date back as far as 200 BCE, from a document known as the *Sefir Yetzirah*. Today, the seminal work on Kabbalah is considered the *Zohar*, dating to the thirteenth century CE. It is the Zohar that introduced the "Tree of Life" as it is known today.

Kabbalah was adopted by Western occultists starting in the fifteenth century CE, and this is known as Hermetic Kabbalah or Hermetic Qabalah. Many modern occultists use the spelling "Qabalah" to distinguish the Hermetic system from Jewish Kabbalah.

Kabbalah is most familiar in its use of the Tree of Life, consisting of ten sephiroth (spheres) and 22 paths between them (see the Tree of Life illustration on page 24. Hermetic Qabalah, in particular, places its entire emphasis on the Tree of Life, while in traditional Jewish Kabbalah it is just one component.

Many Jewish mystics and occultists consider the use of Kabbalah by non-Jews to be a form of cultural appropriation, especially since Hermetic Qabalah originated in antisemitism (kind of "let's take this cool magical system away from those yucky Jews"). While I respect this argument, it is my observation that Kabbalah has been linked with occultism for so long, and on so many levels, that separating it is impossible. Rather than ask people never to use Kabbalah, I ask them to be respectful and supportive of Jewish culture and concerns. It's the least you can do.

Law, The

Gerald Gardner provided a document to his coven called "The Law" or "The Old Laws." Some people call it "The Ardanes" because the phrase "So it be ardane" is repeated in it. The document is a combination of pseudo-history and rules for how to run a coven and how to interact with non-Wiccan society. Most people treat it merely as a historical document—part of the early history of Wicca—and not as laws that must be followed. However, it is full of good advice regarding things like what to do if there's conflict in the coven, or if there's a problem with coven leadership. Unfortunately, it also contains homophobia and sexism.

Lineage

In traditional Wicca, lineage refers to the source, the "pedigree," you might say, of initiation. Your lineage is who initiated you, and who initiated them, and so on back to the origin of the tradition. To say a tradition is "lineaged" is to say it passes lineage and considers it meaningful.

Minoan

The Minoan Brotherhood is a Wiccan tradition for men who love men, founded by the late Eddie Buczynski in 1977. Eddie also helped found the Minoan Sisterhood, for women who love women, around the same time. The Sisterhood ultimately welcomed all women, regardless of orientation. A tradition called the Minoan Fellowship also exists, founded by Minoan brothers and sisters who wanted mixed-gender rituals.

Mojo Bag

A mojo bag is a small bag, often worn as a pendant, containing items combined for a magical purpose. There are many names for such an item. Typically, ingredients are assembled with a goal in mind, placed into the bag, and the whole thing is consecrated and/or charged up. Often, it is used for protection.

Polarity

Polarity is the presence of contrasting energies, forces, or conditions that attract one another, thereby generating power. Not every pair of opposites is a polarity, and not every polarity is exactly a pair of opposites. The important part is the push-pull of energy created by the contrast. Just as protons and electrons have polarity that powers batteries, magical polarity can power spellwork and ritual.

Polytheism

Polytheism is the belief in many deities. There are many varieties of polytheism, which include:

- Soft polytheism: The belief in many deities who are ultimately part of a greater whole.
- Hard polytheism: The belief that all deities are distinct individuals that are not part of a greater whole.
- Henotheism: Devotion to one deity while acknowledging that other deities exist. In henotheism, other deities may sometimes be worshiped, but the focus is always on a primary deity.
- Monolatry: The exclusive worship of only one deity while acknowledging that other deities exist.

Poppet

A poppet is a doll created for magical purposes. It represents the subject of the magic. During the course of a spell, a doll is consecrated as the subject, so that whatever happens to the doll happens to the person. In fiction, the purpose is almost always cursing. While that happens, my real-life experience is that most poppets are used for healing.

Sabbat

A sabbat is one of the eight holidays of Wicca, or a meeting in which one of the eight holidays is celebrated. See *Sabbats: The Wheel of the Year* on page 108.

Skyclad

To be skyclad is to be ritually nude: wearing only the sky. The term was borrowed from Jainism.

Summerland

The Summerland is the resting place for the dead. Wiccan theology tells us that when we die, we go to the Summerland to await rebirth in a new body. The term was borrowed from *Theosophy*.

Funny story, there's a town in California near Santa Barbara that was founded by Theosophists and is called Summerland. My ex-husband and I unexpectedly found ourselves passing through this town on a road trip. Our first sight of it was a sign that said "Summerland" with an arrow pointing right at a 45-degree angle: A normal angle for an exit sign that also happened to be pointing directly at the full moon. We both got quite a chill. On the way home, we stopped in Summerland and took plenty of pictures.

Theosophy

Theosophy is a philosophical religion founded primarily by Madame Helena Blavatsky in 1875. Although many people today consider Blavatsky to be a fraudster, Theosophy remains deeply influential on Western esotericism. It was unique in inserting Hindu concepts into Western occult religion.

Tradition

In Wicca and much of the modern Pagan movement, "tradition" is synonymous with "denomination."

Widdershins

Widdershins (pronounced *WITH-ur-shins*) is an anti-clockwise movement, the opposite direction from the way the sun moves across the sky. Widdershins movement in ritual is used for unwinding and negating. Some people use it very rarely, only for curses or other serious negative work. Other people use it routinely for any unwinding activity, such as closing a circle.

Widdershins movement is frequently used in "negative healing," the most obvious example of which is blasting a tumor with negative energy to heal cancer.

BIBLIOGRAPHY

Bonewits, Isaac. *Real Magic: An Introductory Treatise on the Basic Principles of Yellow Magic*. Creative Arts Book Company, 1979. Originally published 1971.

—. "Varieties of Initiatory Experience (Version 2.2)." *Neopagan.net*, 1984, updated 2005, www.neopagan.net/Initiation.html. Accessed 26 Jan. 2025.

Brain Health University. "Lunar Thinking: Does the Moon Really Influence Mental States?" July 22, 2025. brainhealthuniversity.com/brain-health-insights/lunar-thinking-does-the-moon-really-influence-mental-states/. Accessed 3 September, 2025.

Brau, Jean-Louis, Helen Weaver, and Allan Edmands. *Larousse Encyclopedia of Astrology*. New American Library, 1980. Originally published 1977.

Brigidine Sisters. "Brigid's Fire." *Brigidine Sisters*, 2022, brigidine.org.au/about-us/our-patroness/brigids-light-fire/. Accessed 8 Dec. 2024.

Buckland, Raymond. *Buckland's Book of Saxon Witchcraft*. Red Wheel/Weiser, 2005. Originally published as *The Tree: The Complete Book of Saxon Witchcraft*.

Cajochen, Christian, Songül Altanay-Ekici, Mirjam Münch, Sylvia Frey, Vera Knoblauch, Anna Wirz-Justice. "Evidence that the Lunar Cycle Influences Human Sleep." *Current Biology*, Volume 23, Issue 15, 5 August 2013, Pages 1485-1488. www.sciencedirect.com/science/article/pii/S0960982213007549. Accessed 3 September, 2025.

California Native Plant Society. "White Sage Protection." *California Native Plant Society*, www.cnps.org/conservation/white-sage. Accessed 16 Feb. 2025.

Chanek, Jack. *Queen of All Witcheries: A Biography of the Goddess*. Llewellyn Publications, 2023.

Chen, Ying, Eric S. Kim, and Tyler J. VanderWeele. "Religious-Service Attendance and Subsequent Health and Well-Being throughout Adulthood: Evidence from Three Prospective Cohorts." *International Journal of Epidemiology*, vol. 49, no. 6, 2020, pp. 2030–40. *PubMed Central*, www.ncbi.nlm.nih.gov/pmc/articles/PMC7825951/. Accessed 3 Aug. 2024.

Coughlin, John J. "The Wiccan Rede: A Historical Journey." *The Waning Moon*, 2 Feb. 2002, waningmoon.com/ethics/rede.html. Accessed 2 Mar. 2025.

Crowther, Patricia. *Lid Off the Cauldron: A Wicca Handbook*. Fenix Flames Publishing, 2020.

Culpeper, Nicholas. *Culpeper's Complete Herbal: A Book of Natural Remedies for Ancient Ills*. Wordsworth Editions, 1995.

Cunningham, Scott. *Cunningham's Encyclopedia of Crystal, Gem & Metal Magic*. Llewellyn Publications, 2001.

—. *Cunningham's Encyclopedia of Magical Herbs*. Llewellyn Publications, 1985.

—. *Wicca: A Guide for the Solitary Practitioner*. Llewellyn Publications, 1989.

Ellwood, Taylor. *Pop Culture Magick: A How to Guide to Practical Pop Culture Magic*. Magical Experiments Publications, 2018.

Farrar, Janet, and Stewart Farrar. *A Witches' Bible: The Complete Witches' Handbook*. Phoenix, 1996. Combines *Eight Sabbats for Witches* (1981) and *The Witches' Way* (1984).

Firefox, LaSara. *Jailbreaking the Goddess: A Radical Revisioning of Feminist Spirituality*. Llewellyn Publications, 2016.

Fitch, Ed. *A Grimoire of Shadows: Witchcraft, Paganism, & Magic*. Llewellyn Publications, 1996.

Fitch, Ed, and Janine Renee. *Magical Rites from the Crystal Well*. Llewellyn Publications, 1984.

Forge, Thumper. *The Chaos Apple: Magic and Discordianism for the Postmodern Witch*. Llewellyn Publications, 2025.

Fortune, Dion. *The Sea Priestess*. Samuel Weiser, 1978.

Gardner, Gerald Brousseau. *High Magic's Aid*. Samuel Weiser, 1975.

—. *The Meaning of Witchcraft*. Magickal Childe Publishing, 1991. Originally published 1959 by Rider & Co.

—. *Witchcraft Today*. Magickal Childe Publishing, 1991. Originally published 1954 by Rider & Co.

Harvard Health Publishing. "What Meditation Can Do for Your Mind, Mood, and Health." *Harvard Medical School*, 16 July 2014, www.health.harvard.edu/staying-healthy/what-meditation-can-do-for-your-mind-mood-and-health-. Accessed 28 Dec. 2024.

Heinlein, Robert A. *Stranger in a Strange Land*. Random House, 1961.

Heselton, Philip. *In Search of the New Forest Coven*. Fenix Flames Publishing, 2020.

—. *Witchfather: A Life of Gerald Gardner, Volume 1—Into the Witch Cult*. Thoth Publications, 2012.

—. *Witchfather: A Life of Gerald Gardner, Volume 2—From Witch Cult to Wicca*. Thoth Publications, 2012.

Hutton, Ronald. *The Triumph of the Moon: A History of Modern Pagan Witchcraft*. Oxford University Press, 1999.

Leland, Charles Godfrey. *Aradia, or, The Gospel of the Witches*. Translated by Mario Pazzaglini and Dina Pazzaglini, Phoenix Publishing, 1998.

Lieber, A.L. "Lunar Effect - Biological Tides and Human Emotions." NCJRS Virtual Library, NCJ Number 63700, 1978. www.ojp.gov/ncjrs/virtual-library/abstracts/lunar-effect-biological-tides-and-human-emotions, Accessed 3 September, 2025.

Lipp, Deborah. *Bending the Binary: Polarity Magic in a Nonbinary World*. Llewellyn Publications, 2023.

—. *The Elements of Ritual: Air, Fire, Water, and Earth in the Wiccan Circle*. Llewellyn Publications, 2024.

—. *Tarot Interactions: Become More Intuitive, Psychic & Skilled at Reading Cards*. Llewellyn Publications, 2015.

—. *The Way of Four*. Crossed Crow Books, 2023.

Mankey, Jason. "The Triumph of Mabon." *Raise the Horns, Patheos*, 14 Sept. 2017, 10:28 p.m., www.patheos.com/blogs/panmankey/2014/09/the-triumph-of-mabon/. Accessed 15 Dec. 2024.

—. *Transformative Witchcraft: The Greater Mysteries*. Llewellyn Publications, 2020.

Murray, Margaret. *The Witch-Cult in Western Europe: A Study in Anthropology*. Book Jungle, 2006.

NeuroLaunch editorial team. "Moon's Influence on Human Behavior: Unraveling the Lunar Effect." *NeuroLaunch*, September 22, 2024. neurolaunch.com/how-does-the-moon-affect-human-behavior/. Accessed 3 September, 2025.

Peedikayil, Hannah. "Ecological Damage on White Sage." *California State University Long Beach College of Business Legal Resource Center*, 28 Apr. 2022, www.csulb.edu/college-of-business/legal-resource-center/article/ecological-damage-white-sage. Accessed 26 Feb. 2025.

Rajchel, Diana. *Divorcing a Real Witch: For Pagans and the People Who Used to Love Them*. Moon Books, 2014.

Regardie, Israel. *The Golden Dawn: The Original Account of the Teachings, Rites & Ceremonies of the Hermetic Order*. Llewellyn Publications, 1989.

Slater, Herman, editor. *A Book of Pagan Rituals*. Samuel Weiser, 1978.

Stewart, Dianne M. "The Wedding Tradition of Jumping the Broom Didn't Actually Derive from Africa." *Oprah Daily*, 25 June 2021, www.oprahdaily.com/life/relationships-love/a35992704/jumping-the-broom-wedding-tradition-history-origins/. Accessed 12 Apr. 2023.

Thompson, Tok. "The Ancient Origins of the Easter Bunny: A Scholar Traces the Folk Figure's History from the Neolithic Era to Today." *Smithsonian Magazine*, *The Conversation*, 14 Apr. 2022, www.smithsonianmag.com/history/the-ancient-origins-of-the-easter-bunny-180979915/. Accessed 15 Dec. 2024.

UCLA Health. "Health Benefits of Gratitude." *UCLA Health*, 22 Mar. 2023, www.uclahealth.org/news/article/health-benefits-gratitude. Accessed 18 Nov. 2024.

Ward, Terence P. "A Parting of Companions Around You: Pagans and Divorce." *The Wild Hunt*, 13 June 2017, wildhunt.org/2017/06/a-parting-of-companions-around-you-pagans-and-divorce.html. Accessed 6 Feb. 2025.

Wayman, Erin. "Moonlight shapes how some animals move, grow and even sing," Science News, July 8, 2019. www.sciencenews.org/article/moon-animals-light-behavior-lunar-phases. Accessed 3 September 2025.

Zimecki, Michal. "The lunar cycle: effects on human and animal behavior and physiology." PubMed, NIH National Library of Medicine, National Center for Biotechnology Information, PMID: 16407788. pubmed.ncbi.nlm.nih.gov/16407788/. Accessed 3 September 2025.